THE MULTICULTURAL COOKBOOK FOR STUDENTS

Updated and Revised

Lois Sinaiko Webb and Lindsay Grace Roten

GREENWOOD PRESS
An Imprint of ABC-CLIO, LLC

A B C 🟢 C L I O

Santa Barbara, California • Denver, Colorado • Oxford, England

Library of Congress Cataloging-in-Publication Data

Webb, Lois Sinaiko.
  The multicultural cookbook for students / Lois Sinaiko Webb and Lindsay Grace Roten. — Updated and rev.
    p. cm.
  Rev. ed. of The multicultural cookbook for students / by Carole Lisa Albyn.
  Includes bibliographical references and index.
  ISBN 978–0–313–37558–3 (hard copy : alk. paper) — ISBN 978–0–313–37560–6 (hard copy pbk: alk. paper) — ISBN 978–0–313–37559–0 (ebook)
1. Cookery, International—Juvenile literature. 2. Food habits—Juvenile literature. 3. Food crops—Juvenile literature. I. Roten, Lindsay Grace. II. Albyn, Carole Lisa. Multicultural cookbook for students. III. Title.
TX725.A1A34 2009
641.59—dc22   2009026718

13 12 11 10 9   1 2 3 4 5

This book is also available on the World Wide Web as an eBook.
Visit www.abc-clio.com for details.

ABC-CLIO, LLC
130 Cremona Drive, P.O. Box 1911
Santa Barbara, California 93116-1911

This book is printed on acid-free paper ∞

Manufactured in the United States of America

Copyright Acknowledgments

Contents

Contents

Contents

Contents

Contents

Contents

Contents

Contents

Contents

Contents

Preface

Today, more than any time in the history of our planet, we are aware and concerned about the lives and living conditions of people around the world. The very survival of many plants and animals is at risk. The water we drink and the food we eat are of world-wide concern. We cannot survive without clean water and healthy, nutritious food; this is the core of all human existence. Changes in the ecosystem and global warming affect everyone. We can no longer think of ourselves as isolated people in an isolated country, the United States of America; we are becoming one people on a united planet.

With the help of *The Multiculural Cookbook for Students*, you will better understand what people eat in Africa, Asia, Europe, Latin America, the Caribbean, North America, and the Middle East. Climate, soil conditions, and terrain are the most important factors when it comes to food production, thus, how, why, what, and where people eat what they do.

Today, with advanced farm equipment, refrigeration, packing, and shipping available in many parts of the world, we are more easily able to taste the foods of other cultures. These same advances can also have a negative impact on the environment, causing pollution.

In some parts of the world people still suffer severe malnutrition because of inadequate food supplies. For many this is due to soil erosion, draught, extreme weather changes, or a lack of clean water to grow crops and to use for cooking and drinking. We must find a balance between feeding all the people of the world using modern farming and shipping methods while still protecting our planet. It is up to all of us to join together to help make the planet's water and food supply safe and healthy.

While studying other countries from around the world, a teacher will often request students to enhance their understanding of the foods and cooking traditions. To create a dish from that country is to experience hands-on how, what, and why certain foods are used. If you have been given such an assignment, here are a few things to keep in mind:

- *Be sure to have adult supervision* and involve him or her with the assignment from the beginning.
- Select a few recipes.
- Read the selected recipes carefully and note what you need to buy and how much time is needed to prepare the recipes.
- Schedule a shopping time with whomever is helping you to buy the necessary items to complete your recipes.
- Schedule a time in the kitchen to prepare your recipes when an adult can assist you.

If cooking equipment is available at school, you may ask your teacher to demonstrate or supervise the preparation of some of these recipes for a social studies unit. Some recipes do not even require cooking equipment or might be prepared simply in, for example, an electric frying pan.

We cannot overemphasize the need for caution in the kitchen. Even the most experienced cook has accidents, and so it is essential that you have an adult help you through the completion of the recipe. Please read "Common Sense, Safety, and Cleanliness Tips for Cooks," on pages xxxiii–xxxv. These recipes were designed to teach you about countries, not introduce you to cooking methods in general. We include some recipes that you may want to take to school but that will need refrigeration. Check with your teacher to see whether there is a refrigerator at your school that you can use. Then, store your prepared items in something easily transportable, and refrigerate them.

ABOUT *THE MULTICULTURAL COOKBOOK FOR STUDENTS*

The Multicultural Cookbook for Students contains more than 350 recipes from 152 countries For this new edition, there are more than 140 new recipes and most of the narrative coverage has been revised and updated. The cookbook is arranged geographically, with recipes from countries arranged within these seven continents or regions: Africa, Asia and the South Pacific, the Caribbean, Europe, Latin America, the Middle East, and North America. The book moves from region to region in alphabetical order.

Each section opens with an introductory description of the continent and/or region and gives general information on the recipes offered. For each country, we provide an overview of the country, the lifestyle of the people, and the foods that are grown and eaten.

The Recipes

In almost all cases, we have provided at least two recipes for each country. Each recipe includes the following:

- *Yield*, stating how many servings the recipe makes.
- *Ingredients*, listing how much of which food items are needed.
- *Equipment*, listing the cooking tools and utensils needed, such as pans, bowls, and spoons.
- *Instructions*, explaining exactly how to make the recipe.
- *Serving suggestions*, describing how to serve the food you have prepared.

Special Features

The Multicultural Cookbook for Students includes a glossary of terms—names of food (such as **cassava**), cooking techniques (such as **blanching**), and cooking equipment (such as **serrated knife**)—that may be unfamiliar to U.S. students. Most terms included in the glossary are highlighted in bold type throughout the book.

The book concludes with a comprehensive index to find recipes of interest, listing recipe names, major ingredients, countries, and other terms.

Acknowledgments

Special thanks to Claire Carr, Frankie Camera, Josie Wilson, Jackie Tenny from Nigeria, Hester Mayfield, Barbra Nankivell, Bengie Collazo, Sarkis, Rebecca Salas, Caroline Graham, Jarod Carter, Jean Seltzer, John Roten, Nancy Roten, Barrett North, Barbara and James Dixon, and Amy and Justin Acker.

Getting Started

IMPORTANT. PLEASE READ THE FOLLOWING BEFORE YOU BEGIN TO USE THIS BOOK

SAFETY, COMMON SENSE, AND CLEANLINESS TIPS FOR COOKS

This book will not teach you *how* to cook. There are a number of good books that teach young people cooking techniques; please check your local library for titles.

To make cooking an enjoyable experience it is a good idea to follow a few rules. These rules apply to all cooks, from beginners to professional executive chefs, and they will stay with you throughout your life. The rules concern safety, attention to detail, and cleanliness in the kitchen. Attention to detail means, simply, use "common sense" and think before you act.

Safety:

1. *Make sure that an adult helps you as you select and work on your recipe.* Even apprentice or beginner chefs in restaurants never cook alone; there is always an experienced chef present to answer questions and to help explain how to operate electrical devices and other cooking equipment. It is also important to keep food at the proper temperature at all times, and it takes an experienced eye and nose to tell whether something is usable or has spoiled and should be discarded.

2. Stove-top burners are one of the kitchen's most dangerous appliances and where most home accidents happen. A safety precaution we recommend is having a fire extinguisher (designed for stove fires) in good working condition and hanging within easy reach if an

accident should occur. Because accidents do happen, a first aid kit with burn and cut medication is also good to have on hand. Following the guidelines below will help to prevent accidents:

- *Never* turn your back or walk away from a skillet or pan of hot cooking oil. Have the necessary equipment and ingredients ready to fry before heating the oil in the skillet or saucepan.

- If the oil should begin to smoke or seems too hot, quickly turn off the heat. *Do not move the pan. Do not* throw water in the pan because water will cause the fire to flame up. It is best to turn off heat, if possible cover the fire or pour baking soda over the smoother. Allow it to cool down and begin again.

- Never leave food cooking unattended. All cooking food must be checked from time to time so you are sure the food is not sticking and burning. If the phone rings or there are other distractions while you are cooking, turn the heat off, and using a pot holder, slide the pan to a cold burner and double check to make sure you pushed the correct *off* button before you leave the kitchen. It is very easy to forget that you left something cooking on the stove once you walk away from it. When you return, if it has not been more than a few minutes, just continue where you left off and give your cooking project your undivided attention.

- When you finish cooking, before you leave the kitchen, check to be sure the oven and stove-top dials are "OFF."

3. In each recipe we give a recommended approximate cooking heat and time. This may vary, based on the thickness of the pan you are using, the heat controls on your stove, how thick the cooking ingredients are cut, and the altitude at which you are cooking. Keep dry, heat-proof oven mitts or pot holders handy. All-metal spoons get hot, so use wooden mixing spoons or plastic-handled metal spoons instead. Do not use all-plastic spoons for mixing hot food; they will melt. Never transfer very hot food to plastic containers; some plastic containers are not made to hold hot food and might melt.

4. Dull knives are sometimes more dangerous than sharp knives. A dull knife might slip off food, causing accidents. Always carry a knife by the handle with the blade pointing toward the floor. Never pass a knife to another person blade first. Never put utility knives in a dishwasher or in a sink full of soapy water with other cooking utensils. It is dangerous to yourself and others and is not good for the knives. Wash them by hand and keep them in a safe place.

Cleanliness:

1. Tie your hair back or wear something on your head, such as a bandana.

2. Roll up your sleeves and wear an apron or some protection to keep your clothes clean.

3. Wash your hands with soap and dry them with a clean towel or paper towels before you touch food. Wash your hands as often as necessary while you are handling food. If possible, wear clean rubber gloves. This will prevent cross-contamination.

4. Wash all fresh fruits and vegetables before cutting them.

5. Cooking in a clean kitchen makes the job more pleasant.

6. Make sure all your equipment is ready and in good working order before you begin.

7. Good cooks clean up after themselves and leave the kitchen spotless. Clean up any spills and drips when they happen.

We have made every effort to keep the cooking instructions and procedures throughout this cookbook simple and easy to follow.

EQUIPMENT AND METHODS YOU NEED TO KNOW ABOUT

Almost every recipe in this book will require the following basic equipment:

- A set of **measuring cups**. You will probably need nested cups in different sizes for measuring dry items such as flour, and you will probably need a liquid measuring cup, with lines drawn on the sides to tell you how much liquid you need.
- A set of **measuring spoons** for measuring small amounts of liquid and dry items.
- A **work surface**, such as a counter or table top, where you can put all of your equipment as you prepare your food.
- A set of **sharp knives** for cutting and dicing ingredients.

Each recipe will tell what other equipment you will need—such as bowls, pans, or spoons—to make the food described.

Glossary

Most of the following terms are highlighted throughout this book in **bold** type.

Acidophilus. Live bacteria (or lactic culture) that turns warm milk into yogurt. (See recipe for yogurt making, page 216, Bulgaria). It is available at most supermarkets and health food stores.

Al dente. Italian for "to the tooth." It is a descriptive term used for cooking pasta. "Pasta should be cooked al dente" means the pasta should be firm to the bite, chewy, not mushy and overcooked.

Anise. Spice native to the eastern Mediterranean region and Southwest Asia that adds a licorice flavor to food.

Asafetida. Spice with a pungent garlic smell when raw, but in cooked dishes, it delivers a smooth flavor, reminiscent of leeks.

Basmati rice. Variety of long-grain rice, notable for its fragrance and delicate flavor, used in Indian cooking.

Baste. To moisten food by spooning liquid over it while cooking. It prevents meat or other food from drying out.

Blanch (also Shocking). To put fruit or vegetables in boiling water to soften them, to set color, to peel of skin, or to remove the raw flavor. The fruit or vegetable are first dropped in boiling water for a minute or two and then plunged into cold water to stop the cooking action. (*See also* **Peeling tomatoes.**)

Boned. Bones are removed and discarded.

Bonito flakes. Dried shavings of fish

Bouillon. Broth made from meat, poultry, or vegetables boiled in liquid. The concentrated form of this broth or bouillon comes in dry cubes or granules and is **reconstituted** with liquid, such as water.

Braised. Combination cooking method using both moist and dry heat; typically the food is first seared at a high temperature and then finished in a covered pot with a variable amount of liquid, resulting in a particular flavor.

Breadfruit. Nutritious starchy melon fruit that grows on trees in tropical regions.

Buffet. Style of food service, with an assortment of prepared dishes set out on a table. The food is self-service.

Bulgur Cracked wheat grain. The nutty-textured cereal is ground fine or coarse for use in different Middle Eastern dishes. It is available at health food and Middle Eastern stores.

Bundt pan. Baking pan with scalloped edges and a tube in the center. It is used mostly for cake baking.

Candy thermometer. Calibrated instrument that registers up to 400°F. It shows the exact temperature of a cooking mixture. To properly use the thermometer, the bottom end should be immersed below the surface of the cooking mixture, but not touching the pan bottom. Candy thermometers are available at most supermarkets.

Capers. Tiny olive-green buds of a bush native to North Africa and the Mediterranean region. They are salted and pickled in vinegar and add a zesty flavor to sauces and salads.

Caramelized. Applies to slowly sautéing (usually onions), over medium-low heat, until cooked through and the food becomes soft and turns a caramel color.

Cardamom. Spice made of the dried, ripe seeds of the cardamom plant. The aromatic seeds are ground and used in many dishes, especially curries, breads, and tea. Scandinavians love to add the fragrant spice to pastries. It is an old Chinese custom to chew on a few seeds to sweeten the breath.

Cassava (also called manioc). Edible root from tropical yucca plants. It is almost pure starch, easily digestible, and nutritious. There are two kinds: sweet cassava, eaten as a vegetable; and bitter cassava, which is made into tapioca and manioc, a meal used in cooking. Tapioca is used for thickening soups and puddings. Manioc flour is used extensively in South American cooking. Brazil is one of the world's largest growers of cassava. It is available at some supermarkets and all Latino food stores.

Chickpeas. Round legumes (beans), also known as garbanzo beans, used extensively in Mediterranean, Middle Eastern, Indian, and Mexican cooking. Available dried or cooked and canned at supermarkets.

Chinese cabbage. Bok choy.

Chutney. Condiment (relish) always served with curries. There are hundreds of chutneys made with different fruit or vegetable and spice combinations cooked with vinegar and sugar. Chutneys are easy to make and are also available at most supermarkets.

Cilantro/Coriander. Fresh leaf form, which is an herb, or as dried seeds, a spice. Both are used extensively in Asian, Indian, and Spanish cooking. Cilantro is the Spanish name for fresh coriander.

Coarsely chop. To cut into large bite-sized pieces, about 1/2 to 1-inch square. (*See also* **Finely chop.**)

Colander. Perforated bowl for draining food. It usually has a rounded bottom and feet to stand on.

Core. To cut out and discard the hard center part and the stem of vegetables and fruit, such as apples.

Coriander. *See* **Cilantro/Coriander**

Couscous. Coarsely ground semolina pasta, used in North African cuisine.

Crushed or finely ground nuts Sold in jars and can be purchased in the candy department of most supermarkets. They are a popular topping for ice cream. The finely ground nuts needed for recipes in this cookbook can also be finely chopped. You can grind your own peanuts by hand, putting the nuts in the **mortar** and pressing on them with the pestle, or by finely chopping them with a knife. If you have an electric nut grinder or a food processor, nuts can be finely ground in just seconds. Electric blenders might work if the nuts are very dry; otherwise, we do not recommend them. In a blender, oil is released from the nuts, making them gummy and hard to grind. A hand or electric meat grinder can also be used.

Cube. To cut something into small (about 1/2-inch) squares; compare with **dice**

Curry powder. Blend of spices usually associated with Indian cooking.

Dal. Thick, spicy stew prepared with lentils, a mainstay of Indian, Pakistani, and Bangladeshi cuisine.

Devein. To remove the vein, usually associated with peeled shrimp. It is a black (sometimes white) vein running down the back of shrimp from the head to the tail. It is easily visible and can be removed by cutting the thin membrane covering it, while rinsing the shrimp under cold running water. Use either the tip of a finger nail or tip of a knife to gently pull it out in one piece. It is removed for the sake of appearance only. It is always eaten in very tiny shrimp and is perfectly harmless to eat.

Dice To cut something into very small (about 1/4-inch) squares; compare with **cube.**

Dollop. Small amount or lump.

Double boiler. One pan fitted on top of another. The upper pan holds food that must be cooked at a temperature lower than direct heat. It is cooked by the steam heat of boiling water. The amount of water in the bottom pan is important; it must be enough to cook the food and not boil away. If it is too full, it can boil over and be dangerous. A double boiler can be made out of any two pans that fit together with room between them for the water and steam. A heat-resistant bowl can also be fitted over the pan of water.

Durum wheat. Also called "hard wheat," it is high in gluten. Gluten gives dough its tough, elastic quality. **Semolina** flour is made from the hard portion of wheat that remains after the flour, bran, and chaff have been removed. There are two types of semolina—one is made from hard berries of both hard and soft wheat. When it is coarsely milled into granules, it is used for soups, **groats**, and puddings. The other kind semolina comes from hard durum wheat and is used for all good-quality homemade or commercial pasta. Durum wheat semolina flour is particularly suitable for pasta because it contains a high proportion of protein, which prevents the starch from breaking down during cooking, producing pasta that stays firm and resilient.

Dutch oven. Large, heavy cast-iron pot with a tight-fitting dome cover. It is ideal for slow, stove-top cooking.

Egg beater. Hand or kitchen tool used to whip, mix, and/or beat food.

Eggs, hard cooked or hard boiled. Carefully put eggs into the pan and cover with cold water. Bring them to a boil over high heat and quickly reduce heat to simmer. Cover and cook for about 12 to 15 minutes. Remove from heat, uncover, and place under cold running water to chill eggs before peeling. This prevents the green ring from forming around the yolk.

Eggs, separated Put yolk in one container and the white in another. It is very important to keep the white free of any yolk. Break and separate each egg, one at a time, into small individual bowls before putting them together with other whites or yolks. If the yolk breaks into the white, it can be refrigerated to use at another time.

Fillets. Boneless cuts or slices of meat, poultry, or fish.

Finely chop. Cut food into pea-sized pieces.

Finely ground nuts. *See* **Crushed or finely ground nuts**

Fish. Opaque white and easily flakes means the fish is fully cooked. The flesh appears solid white (versus translucent light grey when raw). When you poke it with a fork it easily separates into small chunks (flakes).

Flakes (fish). *See* **Fish**

Flan. Rich Latin American custard dessert, traditionally served with caramel sauce.

Fluff (rice or grains). Using a fork to stir in a top-to-bottom circular motion, to separate the grains.

Fold. To gently and slowly mix (using a whisk or mixing spoon), in a rotating top-to-bottom motion, allowing air to be incorporated into the mixture.

Frothy. Something that has been beaten or whipped (such as egg whites) just until the surface is covered with small bubbles.

Fusion. Blending food and/or herbs and spices and/or cooking methods and techniques from a different culture, resulting in a new taste.

Ghee. Clarified butter or vegetable oil used in India for cooking. Usli ghee is made from clarified pure butter made from the milk of water buffalo or yak. The advantages of cooking with ghee is it tastes good, it will not burn and turn brown, and it keeps indefinitely even when left unrefrigerated.

Groats. Hulled grains of various cereals, such as oats, wheat, barley or buckwheat

Ground peanuts or grounds nuts. *See* **Crushed or finely ground nuts**

Guavas. Fruit that grows on trees in tropical regions.

Hard-cooked eggs. *See* **Eggs, hard cooked**

Hot pot. Simmering metal pot with stock, placed at the center of the dining table.

Hungarian paprika. Powder condiment made from dried pods of red bonnet peppers. The peppers grow throughout Europe and the best are said to grow in Hungary where they are the national spice. Paprika has a rich, deep red color.

Injera. Sour pancake-like bread native to Ethiopia.

Jalapeño pepper. Green or red pepper grown in southwestern United States and Mexico. A hot pepper. When seeds are removed the pepper becomes less hot.

Julienne. Cutting food, especially vegetables, such as carrots, into matchstick-sized pieces.

Kababs. Grilled or broiled meats and/or vegetables on wood or metal skewers.

Knead. To work a dough until smooth and elastic, preferably with the hands. It is especially important in bread-making. Shape the dough into a ball. Push the "heels" of your hands against the dough, fold the upper half over, and turn it a little bit. Then push the heels of your hands against the dough and repeat the whole procedure many times until dough is smooth.

Leche. Spanish for "milk."

Lemon grass. Aromatic herb is used in Caribbean and many types of Asian cooking.

Lentils. Nutritious legumes (beans). Many varieties of lentil have been a staple in the Middle East and Central Asia for thousands of years. They are available at most supermarkets and all Middle Eastern food stores.

Mace. Spice ground from the outer covering of the nutmeg. The flavor and uses of mace and nutmeg are similar.

Manioc. *See* **Cassava**

Marble. Effect created when two colors of batter are swirled, but not fully mixed together, resembling marble stone.

Marinade. Sauce in which food is marinated.

Marinate. To soak in a sauce made up of seasonings and liquids.

Masa harina. Traditional Mexican corn flour used to make tortillas.

Mascarpone. Soft, mild Italian cream cheese.

Melanga root. Root vegetable popular in the tropics and South America.

Melting chocolate. Requires very little heat. Put chocolate chips in a pan over boiling water or put in heat-proof bowl in warm oven until melted (about 3–5 minutes, depending on quantity).

Millet. Grain grown for human food in different parts of the world, such as Africa, Asia, and India. It seems to grow where nothing else can and has been cultivated in dry, poor soil for over 1,000 years and is said to equal rice in food value. Millet is available at most health food stores either in the form of meal, **groats** or flour. Millet is a "non-glutinous" grain. Gluten gives the elasticity to wheat flour needed in bread-making. Adding some millet to wheat flour makes excellent-tasting bread. Millet has an important place in our economy even though it is not a popular food grain. In the United States, it is cultivated mostly as a forage grass and poultry feed and is especially suitable for chicks and pet birds.

Mince. To finely chop or pulverize.

Mortar and pestle. Bowl (mortar) and a grinding tool (pestle). Both are made of a non-breakable, hard substance such as marble, stone, or wood. The mortar holds something that must be mashed or ground to extract its flavor, such as garlic and fresh or dried herbs and spices. The pestle is held in the hand and is used to do the mashing or grinding. You can make a mortar and pestle; simply use a metal bowl for the mortar and for the pestle use a clean, small, smooth-surface rock, the head of a hammer, or wooden mallet.

Muoc mam. Asian fish sauce.

Naan. Indian flat bread.

Opaque white. *See* **Fish**

Parboiled. Partial boiling of food in order to later finish cooking it.

Peeling tomatoes. Made easy by dropping them in boiling water for about 1 or 2 minutes. Remove with a slotted spoon and hold under cold water to stop the cooking action. If the skin has not already cracked open, poke the tomato with a small knife and the skin easily peels off (also called **blanching**).

Peppercorns. Dried berry of the pepper vine added as a spice to enhance flavor of food.

Pestle. *See* **Mortar and Pestle**

Piloncillo. Mexican dark brown sugar.

Pimento or pimiento. Heart-shaped, sweet-tasting peppers that are almost always canned because they spoil rapidly.

Piri piri. Portugese sauce made from hot chili peppers and olive oil. Used in preparing sauces and marinades for roast and grilled dishes.

Pith. Spongy tissue between the skin and meat of fruit such as oranges, lemons, and grapefruit.

Pitted. Stony seeds or pits from fruit or vegetables, such as avocados, that have been removed.

Plantains or platanos. Cooking bananas with a squash-like taste that come in all sizes and are green, yellow, black, or brown. They are good boiled, baked, fried, and broiled and are either sliced or mashed. They are available year-round from Ecuador and Mexico and are sold in some supermarkets and Latino food stores.

Pork cracklings. Crisp brown skin of pork with all fat rendered.

Prepared mustard. Any creamy mustard spread, readily available at all supermarkets. For the recipes in this book, unless otherwise stated, the mustard can be either regular or Dijon style.

Pulp. Edible solid part of fruit or vegetable.

Punch down. Action performed in bread-making. When the prepared yeast mixer is added to flour it begins to ferment and gasses (carbon dioxide) develop, causing the dough to rise. The gasses are forced out of the dough by a process known as "punching down"; this helps to relax the gluten and equalizes the temperature of the dough. To punch down, take your fist and flatten the dough against the bowl. The best time to "punch down" the dough is when it has doubled in size through fermentation. After the dough is punched, it must rise a second time before it can be made into bread or rolls.

Purée. French word that means to mash, blend, process, or strain food until it reaches a smooth, lump-free consistency. This can be done in a blender of food processor; adding a little liquid will help.

Ramekins. Small glazed ceramic serving bowls used for the preparation and serving of various food dishes.

Reconstitute. To restore to a former condition by adding liquid such as water.

Rose water. Extract distilled from fresh rose petals. It is an important flavoring in the Middle East and India. It is available at Middle Eastern food stores, natural food stores, and most pharmacies.

Roux. Sauce made by stirring a liquid, such as milk or water, into a paste made of fat (usually butter) and flour. For a thin sauce, use 1 tablespoon each of fat and flour for each cup of liquid; for a medium sauce, use 2 tablespoons each of fat and flour for each cup of liquid; for a thick sauce, use 3 tablespoons each of fat and flour for each cup of liquid.

Rub. Mixture of herbs and spices that is rubbed into meat and poultry to enhance their flavor.

Sauté. To fry in a small amount of oil. This term comes from a French word meaning "to jump." The oil must be hot before adding the ingredients. Stir constantly while cooking the "jumping" ingredients; otherwise they absorb too much oil.

Sear. To cook the surface of food, especially meat, quickly over high heat to brown the exterior. Searing does not "seal in" juices, as commonly thought, but it does improve the flavor and appearance.

Seeded. Seeds are removed and discarded before cutting or chopping, usually in a fruit or vegetable.

Semolina. *See* **Durum wheat**

Separated eggs. *See* **Eggs, separated**

Serrated knife. Knife with saw-like notches along the cutting edge, such as on a bread knife.

Shocking. *See* **Blanch**

Shredded. Food, such as cabbage, that has been torn into strips. A grater is often used to shred food. (To shred coconut, see recipe on page 138).

Sift. To shake a dry, powdered substance (such as flour or baking powder) through a strainer/sifter to remove any lumps and give lightness. (*See also* **Sifter.**)

Sifter. Also known as a strainer. Implement used to remove fine particles or lumps from food, such as flour.

Skimmer. Long-handled tool that has a round, slightly cupped, mesh screen or metal disk with small holes for removing food items from hot liquid.

Slurry. Paste made by stirring together water and flour or cornstarch used to thicken hot soups, stews, gravy or sauces. After adding slurry, continue to cook for several minutes for flour to lose its raw taste.

Sofrito. Aromatic mix of herbs and spices used as a base flavoring and seasoning to Latin American cuisine most notably Puerto Rican.

Sorghum Grain related to **millet** and used in Asia and Africa for porridge, flour, beer, and molasses.

Springform pan. Round baking pan with a removable bottom. The sides open by means of a spring hinge, allowing the cake to be easily removed.

Steamer pan or basket. Made of wire mesh or has small holes and sits above a pan of boiling water, allowing food to cook by the steam of boiling water. Steam cooking preserves most of the food's nutrients. A steamer can be made by fitting a wire rack, strainer, or colander in to a large saucepan, allowing room between for the water and steam. Aluminum foil can be scrunched up into a ball and used as a prop to keep the container with food above the water level. The cover must fit tightly over the basket to keep as much steam in as possible.

Stewed. Food that is slowly cooked in a small amount of liquid at low heat in a covered container. This allows flavors to blend and cook together.

Stir-fry food. To cook quickly using very little hot oil. The food is continually stirred, keeping it crisp and firm. Stir-fry originated in China where it is done in a **wok**.

Strain. To put food through a sieve or strainer so that liquid or small parts of food pass through small holes and the large parts are left in the strainer.

Sunni. Branch of Islam.

Tahini. Sesame paste used in Middle Eastern cooking.

Tanjine. Type of stew found in the North African cuisines of Morocco.

Tapioca. *See* **Cassava**

Taro. Several different tropical plants with similar edible starchy tubers and spinach-like leaves. Taro is an important staple in Africa, Asian, and Caribbean cooking. The root has a nutty, potato-like flavor and texture. The leafy green tops are chopped and cooked in vegetable stews. Taro root or flour is available at most Latino food stores.

Teff. Healthy wheat alternative.

Temper. To raise the temperature of a cold liquid gradually by slowly stirring in a hot liquid.

Tenderize. To make meat tender by using a process, such as pounding with a kitchen mallet or adding a marinade, to soften the tissue.

Toasted. Nuts are toasted in oven or skillet. *To toast in oven*: Spread nuts or seeds out on baking sheet and put in preheated 325°F oven until lightly golden, 12–15 minutes. *To toast in skillet*: Heat medium skillet over high heat until a drop of water flicked across its surface evaporates instantly. Add the nuts or seeds and shaking the pan gently, cook for 2–3 minutes, until the seeds are lightly toasted.

Tofu. Bean curd.

Trimmed. Stem or core, or any tough and inedible parts, brown spots, or discoloration of skin or flesh on vegetables or fruit has been removed. To trim meat means to remove fat, gristle, or silver skin.

Turmeric Spice used more for its bright yellow color than flavor. It is used to color curries, pickles, margarine, and cloth.

Vegetarian. One who practices a form of vegetarianism that excludes all meat and poultry from the diet. A vegan is somebody whose diet excludes the use of any animal products, including meat, fish, poultry, dairy products, eggs, or honey.

Vermicelli. Very thin pasta, literally "little worms," often used for soups and puddings.

Wat. Ethopian stew made from chicken, meats, and vegetables.

Whisk. To beat in a fast circular motion. This makes the mixture lighter by beating in air. A whisk is also a light-bulb-shaped kitchen tool made of fine wires held together by a long handle.

Wok. Wide, low metal pan used in Asian countries to cook foods. It is especially useful for quickly frying foods and the **stir-fry** method of cooking.

Yerba. Species of the Holly family native to subtropical Latin American countries.

Yucca. *See* **Cassava**

Zest. Outer peel of citrus fruits, removed by grating or scraping off. It is important to only remove the colored outer peel, not the white **pith** beneath, which is bitter.

1

Africa

Africa is divided into five regions: North Africa, Central Africa, West Africa, East Africa, and Southern Africa. Within each region, the countries are similar in terrain and climate.

While the regions have distinct differences, greens and grains are the primary source of nutrition throughout the African continent. When meat is eaten by Africans it is usually dried, similar to American beef jerky.

In many African countries, serving utensils have been simple things from nature. Dried gourds, in all sizes and shapes, have been used as bowls for serving food. Much of the cooking has been done over open fires. One-pot stews are considered comfort foods of Africa and are the most popular method of cooking throughout the continent. Baking has been done, but not in Western-type ovens; rather, covered barbeque pits are used.

One important point to remember as you read these recipes is that many of the people in Africa depend on the crops they grow within their village to eat. Natural disasters such as famine, floods, and draught or catastrophes such as war may create food shortages, thus relief must be brought in from other countries.

NORTH AFRICA

The North African countries are Algeria, Egypt, Libya, Morocco, Sudan, Tunisia, and Western Sahara. Although Egypt is located in Northern Africa it is more often considered part of the Middle East. (Egyptian recipes are located in the Middle East section.) Most North Africans are Muslim and follow strict Islamic practices and traditions, such as slaughtering animals only after asking God's permission to do so through prayer. Other foods, such as pork and animals that have not been slaughtered, are forbidden according to Muslim tradition. Eating and drinking with only the right hand and praying before meals are other customs.

Along the fertile regions bordering the Mediterranean Sea, crops such as grains, olives, figs, grapes, dates, fruit trees, and vegetables are grown. The most common livestock raised are chickens, sheep, goats, cattle, and horses.

Algeria

Algeria, on the Mediterranean coast of North Africa, was invaded by France in 1830. It was a colony from 1848 until 1962, when the French finally consented to leave after much bloodshed. There are still many French influences, including the spoken language and the preparation of food.

Most Algerians are Sunni Muslim; thus, alcohol is not consumed and pork is not eaten. Sweet mint tea and strong black coffee are popular beverages.

Algerian Couscous (Chicken Stew)

Couscous refers to both the grain as well as stews made with couscous. The North African and Middle Eastern countries each have their own way of cooking couscous. A fiery condiment made with hot **pimentos**, called *Harissais*, is usually served with Algerian couscous. The following recipe is often prepared as a vegetarian dish without the chicken.

Yield: serves 6

2 tablespoons olive oil, more as needed

2 to 3 pounds chicken, cut into serving-size pieces

3 cups chicken broth, homemade or canned

3 carrots, **trimmed**, cut in about 2-inch chunks

2 onions, trimmed, peeled, **coarsely chopped**

2 turnips, trimmed, cut in about 2-inch chunks

3 cloves garlic, trimmed, **finely chopped**, or 1 teaspoon garlic granules

2 teaspoons ground **coriander**

1/4 teaspoon ground red pepper

1/4 teaspoon ground turmeric

3 zucchini, trimmed, cut into 1/4-inch slices

2 cups cooked garbanzo beans, homemade or canned

4 to 6 cups cooked couscous (cook according to directions on package, keep warm)

Equipment: Large saucepan with cover or **Dutch oven**, mixing spoon

1. Heat 2 tablespoons oil in saucepan or Dutch oven over medium-high heat. Add chicken pieces and fry until browned, adding more oil if necessary to prevent sticking, about 6 to 10 minutes per side. Remove from pan and set aside. Fry in batches if necessary.

2. Add chicken broth, carrots, onions, turnips, garlic, coriander, red pepper, and turmeric in same pan. Mix well and bring to boil over high heat. Reduce to simmer and layer zucchini, beans, and chicken on top. Cover and cook slowly for about 1 hour, until chicken is very tender.

3. Mound the couscous in middle of platter and place chicken pieces and vegetables around it.

4. To serve Algerian style, place the platter in the middle of the table. The guests are given a damp towel to wipe their hands. The head of the house eats first, then special guests. They dip their right-hand fingers in the platter of couscous. They then proceed to take a handful and roll it into a ball (using only the right hand).

Different Ways to Serve and Eat Couscous

1. Make a salad of sliced ripe tomatoes topped with morsels of oil-packed canned tuna, chopped onion, and anchovies; drizzle with olive oil and generously splash on lemon juice. Set in the middle of a large platter and spoon the couscous around it.

2. Make a salad of peeled, sliced oranges, thinly sliced radishes, and finely chopped mint leaves. Sprinkle with dressing of orange juice sharpened by a dash of vinegar. Serve on same platter with couscous.

3. For dessert: pour the warm couscous in the center of the platter and sprinkle with chopped sticky dates, shelled almonds, and chopped fresh or dried figs. Serve dessert couscous by dipping the right-hand fingers into mixture and make a small ball with dates, almonds, and figs.

Libya

Libyans import most of their food. The majority of their oil-rich land is desert, with only 1 percent arable along the coast. Before the discovery of oil in 1959, Libya was one of the poorest countries on the African continent. Most people had nothing to eat except beans; fortunately, beans are high in nutrition and low in cost. After the discovery of oil, the sharing of the wealth and foods of the world began to be available to many Libyans. However, old family recipes for bean dishes such as *ful* (recipe page 286) are still a source of pride.

Al Batheeth (Date Candy)

Libyan children, like children everywhere, love sweets. Dates have been cultivated for thousands of years in North Africa, where they are sometimes called the "candy that grows on trees." They are naturally sweet and have excellent nutritional value. To cut dates easily, use scissors, which should be frequently dipped in water to prevent sticking. About 1/2 pound of **pitted** dates yields a little over 1 cup of chopped dates.

Yield: about 20 pieces

1 cup all-purpose flour

1/2 cup melted butter, margarine, or *ghee* (clarified butter) (recipe page 79)

1 teaspoon ground **cardamom**

1/2 teaspoon ground ginger

1 cup **finely chopped pitted** dates (cut with scissors)

1/2 cup confectioner's sugar, more as needed

Equipment: Nonstick cookie sheet, medium mixing bowl, mixing spoon, flat plate, pie pan

1. Preheat oven to 350°F.
2. Spread flour out on cookie sheet and set in oven for about 10 minutes, until flour turns golden brown. Pour flour into mixing bowl.
3. Add butter, cardamom, ginger, and dates. Mix well. Using clean hands form into round or oval shapes. Place side-by-side on flat plate.
4. Spread 1/2 cup confectioner's sugar in pie pan or flat plate and roll each candy to coat, adding more sugar as needed. Place on plate and chill.
5. Serve al batheeth as a candy treat. Store in covered bowl and refrigerate.

Morocco

Morocco is an Arab nation in northwest Africa, bordered by the Atlantic Ocean and the Mediterranean Sea. Moroccans are known for fine food and gracious hospitality. The simplest meal is a ceremony in Morocco. The family and guests sit on floor cushions around a low table. Hands are used to eat with, so before every meal they are wiped with a small, hot, damp towel.

Travelers to Morocco rave about exotic and delicious slow-cooked stews called *tagines* (recipe page 7).

Marak Matisha Bil Melokhias (Braised Okra Stew)

Yield: serves 4 to 6

1 pound okra, washed and **trimmed**   white vinegar, as needed

3 tablespoons olive oil

1 large onion, trimmed, peeled, thinly sliced

2 cloves garlic, trimmed, **minced** or 3 teaspoons garlic granules

2 14-ounce canned chopped stewed tomatoes

2 tablespoons parsley **finely chopped**

1 teaspoon paprika

water, as needed

salt and pepper to taste

Equipment: Medium-large bowl, colander, medium saucepan with cover, wooden mixing spoon, serving bowl

1. Place okra in bowl and pour enough vinegar to cover. Let stand for 20 minutes. Transfer to colander and rinse under cold running water. Set aside.

2. Heat oil in saucepan over medium-high heat. Stir in onions and garlic; stirring constantly, cook for 2–3 minutes or until onions are soft. Stir in tomatoes, parsley, paprika, and okra. Stirring frequently, simmer over medium-low heat for about 20–25 minutes or until okra is tender. If necessary, add a little water to prevent sticking, stir in and heat though. Season with salt and pepper to taste. Transfer to serving bowl.

3. Serve hot or at room temperature with Moroccan bread (see next recipe) for dunking.

❧ Quick Moroccan Bread

Yield: makes 2 loaves

1/4 cup lukewarm water (105°F–115°F)

1 envelope (1/4 ounce) active dry yeast

1/4 teaspoon sugar

3 1/2 cups all-purpose flour

1 cup whole wheat flour (coarse cracked grain, if available)

1 tablespoon salt

1 tablespoon anise seeds

1 1/2 cups cold water, more as needed

1 teaspoon vegetable oil, more as needed

1/2 cup white or yellow cornmeal

Equipment: Small bowl, large mixing bowl, mixing spoon, electric mixer with dough hook (optional), floured work surface, dry or nonstick cookie sheet, kitchen towel

1. Preheat oven to 400°F.

2. Place warm water in small bowl; add yeast and sugar. Let stand 5 minutes or until foamy.

3. Place all-purpose and whole wheat flours, salt, and anise seeds in large mixing bowl. Add yeast mixture and water, a little at a time. Mix continually, using clean hands or electric mixer with dough hook, making dough stiff. Transfer to work surface and, if **kneading** by hand, knead for 10 minutes or until smooth and elastic. (If using electric mixer with dough hook, knead at low speed for 5 minutes.)

4. Divide dough into 2 balls and let rest for 5 minutes. Lightly rub oil on each ball and flatten into disk, 1-inch thick and about 6 inches in diameter.

5. Sprinkle dry cookie sheet with 4 tablespoons cornmeal. Place rounds of dough on it, allowing room between to rise. Cover with dampened kitchen towel and place in warm place for 2 hours to rise. Prick each loaf deeply 4 or 5 times to release the gas.

6. Sprinkle tops of bread with remaining cornmeal. Bake for 10 minutes. Reduce heat to 300°F and bake 40 minutes longer, or until the bread sounds hollow when tapped.

7. Serve bread sliced in wedges, warm or cool.

❧ *Tagine de Poulet aux Pruneauc et Miel* (Chicken with Prunes and Honey)

Tagines can be very sweet or hot and spicy, varying from region to region or family to family.

Yield: serves 4 to 6

2 1/2 to 3 pounds chicken, cut into serving-size pieces

6 cups water, more as needed

1 teaspoon salt

1 teaspoon pepper

1/2 teaspoon ground turmeric

2 teaspoons ground cinnamon

1 onion, **trimmed**, peeled, **coarsely chopped**

1 cup **pitted** prunes or other dried fruit such as peaches, apricots, apples, or combination

1 cup honey

1 cup dark brown sugar

1 cup sliced almonds for garnish

1 tablespoon sesame seeds for garnish

Equipment: Large saucepan with cover or **Dutch oven**, slotted mixing spoon or tongs, heat-proof bowl or pan

1. Place chicken pieces in saucepan or Dutch oven; add water to cover, about 6 cups. Add salt, pepper, turmeric, cinnamon, and onion. Bring to boil over high heat, reduce to simmer, cover, and cook 1 hour or until chicken is tender. Using slotted spoon or tongs, transfer chicken pieces to bowl or pan. Set aside and keep warm.

2. Stir in prunes or other dried fruit, honey, and brown sugar. Bring to boil and mix frequently to prevent sticking. Reduce to simmer. Continue cooking uncovered for 30 minutes or until sauce thickens.

3. Return chicken to pan and coat with sauce. Cover and simmer 10 minutes more to heat through.

4. To serve, transfer chicken pieces to a large platter and spoon over remaining fruit sauce. Sprinkle with almonds and sesame seeds.

❧ *Sesame Cornes de Gazelles* (Almond Crescent Cookies)

Moroccan pastries are works of art. They have incorporated the flair of the French while using Middle East ingredients.

Yield: 20 cookies

1 cup **blanched, finely ground** almonds	1 egg, slightly beaten
1/2 cup confectioner's sugar	1 teaspoon cinnamon
1 cup all-purpose flour, more as needed	1/2 cup butter (at room temperature)
1 teaspoon almond extract	1/2 cup sesame seeds, more if needed

Equipment: Large mixing bowl, mixing spoon, pie pan, lightly greased or nonstick cookie sheet

1. Preheat oven to 350°F.
2. Place ground nuts, sugar, 1 cup flour, almond extract, egg, cinnamon, and butter in mixing bowl and mix well. Using clean hands, **knead** mixture into a dough (it will be slightly sticky).
3. Pour sesame seeds into pie pan. Pinch off walnut-sized pieces of dough (if too sticky, add more flour). Roll dough pieces in seeds to coat; between the palms of your hands, roll pieces into about 2-inch-long-cylindrical shapes, thicker in the middle, tapering at the ends.
4. Place side-by-side on cookie sheet, curving slightly into crescents. Bake in oven for about 30 minutes or until golden brown.
5. Serve sesame cornes de gazelles as a snack with milk or tea.

Sudan

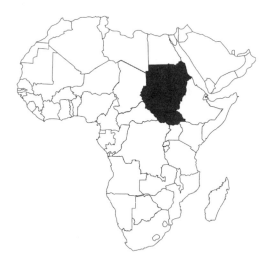

Sudan is in northeastern Africa, and one of the most notable features is the Nile River, which flows from south to north. Fish, mostly Nile perch, is eaten in regions bisected by the Nile and its tributaries. Most of the Sudanese people in the North are Sunni

Muslim, while those in the South follow traditional African beliefs. Yogurt is a favorite food among the nomadic people.

✵ *Fatayer Bil Leban* (**Yogurt Pancakes**)

Yield: serves 4 to 6

3 eggs, **separated**

2 tablespoons corn syrup

2 cups plain yogurt

1 teaspoon baking soda

1 1/2 cups all-purpose flour

2 teaspoons baking powder

1/2 cup butter melted, more as needed

Equipment: Medium mixing bowl, **egg beater** or electric mixer, large mixing bowl, mixing spoon or **whisk**, flour **sifter**, griddle or large skillet, pancake turner or metal spatula.

1. Beat egg whites in medium mixing bowl, using egg beater or mixer, until stiff but not dry. Set aside.

2. Combine egg yolks, corn syrup, yogurt, and baking soda in large mixing bowl and mix well. **Sift** flour and baking powder into egg mixture. Stir continually to blend. Add melted butter; mix well. Fold in egg whites using mixing spoon or whisk.

3. Melt 2 tablespoons remaining butter on griddle or in skillet over medium-high heat; reduce heat to medium. Spoon enough batter on hot skillet to make thin pancakes, about 4-inches wide. Cook until small bubbles appear on surface, about 1 minute. Flip over and cook other side. When done, transfer to platter and keep warm. Continue making pancakes, adding butter as needed.

4. Serve warm with side dishes of yogurt, chopped fruit, and jam or jelly.

✵ *Salata Ma Jibna* (**Salad with Cheese**)

Yield: serves 4 to 6

Dressing:

1/2 cup lemon juice

Salad:

2 red onions, trimmed, thinly sliced

2 cups **shredded** cabbage

1 cup carrots, trimmed, thinly sliced

2 tablespoons white vinegar

2 cloves garlic, **trimmed**, peeled, finely minced

2 cups tomatoes, trimmed, **finely chopped**

1/4 cup olive oil, more as needed

salt and pepper to taste

1/2 cup crumbled feta cheese

Equipment: Small mixing bowl, spoon, medium-large salad bowl, tongs or salad fork, and spoon

1. Make Dressing: In a small mixing bowl combine olive oil, vinegar, lemon juice, and garlic. Stir well and set aside.

2. Place onion, cabbage, carrots, and tomatoes in salad bowl. Pour dressing over mixture. Using tongs or salad fork and spoon, toss to mix well. Salt and pepper to taste. Sprinkle with feta cheese.

3. Serve in individual salad bowls.

Tunisia

Tunisia is located along the Mediterranean Sea. Romans overran the city-state of Carthage (in Tunisia) in 146 BC and controlled the entire Tunisian area until the mid-seventh century. The area provided wheat to the Romans and for centuries was known as the "breadbasket" of ancient Rome. Currently, food is still exported to Europe; however, Tunisians need to import some foods to meet their needs.

Tunisian cooking has been influenced by French, Italian, and Spanish people. Since many Tunisians are Muslims, strict Islamic dietary laws are followed. Many Tunisians eat with their right-hand fingers and everyone eats directly from the same large platter; no forks, knives, or spoons are used.

❧ *Slata de Zaalouk (Cooked Vegetable Salad)*

Yield: serves 4 to 6

2 tablespoons olive or vegetable oil

1 eggplant (about 1/2 pound), **trimmed**, skin on, cut into 1/2-inch **cubes**

2 zucchini, trimmed, cut in 1/2-inch-thick slices

3 cloves garlic, trimmed, peeled, **finely chopped**, or 1 teaspoon garlic granules

3 cups water

1 green bell pepper; trimmed, **seeded**, cut lengthwise into thin strips

1 red bell pepper, trimmed, seeded, cut lengthwise into strips

2 tomatoes, trimmed, **blanched, peeled**, finely chopped

1 teaspoon ground **coriander**

salt and pepper to taste

4 green onions, trimmed, finely chopped, for serving

2 lemons, cut in wedges, for serving

24 black olives, Mediterranean style, for serving

1/4 cup olive oil for serving, to drizzle as needed

Equipment: Large skillet with cover or **Dutch oven**, mixing spoon

1. Heat oil in skillet or Dutch oven over high heat. Add eggplant, zucchini, and garlic. Sauté for 3 minutes and mix well. Add water, bring to boil, cover, reduce to simmer, and cook for 10 minutes.

2. Add red and green peppers, blanched tomatoes, coriander, and salt and pepper to taste. Cook uncovered, stirring frequently, until almost all water evaporates, about 10 minutes. Remove from heat and cool to room temperature.

3. Serve in bowl with little side dishes of green onions, lemons, black olives, and olive oil. Each person adds desired condiments.

Salata Meshwiya (Tuna Fish Salad)

A Tunisian specialty, this salad is popular all along the North African coast.

Yield: serves 2 to 4

2 green bell peppers, **blanched, trimmed, seeded**; cut into thin strips

2 red bell peppers, blanched, trimmed, seeded; cut into thin strips

4 tomatoes, blanched, trimmed, peeled, cut in 1/4-inch-thick slices

6 green onions, trimmed, **finely chopped**

1 cup canned tuna fish (either oil or water pack —drain)

3 tablespoons olive or vegetable oil

1 tablespoon lemon juice

salt and pepper to taste

2 **hard-cooked eggs**, thinly sliced for garnish

1 tablespoon **capers**, drained, for garnish

2 tablespoons chopped flat-leaf parsley, for garnish

Equipment: Salad bowl, mixing spoon, tongs, jar with tight-fitting lid

1. Place green and red peppers, tomatoes, and onions in salad bowl. Crumble tuna, add to vegetables, and toss gently.

2. In jar combine oil, lemon juice, salt, and pepper. Tighten lid and shake well.

3. To serve, pour dressing over salad and toss gently. Garnish with egg slices and capers and sprinkle with parsley.

❧ *Tunisian Tchat-Tchouka* (Baked Egg Casserole)

Yield: serves 4 to 6

2 tablespoons olive oil

4 onions, **trimmed**, peeled, **finely chopped**

4 tomatoes, trimmed, peeled, cut each into 6 wedges

2 green bell peppers, trimmed, **seeded**, cut into 1-inch chunks

1 cup red pimentos, canned, **cubed**

1 clove garlic, trimmed, peeled, **minced** or 1/2 teaspoon garlic granules

6 eggs (1 per person)

1/4 teaspoon paprika

Equipment: Large skillet, mixing spoon, 9-inch shallow ovenproof baking dish or pan

1. Preheat oven to 300°F.
2. Heat oil in skillet over medium-high heat. Add onions and cook until browned, about 3–5 minutes. Add tomatoes, peppers, pimentos, and garlic. Mix well. Reduce to medium heat and cook until vegetables are a soft, pulpy mass, about 20–25 minutes.
3. Transfer mixture to baking dish. Using back of mixing spoon, smooth out top. Again using spoon, make 6 slight indentations about the size of an egg yolk into mixture at equal distances across the top.
4. Break an egg and set it in one of indentations. Repeat using all eggs. Sprinkle eggs with paprika.
5. Bake in oven about 15 minutes or until eggs are cooked through.
6. Serve as the main dish with a side of rice.

❧ *Ghoriba Sablee au Beurre* (Butter Cookies)

Tunisian bakers are famous for melt-in-your-mouth, light-as-air cookies and cakes.

Yield: about 25

6 1/2 cups all-purpose flour, **sifted**

2 cups confectioner's sugar, reserve a little for garnish

2 cups melted butter or margarine

Equipment: Large mixing bowl, mixing spoon, clean hands, nonstick or lightly greased cookie sheet, floured work surface

1. Preheat oven to 350°F.
2. Combine flour and sugar in mixing bowl. Mix well. Make well in center of mixture and pour in melted butter or margarine. Gradually blend with dry ingredients to make dough. Shape into ping-pong-sized balls, place side-by-side on cookie sheet, and chill for about 2 hours.
3. Flatten chilled balls between palms of your hands. Place side-by-side on cookie sheet; bake for about 15 minutes or until golden brown. When cold, dust with confectioner's sugar.
4. Serve as a midday snack with a cool drink or tea.

WEST AFRICA

Most countries in the West Africa region are located on the Atlantic Ocean. The area has been influenced by Western and European settlers and traders. This region earned the name "The Slave Coast" due to heavy slave trading during the seventeenth and eighteenth centuries.

The following countries are considered part of West Africa: Benin, Burkina Faso, Cape Verde, Gambia, Ghana, Guinea, Guinea-Bissau, Ivory Coast (Côte d'lvoire), Liberia, Mali, Mauritania, Niger, Nigeria, Senegal, Sierra Leone, and Togo.

The countries along the West African coast are similar and it is not unusual to find the same foods and cooking customs. Common food crops include corn, palms, taro, cassava, millet, sorghum, sugar cane, peanuts, bananas and plantains, yams, rice, and garden vegetables. Palms are particularly important to this region and every part is used: stalk juice for palm wine, fronds for thatch roofs, and stalk fibers for house construction.

Although palm oil was once very popular for cooking, in more recent years vegetable oil is imported and used instead. Popular snacks throughout Western Africa include melon, pumpkin, sunflower, and squash seeds. Dried melon seeds are very popular and are frequently ground and used to thicken soups and sauces. Coffee and cocoa are major exports and contribute to the success of the economy in the more progressive countries. Livestock raised includes goats, sheep, cattle, pigs, and donkeys.

Benin

Many Benins practice Vodun ("Vodoo"). The rituals and beliefs were brought to the Caribbean Islands and parts of North American during the sixteenth century with the slave trade. Because Benin is a coastal nation, fish and seafood are important to their diet.

🦐 *Ago Glain* (Crab Beninese Style)

The following recipe suggests piri piri (recipe page 16), which is a hot pepper sauce. It was introduced by the Portuguese and is popular in West Africa.

Yield: serves 4 to 6

2 tablespoons palm or vegetable oil

2 large onions, **trimmed**, peeled, **finely chopped**

1/2 cup smooth peanut butter

1 teaspoon piri piri or other hot peppers, to taste (optional)

3 large tomatoes, trimmed, peeled, finely chopped

2 pounds crab meat

salt and pepper to taste

Equipment: Medium-large, heavy-bottomed skillet, wooden mixing spoon, serving dish

1. Heat oil in skillet over medium-high heat. Add onion. Stirring continuously, **sauté** until soft 2–3 minutes. Stir in peanut butter and piri piri or hot peppers. Reduce to medium-low heat. Add tomatoes and mix until well blended. Cook for 5–6 minutes, remove from heat and carefully **fold** in crab meat to keep chunky. Salt and pepper to taste. Transfer to serving dish.

2. Serve warm with rice.

Burkina Faso

Burkina Faso, formerly called Upper Volta, was known as a "paradise of meat" because big game hunting was so popular. The people of Burkina Faso live off the land and any extra food raised is sold as cash crops. Agricultural conditions are hard in Burkina Faso due to frequent droughts and the terrible *tsetse* fly which kills cattle.

✳ *Fo* (Meat Stew)

Stews are popular throughout West Africa, and Burkina Faso is no exception. The national dish is called *fo*. It almost always contains beef, onions, tomatoes, and okra; however, it is up to the individual cooks to add their own special touches. Try adding your own special touch to this recipe. That is what African cooking is all about.

Yield: serves 6

1 1/2 pounds beef, **cubed** (use inexpensive stewing meat)

4 cups water

1 teaspoon salt

1/4 teaspoon ground ginger

1/4 teaspoon ground red pepper

2 onions, **trimmed**, peeled, **coarsely chopped**

4 tomatoes, trimmed, coarsely chopped

2 cups okra, trimmed, coarsely chopped

2 cups squash, peeled, coarsely chopped

salt and pepper to taste.

Equipment: Large saucepan with cover or **Dutch oven**, mixing spoon, medium saucepan with cover, potato masher

1. Place beef, 2 cups water, salt, ginger, red pepper, and onions in a large saucepan or Dutch oven. Bring to boil. Reduce to simmer; cover and cook 1 hour. Add tomatoes and okra, mix well, cover, and simmer 20 minutes.

2. Add remaining 2 cups water and squash in medium saucepan. Bring to boil, reduce to simmer, and cook 15 minutes or until tender. Remove from heat.

3. Mash squash in cooking liquid, using potato masher. Add to meat mixture and mix well. Simmer uncovered for about 15 minutes to thicken; add salt and pepper to taste.

4. Serve *fo* in individual bowls over cooked beans or rice.

✳ *Akara* (Black-Eyed Pea Balls)

CAUTION: HOT OIL USED

Yield: serves 4 to 6

2 cups black-eyed peas, homemade or canned (drain and save liquid)

1 egg

1/2 onion, **trimmed**, peeled, **finely chopped**

1/4 teaspoon ground red pepper

1 teaspoon salt

1 to 3 tablespoons flour

1 cup vegetable oil, more as needed

Equipment: Electric food blender or potato masher, rubber spatula, large mixing bowl, mixing spoon, large skillet, slotted spoon or pancake spatula, paper towels, baking sheet

1. Grind or mash peas into consistency of mashed potatoes using either blender or potato masher. Add a little drained liquid if too dry.

2. Use rubber spatula to transfer to large bowl. Add egg, onion, red pepper, salt, and 1 tablespoon flour and mix well. The mixture should be very firm, not soupy. Add more flour if necessary.

3. Prepare to deep fry: ADULT SUPERVISION REQUIRED. Place two or three layers of paper towels on baking sheet and set aside. Heat 1 cup oil in skillet over medium-high heat. Check temperature either using a food thermometer or handle of a wooden spoon. When oil reaches 350°F on cooking thermometer or small bubbles form at surface on spoon, oil is ready for frying. When ready to fry, hold spoonful of mixture close to oil, and, using another spoon, carefully push mixture off into oil. Flatten slightly with back of spoon. Fry 3 or 4 at a time, in batches, turning to brown each side, about 5 minutes. Remove with slotted spoon or pancake spatula and drain on paper towels.

4. Serve either warm or cold as a side dish with stews, in soup as dumplings, or as a midday snack.

Gambia

The Portuguese were the first traders to settle in Gambia and with them they brought a Portuguese condiment called *piri piri*. It soon became popular throughout most of West Africa. Piri piri is extremely hot and spicy and is added to many foods to enhance their flavor.

❧ *Piri Piri*

Yield: 1 cup

8 red hot chili peppers, **trimmed, seeded, finely chopped**

1/2 cup fresh lemon juice

1 tablespoon cilantro, finely chopped

1 tablespoon parsley, trimmed, finely chopped   1/2 cup olive oil

2 garlic cloves, trimmed, peeled, **minced**

Equipment: blender (if a blender is not available a **mortar and pestle** can be used), rubber spatula, small bowl

1. Combine chilies, lemon juice, cilantro, parsley, and garlic in blender and **puree** until smooth. With blender on low, slowly add olive oil. Blend until smooth. Remove from blender with spatula and place in small bowl.

2. Serve as condiment with seafood, chicken, or meat. *Piri Piri is extremely hot; use cautiously.*

Ghana

Ghana is an agriculturally wealthy country situated on the west coast of Africa. Its varied soils and climates make it possible to grow a wide variety of foods. Ghanaians have developed their own national cuisine that is derived both from the variety of fresh foods available and from the different people who invaded and traded there, such as the Dutch and the British. Ghana is famous for growing high-quality cocoa beans. Almost everyone is involved in some aspect of farming, and nearly every household has a little kitchen garden.

Fishing is a big industry and employs many people in Ghana. Fish is available to everyone throughout Ghana due to coastal fishing, fish farms, inland waters, and Lake Volta, one of the largest human-made freshwater lakes in the world.

Fufu (Plantain, Yam, or Sweet Potato Balls)

Fufu is a national dish of Ghana.

Yield: about 12 to 18 balls

1 pound skin-on plantains, yams, or sweet
potatoes, **trimmed**

water as needed

1 teaspoon ground nutmeg

1 teaspoon ground red pepper, more or less to
taste

salt and pepper to taste

Equipment: Medium sauce pan with cover, large mixing bowl, potato masher or electric
blender, mixing spoon

1. Place plantains, yams, or sweet potatoes in saucepan, cover with water. Bring to boil over
   high heat. Reduce to simmer and cover and cook for about 40 minutes or until tender.
   Remove from heat and allow to cool. Peel and cut into chunks; place in mixing bowl. Using
   potato masher or electric blender, mash into smooth paste. Add nutmeg, red pepper, and salt
   and pepper to taste.

2. Shape mixture into ping-pong-sized balls by moistening hands and rolling mixture in palms.
   Repeat, each time wetting hands, until all of mixture is used. Place balls side-by-side on serving platter. Keep at room temperature until ready to serve.

3. Serve as you would dumplings on top of stew or in soup. *Fufu* is also served as a side dish
   with meat or chicken.

❧ *Hkatenkwan* (One-Pot Meal with Ginger Chicken and Okra)

Yield: serves 6

1/2 to 2 pounds chicken, cut into serving-sized
pieces

1 tablespoon fresh ginger, **trimmed**, peeled,
finely chopped, or 1 teaspoon ground
ginger

1 onion, **trimmed**, peeled, finely chopped

8 cups water

2 tablespoons tomato paste

1 cup tomatoes, trimmed, finely chopped

1 cup chunky peanut butter

1 teaspoon ground red pepper

1 cup eggplant, trimmed, peeled, **cubed**

10 whole okra, trimmed

salt and pepper to taste

Equipment: Large saucepan with cover or **Dutch oven**, slotted spoon

1. Place chicken, ginger, onion, and water in saucepan or Dutch oven and bring to boil. Reduce
   to simmer, cover, and cook 1 hour or until chicken is tender. With slotted spoon remove
   chicken pieces and set aside.

2. Increase heat to medium and add tomato paste, tomatoes, peanut butter, red pepper, eggplant, and okra. Cook for 5 minutes, stirring frequently. Reduce to simmer, cover, and cook
   10 minutes.

3. Return chicken to pan, laying pieces on top of vegetables. Cover and simmer 15 minutes or
   until chicken is heated through. Test chicken doneness. Add salt and pepper to taste.

4. To serve, set saucepan in middle of table and allow everyone to serve themselves.

🦟 *Joffof Ghana* (Chicken and Rice Ghana)

Joffof rice is originally from Senegal, but the people of Ghana have adopted it. Joffof means that the rice is cooked in the same pot with all other ingredients.

Yield: serves 6 to 8

3 to 4 pounds chicken, cut into serving-sized pieces

4 cups **stewed** tomatoes, homemade or canned

2 onions, **trimmed**, peeled, **coarsely chopped**

6 cups water, more as needed

1 cup uncooked rice

1/4 teaspoon ground cinnamon

1/2 teaspoon ground red pepper

1 cup ham, cooked, **cubed**

1 cup sausage, cooked, cubed

3 cups cabbage, coarsely chopped

1 cup green beans, cut in 1-inch pieces, fresh, frozen (thawed), or canned

salt and pepper to taste

Equipment: Medium roasting pan with cover or **Dutch oven**, mixing spoon, oven mitts

1. Preheat oven to 350°F.

2. Place chicken, tomatoes with juice, onions, 6 cups water, rice, cinnamon, and red pepper in roasting pan or Dutch oven. Bring to boil, reduce to simmer, and cover and cook 30 minutes.

3. Layer ham, sausage, cabbage, green beans, and salt and pepper to taste over chicken mixture. Cover and bake in oven for about 45 minutes. Add more water if necessary to prevent sticking.

4. To serve, bring roasting pan or Dutch oven to the table and have guests serve themselves.

🦟 *Akwadu* (Baked Banana with Coconut)

This refreshing dessert is a welcome relief at the end of a spicy Ghana meal. Bananas and coconuts are plentiful and inexpensive all year long in Ghana.

Yield: serves 4 to 6

5 bananas, peeled, cut in half lengthwise

5 tablespoons butter or margarine, melted

2 tablespoons lemon juice

1 cup orange juice

1/2 cup light brown sugar

1 cup **shredded** coconut

Equipment: medium baking pan, small bowl, spoon

1. Preheat oven to 375°F.

2. Place banana slices side-by-side in baking pan and sprinkle with butter or margarine.

3. Mix lemon and orange juice in small bowl. Pour over bananas. Sprinkle with brown sugar and coconut.

4. Bake for 10 minutes or until coconut is golden.

5. Serve warm; spoon bananas and juice into individual bowls.

✵ Peanut Milk

Many children around the world have never tasted a nice, cool glass of milk. There are often no (or hardly any) cows, goats, or sheep to milk in their countries, and even in some countries with available livestock, the thought of drinking milk is quite unpleasant, simply because it is not part of their culture. Such "non-milk-drinking" countries are in Africa, Asia, and some of South and Central America. It has been discovered that even one cup of milk can cause a terrible stomachache or even send someone to the hospital. Extensive research has been done, and scientists have found lactose-deficient people are lacking the body chemicals needed to digest milk. When a protein-rich drink is needed, it is often made with peanuts.

Yield: serves 4 to 6

1/2 cup peanut butter

4 cups water

1/2 teaspoon salt

sugar to taste (optional)

Equipment: Medium saucepan, mixing spoon, **whisk** or **egg beater**

1. Place peanut butter, water, and salt in saucepan. Bring to boil over high heat, stirring until blended. Reduce to simmer and cook for 10 minutes, stirring occasionally.

2. Remove from heat. Add sugar to taste and mix well.

3. Serve either cold or hot in glass or cup; mix well before drinking.

Guinea and Guinea-Bissau

Guinea consists of four regions: the coastal, the inland savanna, the mountainous Fouta Sallon region, and the southeastern forest region. Guinea is a humid tropical country that is known to have extensive rainfall. Most Guineans are involved in agriculture. Cash crops include coffee, bananas, palm products, peanuts, citrus fruits, and pineapples. Nomadic and semi-nomadic herders raise livestock.

❧ Ginger Drink

Poor sanitation is a problem in Guinea, which affects the drinking water. This recipe, with ginger, makes boiled water tasty and gives it a little something extra.

Yield: serves 10 to 12

1/2 cup fresh ginger root, trimmed, peeled, grated

1 teaspoon whole cloves

2 cinnamon sticks

3 cups boiling water

1/2 cup sugar

1/2 cup lime juice

1/2 cup orange juice

4 cups water at room temperature

Equipment: 6- to 8-inch square of cheese cloth with string; large crock pot or enamel or glass container with cover; large, long-handled wooden mixing spoon; ladle

1. Place ginger, cloves, and cinnamon in center of cheese cloth and close tightly with string to make into pouch.
2. Place pouch in crock pot or other container and pour boiling water over. Stir in sugar and set aside at room temperature for an hour, stirring occasionally.
3. When cool, add lime juice, orange juice, and room temperature water. Stir and refrigerate. Before serving, remove and discard pouch.
4. To serve, ladle mixture over ice and garnish each glass with a lime wedge.

❧ Peanut Balls

Yield: about 18 to 24 balls

1 cup **crushed or finely ground** peanuts

2 1/4 cups all-purpose flour

1 cup butter or margarine, at room temperature

1/2 cup confectioner's sugar

2 teaspoons vanilla

18–24 whole peanuts as garnish

Equipment: Medium mixing bowl, mixing spoon, large mixing bowl, mixing spoon or electric mixer, nonstick or greased cookie sheet

1. Preheat oven to 350°F.
2. Mix together peanuts and flour in medium mixing bowl.

3. Combine butter or margarine in large mixing bowl with sugar, using mixing spoon or mixer, and mix until well blended. Add vanilla, then peanut mixture, and mix well.

4. Using clean hands, divide dough into ping-pong-sized balls and place side-by-side on cookie sheet. Leave about 1 inch between. Place a peanut in top center of each ball for garnish.

5. Bake in oven for about 10 minutes or until balls are golden brown.

6. Serve peanut balls as a snack.

Ivory Coast (Côte d'Ivoire)

Côte d'Ivoire, a remarkable nation on the west coast of Africa, has prospered since gaining independence from France in 1960. French influences can still be seen, through the restaurants and shops of major cities. Most people of the Ivory Coast are spread evenly throughout the country, growing food for themselves and export. As a coastal country, saltwater fish is a major food resource that is often exported to other countries.

Calalou (Eggplant and Okra Stew)

Stews, like this calalou, are important one-pot meals in Africa. Everything to be eaten for the day can be thrown in a pot with some water and oil and placed over a fire. Everything cooks together until it is tender and tasty.

Yield: serves 6

1/4 cup peanut or vegetable oil

1 cup onion, **trimmed**, peeled, **finely chopped**

2 tablespoons flour

1/2 cup water, more as needed

2 cups **stewed** tomatoes, homemade or canned

1/2 teaspoon ground red pepper, more or less to taste

1/2 teaspoon thyme

2 bay leaves

1 medium eggplant, trimmed, **cubed** (about 5 cups)

2 cups okra, fresh or frozen, trimmed, cut in 1/2-inch slices

salt and pepper to taste

Equipment: Large skillet with cover, mixing spoon, cup

1. Heat oil in skillet over medium-high heat. Add onions, mix well, **sauté** 3 minutes or until soft.

2. In cup, add flour to water and mix well to dissolve any lumps. Add flour mixture to cooked onions, stirring continually, and cook over medium heat for about 3 minutes until it starts to thicken. Reduce to simmer. Stir in tomatoes, red peppers, thyme, and bay leaves. Mix well. Cover and cook 10 minutes, stirring frequently. Add more water if necessary to prevent sticking.

3. Add eggplant and okra. Cover and simmer about 30 to 40 minutes. Add salt and pepper to taste. Remove and discard bay leaves before serving.

4. Serve in individual bowls as main dish over rice or as side dish with meat or chicken.

❧ *Chicken a la n'gatíetro* (Fried Chicken in Peanut Sauce)

The Ivory Coast is a great producer of peanuts and peanut oil. Peanuts, called groundnuts in Africa, are nutritious and flavorful.

Yield: serves 6

2 to 3 pounds chicken, cut into serving-sized pieces

3 tablespoons peanuts or vegetable oil

1 cup onion, **trimmed**, peeled, **finely chopped**

4 green onions, trimmed, finely chopped

1 large tomato, **coarsely chopped**

2 tablespoons tomato paste

1 teaspoon paprika

1 bay leaf

2 cups water

1/2 cup chunky peanut butter

salt and pepper to taste

Equipment: Large deep skillet with cover or **Dutch oven**, medium mixing bowl, mixing spoon

1. Heat oil in skillet or Dutch oven over medium heat. Add chicken pieces and brown on both sides, about 10 minutes per side. Fry in batches. Return all chicken pieces to skillet or Dutch oven, stacking if necessary.

2. Place onions, green onions, tomato, tomato paste, paprika, bay leaf, water, and peanut butter in bowl. Mix well. Pour mixture over chicken; bring to boil; cover and reduce to simmer. Cook until chicken is tender, about 30 minutes. Turn chicken pieces once while cooking. Season with salt and pepper to taste.

3. Serve on large platter with side dish of rice.

❧ *Tiba Yoka* (Baked Bananas)

A wide variety of bananas grow throughout Africa, from tiny ones just a couple of inches long to enormous specimens several feet in length. Many African-grown bananas are only good to eat when cooked, either fried or baked.

Yield: serves 4 to 6

6 bananas, peeled

1 cup **peanuts crushed or finely ground**

1/2 cup orange marmalade (available at all supermarkets)

1/2 cup melted butter

Equipment: Medium baking pan, small mixing bowl, mixing spoon

1. Preheat oven to 350° F.

2. Roll bananas in peanuts; set in baking pan.

3. In bowl, mix orange marmalade with melted butter. Pour over bananas. Bake in oven until bubbly and hot, about 15 minutes.

4. Serve warm and spoon syrup over bananas. For an added treat, serve with ice cream.

❧ *Kyekyire Paano* (Toasted Cornmeal Cookies)

Yield: about 24 cookies

1 cup cornmeal, yellow or white

1 1/2 cups all-purpose flour, **sifted**

1/2 teaspoon salt

1/2 cup sugar

1/2 teaspoon ground or grated nutmeg

1/2 cup butter or margarine

2 eggs, beaten

1 teaspoon lemon **zest**

Equipment: Medium baking pan, oven mitts, mixing spoon, large mixing bowl, greased or nonstick cookie sheet

1. Preheat oven to 350°F.

2. Spread cornmeal in baking pan. Place in oven for about 20 minutes or until lightly browned. Using oven mitts, stir or shake pan often so cornmeal toasts evenly. Remove from oven. Mix with flour, salt, sugar, and nutmeg in mixing bowl. Blend in butter or margarine with mixing spoon or hands.

3. Add eggs and lemon zest and mix well. Drop dough by spoonfuls on cookie sheet; make each cookie a ping-pong-sized ball.

4. Turn up oven heat to 375°F.

5. Bake in oven for 15 minutes or until golden brown.

6. Serve cookies as a snack with milk.

Mali and Mauritania

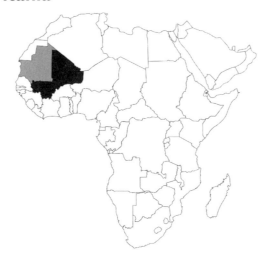

Drought has affected agriculture and livestock in both Mali and Mauritania. This drought has forced Mauritanian nomads to become city dwellers.

Fishing along the coast is a major industry for Mauritania. Mali, an otherwise arid land, has the Niger and Senegal Rivers, providing fish as a source of protein. The fish is often salted and dried and the excess is exported. Using the Niger River water, a massive irrigation project has increased rice production.

Spinach and Peanut Stew

Fresh greens and peanuts are frequently eaten together. In this recipe they are combined into a special stew.

Yield: serves 4 to 6

2 tablespoons vegetable oil, more as needed

1 onion, **trimmed**, peeled, **finely chopped**

1/2 cup peanuts, chopped

2 tablespoons creamy peanut butter

1 tomato, trimmed, finely chopped

1/4 cup tomato paste

3 cups fresh spinach, washed, trimmed, finely chopped, tightly packed or chopped frozen, thawed

1/4 teaspoon ground red pepper, to taste

salt and pepper to taste

Equipment: Large skillet with cover, mixing spoon

1. Heat 2 tablespoons oil in skillet over medium-high heat. Add onion and peanuts. Fry until onion is soft, about 3 minutes, Mix well. Reduce to medium heat and add peanut butter, tomato, tomato paste, spinach, red pepper, and salt and pepper to taste. Mix well. Add more oil if necessary to prevent sticking.

2. Cover and stir frequently; cook 30 minutes.

3. Serve stew hot, in individual bowls over rice or beans or as a side dish.

◈ Peanut and Meat Stew

Yield: serves 6

2 tablespoons vegetable oil, more as needed

1 1/2 pounds beef, **cubed** stewing meat, or chicken, boned and cut into 2-inch chunks

1 bell pepper, **trimmed, seeded, coarsely chopped**

2 onions, trimmed, peeled, coarsely chopped

2 tablespoons creamy peanut butter

1/2 teaspoon salt

1/2 teaspoon thyme

1–2 cups water

1 beef or chicken **bouillon** cube (*Maggi* available at international markets)

1 tablespoon tomato paste (optional)

Equipment: Medium saucepan with cover or **Dutch oven**, mixing spoon, medium mixing bowl

1. Heat 2 tablespoons oil in saucepan over medium-high heat. Add meat or chicken. Mix frequently and brown well, about 5 minutes. Add more oil if necessary to prevent sticking. Reduce to medium heat and add bell pepper and onions. Cook until vegetables are limp, about 4 minutes.

2. Place peanut butter, salt, thyme, 1 cup water, **bouillon**, and tomato paste in medium mixing bowl. Mix well. Pour mixture over meat, mix well. Cover and simmer 30 minutes, mixing frequently. Add more water if necessary to prevent sticking.

3. Serve with mounds of rice.

Niger

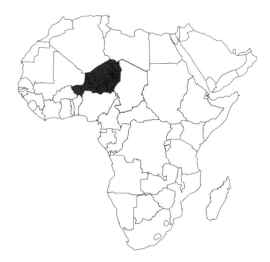

Niger is a landlocked country. Large areas are semi-desert or part of the Sahara Desert. The desert in the north is inhabited mostly by the Tuareg, nomadic herders.

The majority of the people live along a band of land that follows the Niger River in the southeast tip of the country. In this river basin irrigation makes it possible to raise food and livestock with a little more assurance of success. To the west, dry farming techniques are employed, utilizing seasonal rains that make temporary lakes. Livestock is the mainstay of the economy.

Millet and Onions

The best eating **millet** is wholegrain yellow proso variety, available at most health food stores.

Yield: serves 4

1 tablespoon butter or margarine, more as needed

1 cup whole **millet**

2 cups hot water

2 onions, **trimmed**, peeled, **coarsely chopped**

salt to taste

Equipment: Medium skillet with cover or **Dutch oven**, wooden mixing spoon, small skillet

1. Melt 1 tablespoon butter or margarine in medium skillet or Dutch oven over medium-high heat. Add millet, stirring constantly. Toast until grains are light brown, about 5 minutes. Add more butter or margarine if necessary to prevent sticking.

2. Reduce to medium heat and slowly add hot water. Mix well, bring to simmer, cover, and cook about 25–30 minutes, until water is absorbed. (Millet has a nutty aroma as it cooks. The grains stay separate and do not get mushy.)

3. Melt 1 tablespoon butter or margarine in small skillet over medium heat. Add onions and **sauté**, mixing continually until limp and golden brown, about 3–5 minutes.

4. To serve, pour millet into serving bowl and cover with fried onions. Add salt to taste.

Nigeria

Nigeria, on the west coast of Africa, is the world's sixth-leading producer of oil and it has one of the strongest economies in Africa. Agriculture is important to the country's economy.

❧ *Egusi* (Nigerian Melon Seed Soup)

Egusi is an extremely popular Nigerian soup that is made from melon seeds. Shelled melon seeds are available at most African or Latino markets. In this recipe seeds are ground and added to the soup for thickening and add a unique flavor.

Yield: serves 4 to 6

2 tablespoons sunflower, canola, or palm oil

1 pound stewing meat in 1/2-inch cubes, such as lamb, goat, pig, or beef

3 cups water, more as needed

1 onion, **trimmed**, peeled, **finely chopped**

4 hot chili peppers, **trimmed**, finely chopped

3/4 cup ground melon or pumpkin seeds, more if needed

1 pound okra, trimmed

salt to taste

Equipment: Cast-iron skillet, wooden mixing spoon or spatula, large saucepan

1. Heat oil in cast-iron skillet over medium-high heat. Stir in meat and **sauté** until browned on all sides. Stir constantly to prevent sticking. Remove from heat, transfer to saucepan, and add 3 cups water.

2. Stir in onions and chili peppers. Cover and simmer over medium heat until meat is tender, about 1 hour.

3. Stir in ground seeds to thicken; stir until smooth. Add more water if mixture is too thick.

4. Stir in tomatoes and okra and mix through. Cover and simmer over medium-low heat, about 10 minutes until okra is tender. Salt to taste.

5. Serve warm over or along side with *Eba* (recipe page 37).

❧ Toasted Corn and Peanuts

Yield: about 4 cups

1 tablespoon vegetable oil, more as needed

2 cups corn kernels, fresh (cut from about 6 to 8 ears), or frozen (thawed)

2 cups shelled peanuts

salt to taste

Equipment: Medium heavy-bottom skillet, mixing spoon, covered bowl or jar

1. Heat 1 tablespoon oil in skillet over medium heat. Swirl oil to completely coat bottom of pan. Pour corn kernels in pan and cook, stirring continually until lightly browned. Reduce to low

heat and cook about 5 minutes. Do not add more oil unless necessary to prevent sticking. The corn should be on the dry side.

2. Remove from heat. Add peanuts, season with salt to taste, and mix well. Transfer to covered bowl or jar and refrigerate.

3. Serve and eat as a trail mix snack; it is very filling, chewy, and nourishing.

Puff-Puff (Nigerian Doughnuts)

CAUTION: HOT OIL USED.

When the French colonized Nigeria they brought with them their *beignets* (fried fritters) which the Nigerians call "puff-puffs." During the mornings in Nigeria the natives walk around with baskets of puff-puffs on their heads to sell to the people on the streets. This satisfies one's sweet tooth.

Yield: serves 12 to 15

7 cups flour

pinch salt

1/4 cup butter

1 package active dry yeast (each envelope 1/4 oz)

1/2 cup sugar

2 eggs

1 1/2 cups water or palm wine

1 teaspoons vanilla extract

vegetable oil, as needed for deep frying

granulated sugar, as needed

Equipment: Medium-large bowl, wooden mixing spoon or whisk, medium mixing bowl, paper towels, baking sheet, deep fryer or large saucepan, deep fryer thermometer or wooden spoon, slotted metal spatula or metal tongs

1. Sift flour in medium-large mixing bowl and with fingers or back of wooden spoon work butter into flour. Make well in center of flour. Set aside.

2. In medium bowl use fork or whisk to stir together yeast, sugar, eggs, water or palm wine, and vanilla extract. Mix well. Pour mixture into well in center of flour. Using your fingers gradually work in all flour until mixture forms smooth dough.

3. Prepare to deep fry: ADULT SUPERVISION REQUIRED. Have ready several layers of paper towels on baking sheet. Fill deep fryer with oil according to manufacturer's instructions or fill large saucepan, no more than half way, with vegetable oil. Heat oil to 375°F on deep fryer thermometer or place handle of wooden spoon in oil. If small bubbles appear around surface, the oil is ready.

4. To prevent oil from splashing, carefully drop heaping tablespoons of dough into hot oil and fry until golden brown on all sides. Remove with slotted spoon or tongs and drain on paper towel. While still hot, sprinkle each puff-puff with sugar.

5. Serve warm or at room temperature.

Senegal

Senegal, on the west coast of Africa, is mostly low lying and covered with savanna. Most of the Senegalese people live in small villages, farming and raising livestock. The best agricultural areas are to the west where land is fertile.

Because fish is plentiful and cheap, fishing has become a big industry in Senegal.

Tiebou Dienn (also *ceeb u Jen*) (Fish Stew)

Rice, a Senegalese favorite, is combined with fish in the national dish *ceeb u jen*. "Ceeb joints" have sprung up in crowded urban areas where city workers can go to eat ceeb on their lunch breaks. Ceeb joints are small makeshift kitchens outside homes, where the only cooking equipment is a huge iron caldron that sits atop a brush or a wood-burning *brazier* (a large metal pan with room on the bottom for wood to burn, similar to a simple U.S. barbeque oven). Here the housewife cooks for her family then sells what is left to passersby. The ceeb is served to customers in plastic bowls and the "joint" consists of a couple of benches to sit on.

Any combination of in-season vegetables with rice and fish can be used for this hearty dish. Preparing the fish is a little unusual. Deep slits are cut into thick fish steaks or **fillets**, which are then stuffed with herbs and spices. There are three steps to making ceeb: 1. making the fish stuffing (Senegalese call it *roof*), 2. cooking the vegetables, and 3. cooking the rice. In Senegal the rice is cooked after the vegetables in the same caldron. A brown crust of rice called *xoon* forms on the bottom of the pot. This crust is a delicacy and is served with the ceeb. To shorten the cooking time, the rice in this recipe is cooked separately.

Yield: serves 4 to 6

1/2 cup flat-leaf parsley, **trimmed, finely chopped**

4 green onions, trimmed, peeled, finely chopped

1/4 teaspoon ground red pepper, more or less to taste

3 cloves garlic, trimmed, peeled, **minced**, or 1 teaspoon garlic granules

4 (6–8 ounces each) fish steaks, 1-inch thick, or 4 fillets (any firm fish will do)

4 tablespoons vegetable oil, more as needed

1 cup tomato paste

4 cups water

1/2 cup tapioca or 1/2 cup all-purpose flour mixed into a paste with 1/2 cup water

4 cups trimmed, coarsely chopped vegetables, fresh or frozen (thawed), any combination: carrots, turnips, cauliflower, eggplant, okra, green beans, pumpkin, or squash

1/4 small head cabbage, cut into 4 wedges

salt and pepper to taste

3 cups cooked rice (cooked according to directions on package)

2 limes, cut in wedges for garnish

Equipment: **Mortar and pestle** or metal bowl and mallet, paper towels, sharp knife, large saucepan with cover or **Dutch oven**, mixing spoon, slotted spoon, large skillet

1. *Prepare roof*: place parsley, onions, red pepper, and garlic in mortar or metal bowl and grind together using pestle or mallet. Add a few drops of water at a time to make paste.

2. Rinse fish and pat dry with paper towels. Using a sharp knife, cut 1 or 2 deep slits into each piece. Fill with parsley mixture (roof mixture).

3. Heat 2 tablespoons oil in saucepan or Dutch oven over medium-high heat; brown fish on both sides, about 6 minutes per side. Add more oil if necessary to prevent sticking. Remove with slotted spoon and set aside in warm place.

4. *Prepare vegetables*: using same saucepan or Dutch oven, add tomato paste, water, tapioca, and all vegetables. Mix well and bring to boil over high heat. Reduce to simmer. Cover and cook about 45 minutes or until vegetables are tender. Season with salt and pepper to taste.

5. *Prepare rice*: heat 2 tablespoons oil in skillet over medium-high heat. Add cooked rice and fry (DO NOT STIR) about 15 minutes or until bottom becomes crusty brown.

6. To serve, flip rice over with crusty side up in middle of a large platter. Surround rice with fish and vegetables. Serve with lime wedges to sprinkle on fish. To eat, using a clean right hand, pull off pieces of crusty rice and scoop up bite amounts of vegetables and fish. Squeeze together in a ball and pop in your mouth.

Sierra Leone and Liberia

Rice and palm trees are two important food crops in both Sierra Leone and Liberia. Rice is so important it is eaten at almost every meal. Palm oil and heart of palm are favorite foods from the palm tree. Palm oil is used for cooking and palm hearts are added as a vegetable to salads for a crunch. You may find heart of palm, canned, in the specialty section of your super-market. More recently, the popular palm oil is being replaced by vegetable oil for cooking.

❧ Rice Bread

No festive occasion is complete without this tasty heavy bread, favored in Sierra Leone and Liberia.

Yield: serves 6 to 8

1/4 cup oil

1/2 cup water

1/2 cup currants or raisins

3/4 cup sugar

1 cup mashed bananas

2 cups rice flour or instant cream of rice cereal

2 1/2 teaspoons baking powder

1/2 teaspoon baking soda

1/2 teaspoon salt

1/2 teaspoon nutmeg

Equipment: Two mixing bowls, **sifter**, mixing spoon, spatula, greased medium cake pan

1. Preheat oven to 325°F.

2. Mix oil, water, currants or raisins, sugar, and bananas in mixing bowl. Beat mixture well and set aside.

3. In separate bowl, **sift** flour, baking powder, baking soda, salt, and nutmeg. Stir into banana mixture and beat until smooth.

4. Pour into prepared pan, place in oven, and bake approximately 50 minutes. Cake will be heavy, similar to fruit cake.

5. Serve small slices with a glass of milk.

Dried Seeds for Snacking

This recipe can be made with any combination of in-season seeds. Dried seeds and nuts are fun to chew on; however, they are even better if seasoned with sprinkles of garlic granules, red pepper, or curry powder.

Yield: about 4 to 5 cups

2 cups seeds: melon, pumpkin, sunflower, or squash

3 cups water

2 cups cashews and/or peanuts

1 1/2 teaspoons salt

garlic granules, for garnish (optional)

red pepper, for garnish (optional)

curry powder, for garnish (optional)

Equipment: **Colander** or strainer, medium saucepan, mixing spoon, nonstick cookie sheet, oven mitts

1. Preheat oven to 300°F.

2. Place seeds in colander or strainer and rinse off any fibers.

3. Transfer seeds to saucepan and add water and salt. Bring to boil over high heat. Boil 3 minutes and reduce to simmer. Cook about 45–50 minutes. Drain seeds in colander or strainer.

4. Spread seeds and nuts (optional) out on cookie sheet. Bake in oven about 1 hour or until seeds are dry. Shake cookie sheet gently several times during baking in order to dry all seeds. Remove from oven, sprinkle with salt, and cool to room temperature. Store in dry place.

Abala (Savory Steamed Rice)

Abala is a favorite dish among West Africans. It is a dough-like mixture formed into balls, wrapped in warmed banana leaves, and steamed. The banana leaves are not eaten; they simply act as a casing to hold the balls of creamed rice. **Blanched** cabbage or lettuce leaves also work well, as do squares of aluminum foil, which we suggest because it is readily available. For variety, chopped tomatoes or other chopped vegetables, headed and peeled shrimp, or peeled crayfish tails can be added.

Yield: serves 6

1 cup cream of rice cereal

3/4 to 1 cup water

1 green chili pepper, **seeded, finely chopped**

1 onion, **trimmed**, peeled, finely chopped

1/2 cup vegetable oil

1 teaspoon salt

Equipment: Medium mixing bowl, mixing spoon, 6 8-inch squares of aluminum foil, vegetable steamer or deep saucepan, metal colander

1. Pour cream of rice in mixing bowl. Stirring constantly, slowly add boiling water until mixture is thick and smooth. Stir in chili pepper, onion, oil, and salt and mix well. Cool to room temperature.

2. Using clean hands, make 6 balls of mixture and wrap each securely in a square of foil.

3. Fill bottom pan of steamer or deep saucepan with water until it is just below and not touching colander. Bring water to boil over high heat. Place foil-wrapped mixture in colander. Cover tightly to retain steam. Reduce to simmer and cook 2 hours. Check frequently to make sure bottom of pan does not dry out; add boiling water as needed.

4. To serve, each person is given an abala. Each opens the package and begins to eat.

⁂ *Kanya* (Peanut Bars)

Perhaps one of the most popular sweet and crunchy treats in West Africa is a peanut mixture known as *kanya*, *kayan*, or *kanyan*. This simple recipe can be made with fresh roasted peanuts, finely ground or peanut butter. *Kanya* is usually sold by child street peddlers for pennies.

Yield: about 12 pieces

1/2 cup smooth peanut butter

1/2 cup sugar

1/2 cup cream of rice cereal, as needed

Equipment: Small metal bowl, mixing spoon or electric blender, nonstick 9-inch cake pan

1. Place peanut butter and sugar in mixing bowl. Using mixing spoon, beat until well blended.

2. Slowly add cream of rice, stirring continually. If necessary, add more cream of rice to make firm dough.

3. Transfer dough to cake pan. Using back of spoon or clean hands, press evenly to cover bottom. Chill in refrigerator to set.

4. To serve, cut into small rectangular bars and eat as candy.

Ginger Cookies

These cookies have a somewhat unusual ingredient: red pepper.

Yield: about 24 cookies

2 cups flour

6 tablespoons sugar

3 teaspoons ground ginger

1/2 teaspoon salt

1/4 teaspoon ground red pepper, to taste

6 tablespoons butter or margarine

4 tablespoons water or milk

Equipment: Flour **sifter**, large mixing bowl, mixing spoon, floured work surface, rolling pin, cookie cutter or water glass, greased or nonstick cookie sheet

1. Preheat oven to 350°F.

2. **Sift** flour, sugar, ginger, salt, and red pepper together in mixing bowl.

3. Blend in butter or margarine, using mixing spoon or clean hands. DO NOT RUB YOUR EYES; RED PEPPER IN MIXTURE CAN BE IRRITATING.

4. Add water or milk to make firm dough. Transfer to work surface. Using floured rolling pin, roll dough about 1/2-inch thick.

5. Using cookie cutter or top edge of water glass, press into dough to making round cookies. Place side-by-side on cookie sheet. Bake in oven about 15 minutes or until golden brown.

6. Serve ginger cookies as snack.

CENTRAL AFRICA

The Central African countries are Angola, Cameroon, Central African Republic, Chad, Democratic Republic of Congo, Republic of Congo, Equatorial Guinea, and Gabon.

Many people herd cattle, sheep, camels, and goats. Staple foods grown within this region include **millet**, rice, **cassava**, peanuts, beans, sesame seeds, eggplant, **sorghum**, yams, corn, peas, and tomatoes. Bananas of all sizes are grown in the rainforest.

Cassava is a staple crop of the region. It is a root that resembles a yam or sweet potato and in its raw form is poisonous. Although similar in appearance and often confused with it, African yams are botanically different from the North American sweet potato.

Angola

Angola, formerly known as Portuguese West Africa, is located on the lower south-west coast of Africa. Now, according to the United Nations, this country is a part of the Central (Middle) African Region.

Angolans gained their independence from the Portuguese in 1975. The Portuguese influence can be found in the Angolan use of hot spices and their baked goods. Life is changing slowly for the rural people. Agriculture is still practiced by hand, as it has always been. The land is fairly good for agriculture and oil has become the primary export.

Galinha Muamba (Angolan Chicken Dish)

Yield: serves 6

1 teaspoon red pepper flakes

1 teaspoon ground ginger

1 onion, **trimmed**, peeled, **finely chopped**

3 cloves garlic, trimmed, **minced** or 1 teaspoon garlic granules

salt and pepper to taste

1/2 cup lemon juice

2–3 cups water

2 tablespoons vegetable oil, more as needed

2 pounds chicken, cut into serving-sized pieces

Equipment: Small mixing bowl, mixing spoon, gallon plastic bag or bowl with cover, paper towels, large skillet, tongs, large baking sheet, aluminum foil

1. Preheat oven to 350°F.

2. Place red pepper flakes, ginger, onion, garlic, salt and pepper to taste, lemon juice, 2 cups water, and 2 tablespoons vegetable oil in small bowl and mix well. Pour into bag and add chicken pieces. Seal bag and shake vigorously to coat chicken. Rotate bag frequently to coat

chicken. If no seal bags are available, place chicken in large bowl and cover with mixture, making sure all pieces are coated. Cover and refrigerate about 4 hours. Rotate chicken pieces in **marinade** frequently.

3. Remove chicken from marinade and set aside. Save marinade. Heat 2 tablespoons oil in skillet over medium-high heat. Fry chicken in batches, using tongs to turn and brown on both sides. Add more oil if necessary. Transfer browned pieces side-by-side to baking pan.

4. Pour remaining marinade over chicken in pan. Cover tightly with foil and bake for 35 minutes or until tender.

5. Serve chicken with vegetables and rice.

Cameroon

Cameroon is divided by various land forms: to the north are dry plains, the south and central regions are savanna-covered plateaus, and the western region is dominated by highlands and mountains. The coastal region consists of swamps and dense rain forests. Cameroon has a diversified economy and, in terms of food, is self-sufficient.

Eba (Cassava Dumplings)

Eba is made with *garri* (gari), a coarse grain derived from cassava tubers. Cassava is a root resembling a yam or sweet potato and in its raw form is poisonous. An extensive process must take place to cleanse and purify cassava. The cassava tuber is peeled, washed, and grated or crushed to produce a mash which is then placed into porous bags, and heavy stones are placed on top to press out all the water. After fermenting for 1 to 2 days, the mash is then sieved and roasted. The final step is to pound into a flour, which can be stored for long periods of time. When needed, the gari is reconstituted by adding boiling water.

Yield: serves 4 to 6

1 cup gari (available at international markets)   2 cups boiling water

Equipment: Medium-large bowl, mixing bowl

1. Place gari in bowl and slowly stir in boiling water. Continue stirring until thick play-dough-like or soft clay consistency is formed. Make 6–8 golf-sized balls with your hands.
2. Serve with Egusi (recipe page 28). Tear off small pieces with your right hand and eat by dunking into soup or stew.

Central African Republic

The Central African Republic takes its name in part from its location, smack in the middle of Africa. The land consists of a high plateau that covers most of the country with rain forests in the south. Even though Central African Republic is just north of the equator, the high altitudes of the plateaus prevent most of this area from being extremely hot. Agricultural work is done by many people, mostly raising livestock and subsistence farming. The most common method of farming is the slash and burn technique.

✿ Sesame Cakes

Yield: serves 4 to 6

1 cup roasted sesame seeds, ground; use blender, mortar and pestle, or food processor to grind. Buy seeds in bulk at health food stores.

1/4 cup water, as needed   1 tablespoon oil, more as needed

salt to taste

Equipment: Medium mixing bowl, mixing spoon, wax paper, medium skillet, metal spatula

1. Place ground sesame seeds in mixing bowl. Add just enough water to make firm dough. Add salt to taste. Shape into ping-pong-sized balls and place side-by-side on wax paper.
2. Heat oil in skillet over medium-high heat. Slightly flatten balls into patty shape and fry on both sides in skillet until golden brown, about 6 minutes.
3. Serve either warm or cold as snack with honey or peanut butter.

Chad

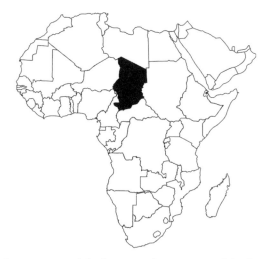

Chad is a landlocked country with three major geographical regions: a desert zone in the north, known for Islamic nomads; an arid Sahelian belt in the center; and a more fertile Sudanese savanna zone in the south that is excellent for farming.

Lake Chad, the second largest lake in Africa, supplies large quantities of fish to the local Buduma people. Fish is most popular smoked and dried.

Sugar cane was introduced by the French in the 1970s. Children in Chad will chew on a length of sugar cane as a sweet treat.

Peanuts are among the biggest exports of Chad.

Sweet Potato and Peanut Salad

Yield: serves 6

4 cooked sweet potatoes; fresh, **trimmed**, peeled or canned, drained, cut into 1/4-inch slices

1/2 onion, **trimmed**, peeled, **finely chopped**

1/2 cup lemon juice

2 tablespoons peanut or vegetable oil

1 cup roasted peanuts, shelled

salt and pepper to taste

3 tomatoes cut in 4 wedges, for garnish

Equipment: Medium bowl, mixing spoon or tongs, cup, mixing spoon

1. Place sweet potato and onion in bowl. Using spoon or tongs, lightly toss to mix.

2. Mix lemon juice and oil in cup and pour over potato mixture; mix well. Add peanuts and salt and pepper to taste. Lightly toss and transfer to serving bowl. Garnish with tomato wedges around edge of bowl and chill.

3. Serve salad as a side dish along with stew.

Squash and Peanut Dessert

Yield: serves 4 to 6

4 tablespoons butter or margarine

1 cup peanuts, shelled, **coarsely chopped**

3 tablespoons dark brown sugar, more as needed

3 cups acorn squash fresh, cooked, mashed, or frozen, thawed and mashed

Equipment: Medium skillet, mixing spoon

1. Melt 2 tablespoons butter or margarine in skillet over medium-high heat. Add peanuts and cook 3 minutes until lightly browned. Add 3 tablespoons brown sugar and mix well. Stir in squash and remaining 2 tablespoons butter or margarine and mix well. Taste to adjust sweetness and add sugar if necessary.

2. Cook over low about 4–6 minutes to heat through.

3. Serve as dessert in individual bowls.

Democratic Republic of Congo and Republic of Congo

In Central Africa these two countries have similar names but were settled by different people and have different histories. King Leopold II of Belgium acquired the area known as the Democratic Republic of Congo in 1885 and named the land Congo Free State. Since then the country has had several names including that of Zaire. After the overthrow of Zaire President Mobutu in 1997, the name changed back to the Democratic Republic of Congo (DR Congo).

The Republic of Congo sits to the west of the DR Congo and it was explored by the Portuguese and then later taken over by the French. The capital of the Republic of Congo, Brazzaville, was named after Pierre Savorgnan de Brazza, a man who worked on behalf of the French. In the region it is said that the two countries distinguish themselves as ''Congo-Leopoldvile'' (Democratic Republic of Congo) and ''Congo-Brazzaville'' (Republic of Congo).

❧ *Babute* (Curried Beef Meatloaf)

The dish is named after the region Babute in which it originated. Babute is located in the north central region of the Democratic Republic of Congo.

Yield: serves 6 to 8

2 pounds lean chopped beef	2 1/2 cups evaporated milk
1/2 teaspoon salt	3/4 cup dried apricots, **finely chopped**
1 1/2 tablespoons curry powder	6 bay leaves
4 eggs, beaten	2 teaspoons butter, more as needed

Equipment: Medium-large mixing bowl, medium mixing bowl, fork or whisk, mixing spoon, greased 4×8×4-inch loaf pan

1. Preheat oven to 350°F.
2. Place beef in medium-large mixing bowl. Using fingers, break meat into small pieces. Sprinkle in salt and curry powder and mix well.
3. In medium mixing bowl combine eggs and evaporated milk. Using fork or whisk, mix well. Add half egg mixture to beef and mix well. Stir in apricots. Transfer mixture to greased loaf pan and gently smooth top. Pour remaining egg mixture over meatloaf. Float bay leaves in milk and dot with butter.
4. Bake in oven 30–40 minutes or until top resembles baked custard.
5. To serve, remove and discard bay leaves and spoon meatloaf over rice.

❧ Congo Green Papaya Soup

Yield: serves 4 to 6

2 chicken bouillon (in Africa the *Maggi* brand is popular)

2 cups boiling water or vegetarian broth or vegetable broth

2 tablespoons butter or margarine

1 small onion, **trimmed**, peeled, **finely chopped**

2 large green papayas (also known as *paw-paws*), trimmed, peeled, **seeded**, diced (about 2 cups)

1 teaspoon salt

1/2 teaspoon hot red pepper

1/4 cup milk

1 teaspoon cornstarch

Equipment: Medium saucepan, mixing spoon, small bowl, small spoon

1. Dissolve bouillon in boiling water. Set aside.

2. Over medium-high heat, melt butter or margarine in saucepan. Add onion and **sauté** until soft about 2–3 minutes. Stir in bouillon broth. Stir in papaya, salt, and red pepper. Simmer until papaya is tender, about 8 minutes. Transfer to blender or food processor and blend until smooth. Transfer back to saucepan and set over medium-low heat.

3. Make **slurry**: Place cornstarch in small bowl and slowly stir in milk until smooth. Using mixing spoon, slowly stir slurry mixture into soup. Stirring frequently, simmer until soup thickens, about 5 minutes.

4. To serve, pour into individual cups or bowls and accompany with Eba (recipe page 37).

Equatorial Guinea and Gabon

Equatorial Guinea is the smallest country on the continent of Africa. It is so named because of its proximity to the equator and was formerly part of the Spanish Guinea colony.

Similar to the Republic of Congo, Pierre Savorgnan de Brazza explored and settled in Gabon, giving the country a deep French influence in its cooking.

Poulet Nyembwe (Chicken Course)

This is considered the national dish of Gabon.

Yield: serves 6 to 8

2 tablespoons vegetable oil, more as needed

1 1/2 to 2 pounds chicken, cut into serving-sized pieces

1 onion, **trimmed**, peeled, **finely chopped**

2 garlic cloves, trimmed, **minced**

1 hot chili pepper, trimmed, finely chopped

1 ripe tomato, trimmed, finely chopped

20 pieces okra, trimmed, finely chopped

1 cup water

2 cups *nyembwe* sauce (also known as palm butter) or Palm Soup Base (*Sauce Graine* or *Noix de Palme* available at African supermarkets or international markets)

salt, black pepper, and cayenne pepper to taste

Equipment: **Dutch oven** or heavy-bottomed saucepan with cover, tongs or mixing spoon, large bowl, medium bowl

1. In Dutch oven or heavy-bottomed saucepan heat 2 tablespoons oil over medium high heat. Add chicken and **sauté** until browned on all sides. Remove from pan using tongs or large spoon and transfer to large bowl. Set aside and keep warm.

2. In same Dutch oven or saucepan, over medium heat, stir in onions, garlic, and chili pepper and sauté until soft, about 2–3 minutes. Add more oil if necessary to prevent sticking. Stir in tomato and okra. Reduce to medium heat. Stirring frequently, sauté until okra is soft, about 5 minutes. Return chicken to Dutch oven or saucepan.

3. In medium bowl add water to nyembwe sauce or Palm soup base. Mix well and pour over chicken. Bring to simmer over medium-high heat. Stir in salt, pepper, and cayenne pepper to taste. Reduce to medium-low heat. Cover and cook for 40–50 minutes or until chicken is tender. Transfer to large serving bowl.

4. Serve with fufu (recipe page 17).

SOUTHERN AFRICA

The southern region is dominated by the Republic of South Africa and has received worldwide recognition post-Apartheid. The southern African region includes Botswana, Lesotho, Namibia, South Africa, and Swaziland.

Botswana

Since gaining independence from the British in 1966, Botswana transformed itself from one of the poorest countries in the world to a middle-income status. Mineral exports such as diamonds and gold assisted in this dramatic turnaround. As one of Africa's largest cattle exporters, cattle raising is one of the most important food-producing activities in Botswana.

Botswana has a diverse terrain, from the Okavango Delta in the northeast to the Kalahari Desert in the southeast. It has rich grasslands and savannas throughout with an abundance of wildlife, including a large population of the endangered African wild dog.

Potjie (Vegetable Stew)

This is a traditional southern African stew.

Yield: serves 6 to 8

2 tablespoons vegetable oil

3 yellow onions, **trimmed**, peeled, **coarsely chopped**

6 garlic cloves, trimmed, peeled, coarsely chopped

5 medium potatoes, washed, trimmed, coarsely chopped

1 medium butternut squash, washed, trimmed, coarsely chopped

5 large carrots, washed, trimmed, coarsely chopped

2 ears of corn, shucked and rinsed and cobs cut crosswise into 2 pieces

1 small turnip, washed, trimmed, coarsely chopped

1 stalk celery, washed, trimmed, coarsely chopped

8–10 cups vegetable broth

2 teaspoons dried oregano

2 teaspoons dried basil

salt and pepper to taste

Equipment: Large heavy-bottom pot with lid, wooden mixing spoon, serving bowls, ladle

1. Heat oil in broth pot over medium-high heat. Add onion and garlic. Stirring constantly, **sauté** until soft and light brown, about 3–5 minutes.
2. Add chopped vegetables and cover with vegetable broth. Stir in oregano, basil, and salt and pepper to taste. Cover and simmer on medium-high heat until vegetables are soft, about 30–40 minutes.
3. Serve hot in individual bowls with fufu (recipe page 17) for dunking.

Lesotho and Swaziland

Both Lesotho and Swaziland are small independent countries located within the eastern coast of South Africa. In Lesotho many people work in South African mines to support their families. Food needs to be imported because of the overworked and poor soil. Many households have small vegetable gardens. The economy and terrain of Swaziland is similar to South Africa and it is a very poor country.

Setjetsa (Cooked Pumpkin)

Cereals, inexpensive and nutritious, are important to the people of Lesotho.

Yield: 6 to 8

4 cups pumpkin, **trimmed**, peeled, washed, cut into small pieces or canned, drained

3 cups water

1 tablespoon sugar

1 tablespoon butter, margarine, or vegetable oil

salt to taste

2 cups cornmeal

Equipment: Medium saucepan, mixing spoon

1. Combine pumpkin and water in saucepan, cook over medium until pumpkin is soft.
2. Add sugar and butter, margarine, or vegetable oil. Mix well. Slowly add cornmeal, mixing continually until well blended and smooth.
3. Reduce to low heat and continue cooking 30 minutes. Add salt to taste.
4. Serve as a side dish with meat and vegetables.

❧ Pap (Porridge)

Pap is an Afrikaans word that means "porridge" or "gruel." In South Africa pap is served along with a main dish such as a stew.

Yield: serves 6 to 8

2 cups water

salt to taste

2 cups polenta or maize (available in the international food section of most supermarkets)

Equipment: Medium saucepan, stirring spoon

1. Bring water to boil in medium saucepan, stir in polenta. Reduce to medium heat and stir frequently to prevent sticking. Cook for 20–25 minutes or until all water is absorbed. Add salt to taste.
2. Serve with a medley of vegetables, such as the following recipe.

❧ Lesothan Chakalaka (Medley of Vegetables)

Yield: serves 6 to 8

2 tablespoons vegetable oil

2 tomatoes, trimmed, peeled, finely chopped

1 carrot, **trimmed, finely chopped**

salt to taste

1 bell pepper, trimmed, finely chopped

crushed red pepper to taste (optional)

1 onion, trimmed, peeled, finely chopped

Equipment: Medium-large skillet with lid, mixing spoon

1. Heat vegetable oil in skillet over medium-high heat. Add carrot, bell pepper, and onion, stirring frequently. **Sauté** until soft, about 5 minutes. Stir in tomatoes, cover, and cook until mixture is well blended, about 5 minutes.

2. Add salt and crushed red pepper to taste.

3. Serve hot over pap (previous recipe).

Namibia

Namibia received gained independence from the Republic of South Africa in 1990. It is a high desert plateau land that supports cattle and ostrich raising but little agriculture. Both cattle and ostriches are raised in the northern and central parts of Namibia where it is dry and arid.

White Namibians, mostly descendants of Germans who ruled for many years, dominate this region. German customs and eating habits have been adapted to their new surroundings. For example, in Germany chicken eggs are used while in Namibia ostrich eggs are used. The San, a dwindling group of people who still forage for food, eat ostrich eggs, then use the shell to carry water.

Fishing along the coast provides food and export income. Ovambo tribe people, who live in both Namibia and Angola, raise **millet** as a staple crop. The millet is pounded into a flour, then made into a thick porridge (recipe follows).

Thick Millet Porridge

Yield: serves 4

1 cup **millet**, available at most health food and Asian food stores

3 cups water

1/4 teaspoon salt

milk and honey or sugar to taste

Equipment: Electric blender, mixing spoon, saucepan

1. Grind millet in blender until powdered (or buy in powdered form).

2. In saucepan bring water and salt to boil. Stir in powdered millet and reduce to medium-low heat. Stir constantly until smooth. Cook 10 minutes.

3. Serve porridge in bowls with milk and sugar.

South Africa

The foods and cooking methods of South Africa were influenced by the early Dutch and other European settlers. At the southern tip of Africa, The Dutch East India Company founded a settlement in 1652 called Cape Town. The original intention was to provide a resupply point for traveling ships. Upon settling the area, these Europeans cultivated farms with fresh food and livestock, providing an abundance of food for the ship crews. The blending of East Asian, Malay, and Indian cooking styles and ingredients with the European touch has created a unique South African style.

Mushroom Soup

Yield: serves 4 to 6

1 pound (16 ounces) fresh mushrooms, **trimmed**, cut into 1/4-inch thick slices

5 tablespoons butter

1/2 teaspoon curry powder

3 tablespoons cake flour

4 cups chicken or vegetable broth, homemade or canned

1 6-ounce can evaporated milk

salt and pepper to taste

Equipment: Damp kitchen towel, knife, cutting board, large saucepan, mixing spoon, blender

1. In skillet melt butter or margarine and add mushrooms. On medium-high heat, stirring constantly, **sauté** mushrooms until soft, about 4–6 minutes.

2. Sprinkle and stir in curry powder and flour. Slowly pour in broth and allow mixture to boil for 2–3 minutes.

3. Remove from heat and in batches spoon mixture into blender. Blend until smooth. Return mixture to saucepan. Stir in evaporated milk, salt and pepper to taste and return to boil. Cook about 5 minutes until heated through.

4. Serve hot in individual soup bowls.

﹪ **Vegetarian Hot Rice Salad**

In South Africa, hot rice salad is a very traditional dish and can be prepared in a variety of ways. It usually accompanies a meat dish.

Yield: 6–8 servings

4 cups vegetable broth

2 cups rice

3 onions, **trimmed**, peeled, **finely chopped**

1 clove garlic, trimmed, **minced**

1 green bell pepper, trimmed, **seeded, coarsely chopped**

1 tablespoon sunflower or canola oil

8 ounces mushrooms, cleaned, trimmed, coarsely chopped

1 large tomato, trimmed, peeled, coarsely chopped

salt and pepper to taste

Equipment: Large saucepan with tight-fitting lid, stirring spoon, large skillet, slotted spoon, large fork, serving dish

1. Bring vegetable broth to boil in saucepan and add rice. Cook according to directions on package until firm but not mushy.

2. Heat oil in skillet over medium-high heat. When hot, add onion, garlic, and bell pepper. Cook until soft, about 6–8 minutes. Add mushrooms and chopped tomato, stirring frequently until all vegetables are tender, about 12–15 minutes. Add salt and pepper to taste.

3. Stir vegetable mixture into rice with large fork.

4. Serve hot on individual plates.

﹪ *Engelegte (Curry Pickled Fish)*

Combining curry seasonings with pickling spices is an easy and tasty way to preserve fish. The fish keeps for several days without refrigeration. Sailors on the Dutch spice ships learned of this preserving process from the Malaysians. When the South Africans heard about a new way of preserving food, curry pickled fish soon became very popular.

Yield: serves 6 to 8

3 tablespoons vegetable oil, more as needed

6 skin-on fish **fillets**, fresh or frozen, washed, patted dry

3 cups vinegar

1 teaspoon curry powder

1 teaspoon **turmeric**

1 teaspoon salt

2 onions, **trimmed**, peeled, thinly sliced

3 tablespoons sugar

Equipment: Large skillet, pancake turner or spatula, glass or earthenware bowl with lid or plastic wrap, small saucepan, mixing spoon

1. Heat 3 tablespoons oil in skillet over medium heat. Add fish fillets and fry on both sides until fish is done (about 8 minutes per side—the flesh becomes **opaque** white and **flakes** easily when poked with fork). Add more oil if necessary. With pancake turner or spatula, carefully transfer fillets to bowl. Slightly overlap fillets to cover bottom of bowl.

2. Heat vinegar, curry powder, turmeric, salt, and sugar in saucepan over medium-high heat. Mix well and bring to boil. Add onion slices. Reduce to simmer and cover and cook 8–10 minutes. Remove from heat and cool to room temperature.

3. Pour vinegar mixture over fillets, cover with lid or plastic wrap, and refrigerate about 12 hours before serving.

4. Serve engelegte cold, with onion slices, on a bed of lettuce as an appetizer or salad.

EAST AFRICA

During the nineteenth century, the eastern region of Africa was heavily influenced by Europeans, particularly the Portuguese. In the last century the neighboring Islamic Middle East countries have had a strong influence on East African cooking and traditions.

The countries within this region include Burundi, Djibouti, Eritrea, Ethiopia, Kenya, Madagascar, Malawi, Mauritius, Mozambique, Rwanda, Somalia, Tanzania, Uganda, Zambia, and Zimbabwe.

Crops include **millet**, **sorghum**, barley, wheat, corn, **plantains**, potatoes, peanuts, sugar cane, and peas.

Burundi and Rwanda

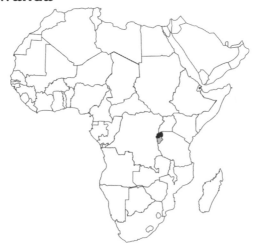

Burundi is a small landlocked country and said to be the poorest country in Africa with little resources. By contrast the neighboring country, Rwanda, is hilly and fertile, allowing most Rwandans to farm their own land.

Beans and Plantain Medley

Very little meat is eaten in Burundi and Rwanda, thus beans and plantains are very popular in order to attain essential vitamins and proteins.

Yield: serves 4

2 tablespoons palm or vegetable oil, as needed

1 small onion, **trimmed**, peeled, **finely chopped**

4 green plantains or green bananas, peeled, finely chopped

2 15-ounce cans red kidney beans

salt and chili pepper to taste

Equipment: Medium-large skillet, mixing spoon, colander

1. Heat 2 tablespoons oil in skillet over medium-high heat. Stir in onion and plantains. Stirring frequently, **sauté** until soft, about 3–5 minutes. Add more oil as needed to prevent sticking.
2. Place beans in colander and rinse under cold water. Transfer to skillet with sautéed onion and plantains. Reduce to medium heat, stirring frequently and continue to cook until heated through.
3. Serve hot as a side dish.

Djibouti and Eritrea

The northeast corner of Africa, referred to as the Horn of Africa, was greatly influenced by the ancient spice traders.

❧ *Berbere (Mixed Spices)*

This is a traditional spice combination used to flavor many dishes within this region.

Yield: 1/2 to 1 cup

2 teaspoon whole cumin seeds	10 small dried red chilies, **trimmed**
4 whole cloves	1 teaspoon ground ginger
3/4 teaspoon cardamom seeds	1/4 teaspoon turmeric
6 whole black peppercorns	1 teaspoon salt
6 whole allspice	1/4 teaspoon cinnamon
1 teaspoon fenugreek seeds	1/4 teaspoon ground cloves
1/2 teaspoon whole coriander	

Equipment: Small skillet, mixing spoon, spice grinder (a coffee grinder can be used) or mortor and pestle, 10–12 ounce jar with tight-fighting lid

1. In skillet on low heat, toast cumin, cloves, cardamom, peppercorns, allspice, fenugreek, and coriander for 2 minutes, stirring constantly. Remove from heat and set aside to cool.

2. Transfer toasted spices from skillet to spice grinder or mortar and pestle. Add chilies. Grind together to fine powder.

3. Transfer to jar. Mix in ginger, salt, cinnamon, and ground cloves. Close with lid and shake well to mix. Store in refrigerator until needed.

4. To serve, add to soups and stews to enhance flavor (typical recipe using berbere follows).

❧ *D'Nish Zigni (Fiery Potato Stew)*

Yield: serves 4 to 6

2 tablespoons olive oil	4 cups chicken broth homemade or canned (available in most supermarkets)
1 medium onion, **trimmed**, peeled, **coarsely chopped**	4 tablespoons tomato paste
4 tablespoons berbere (previous recipe)	salt to taste
6 medium potatoes, peeled, **cubed**	

Equipment: Large saucepan or **Dutch oven**, wooden mixing spoon

1. Heat oil in saucepan or Dutch oven over medium-high heat. Add onion and stirring constantly **sauté** until soft, about 4–6 minutes. Stir in berbere and potatoes. Stirring frequently, sauté for 5 minutes.

2. Stir in broth and tomato paste. Mix well. Reduce to medium heat. Cover and simmer, stirring occasionally, 15–20 minutes or until potatoes are tender. Salt to taste.

3. Serve warm or room temperature with *injera* (recipe page 54).

Ethiopia

Ethiopia is an independent nation located in the Horn of Africa. Ethiopians have their own unique style of cooking, which is very popular in many countries.

Ethiopia has a variety of terrains ranging from high plateaus to lowland valleys. The best areas for agriculture are the plateaus, which provide fertile soil and a year-round growing season. This enables most people to farm in Ethiopia.

An important cash crop is coffee. Ethiopia is the birthplace of coffee: it is in the forests of the Kaffa region that coffee Arabica grows wild. Coffee is *"bun"* or *"buni"* in Ethiopia. *Tef* or *teff* (wheat alternative) is another important crop that is unique to this country. It is the source from which the bread *injera* is made. *Wats*, fiery hot stews, are served on injera.

✤ *Doro Wat (Chicken Stew)*

The national dish of Ethiopia is doro wat, made with chicken and **hard-cooked eggs**. Wats (stews) can also be made with beef, fish, **lentils**, or **chickpeas**.

Yield: serves 4 to 6

1/2 cup butter or margarine

2 cups onions, **trimmed**, peeled, **finely chopped**

3 cloves garlic, trimmed, peeled, **minced** or 1 teaspoon garlic granules

1 cup tomato paste

3 cups chickens broth, homemade or canned, more as needed

1 teaspoon ground ginger

1/2 teaspoon ground cinnamon

1/4 teaspoon ground cloves

1 teaspoon ground red pepper, or to taste

1 chicken, cut into serving-sized pieces

6 peeled, hard-cooked eggs

salt and pepper to taste

Equipment: Large saucepan or **Dutch oven**, mixing spoon

1. Melt butter or margarine in saucepan or Dutch oven over medium-high heat. Add onions and garlic, stirring frequently. **Sauté** until onions are golden brown, about 3–5 minutes. Reduce heat to simmer. Add tomato paste, broth, ginger, cinnamon, cloves, and red pepper to taste. Mix well.

2. Add chicken pieces and coat well with sauce. Bring to boil, cover, reduce heat to simmer, and cook for about 45–50 minutes. Add more broth if necessary to prevent sticking. Turn chicken pieces over to prevent sticking. Add eggs, cover with sauce, and continue cooking for 10 minutes or until chicken is tender. Remove from heat and add salt and pepper to taste.

3. To serve, place pot of stew in middle of table and have guests help themselves, using fingers of the right hand. Serve with rice and injera bread (next recipe).

Injera (Ethiopian Bread)

Teff or teff, the **millet** used by Ethiopians, is not easy to find outside of this region, so we have adapted a recipe that closely resembles real injera. Baked on a griddle or in a skillet, this thin, pancake-like bread makes a perfect scoop for Ethiopian wats (stews).

Yield: about 18 pieces

4 cups self-rising flour

1 cup whole wheat flour

1 teaspoon baking powder

2 cups club soda

4 cups water, more as needed

2 tablespoons vegetable oil, more as needed

Equipment: Large mixing bowl, mixing spoon, 9-inch nonstick skillet, ladle, clean kitchen towel, 12-inch square aluminum foil

1. Place self-rising and whole wheat flour in bowl. Add baking powder and mix well. Add club soda and 4 cups water and mix into smooth, thin batter.

2. Heat 2 tablespoons oil in skillet over medium-high heat. With ladle, thinly spread 1/2 cup of batter into skillet. Remove from heat and swirl batter so that it makes a very thin pancake; return to heat. When moisture evaporates and small holes appear, similar to a pancake, remove from heat. Do not brown or make too crisp. Cook one side only.

3. Flip skillet over to release bread onto clean kitchen towel (spread out and covering work surface). If pancake sticks to skillet, lightly tap pan rim against work surface. If batter is too pasty, add water to thin. Add oil to skillet for each batch to prevent sticking, and repeat until all batter is used. When bread is cool, stack, and cover with foil to prevent drying out.

4. To serve, set platters of injera on the table. Everyone helps themselves, tearing off a piece of injera to help them scoop up the food. Serve with *doro wat* (recipe page 53).

Kenya

Nomadic herders live in the northern part of Kenya where most of the country's livestock is raised. The eastern plateau is the most usable land for farming. Kenyans see livestock as a form of wealth. For this reason meat is not traditionally a major part in the Kenyan's diet. People instead consume grains and vegetables and by-products of their livestock, such as milk. British settlers established Western farming and ranching methods in the fertile agricultural region of the eastern plateau that are still used today. Corn was introduced to Africa over 100 years ago by Europeans and is now an important food throughout most of Africa.

Ugali (Cornmeal Porridge)

The national dish of Kenya is a cornmeal mush called ugali. It is cornmeal cooked with water to a thick consistency and poured out onto a board or plate for everyone to eat from. The following recipes for ugali could be made over an open fire outside or in a kitchen. Beef broth with vegetables can be poured over it, and on special occasions chunks of meat are added to the broth.

Yield: serves 4 to 6

1 cup cold water

1 cup yellow cornmeal

1 teaspoon salt, more or less to taste

3 cups boiling water

Equipment: Medium saucepan, mixing spoon or whisk

1. Place cold water in saucepan. Mixing continually, add cornmeal and salt. Bring to a boil over high heat. Mixing continually, slowly add 3 cups boiling water to prevent lumps.

2. Reduce to simmer, cover, and cook for about 8 minutes, mixing frequently to prevent sticking. Add salt to taste and mix well.

3. Serve ugali in individual bowls with cream, sugar, syrup, **ghee** (recipe page 79), or butter poured over it.

Sukuma Wiki (Collard Greens)

The dish sukuma wiki literally means "stretch the week." In Africa this recipe would also be made with **cassava** leaves or potato leaves if collard greens were not available. Any other greens can be substituted. "Doing your own thing" is typical in African cooking—following the basic recipe using what is on hand and easily available.

Yield: serves 4 to 6

6 cups tightly packed, chopped collard greens (if collard greens are not available, spinach or kale can also be used), fresh, washed, **trimmed**, drained or frozen, thawed

2 tablespoons vegetable oil, more as needed

1 onion, trimmed, peeled, **coarsely chopped**

1 cup **stewed** tomatoes, chopped

1 green chili pepper, **seeded, finely chopped** or 1 teaspoon ground red pepper

3 tablespoons lemon juice

1 tablespoon all-purpose flour

1/2 cup water, more as needed

salt and pepper to taste

Equipment: **Steamer pan or basket** or large saucepan with a cover, fitted with a metal **colander** or strainer; mixing spoon; large skillet

1. Fill bottom of steamer or saucepan with water so that when water boils it does not touch steamer rack or basket. Fit steamer rack, strainer or colander filled with greens into saucepan and bring to boil. Reduce heat if necessary so water boils but does not evaporate. Add more hot water if necessary. Cover and steam about 8 minutes.

2. Heat 2 tablespoons oil in skillet over medium-high heat. Add onion, tomatoes, and pepper. Cook 3 minutes or until onion is soft. Mix well. Reduce to low heat, if necessary. Add oil to prevent sticking.

3. Add lemon juice, flour, and water in cup and mix well. Pour into onion mixture. Mix well. Add remaining 1/2 cup water, cooked greens, salt, and pepper to taste and mix well. Increase to medium heat. Cover and cook 3–5 minutes or until heated through.

4. Serve greens as side dish with meat stew.

Madagascar

Madagascar, the fourth largest island in the world, is located in the Indian Ocean just off the east coast of Africa. Many different kinds of crops can be raised due to its varied climates and soils. Vanilla beans are an abundant cash crop. Rice is a staple crop.

France colonized Madagascar from 1896 to 1960, leaving strong influences on the country's cooking style. The vegetables in these recipes would actually be mashed together in Madagascar, but we suggest that you finely chop them; the result will be almost the same with less work and better texture.

❧ *Soupe a la Malgache* (Soup of the Malagasies)

Yield: serves 6 to 8

2 pounds veal or beef bones

8 cups water

2 cups **stewed** tomatoes, homemade or canned

3 white potatoes, **trimmed**, peeled, **finely chopped**

2 onions, trimmed, peeled, finely chopped

3 carrots, trimmed, peeled, finely chopped

1 turnip, trimmed, peeled, finely chopped

1 leek, trimmed, finely chopped, washed, drained

1 cup finely chopped string beans, fresh, **trimmed** or frozen, thawed

salt and pepper to taste

4 cups cooked rice (cooked according to directions on package)

Equipment: Large saucepan with cover, mixing spoon

1. Place meat bones in saucepan. Add water and bring to boil. Cover and reduce heat to simmer. Cook about 1 hour.

2. Add tomatoes, potatoes, onions, carrots, turnip, leek, and string beans. Cover and continue simmering additional 45–50 minutes or until vegetables are tender and meat is cooked through. Add salt and pepper to taste and mix well.

3. Serve soup thick and hot over large servings of cooked rice.

❧ *Tomatoes Rougaille* (Tomato Sauce)

Yield: serves 4 to 6

2 cups green bell peppers, **trimmed, seeded, finely chopped**

2 cups **stewed** tomatoes with juice

1 onion, trimmed, peeled, finely chopped

few drops liquid hot pepper sauce, or to taste

salt and pepper to taste

6 cups cooked rice (cook according to directions on package); keep warm

Equipment: Medium bowl, mixing spoon

1. Place green peppers, tomatoes, onion, hot sauce, and salt and pepper to taste in the bowl. Mix well. Adjust seasonings (salt and pepper) and refrigerate.

2. Serve rougaille chilled over cooked warm rice.

Mozambique

Mozambique, an independent nation, was formerly called Portuguese East Africa. Portugal set up outposts in Mozambique beginning in 1505 AD, colonized the country, and were forced to leave after an independence movement in 1974. The Portuguese imported a vast assortment of fruit trees and vegetable plants to Mozambique and cultivated them in climates and soils similar to Portugal. Some of the most popular foods grown are oranges, lemons, limes, pineapples, chilies, pepper, corn, tomatoes, sweet potatoes, **cassavas**, and bananas.

❧ *Arroz de Coco* (Coconut Milk Rice)

Yield: serves 4 to 6

2 tablespoons vegetable oil

1 green bell pepper, **trimmed, seeded, finely chopped**

1 cup onion, trimmed, peeled, finely chopped

1 cup uncooked rice

3 cups coconut milk, canned, frozen, or homemade (recipe page 138)

2 tomatoes, trimmed, **peeled**, finely chopped or 1 cup canned stewed diced tomatoes

salt to taste

1/2 teaspoon ground red pepper, more or less to taste

Equipment: Large skillet with cover or **Dutch oven**, mixing spoon

1. Heat oil in skillet or Dutch oven over medium heat. Add bell pepper and onion. Stirring frequently, **sauté** 3–5 minutes or until vegetables are soft but not brown.

2. Reduce heat to low and add rice. Stir constantly until grains are evenly coated. Add coconut milk and tomatoes. Bring to boil. Reduce heat to simmer, cover, and cook for 20–25 minutes or until liquid is absorbed and rice is tender.

3. Remove skillet or Dutch oven from heat and season with salt and ground red pepper to taste. Cover mixture and set aside for 10 minutes.

4. To serve, **fluff** rice with fork and serve directly from skillet or Dutch oven or transfer to serving bowl.

❧ *Ovos Moles de Mango* (Mango and Egg Pudding)

Mangos were introduced to Africa by way of India, where they are thought to have originated. They are nutritious and delicious.

Yield: serves 4 to 6

2 ripe mangos, **trimmed**, peeled, **seeded, coarsely chopped**

1/4 cup fresh lemon juice, strained

1/4 cup water

2 cups sugar

1 teaspoon ground cinnamon

1 teaspoon ground clove

5 egg yolks (refrigerate egg whites to use at another time)

whipped cream or prepared whipped topping for garnish

Equipment: Large mixing bowl, potato masher or electric blender, medium saucepan, wooden mixing spoon, **egg beater** or electric mixer

1. Mash mangos, lemon juice and water in mixing bowl using potato masher or place in electric blender and blend until smooth.

2. Pour mixture into saucepan. Add sugar, cinnamon, and cloves. Stirring continually, bring to boil. Reduce heat to simmer and cook until mixture thickens, about 10–12 minutes, stirring frequently to prevent sticking. Remove from heat.

3. Place egg yolks in large mixing bowl. Using mixer, mix yolks until slightly thick, about 2–3 minutes. Continue mixing while slowly pouring hot mixture into yolks. Beat until smooth and thick, about 5 minutes. Cool to room temperature and refrigerate for 2 hours before serving. The dessert will thicken as it cools.

4. Serve pudding in small individual bowls as dessert. Top with whipped cream.

﷯ *Bolo Polana* (Potato and Nut Cake)

Yield: 10 to 12 slices

11/2 cups cake flour

2 teaspoons baking powder

1 teaspoon ground cinnamon

1/2 teaspoon ground cloves

1 cup butter or margarine at room temperature

2 cups sugar

4 eggs, **separated**

1/2 cup heavy cream

1 cup cooked mashed potatoes, fresh or instant

1 cup nuts, **finely chopped**: cashews, **blanched** almonds, or pecans

4 teaspoons lemon **zest**

1 teaspoon almond extract

Equipment: **Sifter**, medium mixing bowl, large mixing bowl, electric mixer, mixing spoon, **whisk**, greased 9-inch **springform pan**

1. Preheat oven to 350°F.

2. Sift flour, baking powder, cinnamon, and cloves into medium mixing bowl.

3. Using mixer, blend butter and sugar in large mixing bowl. Add egg yolks (one at a time), mixing continually until smooth and creamy. Stirring constantly, add cream, mashed potatoes, flour mixture, nuts, lemon peel, and extract until mixture is smooth and lump-free.

4. Place egg whites into clean, dry, medium mixing bowl. Beat with electric mixer until egg whites are stiff and form peaks.

5. Gently **fold** whites into batter until well blended, using spoon or whisk.

6. Pour mixture into springform pan and bake in oven for 60 minutes or until toothpick inserted into center of cake comes out clean.

7. Serve cake slightly warm or at room temperature.

Somalia

Somalia is a poor country situated in the Horn of Africa that suffers frequent droughts, making farming a challenge. Many Somalis are nomadic herders of camels, which are a major source of pride and wealth. They drink camel milk, eat camel meat, and use camels as their beast of burden. Herding animals is a long-standing tradition in Somalia.

Due to the fertile land in the south, many Somali herders have transitioned from herding to farming. Many people along the Jubba and Shabeele rivers grow bananas, sugar cane, corn, vegetables, and **sorghum**. In this region fishing is also an important source of food, and what is not eaten is exported. Most Somalis are Sunni Muslim and follow the traditions of Islam.

✸ Curry in a Hurry

Yield: 6 servings

2 tablespoons vegetable oil, more as needed

1 onion, **trimmed**, peeled, **coarsely chopped**

2 tablespoons curry powder

1/2 cup all-purpose flour

1/2 cup cold water

3 cups beef or chicken broth, homemade or canned

3 cups cooked beef, pork, lamb, chicken, turkey, or combination, cut into bite-sized **cubes**

salt and pepper to taste

Equipment: Large saucepan, mixing spoon

1. Heat 2 tablespoons oil in saucepan over medium-high heat. Add onions. **Sauté** until soft, about 2 to 3 minutes. Add curry powder and mix well. Add more oil if necessary to prevent sticking.
2. Mix flour with 1/2 cup cold water and blend to a smooth paste. Add to skillet, mixing continually to prevent lumps. Cook 2 to 3 minutes. Add broth, mix well, and bring to boil. Reduce heat to simmer.
3. Slowly add cubed meat, vegetables, and salt and pepper to taste. Mix well. Cook until heated through, about 5 minutes.
4. Serve with injera bread (recipe page 54).

Tanzania

Tanzania is located on the eastern coast of Africa. The people are fortunate to have many natural resources and a climate suited for agriculture. Many people farm to provide their own food and cash crops. A popular cash crop is coffee and the unique flavor is popular in many Western countries.

Tanzanians combine grains and legumes to replace meat. Another source of protein is fishing from abundant rivers, lakes, and coastal waters.

Spiced Papaya

This dish is commonly eaten as an accompaniment to meat.

Yield: 6 servings

2 papayas, about 1 pound each, firm to the touch, **trimmed**, peeled, **seeded**, and cut into 1-inch cubes

2 tablespoons butter, margarine, or vegetable oil, more as needed

salt to taste

1 teaspoon ground nutmeg

Equipment: **Steamer pan** and rack or large saucepan with cover, strainer, or **colander**; large skillet

1. Fill bottom pan with water so that when water boils it does not touch steamer rack. Fit steamer rack, strainer or colander into large saucepan, add papaya cubes, and cover tightly. Bring water to boil over high heat, reduce to medium heat, and cook for about 10 minutes or until papaya is tender, not mushy.

2. Heat 2 tablespoons butter, margarine, or vegetable oil in skillet. Add nutmeg and mix well. Add steamed papaya and salt to taste. If necessary add more butter, margarine, or vegetable oil. Carefully toss to coat.

3. Serve hot as a side dish with meat.

✸ Meat Cakes

Yield: serves 6

1 pound ground meat

4 cups potatoes, **trimmed**, grated

1 cup carrots, trimmed, grated

1 egg, beaten

1/2 cup milk

1/2 cup flour

2 tablespoons sugar

1/2 teaspoon salt

1 teaspoon curry powder, or more to taste

1 teaspoon baking powder

2–4 tablespoons vegetable oil

Equipment: Grater, skillet, large and medium mixing bowls, mixing spoons, spatula

1. Place meat, potatoes, and carrots in large mixing bowl. Add egg and milk. Using mixing spoon or clean hands, blend well.

2. Mix together flour, sugar, salt, 1 teaspoon curry powder, and baking powder in medium mixing bowl. Slowly add flour mixture to meat mixture and mix constantly using clean hands.

3. Heat 2 tablespoons oil in skillet over medium-high heat. Using clean hands, shape about 1/2 cup mixture to make each patty and place side-by-side in hot skillet. Allow space between patties to turn. Fry for about 5 minutes on each side, or to desired doneness. Continue frying patties until all of mixture is used. Add more oil if necessary to prevent sticking. Keep patties in warm place until serving time.

4. Serve as the main dish, in a sandwich, or as a light snack.

Uganda

Uganda is a landlocked country that sits on the equator in East-Central Africa. Many Ugandans cultivate the land and grow their own food. The bulk of the crops are grown in the fertile region south of Lake Kyoga.

Peanut Butter Candy

One of the principal crops of Uganda, as well as most of Africa, is peanuts. They are nutritious and hardy, making them a first-rate survival food. In this recipe peanuts and highly prized honey are combined to make a sweet treat.

Yield: 24 to 30 pieces

1 cup peanut butter, either smooth or chunky

1 cup honey, slightly warm

1 cup powdered milk or toasted wheat germ or combination, more as needed

1/2 cup finely grated coconut

Equipment: Medium mixing bowl, mixing spoon, pie pan, flat plate, plastic wrap or foil to cover plate

1. Place peanut butter and honey in bowl. Using mixing spoon mix well. Stir in 1 cup powdered milk and/or wheat germ. Mix into stiff dough, adding more powdered milk or wheat germ as needed. Form mixture into 1-inch ping-pong-sized balls or patties.
2. Place coconut in pie pan. Roll balls or patties in coconut to coat. Place side-by-side on plate, cover with plastic wrap or foil, and refrigerate.

⁂ Ground Nut Sauce with Greens

Yield: serves 4 to 6

2 tablespoons vegetable oil

1 onion, **trimmed**, peeled, **finely chopped**

2 tomatoes, trimmed, finely chopped

1 cup okra, trimmed, **coarsely chopped**, fresh or frozen and thawed

1 cup peanuts, finely chopped

1/4 cup sesame seeds

4 cups chicken broth, homemade or canned

1 teaspoon curry powder

salt to taste

4 cups collard greens or spinach, chopped, fresh, washed, trimmed, **blanched** or frozen and thawed.

Equipment: Large skillet with cover, mixing spoon

1. Heat oil in skillet over medium high heat. Add onion and cook 2–3 minutes or until soft. Stir in tomatoes and okra, stirring frequently until okra is soft, about 5–8 minutes.

2. Add nuts, seeds, and chicken broth. Bring to boil, reduce to simmer, and cook about 10 minutes. Stir frequently, until mixture slightly thickens. Add curry powder and salt to taste. Mix well.

3. Add greens to mixture and mix well to coat greens with sauce. Cover and cook for about 10 minutes or until greens are heated through and limp.

4. Serve greens as a side dish with meat or beans.

Zambia

Zambia rests on a high plateau, which kept it free from European settlers until the nineteenth century. The country has been inhabited by tribes of hunters and gatherers, including the Ndembu tribe.

In more recent years, the transition from subsistence farming to commercial farming has improved the economy. The growing and commercial canning of pineapples and tomatoes has assisted in this turnaround.

❧ *Nshima* (Corn Meal Dumpling)

Nshima, cooked from plain maize or maize flour, is deeply rooted within the country's traditions, customs, rituals, and folklore. When harvest is plentiful, Nshima is eaten at almost every meal.

Yield: serves 6 to 8

5 cups cold water   2 cups cornmeal

Equipment: **Dutch oven** or large saucepan with lid, wooden mixing spoon

1. Pour water into Dutch oven or saucepan, heat over medium-high heat until water boils. Reduce heat to medium. Stirring continuously with wooden spoon, slowly add cornmeal one spoonful at a time.
2. Continue cooking and stirring until mixture thickens and all liquid is absorbed. The mixture should be smooth with no lumps.
3. Once desired consistency is reached, remove from heat, cover, and let sit for 10 minutes before eating.
4. Serve hot with stew of choice. For a traditional Zambian meal, wash hands prior to eating and using your right hand take a clump of Nshima and dip into stew.

❧ *Ifisashi* (Greens in a Peanut Sauce)

Greens in peanut sauce is traditional within Central and South African countries. Zambia natives call this dish ifisashi, It is usually served as a vegetarian dish, but cooked chicken, beef, or fish can be added if desired. The most popular type of greens used in Zambia are collard greens, pumpkin leaves, sweet potato leaves, beet greens, mustard greens, spinach, and kale.

Yield: serves 6 to 8

2 cups of water, more as needed

2 cups raw peanuts, shelled, skinned; use a **mortar and pestle** to pound until smooth or use a food processor to grind until smooth or use 2 cups natural, sugar-free peanut butter

1 onion, **trimmed**, peeled, **finely chopped**

2 tomatoes, trimmed, peeled, finely chopped

2–3 pounds greens, trimmed, washed, rinsed, and finely chopped

salt to taste

Equipment: Mortar and pestle or food processor, large heavy-bottom saucepan with lid, mixing spoon, individual serving bowls

1. In saucepan bring 2 cups water to boil over medium-high heat. Stir in peanuts or peanut butter. Mix thoroughly. Stir in onion and tomatoes and **sauté** over medium-high heat until onions are soft, about 3–4 minutes.

2. Stir in greens and mix well. Reduce to medium-low heat. Cover and cook for 30 minutes, stirring frequently. Add more water as needed to prevent sticking. Mixture should be the consistency of thick sauce. Add salt to taste.

3. Serve hot in individual bowls with *nshima* (previous recipe).

Zimbabwe

Zimbabwe, formerly Rhodesia, is a landlocked country. The Shona people of Zimbabwe make up a majority of the population. Many are moving from farming and cattle-raising to living in cities in search of a better life. Corn is a major staple in their diets as in other African countries; meat is eaten but plays a minimal role. Fish from lakes and rivers are enjoyed both fresh and in dried form. Dried fish is extremely popular because it needs no refrigeration and is a rich source of protein.

The *Ndebele* people, another group in Zimbabwe, traditionally lived by growing **millet** and hunting. They make a thick porridge called *isitshwala* that is served with soured milk or mixed with locally grown wild greens. Corn has taken the place of millet. When ground, it is also called *sadza*, the national food of Zimbabwe. Stews of beef, chicken, or vegetables are poured on top of the sadza.

There are strong English influences in Zimbabwe cities due to years of British rule. Many Zimbabweans still enjoy English tea. In the cities the people follow European customs and eating habits.

❧ **Breedie (Beef Stew)**

Yield: serves 4 to 6

2 tablespoons vegetable oil, more as needed

1 pound lean stewing beef, **cubed**

2 onions, **trimmed**, peeled, **finely chopped**

2 cups **stewed** tomatoes, homemade or canned

1 cup corn kernels, fresh, cut from the cob or frozen and thawed

1/2 pound green beans, fresh or frozen, cut in 1/2-inch pieces

1/2 cup seedless raisins

3 teaspoons sugar

salt and pepper to taste

Equipment: Large saucepan with cover or **Dutch oven**, mixing spoon

1. Heat 2 tablespoons vegetable oil in a saucepan or Dutch oven over medium-high heat. Add meat and cook until browned, about 8 minutes, stirring frequently. Reduce to medium heat. Add onions and **sauté** until soft, about 3–5 minutes. Add more oil if necessary to prevent sticking.

2. Add tomatoes, corn, green beans, raisins, sugar, and salt and pepper to taste. Mix well; reduce to simmer. Cover and cook 30 minutes or until meat is tender. Reduce to simmer, cover, and cook 30 minutes or until meat is tender.

3. Serve breedie hot over a mound of snowy white rice.

❧ **Cornmeal Cake**

Yield: serves 6

4 cups milk

2 eggs, beaten

3/4 cup butter or margarine

1/2 cup sugar

1 cup yellow cornmeal

1 tablespoon vanilla extract

1/2 cup sour cream

Equipment: Medium saucepan, wooden mixing spoon, 8-inch cake pan, spatula

1. Preheat oven to 350°F.

2. Place milk, eggs, 1/2 cup butter or margarine, and sugar in saucepan. Bring to boil over medium-high heat. Remove from heat and add cornmeal, stirring continually to prevent lumps. Reduce to low heat and continue cooking for 20 minutes or until thickened. Stir frequently to prevent sticking. Add vanilla and mix well.

3. Melt remaining 1/4 cup butter and coat bottom and sides of cake pan. Add mixture. Bake for 30 minutes, until cake is golden brown and toothpick inserted in center comes out clean. Remove from oven. Using spatula, carefully cover top with sour cream and return to oven for 15 minutes more or until top is bubbly and lightly browned.

4. Serve cake for dessert while still warm, cut into squares.

2

Asia and the South Pacific

The foods of Asia and the South Pacific are as diverse as the people. The largest concentration of the earth's population lives in this part of the world.

ASIA

All the countries within Asia, except for Australia and New Zealand, have one food in common: rice. Asians have a great respect for rice growing, a painstaking, hands-on, labor-intensive task. Even today, with modern technology, the only tool many rice growers have to harvest the rice patties with is a handheld hoe. There are over 2,000 varieties of rice grown throughout the world to suit different types of soil, terrain, climate, and cultures.

Countries such as China, Japan, and India each have a unique cooking style.

In most Asian countries, retaining the natural flavor of the main ingredient is very important. Steaming (a very healthy way to cook) and **stir fry** are the most common cooking methods. Spices are added with a sense of balance and harmony, never with a "heavy hand."

Afghanistan

Afghanistan, located in central Asia, is a mountainous, landlocked country that experiences periods of extreme drought. With less than 10 percent of farmable land, it was necessary to develop an underground water irrigation system. This has improved the harvest of major crops such as wheat, corn, barley, and rice. Afghanis are currently plagued by ongoing war.

The food and eating habits of Afghanis are similar to those of their neighboring countries: Pakistan, Iraq, and Iran. Favorite foods are soups, rice dishes, yogurt, kebabs, *naan* (bread), and tea. In this mostly Muslim society, lamb and chicken are the primary meats eaten and they are often seasoned with saffron, mint, **coriander**, **cilantro**, cardamom, and black pepper. Fruits and vegetables are important to the diet; however, they must be dried and stored to preserve them for cold winter months. The national drink of Afghanistan is tea, flavored with the spice cardamom.

Bonjan Borani (Eggplant and Yogurt Casserole)

Yield: serves 6

4 tablespoons vegetable oil, more as needed

1 onion, **trimmed**, peeled, finely sliced

1 eggplant, trimmed, (about 1 1/2 to 2 pounds) cut into 1/2-inch, skin-on **cubes**

1 cup plain yogurt

3 cloves garlic, trimmed, peeled, **minced** or 1 teaspoon garlic granules

3 tablespoons chopped fresh mint, finely
   chopped or 2 teaspoons crushed dried mint

paprika for garnish

salt and pepper to taste

Equipment: Large skillet, slotted mixing spoon, baking casserole or 9-inch baking pan, small bowl

1. Preheat oven to 350°F.

2. Heat 4 tablespoons oil in skillet over medium-high heat. Add onion and eggplant. Stirring frequently, **sauté** until golden, about 8–10 minutes. Add more oil if necessary to prevent sticking.

3. Using slotted spoon, transfer mixture to baking casserole and set aside.

4. Bake in oven about 20–25 minutes or until bubbly and lightly browned on top.

5. Serve directly from the oven with side dish of rice and plenty of bread.

Firnee (Pistachio Pudding)

Yield: Serves 4 to 6

1/2 cup whole milk, more as needed

1/2 cup cornstarch

1/4 cup cold water

1/2 cup sugar, more to taste

1 pinch salt

1/2 teaspoon freshly ground **cardamom**

1/2 teaspoon saffron threads (available at most supermarkets)

2 tablespoons pistachios, shelled, crushed

Equipment: Small mixing bowl, mixing spoon, medium saucepan, medium serving bowl

1. In small mixing bowl, mix 1/2 cup milk, water, and cornstarch and stir until smooth. Set aside.

2. Heat 2 1/2 cups milk in medium saucepan over medium heat. Stirring constantly, add salt and sugar. Stir continuously until sugar dissolves.

3. Stir in cornstarch mixture until well blended. Stirring constantly add cardamom and saffron. Continue stirring until mixture thickens, about 3–5 minutes. Adjust sweetness to taste, add more sugar if necessary. Remove from heat and pour into a medium serving bowl. Sprinkle with pistachios and refrigerate for at least an hour before serving.

4. Serve in individuals bowls as a dessert.

Bangladesh

Bangladesh, formerly known as East Pakistan, was formed in 1971 after breaking away from Pakistan, more than 1,000 miles away. Rice is their main cash crop, accounting for the majority of the cultivated land. Fishing and seafood harvesting are important to the Bangladesh economy, as well. Low-lying marshes are home to millions of frogs, whose tasty legs show up on fancy restaurant menus around the world.

A typical Bengali meal consists of highly seasoned vegetables, fish, or seafood, followed by a soup made from *dal* (see recipe page 108). To gently end the meal, dessert is often a mild, sweetened, soft white cheese sprinkled with rose water.

In the past decade, natural disasters, affecting agriculture, have had a negative impact on Bangladesh's economy. Today, however, the country is showing greater self-reliance. Exports have continued to improve and the government is making an effort to attract foreign investors.

❧ *Bhapa Ilish Patey* (Steamed Fish Fillets)

Hilsa fish is the national fish of Bangladesh. This unique tropical fish lives in the sea for most of its life then migrates up river for spawning. Economically, this is essential for fisherman within river regions of Bangladesh. (This fish is steam cooked; please refer to glossary for details on cooking with a **steamer pan or basket**.)

Yield: serves 4 to 6

6 fish **fillets**, about 5 ounces each, hilsa, shad, tilapia, or any firm white fish (available at local fish markets)

1 1/2 teaspoons turmeric powder, more as needed

salt to taste

3 tablespoons ground mustard

2 green chili peppers, **trimmed, minced**, more   1 tablespoon mustard or vegetable oil
as needed for garnish

1/2 cup heavy cream

Equipment: Small bowl, mixing spoon, pie pan, **steamer pan or basket**

1. In small bowl combine salt and turmeric powder. Rub fish fillets with turmeric and salt mixture and set aside, about 20 minutes.

2. Prepare **steamer**: fill steamer with water, allowing at least 1 inch of space between water line and bottom of steamer basket. Bring water to boil.

3. In pie pan mix together ground mustard, green chilies, 1/2 teaspoon turmeric, cream, and oil. Mix well. Dip and coat each fish fillet into mixture and place in steamer basket.

4. Set steamer basket filled with fish fillets over boiling water; cover tightly. Reduce to medium heat and cook about 8–12 minutes or until fish is opaque white and **flakes** easily when poked with a fork.

5. Serve hot with rice and garnish with chopped green chilies.

Cambodia

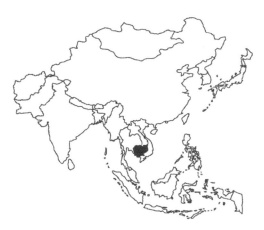

Political stability has only recently returned to Cambodia, a tiny country tucked between Thailand, Laos, and Vietnam. The Cambodians are mostly village people whose lives have been plagued with war and malnutrition.

Most of the people live in the center of the country where monsoon season (from May to October) causes annual flooding making the land rich and fertile for growing rice. The Mekong River and the Tonle Sap Lake (where fish farming is practiced) are centrally located, making fish a primary source of food for the people. Fish is eaten fresh or can be dried or salted to preserve and eat later. To eat salted fish it must first be soaked in water to leach out the salt. Famous sauces are made of fish and are called *tuk trei*; these sauces and fish paste (*prahoc*) are used in cooking to enhance flavors.

People living along the Cambodian coast love their squid. A common sight is thousands of squid drying in the sun on bamboo poles suspended over boat decks. The drying squid look like crystal prisms hanging from a chandelier. The common crops grown are sweet potatoes, onions, chili peppers, oranges, bananas, pineapple, coconuts, tomatoes, and corn. Seasonings include chilies, mint, and garlic.

Similar to other Asian countries, Cambodians squat around low tables and eat with chopsticks. Tea is the main drink while meals consist of steamed or fried rice mixed with fish. Roasted sunflower seeds are often eaten as a tasty snack.

Trey ang swai chei (Grilled Fish with Green Mango Slaw)

In Cambodia trey ang swai chei is made with Asian catfish; however, any firm white fish fillets can be used.

Yield: serves 2 to 4

2 whole catfish (about 1 pound each), scaled, cleaned, filleted (available fresh or frozen at supermarkets)

1–2 green mangos, peeled, **pitted, shredded**

1 tablespoon fresh lime juice

1 tablespoon sugar

3 hot chili peppers, **trimmed, finely chopped,** to taste

salt to taste

Equipment: Small mixing bowl, mixing spoon, large platter, grill, spatula, fork

1. In a small bowl, mix together lime juice, sugar, hot chili pepper, and salt to taste.

2. Spoon shredded mango in center of large platter. Pour lime mixture evenly over the top. Set aside.

3. Grill fish on both sides until golden brown, using spatula to flip fish over. To test doneness: fish flakes easily when poked with a fork.

4. To serve, arrange fish on top of the green mango and serve with rice.

China

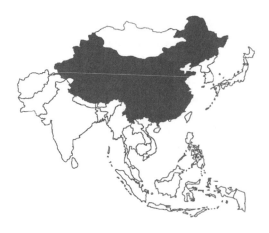

The vast land of China is divided into eight regions, each with its own distinct cuisine. The regions are Anhui, Cantonese, Fujian, Hunan, Jiangsu, Shandong, Sichuan, and Zhejiang. The most popular foods of China enjoyed worldwide are Cantonese from southeastern China, Hunan from the south-central region, and Sichuan from the mid-western region.

Chinese culture and cooking traditions date back over six millennia. China also has the world's largest population with well over one billion people. Fishing is a productive industry while chief food crops include rice, corn, and wheat. The national food of China is rice and it is so integrated into their culture that the Chinese word for rice, "*fan*" also means "meal." During a Chinese meal each individual is given a bowl of rice and accompanying dishes are usually placed on a lazy Susan in the center of a round table for all guests to share.

Jook Congee (Rice Porridge)

When rice is soupy, as in porridge, it is called *congee*. Congee is well known throughout China; however, each region has its own distinct way of preparing the soupy rice. The Cantonese use white rice and add lots of water, boiling it until the rice breaks down and becomes a thick white porridge. Other regions might use different types of rice or different proportions of water, changing consistency and taste.

When nothing chunky has been added to congee it is called *jook*. The following recipe is for basic jook.

Yield: serves 4 to 6

1 cup glutinous rice (available at many super-markets and Asian stores)

4 cups water

4 cups chicken or vegetable broth, homemade or canned

salt and pepper to taste

Equipment: Strainer, medium saucepan with cover, mixing spoon

1. Place rice in strainer and rinse under cold running water.

2. Place water and broth in saucepan. Add rice and bring to boil over high heat. Reduce to simmer, cover, and cook about 1 hour, stirring frequently to prevent sticking. Remove cover and cook about 30 minutes more until jook is soupy thick. Add salt and pepper to taste.

3. Serve warm and garnish with chopped green onions and serve jook in soup bowls. Congee can be seasoned with grated ginger, sugar, salt, pepper, and soy sauce according to your tastes. As in China, beef, lettuce, bok choy, fish, pork, or preserved eggs can be added for additional taste and texture.

❧ *Xiao Sun Zi Chao Rou Mo* (Bamboo Shoots with Ground Meat)

This is a typical Hunan or Xiang-style recipe where chili peppers, shallots, and garlic are added, creating a "dry heat."

Yield: serves 4 to 6

2 tablespoons peanut oil, more as needed

14 ounces canned bamboo shoots, drained, **julienned**

2 cloves garlic, **trimmed**, peeled, **minced**

1 fresh red chili, **seeded, finely chopped**

1/2 teaspoon dried chili pepper flakes

3 ounces ground meat (such as turkey, beef, or pork) or textured vegetable protein (a meat substitute available at health foods stores)

1 tablespoon rice wine vinegar

1 tablespoon soy sauce

salt to taste

3 tablespoons chicken or vegetable broth or water

3 green onions, trimmed, finely sliced

1 teaspoon sesame oil

Equipment: Chinese wok or large skillet with cover, wooden mixing spoon, plate

1. Heat 2 tablespoons peanut oil in wok or large skillet over medium-high heat. Add bamboo shoots. Stirring constantly, cook 2–3 minutes, until heated through. Remove from pan and set aside on plate.

2. In wok or large skillet, heat 1 tablespoon peanut oil over medium-high heat. Add garlic, fresh chili, and dried chili pepper flakes. **Stir-fry** until fragrant, about 1–2 minutes. Crumble in ground meat or textured vegetable protein and continue to stir until cooked through, about 5–6 minutes.

3. Return bamboo shoots to wok. Stir constantly until hot and sizzling, about 2 minutes. Add vinegar, soy sauce, and salt to taste. Stir in broth or water and stir-fry about 1–2 minutes longer, allowing flavors to blend. Toss in green onions, remove from heat, and stir in sesame oil.

4. Serve warm with side of white rice.

❧ Broccoli and Carrots with Firm Tofu

Combining fresh vegetables with *tofu* (bean curd) is one of China's most popular dishes. Tofu is a white, soft, and easily digestible dried soybean product. It is high in protein, low in calories, and cholesterol free. (For more information about tofu, refer to page 88.)

Yield: serves 6

4 tablespoons vegetables oil, more as needed

1 tablespoon ginger root, **trimmed**, peeled, **finely chopped** or 1 teaspoon ground ginger

2 cloves garlic, trimmed, peeled, **minced** or 1 teaspoon garlic granules

1 pound tofu (firm), drained, cut into bite-sized cubes (available at most supermarkets and Asian markets)

2 cups broccoli flowerets, trimmed

1 cup carrots, trimmed, peeled, thinly sliced

1 onion, trimmed, peeled, sliced, separated into rings

1 cup chicken broth, homemade or canned

1 tablespoon cornstarch

1 tablespoon water

Equipment: Wok or large skillet with cover, slotted mixing spoon, paper towels, cup

1. Heat oil in wok or large skillet over high heat. Add ginger root and garlic, stirring continually, about 1 minute. Cook until lightly browned. Reduce to medium heat. Add tofu and **sauté** until golden brown, about 10 minutes. Stir frequently. Remove tofu, drain on paper towels, set aside.

2. Increase to medium-high heat, adding more oil if necessary to prevent sticking. Stir in broccoli, carrots, and onion and fry about 1 minute, stirring continually. Add chicken broth, cover, and cook, about 3 minutes or until carrots are tender.

3. Mix cornstarch with water in a cup. Add to vegetable mixture and mix well. Reduce heat to simmer. Add fried tofu to mixture. Toss gently and cook until mixture thickens and bean curd is heated through, about 2–3 minutes.

4. Serve **stir-fry** vegetables in bowl with extra soy sauce. It is customary to serve other dishes at the same time and always include a bowl of rice.

Dandan Mian (Spicy Peanut Noodles)

Dandan mian was sold from buckets (*dandan*) suspended from each end of a pole carried across the shoulders of street vendors in the city of Chengdu. The distinct flavor of this dish comes from the Szechuan peppercorns (available at Asian markets), also known by the Chinese name "*huajiao*" (flower pepper). Cayenne or red chili peppers are NOT interchangeable with the Szechuan peppercorns.

Yield: serves 2 to 4

1/2 pound Chinese flat wheat noodles (available at Asian markets) or linguine

cook according to directions on package

2 tablespoons peanut butter

1 tablespoon ground Szechuan red peppercorns

1 tablespoon garlic, **trimmed**, peeled, **minced**

1 teaspoon brown sugar

2 teaspoons Chinese or white vinegar

2 teaspoons soy sauce

1 tablespoon dark sesame oil

1 tablespoon crushed roasted peanuts

Equipment: colander, medium serving bowl, small mixing bowl, tongs

1. Drain noodles in colander and transfer to serving bowl. Cover and keep warm.

2. In small mixing bowl combine peanut butter, Szechwan peppercorns, garlic, sugar, vinegar, soy sauce, and sesame oil. Stir until well blended and smooth.

3. Add peanut butter mixture to noodles and using tongs toss until well blended. Sprinkle with peanuts.

4. Serve at once.

India

India is the second most populous nation in the world, after China. Agriculture is very important in India, with a large majority of the population involved in growing rice, cereals, and legumes.

The cuisine of India varies according to region. The northern region includes dairy products: milk, **ghee**, *paneer* (a common Persian and South Asian cheese similar in texture to tofu), and yogurt are predominant. An abundance of coconut, fresh fruits, and rice are used in the southern region. Eastern cuisine is influenced by neighboring countries China and Mongolia. And western cuisine is known for fresh fish and a slightly sweet flavor, due to a pinch of sugar added to most dishes.

Indians have combined and blended spices for thousands of years. Spices, initially used only for medicinal purposes, are now used mostly for flavoring. In India, cooks blend their own spice to make curry powder, unlike Western countries where curry powder is preblended and sold in supermarkets.

A curry meal consists of mountains of rice and a variety of condiments, each served in its own little dish and used to awaken the taste buds. The condiments (*sambals*) include **chutney**, **shredded** coconut or raisins for sweetness, lemons for a sour flavor, salted nuts or **capers** for a salty flavor, slices of fresh melon or yogurt for a cooling flavor, pickles for pungent, and sliced apples for a tart flavor.

Most Indians are vegetarian and an interesting group of Hindus, Jains, believe that all living things have souls. Thus, they sweep the ground in front of them to avoid stepping on bugs. Jains also avoid eating root vegetables, such as sweet potatoes, because they fear an insect may be harmed while pulling up the plant.

Ghee (Indian Butter)

Ghee is clarified butter. Water and nonfat solids are separated and removed by gentle heating. There are several advantages to cooking with ghee: it does not sputter, it has excellent flavor, and it keeps for a long time, even when left unrefrigerated.

Usli ghee is clarified butter made from water buffalo and also yak milk. For centuries it has been used for cooking as well as for religious ceremonies. During the "Festival of Lights," thousands of clay lamps are fueled with ghee, and every Indian, rich and poor alike, gathers to celebrate the festival that symbolizes the start of the winter season. Every home glows from the flickering lights of these simple lamps.

Ghee is available at supermarkets that carry foreign foods and at Indian food markets or you can make it at home following this recipe.

Yield: about 1 cup

1 pound butter

Equipment: Medium saucepan, spoon, bulb baster or fine-hole strainer lined with cheese cloth, small bowl

1. Melt butter in saucepan over low heat without browning. Cook undisturbed about 45 minutes or until it separates, with solids on bottom and clear oil on top.
2. The clear oil (ghee) can be carefully spooned off, removed with bulb baster, or slowly poured through the strainer and into the bowl. Save the solid to add to and enrich soups or sauces. Cool ghee (oil) to room temperature, cover, and refrigerate.
3. Serve ghee over vegetables or fish, use it in making many sauces, or use it in place of oil for stir-frying.

Chapati (Flat Bread)

Bread and grains are used in sacred rituals and ceremonies marking major life events, from birth to death. Chapati is unleavened bread, made today as it was in ancient times. The flour has become more refined, but the end result is pretty much the same.

Yield: makes 6

3/4 cup unbleached all-purpose flour (set aside 1/4 cup)

1 cup whole-wheat flour

3/4 cup warm water

2 tablespoons butter, margarine, or **ghee**, more as needed

Equipment: Large mixing bowl, floured work surface, large griddle or heavy-bottomed skillet, metal spatula or pancake turner

1. Combine all-purpose and whole-wheat flours in bowl, make a well in center and add water. Mix flour into water, using clean hands **knead** into very smooth dough about 5 minutes.

2. Divide dough into 6 equal egg-sized balls. Press each piece between palms of hands or on work surface. Each ball should flatten out to a circle of about 6 inches in diameter. If balls seem sticky, dust lightly with flour.

3. Heat butter, margarine, or ghee on griddle or skillet over high heat. Cook dough circles, one at a time, about 15 seconds per side. Brown spots will appear on underside. Press chapati down around the edges with spatula or pancake turner. The center should bubble up.

4. To serve, brush one side with butter, margarine or ghee and eat while warm.

❧ *Am Ki Chatni* (Fresh Mango and Coconut Chutney)

Curries without **chutneys** are incomplete; they lack sparkle and the finishing touch.

Yield: about 2 cups

1 mango (about 1 pound), **trimmed**, peeled, **seeded**, cut in chunks

1/2 cup **shredded** coconut, fresh (recipe page 138), frozen, or canned

1/4 cup fresh **coriander** leaves **finely chopped**

1 tablespoon fresh ginger, trimmed, peeled, finely chopped or 1 teaspoon ground ginger

1/2 teaspoon salt

1/2 teaspoon dried red pepper flakes

Equipment: Small bowl, mixing spoon

1. Place mangos, coconut, coriander, ginger, salt, and red pepper in bowl. Toss gently until completely mixed.

2. Serve in a separate bowl as a condiment with curries. With every mouthful of curry, add a dab of chutney.

❧ *Palak Raita* (Spinach and Yogurt Salad)

Yield: serves 2 to 4

1 1/2 cups plain yogurt

1/2 cup sour cream

1 teaspoon ground cumin

1 teaspoon ground coriander

1/4 teaspoon each black and red pepper

Kosher salt to taste

1 cup cooked spinach; fresh coarsely chopped or frozen thawed

paprika to taste, for garnish

Equipment: Medium mixing bowl, mixing spoon, serving dish

1. Place yogurt, sour cream, cumin, coriander, and black and red pepper in medium bowl and mix thoroughly. Add kosher salt to taste. Cover and refrigerate until ready to serve.

2. When ready to serve, carefully **fold** spinach into seasoned yogurt and transfer to serving bowl.

3. To serve, sprinkle with paprika to taste.

Brinjal Curry (Eggplant Curry)

Yield: serves 6 to 8

1 tablespoon turmeric

salt to taste

water, as needed

1 *brinjal* (eggplant), **trimmed**, cut into 1-inch **cubes**

2 tablespoons ghee or vegetable oil, more as needed

2 onions, trimmed, peeled, **finely chopped**

2 tablespoons mustard seeds

2 curry leaves (available at international food markets)

1 tablespoon ground coriander

2 cloves garlic, trimmed, peeled, **minced**

1/2 teaspoon ground cumin

1 teaspoon ground red chili flakes

1 12-ounce can coconut milk

2 green chilies, trimmed, finely chopped

2 tablespoons fresh ginger root, trimmed, peeled, finely grated

3 tablespoons cider vinegar

Equipment: Large mixing bowl, mixing spoon, large skillet with cover, large saucepan, serving dish

1. In large mixing bowl blend together turmeric with pinch of salt and just enough water to form thin paste. Add eggplant and toss to coat. Set aside.

2. In large skillet heat 2 tablespoons ghee or vegetable oil over medium-high heat. Add eggplant. Stirring frequently, cook until soft and lightly browned, about 3–5 minutes. Remove from heat, set aside, and keep warm.

3. Heat 2 tablespoons ghee or vegetable oil in large saucepan over medium-high heat. Add onions, curry leaves, and mustard seeds. Reduce to medium-low heat. Stirring frequently, **sauté** until onions are **caramelized**, about 8–10 minutes. Stir in coriander, cumin, dried red chili, garlic, and 1/4 cup coconut milk. Bring to boil, reduce heat to simmer, and cook about 3–5 minutes.

4. Stir in green chilies, ginger, vinegar, and remaining coconut milk. Return to simmer and add prepared eggplant. Stir to coat and heat through. Add salt to taste. Transfer to serving bowl.

5. Serve at once with side dishes of rice, yogurt, and *Am Ki Chatni* (recipe page 80).

✌ *Gajar Halva* **(Sweet Carrot Pudding)**

Yield: serves 6 to 8

6 carrots (about 1 pound), trimmed, peeled, finely **shredded**

2 cups half-and-half

1/2 cup dark brown sugar

1/2 cup golden seedless raisins (soaked in warm water for 20 minutes and drained well)

1/4 cup butter, margarine, or **ghee**

1/2 teaspoon ground **cardamom**

salt to taste

1 cup **finely chopped** almonds or pistachios, **blanched**

1/2 cup chopped cashew nuts

Equipment: Medium saucepan with cover, mixing spoon, platter

1. Place carrots and half-and-half in saucepan and bring to boil over medium-high heat. Reduce heat to simmer, cover, and cook until liquid is almost absorbed, about 40–50 minutes.

2. Add brown sugar, raisins, butter or margarine, or ghee, cardamom, and salt. Mix well. Reduce to low heat and stir constantly until sugar is dissolved, about 2 minutes.

3. To serve as they do in India, spoon the carrot pudding into a mound in the center of a platter, garnish with chopped nuts, and serve warm.

Indonesia

For centuries Indonesia, now a nation of 3,000 islands including Java, Sumatra, Sulwesi, parts of Borneo and New Guinea, and Baki, was known to Westerners as the source of spices. The Moluccas, a small string of islands in Indonesia, are often referred to as the original "spice islands" since nutmeg and clove originated from here. Today, Indonesia not only exports cloves and pepper, but it is also a fertile supplier of rice, sweet potatoes, coffee, tea, peanuts, soybeans, and sugar cane. The Dutch controlled the Indonesian archipelago from the seventeenth century to 1949, when under internal and international pressure they granted Indonesia independence. To this day, Dutch remains the common language of many islanders. Rather than bring Dutch food to Indonesians, the Dutch brought Indonesian food to the world, creating a style of dining known as *rijsttafel*, meaning "rice table." At times as many as 30 dishes are placed on a large table and guests serve themselves. Most dishes are vegetarian; very little meat is eaten, and when it is, a little goes a long way. Huge bowls of cooked, white rice are served with every meal, and some of the dishes are simply bowls of fresh sliced pineapple, fresh and fried bananas, peanuts, pistachios, fresh coconuts, mango, cucumbers, and fish. Vendors sell many foods on the streets: cakes and breads, noodles and meatballs, and rice with fish are just a few of the offerings.

❧ Timor Achar (Pepper Salad with Sesame Seeds)

Yield: serves 6

1/4 cup apple cider vinegar

1 teaspoon sugar

1/2 teaspoon salt

2 tablespoons sesame seeds

1/4 pound snow peas, **trimmed** or frozen, thawed, **julienned**

1 red onion, trimmed, peeled, thinly sliced

1 green bell pepper, trimmed, **cored, seeded,** finely sliced

1 red bell pepper, trimmed, cored, seeded, finely sliced

1 tomato, trimmed, cut in 6 wedges

Equipment: Small jar with cover, small skillet, salad bowl, tongs or salad fork and spoon

1. Place vinegar, sugar, and salt in jar, cover, and shake to blend; refrigerate.

2. Heat sesame seeds in small skillet over medium heat, tossing until browned, about 3 minutes. Set aside.

3. Place snow peas, onion, and green and red bell peppers into salad bowl. Pour over dressing and toss to blend, using tongs or salad fork and spoon. Sprinkle with sesame seeds.

4. Serve the salad chilled with rice and other dishes.

❧ Gado-Gado (Cooked Vegetable Salad)

This traditional cooked vegetable salad with savory peanut dressing makes a refreshing lunch on a hot summer day.

Yield: serves 6

1 tablespoon vegetable oil

1 cup bean curd (firm tofu), **cubed**

1 cup fresh cabbage, **trimmed, shredded, blanched**

1/2 cup sliced carrots, fresh, trimmed, blanched or frozen, thawed

1/2 cup diagonally sliced green beans, fresh, trimmed, blanched or frozen, thawed

2 tomatoes, trimmed, thinly sliced

1 cucumber, trimmed, peeled, thinly sliced

2 **hard-cooked eggs**, peeled, thinly sliced
Peanut sauce (*katjang saos*) (next recipe)

3 cooked potatoes, trimmed, peeled, thinly sliced

salt and pepper to taste

Equipment: Small skillet, slotted spoon, paper towels, salad bowl, tongs or salad fork and spoon

1. Heat oil in skillet over medium-high heat. Add bean curd and **sauté** about 6–8 minutes until lightly browned. Remove with slotted spoon and then drain on paper towels. Arrange cabbage, carrots, green beans, tomatoes, cucumber, and potatoes in salad bowl.

2. Add salt and pepper to taste and eggs for garnish. Drizzle with katjang saos (peanut sauce) and serve.

Katjang Saos (Peanut Sauce)

This sauce is available at most supermarkets and Asian food markets.

Yield: about 1 cup

1/2 cup peanut butter, chunky or plain

3 tablespoons fresh lemon juice

3 tablespoons sugar

2 tablespoons soy sauce

1 teaspoon fresh ginger, **trimmed**, peeled, grated or 1/4 teaspoon ground ginger

2 cloves garlic, trimmed, peeled, **minced** or 1 teaspoon garlic granules

1/2 teaspoon ground red pepper

1/4 cup water

Equipment: Electric blender, rubber spatula

1. Using blender, combine peanut butter, lemon juice, sugar, soy sauce, ginger, garlic, red pepper, and water into a smooth paste.

2. Serve sauce in little individual bowls. Have guests dip sate ajam (next recipe) in their dishes of sauce. The sauce is also used as a salad dressing on the gado-gado (recipe page 83).

Sate Ajam (Skewered Chicken)

The chicken is eaten off the stick, like eating a corn dog.

Yield: serves 4 to 6

2 tablespoons soy sauce

1 tablespoon sugar

1 tablespoon peanut oil

1 clove garlic, **trimmed**, peeled, **minced**

1 tablespoon fresh ginger, peeled, finely chopped, or 1 teaspoon ground ginger

4 chicken breasts, skinless and boneless, cut in
  1-inch cubes

Equipment: Medium bowl, mixing spoon, 8 or 10 12-inch wooden skewers (or metal skewers), either lightly greased oven broiler pan or lightly greased baking sheet with raised edge, tongs, oven mitts

1. Preheat broiler: set broiler rack about 4 inches under heat.

2. Place soy sauce, sugar, oil, garlic, and ginger in medium bowl and mix well. Add chicken. Mix well and **marinate** for 1 hour in refrigerator. While in refrigerator, mix to coat with **marinade** several times.

3. To broil: If using wooden skewers, you must first soak skewers in water for about 30 minutes. Thread about 6 chicken cubes on each skewer and place side-by-side on broiler pan or baking pan. Place under broiler to broil for about 3 minutes on each side. Turn chicken once it browns, using tongs and oven mitts. Do not overcook.

4. Serve sate ajam with katjang saos (peanut sauce) for dipping (previous recipe) and rice.

⁂ *Lontong* (Indonesian Rice Rolls)

Lontong is the traditional bread dish served at a buffet.

Yield: serves 6

3 cups water, more as needed   1 cup uncooked long-grain rice, rinsed in cold
                                               water

Equipment: Medium saucepan with cover, 2 (10˝ × 16˝) aluminum foil sheets, large saucepan with cover, pot holder or oven mitts

1. Place rice and water in saucepan and bring to boil over high heat. Reduce to simmer, cover, and cook for 15 minutes. Remove from heat, keep covered, and set aside for 10 minutes. Uncover and cool at room temperature about 15 minutes.

2. Place 2 sheets of foil side-by-side on work surface and divide cooked rice equally between them. Moisten hands and one at a time, form each mound of rice into a sausage shape, about 2-inches thick and 6-inches long down center of foil. To wrap rice, bring 2 long edges of foil up over rice. Holding them together, fold over several times and press each fold to tightly seal in rice. Twist ends and bend them over, making package waterproof.

3. Fill large saucepan with 2 1/2 quarts water. Bring to boil over high heat, and add foil-wrapped rice. Bring back to boil, reduce heat to simmer, cover, and cook for 1 hour. Wearing oven mitts and using tongs, remove packages of rice from water and place on work surface to cool to room temperature. Refrigerate wrapped until ready to serve.

4. To serve, carefully unwrap and discard foil. Place lontong on service dish and cut into 1-inch slices (a moistened knife helps with cutting). Serve at room temperature.

Japan

Japan consists of four separate islands located off the coast of eastern Asia. The Japanese are known worldwide for their artistic presentation of food. *Sushi*, which means "vinegar rice," is one of Japan's most famous and well-known creations. The Japanese often eat sushi and *sashimi* (sliced raw fish) as appetizers.

Stir-frying, an important Asian method of cooking, retains the natural flavor of food. Japanese rice has a sticky consistency and is served at every meal. A home-cooked Japanese meal is simple and frugal, usually consisting of rice, soybeans in some form such as *miso* soup, pickles, fish, and seaweed. However, for special occasions it is not unusual for the Japanese to serve up 15 side dishes at one meal.

Fishing is an important industry and fish is essential to the Japanese diet. A specialty in Japan is Kobe beef, which is unique and highly prized for its tenderness and delicate flavor. Fresh fruit is the preferred end to a meal, and while a variety of fruit is available, mangos are a favorite. Mangos are simply peeled, sliced, and served with a bit of lemon juice. Orange trees and golden persimmon seem to grow in every yard.

✌ Chicken Egg Soup

Yield: serves 4 to 6

6 cups chicken broth, homemade or canned

1/4 cup celery, trimmed, **finely chopped**

1/4 cup carrots, trimmed, peeled, finely chopped

1/4 cup onion, trimmed, peeled, finely chopped

1 egg, beaten

salt and pepper to taste

1 green onion top, finely sliced diagonally, for garnish

Equipment: Medium saucepan, strainer, medium bowl, mixing spoon

1. Place chicken broth, celery, carrots, and onion in saucepan. Bring soup to boil, reduce heat to simmer, and cook for 1/2 hour.
2. **Strain** soup into bowl. (Refrigerate or freeze vegetables to use at another time.) Pour liquid back into saucepan, bring to boil, then reduce heat to simmer. Stirring continually, slowly pour egg into soup, heat through, add salt and pepper to taste, and serve.
3. To serve soup, ladle into bowls and float green onion garnish on top of each.

Tempura (Japanese-Style Frying)

Tempura, a Japanese method of cooking, is believed to have been introduced to Japan by Portuguese missionaries and sailors during the late sixteenth century. As the story goes, Catholic missionaries would eat fried fish on Fridays, so the Japanese associated this style of cooking as a religious custom. Therefore, they named this type of frying *tempura*, derived from *templo*, meaning temple or church. Tempura became so popular over the next two centuries that wheeled carts with hot oil for frying dominated the streets in small villages. To enjoy the best flavor, this trendy "street food" was consumed immediately after frying.

Tempura is very different from American deep frying. Fresh batches of batter are continuously made immediately before frying to ensure an airy, light texture essential for the best tempura. In Japan only the freshest garden vegetables and seafood are used for tempura.

CAUTION: HOT OIL USED

Yield: serves 4 to 6

vegetable oil as needed

12 large jumbo shrimp, tail on, peeled, **deveined**

6 shitake mushrooms, cleaned, stems removed

1 sweet potato, **trimmed**, peeled, thinly sliced into 1/4-inch-thick strips

1 carrot, trimmed, sliced into 1/4-inch-thick strips

12 green beans, washed, trimmed

1 red bell pepper, seeded, sliced into 1/4-inch-thick strips

Dipping sauce (next recipe)

For the batter:

1 egg

1/2 cup iced water

3/4 cup all-purpose flour

1/2 teaspoon baking powder

2 ice cubes

Equipment: 2 large plastic sealable bags, medium bowl, fork, deep fryer, wok or tall pot, wooden spoon, metal tongs or skimmer, plate with several layers of paper towels

1. Place vegetables in large plastic bag and shrimp in second plastic bag. Seal and refrigerate until ready to fry.

2. Prepare batter: Place egg in medium mixing bowl and stir with fork. Add water, flour, and baking powder. Stir two or three times, leaving some flour unblended. Set aside. Immediately before frying, add ice cubes to chill mixture and stir gently.

3. Prepare to deep fry: ADULT SUPERVISION REQUIRED. Have ready several layers of paper towels on plate. Fill deep fryers with oil according to manufacturer's directions or fill wok or tall pot with about 3 inches of vegetable oil. Heat oil to 375°F on deep fryer's thermometer or place handle of wooden spoon in oil; if small bubbles appear around surface of inserted spoon, oil is ready for frying.

4. Place shrimp and vegetables one by one in batter mixture and then carefully drop into hot oil. Fry about 2–3 minutes, until golden. Remove with metal tongs or skimmer and place on paper towel on plate.

5. Serve immediately with dipping sauce (next recipe).

Dipping Sauce

3/4 cup water

3 tablespoons *mirin* (sweet rice wine, available at most supermarkets)

1/2 tablespoon *bonito* flakes (available at Asian markets)

3 tablespoons Japanese soy sauce

Equipment: Small saucepan, wooden mixing spoon, strainer, 4–6 individual bowls for serving

1. Combine all ingredients in saucepan. Bring to boil over medium-high heat. Set aside to cool.

2. Strain and serve in individual bowls with tempura.

Tofu (Bean Curd)

It is believed that during the tenth century Japanese Buddhists discovered tofu while on missionary work in China. Vows taken by the Buddhists prevent them from eating meat, thus tofu became a nutritious dietary supplement. Over the years, the Japanese have cultivated soybeans resulting in fine-quality tofu.

There are different methods of processing tofu, therefore giving it a variety of textures. Two major types of tofu are referred to as "silk" and "cotton." "Silk" (also called soft) tofu is smooth and silky in appearance, crumbles easily, and should not be cooked at high temperatures, while "cotton" tofu is firm. "Cotton" (also called firm) tofu received its name from the cotton cloth used to strain out excess liquid during processing. Silk tofu is best used in soups or sweet desserts, while cotton tofu is best used for sautéing and deep frying. Since tofu has little to no flavor when cooking, it is important to use strong seasonings such as garlic, ginger, scallions, chilies, soy sauce, oyster sauce, shrimp paste, or sesame oil.

Tofu is a healthy meat alternative, high in protein but inexpensive.

❧ *Shiraae* (Mashed Tofu and Vegetable Salad)

Yield: serves 4

1 block *momendofu* tofu (firm)

1/4 pound carrots (about 2 carrots), **trimmed**, thinly sliced into strips about 2-inches long, **blanched**

4 shiitake mushrooms, trimmed, **finely sliced**, blanched

1 bunch of baby spinach, trimmed, blanched

3 tablespoons sugar

1 tablespoon sesame oil

2 tablespoons Japanese soy sauce

Equipment: Medium saucepan, slotted spoon or skimmer, 4 paper towels, colander or strainer, large bowl, cutting board, sharp knife, large salad bowl, medium mixing bowl, wooden spoon, tongs or salad fork, and spoon

1. Fill medium saucepan halfway with water and bring to boil. Add tofu and boil 2 minutes; remove with slotted spoon. When cool enough to handle, wrap tofu in paper towels and place in colander. Set large bowl on top of tofu to act as a weight and allow excess water to drain for 30 minutes. Remove from paper towels and place on cutting board. Using knife, cut into bite-sized pieces.

2. Using knife and cutting board, cut blanched spinach into bite-sized pieces. In large salad bowl combine blanched vegetables.

3. In medium mixing bowl combine sugar, sesame oil, soy sauce, and tofu. Toss to mix well. Transfer tofu mixture to salad bowl with blanched vegetables and toss well with tongs or salad fork and spoon.

4. Serve cold in individual salad bowls.

❧ *Teriyaki* (Marinated Beef)

Yield: serves 4 to 6

1/2 cup teriyaki sauce, available at most supermarkets

1 tablespoon peeled, **finely chopped** fresh ginger or 1 teaspoon ground ginger

2 pounds lean beef, sirloin, or round steak, cut into 3–4-inch strips, 1/4-inch thick

Equipment: Large mixing bowl or large plastic bag, mixing spoon, tongs or long-handled fork

1. Preheat broiler: set broiler tray about 6 inches under heat.

2. Place teriyaki sauce and ginger in bowl or bag and mix well. Add beef strips and coat with mixture for at least 30 minutes, stirring frequently.

3. Place meat strips side-by-side on broiler pan. Broil on one side for about 3 minutes. Using tongs or long-handled fork, turn meat, and broil on other side about 3–5 minutes, or to desired doneness.

4. Serve teriyaki on platter with side bowls of boiled rice. Guests help themselves using chopsticks.

Gohan (Boiled Rice)

Japanese rice is short grained and cooks to a very sticky consistency, making it ideal to eat with chopsticks.

Yield: serves 4

1 cup Japanese uncooked short-grain rice   11/4 cups water
(available at most supermarkets and Asian
food stores)

Equipment: **Colander** or strainer, medium saucepan with cover

1. Place rice in strainer or colander and rinse under running water about 2–3 minutes.

2. Transfer to saucepan and add water. Bring to boil over high heat. Reduce heat to simmer, cover, and cook about 15 minutes or until water has been absorbed by rice. Reduce to warm heat. Keep covered, allowing rice to steam about 15 minutes.

3. Serve rice in individual bowls to be eaten with chopsticks. The rice bowl is held in the left hand, close to the mouth. The chopsticks are used to push the rice into your mouth as the bowl is slowly rotated in your hand.

North Korea and South Korea

Korea is a peninsula attached to the northern most part of China. Bordering Korea is the Yellow Sea to the west, the Sea of Japan to the east, and the Korean Strait to the south. North Korea and South Korea border each other geographically; however, the countries are divided with opposing political differences. The culture and cuisine of North Korea remains an undisclosed secret to the outside world. What is known about North Korea is that they use cold noodles, *naengmyeon*, in abundance served in ice water with vegetables and an egg. Other popular ingredients in the north include seaweed, red and green peppers, soy sauce, onions, garlic, ginger, and vinegar.

South Koreans have their own distinguished dishes such as *kimchi*. For thousands of years pickled cabbage or kimchi has been Korea's national dish. Koreans often organize work parties and help each other prepare huge batches of this pungent-smelling dish. Throughout Korea, from every city-dweller balcony to farmhouse roof, vats of Chinese cabbage are fermenting, turning into beloved kimchi.

Shigumchi Namul (Stir-Fried Spinach and Mung Bean Sprouts)

Yield: serves 4 to 6

2 teaspoons vegetable oil

2 teaspoons sesame oil

1 bunch spinach, **trimmed**, washed, patted dry with paper towel

2 cups mung bean sprouts (available at Asian markets)

1 teaspoon sea salt

1/4 teaspoon sesame seeds, **toasted** (available at supermarkets)

1/4 teaspoon black sesame seeds (available at Asian markets)

Equipment: Wok or skillet, two serving bowls, wooden serving spoon

1. In wok or skillet heat 1 teaspoon each of vegetable and sesame oil over medium-high heat. Add spinach, season with salt, and **stir-fry** until leaves are wilted, about 2–4 minutes. Transfer to serving bowl and set aside.

2. In wok or skillet add remaining sesame and vegetable oil. Stir in mung bean sprouts, season with salt, and stir-fry until tender but firm, about 2–4 minutes. Remove from heat and transfer to serving bowl.

3. To serve, sprinkle spinach with toasted sesame seeds and sprinkle mung bean sprouts with black sesame seeds. Serve as side dish with kimchi (next recipe) and rice.

Kimchi (Pickled Cabbage)

There are many variations for kimchi. It can also be made hotter and spicier. The longer kimchi ferments, the stronger the flavor and odor.

Yield: about 4 cups

2 cups chopped Chinese cabbage (*bok choy*), washed, drained

1/2 cup coarse (kosher) salt

4 green onions (including tops), **trimmed, finely chopped**

1 cup carrots, trimmed, finely shredded

1 tablespoon fresh ginger, trimmed, peeled, grated or 1/2 teaspoon ground ginger

3 cloves garlic, trimmed, peeled, **minced** or 1 teaspoon garlic granules

1 teaspoon sugar

4 tablespoons dried red pepper flakes

Equipment: Large mixing bowl, **colander** or strainer, 2-quart crock or glass jar with cover

1. Toss cabbage with salt in large mixing bowl to coat evenly. Set aside about 30 minutes; toss frequently.

2. Transfer cabbage to colander or strainer. Rinse under cold water and drain well. Return to bowl and add green onions, carrots, ginger, garlic, sugar, and red pepper flakes. Mix well.

3. Pack mixture in crock or jar, cover, and keep at room temperature about 2 days, then refrigerate.

4. Serve as a relish.

Laos

Laos is very mountainous and the only low flatland is on the eastern shore of the Mekong River, where the majority of the natives live. It is here that the staple crop, rice, is grown using wet-rice farming techniques. Laotians practice subsistence agriculture, growing just enough food to feed their families and pay taxes.

Laos, along with Vietnam and Cambodia, was once part of French Indochina, yet the cooking in Laos reflects little of the French style. It is a blend of neighboring southern

Chinese cooking and Thai spices and foods. The foods of Laos are simple, spicy, and always colorful. Unlike many other Asian countries, Laotians only use chop sticks when eating noodles and spoons are used when eating soups. Sticky rice, the country's staple food, is eaten with the hands. Rice is taken little by little with the fingers, **kneaded** into a ball, and dipped into sauces. Sauces are eaten to enhance flavors in the main dish.

The day begins with a hearty bowl of rice porridge referred to as "national breakfast soup." In Laos, it is made of spiced coconut milk and rice-like noodles, called *khao poon*. In cities khao poon stands are set up early each morning where Laotians can hurriedly buy and eat bowls of porridge on their way to work or school.

Khao poon means "rice vermicelli." Italian vermicelli noodles are made with wheat flour while Asian vermicelli noodles are made with rice flour. Italian vermicelli should not be used in place of rice noodles. It is not necessary to cook dried rice noodles since they are already cooked. The noodles are **reconstituted** by soaking in water for about 15 minutes to soften and remove starch. Once noodles are soft they may be added to hot broth or **stir-fry.**

✿ *Khao Poon* with Chicken

Yield: serves 4 to 6

1 chicken, quartered

3 cups water, more or less as needed

2 teaspoons fresh ginger, **trimmed**, peeled, grated or 1 teaspoon ground ginger

2 tablespoons **cilantro**, trimmed, **finely chopped** or 1 teaspoon ground coriander

6 green onions, **trimmed** and finely chopped (set aside half for serving)

3 tablespoons fish sauce (*nuoc mam*), home-made or bottled (available at Asian markets)

6 ounces rice vermicelli (prepare according to directions on package, available at some supermarkets and all Asian markets)

1 cup Chinese cabbage, trimmed, finely chopped

1 small papaya, trimmed, peeled, **seeded**, thinly sliced

1/2 cup chopped canned bamboo shoots (available at most supermarkets)

1 teaspoon ground hot red pepper, more or less to taste, for serving

salt to taste, for serving

Equipment: Large saucepan with cover, mixing spoon, large serving bowl, strainer

1. Place chicken in saucepan and add water to cover. Add ginger, coriander, half green onions, and 1 tablespoon fish sauce. Bring to boil over high heat, reduce to simmer, cover, and cook about 45–50 minutes or until tender. Remove chicken from broth and set aside to cool. Continue simmering broth, uncovered, about 1/2 hour more or until broth is reduced to about 2 cups.

2. Using clean hands, remove skin from cooled chicken and discard. Pull meat off bones and cut into bite-sized strips. Set aside.

3. Arrange cabbage, papaya slices, and bamboo shoots in center of serving bowl and cover with noodles and top with shredded chicken. Pour about 1 cup strained broth over mixture and sprinkle with remaining green onions.

4. Serve with a bowl of rice.

⚜ *Larb* (Spicy Minced Meat Salad)

Larb is the unofficial national dish of Laos.

Yield: serves 4

1 head leaf or bib lettuce, rinsed, **cored**, drained

2 tablespoons peanut oil

3 stems lemon grass (white part only), **trimmed, finely chopped**

2 fresh green chilies, trimmed, finely chopped

4 cloves garlic, trimmed, peeled, **minced**

1 pound finely ground meat, chicken, beef, duck, pork, turkey, or fish

1/4 cup lime juice

2 teaspoons lime rind, minced

6 teaspoons green chili sauce (condiment) (available at Asian markets)

1/4 cup coriander leaves, finely chopped (condiment)

1/4 cup mint, finely chopped (condiment)

1 red onion, trimmed, peeled, finely chopped (condiment)

1/4 cup unsalted peanuts

Equipment: Paper towels, wok or medium skillet, wooden mixing spoon, medium bowl, serving platter, small individual bowls for condiments

1. Pat lettuce leaves with paper towels, place on platter and refrigerate until ready to serve.

2. Heat oil in wok or skillet over medium-high heat. Add chilies, lemon grass, and garlic. Stir-fry about 2–3 minutes or until garlic is lightly browned. Crumble in meat, stir constantly, and stir-fry until meat is cooked through. Stir in lime juice and lime rind and mix well. Transfer to bowl and cool to room temperature.

3. To serve, place bowl of larb in center of platter and surround with lettuce leaves. Place condiments—chili sauce, coriander leaves, mint, red onion, and peanuts—in small individual bowls.

4. To eat: cup a lettuce leaf in your hand, fill with 2–3 spoonfuls of meat mixture, and add desired condiments. Encase lettuce around meat, roll up, and eat.

Malaysia and Singapore

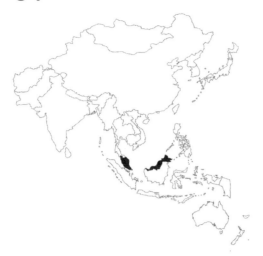

Malaysia is a long, narrow peninsula, part of the island of Borneo. Being just north of the equator it is extremely hot and humid. Due to abundant rainfall people must build their homes on high posts to keep dry. Most Malaysians have small plots of land where they can grow staples: rice, sweet potatoes, and sago (a starch extracted from sago palm). Seafood is popular throughout the island and often salted and dried. Fruit trees such as coconut, banana, guava, and papaya thrive in the tropical climate. A popular fruit is *durian*, which has a highly offensive odor.

Three ethnic groups live side-by-side in Malaysia: Chinese, Indians, and native Malaysians. Each group has its own distinct habits and traditions. Yet, they are known to borrow from each other at times, while still retaining their unique cooking customs. A Malay specialty is *satay*, a grilled kebab of **marinated** chicken, beef, or mutton, similar to Thai food with the same name (see recipe page 111).

Singapore, a small, independent nation south of the Malay Peninsula, comprises the main island of Singapore as well as 60 islets. A cooking style unique to Singapore is *Peranaken*, a multiethnic fusion of old Chinese immigrant cooking with Indonesian, Malaysian, and Indian traditions. Coconut milk is used in many dishes. "Hawker food," for which Singapore was famous, was sold by street vendors who trundled their carts through the streets of Singapore. Because of health safety concerns, this is no longer done.

✑ *Keoh Char Huan Cheo* (Spiced Eggplant)

Yield: serves 4 to 6

1 to 1 1/2 pounds eggplant, **trimmed**, cut into cubes

2 tablespoons vegetable oil, more as needed

Spice mixture:

1–5 fresh chilies, trimmed, **finely chopped**

2 tablespoons dried red chili flakes

3 tablespoons shrimp paste (available at Asian markets)

1 clove garlic, trimmed, peeled, **minced**

12 shallots, trimmed, peeled, finely chopped

1/4 cup macadamia nuts

2 tablespoons water, more as needed

2 tablespoons sugar, or to taste

sea salt to taste

Equipment: Medium bowl, colander, **wok** or large skillet, wooden mixing spoon, paper towels, food processor or blender, rubber spatula

1. Place cubed eggplant pieces in bowl and cover with salted water, about 10–15 minutes. Drain in colander and set aside.

2. Heat oil in wok or skillet over medium heat. Add eggplant and stir-fry until lightly browned, about 6–10 minutes. Remove from wok or skillet and drain on paper towels.

3. In food processor or blender, blend together fresh chilies, dried chili flakes, shrimp paste, garlic, shallots, nuts, water, and sugar. Blend well.

4. In wok, add more oil if necessary, add spice mixture, and stir-fry over medium-low heat until fragrant, about 2–3 minutes. If mixture seems dry add more water to prevent sticking. Add cooked eggplant and stir-fry until heated through, about 3–5 minutes. Carefully toss and coat eggplant thoroughly with spice mixture. Add salt to taste.

5. Serve warm as side dish with rice.

Pengat Pisang (Banana Porridge)

Yield: serves 4 to 6

4 cups coconut milk, homemade (recipe page 138), canned, or frozen (thawed)

3 teaspoons fresh ginger, **trimmed**, peeled, grated or 1 1/2 teaspoons ground ginger

1 cup sugar, more or less to taste

4 ripe bananas, peeled, sliced into 1/4-inch rounds

1 tablespoon **tapioca** (available at all supermarkets)

Equipment: Medium saucepan, mixing spoon, medium serving bowl

1. Place coconut milk and ginger in saucepan, bring to boil over medium-high heat, reduce heat to simmer. Add sugar, bananas, and tapioca, stirring continually until mixture thickens, about 6 minutes. Remove from heat, pour into serving bowl, and cool to room temperature.

2. Serve porridge hot or cold, for dessert or breakfast.

Biryani (Lamb in Yogurt)

Biryani, an Indian dish, was brought by Sikh Indians when they migrated from Singapore.

Yield: serves 4 to 6

1 pound boneless lamb shoulder cut into 1-inch **cubes**

1/2 cup plain yogurt, homemade (recipe page 216) or commercial

2 tablespoons vegetable oil

1 cup onion, **trimmed**, peeled, **finely chopped**

3 cloves garlic, trimmed, peeled, **minced** or 1 teaspoon garlic granules

2 cups chicken broth, homemade or canned

2 teaspoons ground cinnamon

1 tablespoon ground cumin

2 teaspoons fresh ginger, trimmed, peeled, minced or 1 teaspoon ground ginger

salt and pepper to taste

Equipment: Medium bowl, mixing spoon, medium skillet with cover

1. Place lamb in bowl, add yogurt, and mix well. Set aside to **marinate** about 30 minutes.

2. Heat oil in skillet over high; add onion and garlic. Stirring constantly, fry about 3–5 minutes until golden. Add meat and yogurt mixture, chicken broth, cinnamon, cumin, ginger, and salt and pepper to taste in skillet. Mix well. Bring to boil, reduce heat to simmer, cover and cook about 40 minutes or until meat is tender.

3. Serve over biryani rice (next recipe).

❧ *Biryani* (Rice)

Yield: serves 4 to 6

1 cup basmati rice (available at most super-markets and Middle East stores)

3 cups water

1 teaspoon ground cinnamon

1/2 teaspoon ground cloves

1/4 teaspoon ground **turmeric**

salt to taste

4 **hard-cooked eggs**, peeled, quartered, for garnish

Equipment: Strainer, medium saucepan with cover, wooden mixing spoon

1. Place rice in strainer and rinse under running water. Drain well.

2. Place water in saucepan, add rice, and bring to boil over high heat. Reduce heat to simmer. Add cinnamon, cloves, turmeric, and salt to taste. Mix well. Cover and cook about 10 minutes or until water is absorbed. Stir frequently to prevent sticking. Reduce to low heat and keep covered to steam rice, about 20 minutes or until tender. **Fluff** rice with fork before serving.

3. To serve, transfer rice to large bowl and garnish with hard-cooked egg wedges.

Mongolia

Throughout most of history Mongolians were known as nomads, herding sheep, yaks, goats, camels, cattle, and horses on their windswept, flat grasslands. Today, political boundaries prevent free movement and Mongols are settled in more stable communities, allowing them to grow their own fields of grain to feed their livestock.

The Mongolians are hearty meat eaters, preferring lamb with vegetables such as potatoes, cabbage, and onions. Tea is a favorite beverage prepared the traditional Tibetan way with butter and roasted barley.

Meng Ku Shua Yang Jou Kuo (Mongolian Hot Pot)

The Mongolian hot pot is a method of cooking that dates back 400–500 years. Nomadic tribes gathered around the "hot pot" where the heat from cooking would keep them warm. The hot pot cooking is similar to fondue. The hot pot is placed in the center of the table where raw meats and vegetables are dipped into broth or other liquid and cooked to desired doneness.

Yield: serves 4 to 6

3 ounces bean thread noodles (available at Asian markets)

1 quart chicken or vegetable broth

1 teaspoon ginger root, **trimmed**, peeled, **finely chopped**

2 tablespoons scallions, trimmed, finely chopped

1 teaspoon garlic, trimmed, peeled, **minced**

1 tablespoon cilantro, trimmed, finely chopped

3 pounds lamb, very thinly sliced

1/2 pound spinach, washed, trimmed

1/2 pound Chinese cabbage, trimmed, cut into 3-inch slices (available at Asian markets)

Equipment: Medium bowl, colander, knife or scissors, medium saucepan, ladle, heat-proof pad, hot pot or fondue pot (use either according to manufacturer's directions), serving plates, chop sticks or long-handled fondue forks, 4–6 individual soup bowls and spoons

1. In medium bowl soak noodles in warm water about 5 minutes. Strain in colander. Using knife or scissors cut noodles into 5-inch lengths. Transfer to bowl and set aside.

2. Make dipping sauce (next recipe).

3. A small bowl of dipping sauce is placed in front of each guest along with a plate of uncooked lamb, spinach, and Chinese cabbage (bok choy).

4. Place hot pot or fondue pot in center of table on top of heatproof pad.

5. In medium saucepan bring broth to boil over high heat; boil 1 minute. Ladle broth into hot pot or fondue pot. Add ginger, scallions, garlic, and cilantro.

6. To serve: Food is picked up using chop sticks or fondue fork and dipped into hot broth. When all meat and vegetables have been eaten, add noodles to remaining broth, heat through, then ladle noodle soup into individual soup bowls.

7. Serve with dipping sauce (next recipe).

🥢 Dipping Sauce

2 tablespoons sesame paste (available at Asian markets)

1 tablespoon soy sauce

1 tablespoon rice wine vinegar (available at supermarkets)

Yield: serves 4 to 6

2 teaspoons chili bean sauce (available at Asian markets)

1 tablespoon sugar

1 tablespoon water

Equipment: Small mixing bowl, whisk, small individual serving bowls

1. In small mixing bowl whisk together sesame paste, soy sauce, rice wine vinegar, chili bean paste, sugar, and water. Stir well.

2. Serve as aforementioned.

Myanmar (Burma)

Once known as Burma, Myanmar was at one time the richest country in Southeast Asia. It was ruled by the British as part of India until 1937, when it became an independent country. It was originally settled by Tibetans, around the ninth century, and follows Buddhist teachings. Most natives are vegetarians; however, many do eat fish. The cuisine is a **fusion** of Indian curries with Chinese **stir-fry**, using native tropical fruits and vegetables.

Rice is a staple of the Myanmar diet. Small farms with rice paddies dot the countryside, and all work, from seeding to harvesting, is done by hand. Burmans follow many Chinese customs, except they eat with their hands and are offended if chopsticks are suggested. They like using Indian ingredients, such as **ghee**, with Chinese cooking equipment, such as the **wok**, a very efficient cooking utensil.

✑ *Thanatsone* (Vegetable Salad with Sesame Seeds)

Any of the following vegetables may be used in this recipe: beans, cabbage, cauliflower, okra, carrots, bamboo shoots, spring onions, bean sprouts, cucumber, or zucchini.

Yield: serves 4 to 6

4 cups mixed vegetables, **trimmed**, cut into bite-sized pieces, **blanched**

1/2 cup vegetable oil

1 tablespoon sesame oil (available at all supermarkets)

1/2 teaspoon ground turmeric

2 onions, trimmed, peeled, finely sliced

4 cloves garlic, trimmed, peeled, **minced**

2 tablespoons white vinegar

salt to taste

3 tablespoons sesame seeds

Equipment: Medium-large saucepan, **skimmer** or slotted spoon, medium-large bowl filled with iced water, colander, large skillet or **wok**, serving bowl, tongs

1. Heat 2 tablespoons oil in skillet or wok over medium-high heat. Stir in turmeric, onions, and garlic. Stirring constantly, **sauté** until onions and garlic are browned, about 2–3 minutes.
2. Add drained vegetables, mix, and stir-fry about 2–4 minutes. Season with vinegar and salt taste. Sprinkle sesame seeds over top of vegetables before serving.
3. Serve at room temperature as side dish with rice and curry.

❧ *Tupa Menda* (Buttered Fruit Rice)

Yield: serves 4 to 6

1/4 cup butter or **ghee** (recipe page 79.)

1 cup uncooked rice, rinsed, drained

13/4 cups water

1/4 teaspoon salt

1/2 cup seedless raisins

1/2 cup dried apricots, **finely chopped**

Equipment: **Wok** with cover or medium skillet with cover, mixing spoon

1. Melt butter or ghee in wok or skillet over medium heat. Add rice and stir until golden, about 3 minutes. Add water and salt, mix well, and bring to boil. Reduce heat to simmer, cover, and cook 5 minutes.
2. Add raisins and apricots and mix well. Cover and continue simmering until rice is dry and soft, about 10–15 minutes.
3. Turn off heat and let rice stand covered 15 minutes before serving.
4. Serve rice as a side dish with **stir-fry** vegetables.

Pakistan

Pakistan, once part of the British-India Empire, has experienced ongoing conflicts between the Islamic Pakistanis and Hindus who migrated from India. Many Pakistanis are Muslim with a lesser number of Hindus, Sikhs, Buddhists, Parsis, and Christians.

Pakistanis traditionally sit on the floor to eat using the fingers of their right hands. Today, however, with strong European influences, some choose to sit at tables, using chairs, flatware, and china.

Fishing and agriculture are essential to the Pakistan economy. Pakistanis grow wheat, rice, and sugar cane and raise sheep, cattle, water buffalo, and donkeys.

Chapli Kabab (Meat Patties)

Chapli kababs are not *kababs* but rather meat patties. Adding curry powder is a unique characteristic of Pakistani cooking.

Yield: serves 2 to 4

1 pound finely ground beef or lamb

1 egg

2 teaspoons curry powder

juice of 1/2 lemon

1 green chili pepper or jalapeño fresh or canned, **cored, seeded, finely chopped**

3–5 tablespoons **ghee** or vegetable oil

1 onion, **trimmed**, peeled, thinly sliced, for garnish

1 tablespoon chopped fresh **coriander**, for garnish

Equipment: Medium mixing bowl, mixing spoon or electric mixer, medium skillet, metal spatula or pancake turner

1. Place meat, egg, curry powder, lemon juice, and chili pepper in bowl, and using spoon or electric mixer, mix into smooth paste. Divide mixture into 4 oval-shaped patties, each 1/2-inch thick.

2. Heat 3 tablespoons ghee or oil in skillet over medium-high heat. Add patties, reduce heat to medium, and fry about 8 minutes on each side or until browned on both sides. Add more oil if necessary to prevent sticking. Transfer to serving platter, garnish with onion slices, and sprinkle with coriander.

3. Serve with chopped pickles, **chutney**, peanuts, coconut, and chopped tomatoes. To fully enjoy, sprinkle a dab from each side dish with every mouthful.

Tikka Boti (Grilled Beef)

Yield: serves 4 to 6

1/2 cup fresh papaya, **trimmed**, peeled, **pitted**, mashed

1 teaspoon ground ginger

2 cloves garlic, trimmed, peeled, **minced**

1 cup yogurt, more as needed

2 tablespoons green chilies, trimmed, **finely chopped**

salt to taste, more as needed

3 pounds beef, **cubed**

For serving: mint chutney and naan (bread, available at most supermarkets and most Middle Eastern stores)

Equipment: Medium mixing bowl with cover or plastic wrap, mixing spoon, 10–12 skewers (soaked in water overnight to prevent burning), flat plate, grill or barbeque (use according to manufacturer's directions), tongs

1. In medium bowl mix together papaya, ginger, garlic, 1 cup yogurt, chilies, and salt to taste. Add beef cubes and coat well. Cover and refrigerate overnight.

2. Heat and prepare grill. Skewer beef and place on flat platter. When grill is hot place skewered meat on grill. Using tongs, turn frequently until desired doneness.

3. Serve immediately with naan and side dishes of mint chutney and yogurt.

Kachoomber (Raw Vegetable Salad)

Sambals are side dishes consisting of hot and cool flavors, smooth or crisp textures, and color contrasts. Sambals are often more important than the main dish. They can be simply pickles and **chutneys**, cooked dried peas, beans, or any selection of fruit and vegetables.

Yield: about 1 1/2 cups

1 green bell pepper, trimmed, **cored, seeded, finely chopped**

1 small cucumber, trimmed, finely chopped

1 tomato, trimmed, finely chopped

1 white onion, trimmed, peeled, finely chopped

1 green chili pepper, fresh or canned, **cored**, seeded, finely chopped

2 tablespoons white vinegar, more as needed

1 tablespoon fresh **coriander** finely chopped leaves or 1 teaspoon dried ground coriander

sugar and salt to taste

Equipment: Large bowl with cover, mixing spoon

1. Place green pepper, cucumber, tomato, onion, chili pepper, vinegar, coriander, and sugar and salt to taste in bowl and mix well. Cover and refrigerate. Mix before serving; add more vinegar if necessary.

2. Serve in small bowl as salad or condiment to other dishes.

Philippines

The Philippines are a group of islands in Southeast Asia across the South China Sea from Cambodia, Laos, and Vietnam. The Philippines are a melting pot of people from around the world. The first Filipino settlers were Austronesian (Malayo-Polynesian), then Spanish settlers arrived during the sixteenth century, claiming the islands as their own. Spaniards unified the country with Christianity and a common language, Spanish. Later the Americans came and "Westernized" the country. Together these diverse cultures have created a **fusion** of tastes and flavors unique to Philippine cuisine. Similar to Latin American and Spanish cultures, families are closely knit, with strong family ties. Pineapples, coconuts, sugar cane, rice, and corn are among the crops grown. Fish and shellfish are plentiful while chicken and pork are favored meats.

Adobong Manok (Marinated Chicken)

This is the national dish of the Philippines and is often made with chicken or pork.

Yield: serves 4 to 6

4–6 chicken thighs or breasts, or 2 pounds pork, **cubed**

1/2 cup soy sauce

3/4 cup white vinegar

4 cloves of garlic, **trimmed**, peeled, crushed

2 bay leaves

1/2 tablespoons peppercorns

salt to taste

Equipment: Large plastic bag, large saucepan with cover, tongs, broiler pan, over mitts

1. Preheat broiler to high.

2. Place chicken or meat in plastic bag. Add soy sauce, vinegar, garlic, bay leaf, and peppercorn. Seal and refrigerate for at least 1 hour. Turn several times to coat evenly.

3. Pour marinated meat into saucepan. Add just enough water to cover. Bring to boil, cover, reduce to simmer and cook 30 minutes or until meat is cooked through.

4. Using tongs, transfer meat to broiler pan. Place in oven and broil on high about 10 minutes or until golden.

5. Continue cooking vinegar-soy sauce mixture uncovered over medium-high heat until reduced by half. Add salt to taste.

6. Transfer meat to serving platter. Pour sauce over meat.

7. Serve hot with side of rice.

Misua (Angel Hair Noodles in Soup)

Noodle shops are a fast-food craze in the Philippines. For a few pesos a plate of noodles is quickly served with one's choice of toppings. Philippine noodles used in the following recipe are extremely thin. We suggest substituting angel hair noodles, available in most supermarkets.

Yield: serves 4 to 6

2 tablespoons vegetable oil

3 cloves garlic, **trimmed**, peeled, **minced** or 1 teaspoon garlic granules

4 green onions, trimmed, peeled, **finely chopped**

1 yellow onion, trimmed, peeled, finely chopped

6 cups chicken broth, homemade or canned

2 cups spinach, trimmed, finely chopped fresh or frozen, thawed

salt and pepper to taste

3 ounces angel hair noodles or Filipino fine wheat vermicelli noodles

Equipment: Large saucepan with cover, mixing spoon, ladle

1. Heat oil in saucepan over medium-high heat. Add garlic, green onions, and yellow onion. Fry about 3 minutes or until soft. Add chicken broth, mix well, and bring to a boil. Add spinach, reduce heat to simmer, and cook for about 2 minutes. Add salt and pepper to taste. Mix well.

2. Remove from heat and add noodles over top of soup. Do not mix. Push noodles down with back of spoon as they soften and absorb liquid. Cover and simmer about 5 minutes or until soft. Remove from heat. Keep covered until soft, not soggy, about 5 minutes.

3. Serve immediately in individual soup bowls.

Maja Blanca (Coconut Cake)

In the Philippines, coconuts are used in or on everything. The following recipe is a firm, custard-like cake requiring no baking—the oven is used only to toast grated coconut. The cake is very unusual but easy to make.

Yield: serves about 6–8

2 cups tightly packed, finely **shredded** coconut, fresh (recipe page 138), frozen, or canned (sweetened)

3 tablespoons granulated sugar, more or less to taste

4 tablespoons butter or margarine, melted

1/2 cup cornstarch

1/2 cup tightly packed light brown sugar

1/4 cup water

2 cups coconut milk, fresh (recipe page 138), frozen, or canned (unsweetened)

3 egg yolks (refrigerate egg white to use at another time)

whipped topping for garnish

Equipment: Medium mixing bowl, 9-inch pie pan, **whisk** or mixing spoon, medium saucepan

1. Preheat oven to 325°F.

2. If using freshly grated unsweetened coconut, add about 3 tablespoons of granulated sugar, more or less to taste. No sugar is needed if canned sweetened coconut is used.

3. Place coconut and melted butter or margarine in medium mixing bowl. Using clean fingers, blend well. Press coconut onto pie pan bottom and up sides, making a pie crust. Place in oven and bake about 5–10 minutes or until lightly golden. Remove from oven and cool to room temperature.

4. Place cornstarch and sugar in medium saucepan, add water, and mix well to dissolve cornstarch. Add coconut milk and egg yolks, and, stirring continually, heat over medium-high heat until mixture boils. Reduce to low and stir vigorously until smooth and thick, about 5 minutes. Remove from heat and pour mixture into coconut pie crust. Cool to room temperature and refrigerate about 3 hours to set.

5. To serve, cut into wedges and add dollop of whipped topping.

Philippine Fruit Salad

The following fruit salad is a mixture of many different fruits growing in the tropical Philippines. It makes a colorful and delicious salad or dessert as well as a decorative **buffet** presentation. Slice and add bananas just before serving for best flavor and color.

Yield: serves 4 to 6

2 pineapples, cut each pineapple in half, scoop out flesh, leaving 1/2-inch shell for making pineapple boats

1 pint strawberries, rinsed, hulled, halved (leave 4 whole for garnish)

1 cantaloupe, cut in half, **seeded**, cut into balls

1 honeydew melon, cut in half, seeded, cut into balls

2 kiwifruits, peeled, sliced in rounds, about 1/4 inch thick

1 cup **shredded** coconut, fresh (recipe page 138), frozen, or canned

2 bananas, peeled, sliced in rounds, about 1/4 inch thick

1 cup heavy cream, whipped, or frozen whipped topping (thawed)

Equipment: Melon baler, large **serrated knife**, grapefruit knife or sharp paring knife, large bowl with cover, mixing spoon

1. Cut scooped-out pineapple flesh into bite-sized pieces and place in mixing bowl. Add strawberries, melon balls, kiwi, and coconut. Using clean hands, toss gently. Cover and refrigerate until ready to serve.

2. Set pineapple shells on large round serving platter with tops hanging over outer edge. Remove fruit from refrigerator, add bananas and whipped cream or whipped topping, toss gently to blend. Transfer mixture to pineapple shells and pile high. Garnish with whole strawberries.

3. Serve with a large serving spoon as salad or dessert for a luncheon or **buffet.**

Sri Lanka

Sri Lanka, an island nation just off the southern coast of India, is mostly flat with rolling hills and mountains. Located in the Indian Ocean, fish are plentiful year-round and are important to the Sri Lankan diet. Tropical fruit such as oranges, bananas, mangos, plums, kiwi, and melons are grown in abundance and often served to give a cool, pleasing contrast to the hot, spicy curries. "White curry," made with coconut and coconut milk, is a specialty of Sri Lankans. Rice, a staple grain, provides a nutritious base for meals and is eaten by most Sri Lankans on a daily basis. To improve the production of cash crops, rice and tea, irrigation systems were and continue to be developed and improved.

Tea, a valuable cash crop, was brought by the British during the 1800s. Today, Sri Lanka is known for fine tea.

⁂ *Meen Molee* (Fish Coconut Curry)

Molee is a coconut milk curry made with precooked vegetables, fish, or poultry. The following recipe can be made with poultry (4 chicken breasts) or vegetables cut into chunks (4 cups) or shrimp instead or fish **fillets**. Just reduce the cooking time.

Yield: serves 4 to 6

1 teaspoon **turmeric**

1 teaspoon salt

6 fish fillets, skin on, about 6–8 ounces each, washed, patted dry

2 tablespoons butter, margarine, or ghee (recipe page 79), more as needed

2 onions, **trimmed**, peeled, **finely chopped**

4 green chili peppers, **seeded**, cut in thin strips

1 tablespoon fresh ginger, trimmed, peeled, grated or 1 teaspoon ground ginger

1 teaspoon curry powder

1 cup coconut milk, fresh (recipe page 138), frozen, or canned

1/4 cup lemon juice

1/2 cup shredded coconut, for garnish

Equipment: Large skillet, pancake turner or metal spatula, mixing spoon, large baking pan

1. Preheat oven to 350°F.

2. Mix turmeric and salt in small bowl and rub on fish fillets.

3. Heat 2 tablespoons butter, margarine, or ghee in skillet over medium heat. Add fillets and fry about 5 minutes per side or until golden brown. Transfer to baking pan and place fillets side-by-side, skin side down. Do not stack fish.

4. In same skillet, add more butter, margarine, or *ghee* if necessary. Add onions, chilies, ginger, and curry powder. Mix well. Fry over medium heat about 2–3 minutes or until onions are soft. Remove from heat. Stir in coconut milk and lemon juice, mix well, and pour over fish.

5. Place fillets in oven for 10 minutes or until heated through. Remove and sprinkle with shredded coconut for garnish.

6. Serve hot with side dishes of lentils, rice, and condiments of your choice.

⁂ *Dal* (Spicy Lentils)

Hindus call legumes *dal* and there are over 60 varieties available. Some of the most common are red kidney beans; yellow, red, and brown **lentils**; split, black-eyed, and pigeon peas. Dals, a protein-rich meat substitute, are inexpensive, tasty, nutritious, and easy to cook. A good buffer for hot and spicy curries, dals can be spooned over rice or served separately as side dishes. Soup can be made from leftover dal by just adding water or broth.

Yield: serves 4 to 6

1 cup dried **lentils** (red, brown, or yellow) or split peas

3 cups water

2 tablespoons vegetable oil

1 teaspoon salt

1 teaspoon ground cumin

1 teaspoon ground **turmeric**

3 cloves garlic, **trimmed**, peeled, **minced** or 1 teaspoon garlic granules

1 onion, trimmed, peeled, **finely chopped**

4–6 lemon wedges

Equipment: Large saucepan with cover, mixing spoon, small skillet

1. Place lentils or split peas and water in saucepan and bring to boil over high heat. Reduce to simmer, cover, and cook, about 45 minutes or until tender. Stir frequently.

2. Heat oil in skillet over medium-high heat. Add salt, cumin, turmeric, garlic, and onion. Mix well and cook until tender, about 3–5 minutes.

3. Stir onion mixture into lentils and simmer, uncovered, about 20 minutes, stirring frequently to prevent sticking.

4. Serve warm as a side dish.

✳ Coconut Rice

Yield: serves 4 to 6

2 cups brown rice

2 cups coconut milk, homemade (recipe page 138) or canned

4 small onions, **trimmed**, peeled, **finely chopped**

1/2 teaspoon ground turmeric

1/2 teaspoon ground cloves

3 cloves garlic, trimmed, peeled, **minced**

1/2 teaspoon ground cardamom

salt and pepper to taste

Equipment: Small saucepan with tight-fitting lid, wooden spoon

1. Place coconut milk and rice in small saucepan. Over medium-high heat bring to boil. Stir in onions, turmeric, cloves, garlic, and cardamom. Cover and reduce heat to simmer. Cook until rice is tender, about 20–25 minutes. If coconut milk evaporates, add just enough water to prevent sticking. When rice is tender remove from heat and add salt and pepper to taste.

2. Serve with curry and yogurt or pickles and chutney.

Thailand

Thailand lies in the heart of Southeast Asia and experiences monsoon season from May to mid-September. Thai people have a reputation for being mellow, easygoing, and very hospitable. Thais maintain their cultural identity while embracing modernization and foreign influences.

The soil of Thailand is very fertile and a majority of people are involved in agriculture. During the mid-1980s, agro-industrial farms brought foreign investors and modernized farming.

Rice (a staple crop) and cucumber salad (marinated in rice-wine vinegar) are usually served as a cool contrast to hot and spicy curries. Popular spices are similar to those found in other Asian countries. Favorite desserts are often made with sweet rice or bananas and cooked with shredded coconut and/or coconut milk.

Goong Curry (Shrimp in Green Curry)

Chili peppers, kaffir lime leaves, and lemon grass are used in Thai curries, making them more aromatic than Indian curries. Curries in Thailand are often referred to by their color: red curry is usually mildly spicy, yellow curry tends to be creamy due to the use of coconut cream, and green curry adds fresh chilies and tends to be spicier than the other two.

Yield: serves 4 to 6

2 ounces coconut milk homemade (recipe page 138) or canned

2 tablespoons corn or peanut oil

5 tablespoons green curry paste (available at international markets)

11/2 tablespoons fish sauce (*nam pla*) (available at Asian markets)

1/2 cup water

1 teaspoon lemon juice

1 teaspoon brown sugar

1 1/2 pounds raw headless shrimp, peeled, **deveined**

1 teaspoon lemon rind, **julienned**

15–20 fresh sweet basil leaves (*bai horappa*) (available at international markets)

Equipment: Measuring cup or clear glass, spoon, small bowl or cup, medium saucepan with cover, wooden mixing spoon

1. Transfer coconut milk to measuring cup or clear glass and leave undisturbed for 3 hours or more. A thick cream will accumulate at top of coconut milk. Using measuring spoon, scoop off top 4 tablespoons cream and place in bowl or cup. Set aside. Discard remaining cream.

2. Heat oil in saucepan over medium-high heat. Add green curry paste. Stirring constantly, stir in thick cream. Stir and simmer until oil separates and paste is lightly browned.

3. Reduce heat to low. Stir in fish sauce, tamarind paste, sugar, and 1/2 cup water. Stirring constantly, bring to simmer and adjust seasoning. If needed, add more fish sauce, sugar, or lemon juice.

4. Stir in shrimp. Bring to simmer, cover, and gently cook 3–5 minutes or until shrimp are **opaque white.** Remove from heat and just before serving sprinkle lemon rind and basil leaves over top of shrimp curry.

5. Serve warm with fresh rice noodles or jasmine rice.

⁂ Meat Satay

Mention Thailand cooking and everyone seems to know about the famous and delicious thinly sliced, **marinated**, skewered, and grilled meat-on-sticks served with dipping sauces.

Cooking tip: Cut meat while slightly frozen; it will be easier to cut into thin strips.

Yield: serves 6 to 8

1/2 pound skinless, boneless chicken breast cut as thinly as possible into strips

1/2 pound boneless beef or pork loin, cut as thinly as possible into strips

1 teaspoon curry powder

salt and pepper to taste

1/2 cup unsweetened coconut milk, home-made (recipe page 138), canned, or frozen (thawed)

1/2 cup apple cider vinegar

2 tablespoons sugar

2 tablespoons dried, crushed red pepper, more or less to taste

1 onion, **trimmed**, peeled, **finely chopped**

1 tablespoon fresh **coriander**, finely chopped or 1/2 teaspoon dried

Equipment: Large shallow dish, medium bowl, 24 6–12-inch-long water-soaked bamboo skewers (as needed, or use metal skewers), baking sheet

1. Preheat broiler.

2. Place strips of chicken and meat in large shallow dish.

3. Place curry powder, salt and pepper to taste, coconut milk, vinegar, sugar, red pepper, onion, and coriander in medium mixing bowl. Add strips and mix well to coat. Refrigerate for 1 hour, mixing frequently to coat strips.

4. Set oven rack about 6 inches under broiler and preheat to high.

5. If using wooden skewers, you *must* soak skewers in water for about 30 minutes. Thread chicken and meat strips onto separate skewers. Place skewers side-by-side on baking sheet and broil for about 3 minutes, until lightly browned. Turn strips over and broil other side until cooked through and browned, about 3 minutes.

6. To serve satays, place skewers on large platter and give each person a small dish of peanut dipping sauce. Everyone picks up a skewer and dips the end to be eaten in the dipping sauce.

Peanut Dipping Sauce

Cooks in Thailand and other Asian countries prepare many different dipping sauces to use with satays, but peanut sauce is the most popular. Thais usually grind peanuts to a paste for the following recipe, and coconut milk is sweetened. We suggest a simpler procedure that will provide similar results.

Yield: about 1 1/8 cup

1/2 cup smooth peanut butter   3 tablespoons soy sauce

1/2 cup coconut cream, canned

Equipment: Mixing spoon or electric blender, small bowl

1. Use mixing spoon or blender, combine peanut butter, coconut cream, and soy sauce until thoroughly mixed. Refrigerate until ready to serve.

2. Serve each person about 2 tablespoons of dipping sauce with satay.

Vietnam

Vietnam is a long, narrow country bordering the South China Sea. Vietnamese people are of Chinese descent. They migrated from the north, bringing with them the cooking of their homeland and applying it to the native tropical foods of their new surroundings. The Vietnamese dishes and flavors are unique and distinctive, unlike any others, and are often made with fish, shellfish, or duck. Vegetables are eaten with rice at almost every meal. Rice is served either as a grain or noodles made from rice flour. *Pho* is a favorite soup made with "rice sticks," a brittle noodle. Popular spices are ginger, lemon grass, chilies, garlic, and star anise. Besides rice, sweet potatoes, corn, **sorghum**, citrus fruits, bananas, melons, and garden vegetables are grown. The best locations for farming are along the rich soils of the Red River delta and the Mekong River delta.

Fishing is a very important industry. Nothing is wasted. Sauces are made from crustacean shells, fish heads, and bones to add flavor to soups and stews. It seems as though every Vietnamese recipe includes a few spoonfuls of fish sauce called *nuoc mam*. Nuoc mam is made from salt and fish that has fermented for 9–12 months.

Pho Ga (Chicken Rice Noodle Soup)

Yield: serves 2 to 4

3 celery stalks, **trimmed, finely chopped**

3 green onions, trimmed, finely chopped

3/4 pound cooked chicken breast, finely **shredded**

1/2 pound rice noodles (available at Asian markets), cooked according to directions on package, drained well

2 cups chicken broth, homemade or canned

nuoc mam, as needed (available at supermarkets and Asian markets)

2 wood-ear or portobella mushrooms, trimmed, **coarsely chopped**

Equipment: 2 medium bowls, medium saucepan, 2–4 individual serving bowls, tongs, chopsticks

1. Place celery and green onion together in bowl and refrigerate until ready to serve.

2. Place cooked shredded chicken in separate bowl and refrigerate until ready to serve.

3. In saucepan bring chicken broth to boil over medium-high heat Add wood-ear or portobella mushrooms, reduce to simmer, and cook for 15 minutes. Add nuoc mam to taste. Stir in noodles and heat through.

4. To serve, each guest receives a soup bowl and adds desired amount of celery-green onion mix and shredded chicken. Then ladle hot chicken noodle soup into individual bowls, using tongs to pick up noodles. To eat, use chopsticks for noodles and spoon for broth.

✻ *Nam Nyong* (Grilled Meatballs)

Very often, hot, spicy meat is wrapped in lettuce leaves and eaten like a sandwich. The meat and ingredients are pulverized to a smooth paste. We suggest chopping ingredients as fine as possible; you will still taste the flavors of Vietnam with an added pleasant crunchiness.

Yield: serves 4 to 6

1 pound extra finely ground pork

1 onion, **trimmed**, peeled, **finely chopped**

2 cloves garlic, trimmed, peeled, **minced** or 1/2 teaspoon garlic granules

1 teaspoon sugar

1 tablespoon all-purpose flour

salt and pepper to taste

6 or 8 large leaf lettuce, washed, dried

Equipment: Medium mixing bowl, mixing spoon, aluminum foil, broiler pan with rack, oven mitts, tongs

1. Place broiler tray on top shelf in oven, about 6 inches under broiler heat, and preheat broiler to medium hot

2. Place pork, onion, garlic, sugar, flour, and salt and pepper to taste in mixing bowl and mix until well blended.

3. Using wet hands, form meat into ping-pong-sized balls.

4. Place meatballs side-by-side on broiler pan rack. Broil in oven until firm and fully cooked. Using metal tongs, turn to brown evenly on all sides.

5. Serve meatballs on platter surrounded with lettuce leaves with rice and dipping sauce. To eat meatballs, slide onto lettuce leaf, add a spoonful of rice, and sprinkle with nuoc mam. Wrap leaf around mixture and eat with hands.

THE SOUTH PACIFIC

Australia

Australia is divided into seven regions: Western Australia, Southern Australia, Northern Territory, Queensland, New South Whales, Victoria, and Tasmania. Australia has a very dramatic landscape ranging from the well-known "outback" (a remote and barren interior where it is too hot and dry for people to live) to lush grasslands of the eastern coast (where there are many sheep and cattle ranches). Throughout Australia there is a diverse mix of immigrants who brought with them foods and traditions from their homeland.

Australia is surrounded by waters brimming with wonderful fish and seafood. Beef and lamb are important in the Australian diet and a local favorite is kangaroo meat.

Australia was originally inhabited by two groups of people, Native Aborigines, and prisoners brought from Great Britain who settled in penal colonies. Traditionally Aborigines were hunters and gatherers. Kangaroos, snakes, lizards, and wombats were favorite meats.

Kangaroo Fillet with Red Currant Sauce

Yield: serves 4

4 6–8-ounce kangaroo fillets or strip sirloin steak

2 tablespoons vegetable oil, more as needed

2 cups beef broth

1/2 cup water

4 tablespoons red currant jelly, more as needed

Equipment: Basting brush, large skillet, small saucepan, mixing spoon, sharp knife

1. Using basting brush, brush both sides of steaks with oil. Pan fry in skillet over medium-high heat until browned on both sides, about 8–12 minutes.

2. In saucepan over medium-high heat, combine beef broth, water, and red currant jelly and stir well. Cook until reduced to thick, syrupy sauce.

3. To serve, slice meat into serving-sized pieces and spoon red currant sauce over meat.

Pineapple and Cabbage Salad

Exceptional exotic fruits grow in Australia's tropical climate. Fresh fruit salads and desserts are popular throughout the country.

Yield: 4 to 6

2 cups cabbage, **trimmed**, finely **shredded**

1 large ripe pineapple, trimmed, peeled, **cored, cubed**

1 grapefruit, peeled, separated into segments

1 orange, peeled, separated into segments

1/2 cucumber, trimmed, peel on, sliced into thin rounds

1 red bell pepper, trimmed, seeded, cored, sliced into thin strips

1 cup cooked ham, **finely chopped**

Equipment: Medium salad bowl, tongs or salad fork and spoon

1. Place cabbage, pineapple, grapefruit, orange, cucumber, bell pepper, and ham in salad bowl. Toss gently using tongs or salad fork and spoon. Refrigerate until ready to serve.
2. Pour dressing (next recipe) over salad and toss gently to blend.

⁂ Dressing

Yield: about 1 cup

1 tablespoon grated orange rind

4 tablespoons olive oil or vegetable oil

2 tablespoons apple cider vinegar

2 tablespoons mayonnaise

2 tablespoons heavy cream

salt and pepper to taste

Equipment: Small bowl, **whisk** or mixing spoon

1. Place orange rind, oil, vinegar, mayonnaise, and cream in small bowl and add salt and pepper to taste.
2. Mix well with whisk or mixing spoon.
3. Serve salad on individual plates lined with lettuce leaves.

⁂ Toad-in-the-Hole (Meat Baked in Batter)

Toad-in-the-hole, a traditional English recipe brought to Australia by early settlers, is a great way to use leftover cooked meat. In England it is traditionally made with sausage.

Yield: serves 6

1 1/2 cups all-purpose flour

1/2 teaspoon baking powder

2 cups milk

2 eggs, beaten lightly

3 cups cooked chicken, sausage, or roast beef, cut into bite-sized pieces

3 tablespoons parsley, **finely chopped** fresh or dried

salt and pepper to taste

Equipment: Flour sifter, medium mixing bowl, **whisk** or egg beater, mixing spoon, greased medium baking dish, oven mitts

1. Preheat oven to 375°F.

2. **Sift** flour and baking powder into mixing bowl. Add milk and eggs, mix until smooth using whisk or egg beater.

3. Cover bottom of baking dish with meat and sprinkle with parsley flakes. Add salt and pepper to taste. Pour batter over meat and spread smooth. Bake in oven until puffed and golden brown, about 45 minutes.

4. Serve either hot or cold, cut into squares.

Pasties (Meat Pies)

Pasties, the country's favorite fast food, are a combination of meat and vegetables encased in pie crust dough. The variety of sizes, shapes, and fillings are endless and any combination of meat and vegetables can be used.

Yield: serves 2 or 3

2 tablespoons vegetable oil, more as needed

1/2 pound lean ground beef

2 carrots, **trimmed, finely chopped**

1 onion, trimmed, peeled, finely chopped

1 potato, trimmed, finely chopped

salt and pepper to taste

1 prepared 9-inch pie crust, homemade or frozen, thawed

1 egg, beaten

Equipment: Medium skillet, mixing spoon, nonstick or lightly greased baking sheet, fork pastry brush, aluminum foil

1. Preheat oven to 350°F.

2. Heat oil in skillet over medium heat and add meat. Stirring continually, fry for 3–5 minutes or until brown. Add carrots, onion, potato, and salt and pepper to taste. Mix well and cook for about 3 minutes more.

3. Place prepared pie crust on baking sheet. Spoon meat mixture onto 1/2 of the pie crust and about 1 inch inside edge. Moisten edge of crust with a slightly wet finger. Fold unfilled side over filling, making half circle. Using fork tines, press edges together to seal in filling and poke about 5 vents into top crust.

4. Using pastry brush, brush top with beaten egg. Bake in oven about 30 minutes or until crust is golden.

5. Serve pasties hot with plenty of catsup as they do in Australia

Dandenong Squares (Cookies from the City of Dandenong)

Yield: about 15 pieces

1/4 cup butter or margarine

1/4 cup sugar

1 cup pitted, chopped dates (cut with scissors for best results)

3 cups Rice Krispies   2 cups chocolate chips, melted

Equipment: Medium saucepan, wooden mixing spoon, medium mixing bowl, medium non-stick baking pan, metal spatula or spoon

1. Place butter or margarine, sugar, and dates in saucepan and cook over low heat stirring continually until mixture thickens. Remove from heat.
2. Place Rice Krispies in mixing bowl and add date mixture. Mix well. Transfer mixture to baking pan and press down to cover bottom.
3. Pour melted chocolate over mixture, using metal spatula or back of spoon to spread evenly. Refrigerate to set, about 1 hour.
4. To serve, cut into squares.

Fiji

In the South Pacific, between Australia and Hawaii, sits a group of tiny islands known as Fiji. The islands are home to Melanesian and Polynesian natives and a very large group of East Indians, brought to the islands by the English in the nineteenth century to work the sugar cane plantations. There are many cultural differences between the Indian descendants, following the Muslim and Hindu rituals of their homeland, and native Fijians, who prefer to live in underdeveloped communal villages, much as their ancestors have done for hundreds of years. Rice, coconuts, and sugarcane are the main island cash crops. Coconuts are prominent throughout the islands and coconut oil is very popular when cooking. Pork is a favorite meat and seafood is plentiful. Most foods are prepared simply and often wrapped in native plant leaves and then cooked in a pot over steam. During the twentieth century, the growth of urbanization has caused an increase in environmental concerns on the islands of Fiji. As with so many environmental issues, the destruction has created a ripple effect: slash and burn methods are used for farming, topsoil is washed into the ocean, and coral dies causing a decrease in the number of fish species. To counterbalance this effect, local organizations and government are encouraging eco-tourism and sustainable methods of farming.

I'A (Steamed Fish with Sweet Potatoes)

Fijians prefer their fish whole, heads on, bones in; however, fish fillets are suggested for this recipe.

Yield: serves 4

4 skin-on fish **fillets**, such as red snapper or sea bass, about 8 ounces each

4 sweet potatoes, peeled, cut into 1/2-inch chunks

2 tablespoons vegetable oil, more as needed

juice of 1 lemon

1/2 cup butter or margarine, more or less as needed

salt and pepper to taste

Equipment: Aluminum foil, paper towels, roasting pan with wire rack and cover, medium skillet with cover or **Dutch oven**

1. Preheat oven to 350°F.

2. Cut foil into 4 (8-inch) squares and place side-by-side on work surface.

3. Rinse fish fillets and pat dry, using paper towels. Rub both sides with oil and place fillet, skin side down, in center of each foil square. Sprinkle with lemon juice and salt and pepper to taste. Wrap each fillet securely in foil, tightly sealing edges.

4. Set foil packages, seam side up, on wire rack in roasting pan., Pour about 1 or 2 inches of boiling water into pan. (Water can touch, but not cover, foil packages.) Cover and place in oven for about 20 minutes or until fish **flakes** easily when poked with fork.

5. *Preparing sweet potatoes*: Melt butter or margarine in skillet or Dutch oven over medium-high heat, add potatoes, and brown on all sides, mixing gently, about 5–8 minutes. Reduce heat to low, cover, and cook until tender, about 10–12 minutes. Add more butter or margarine, if necessary, to prevent sticking.

6. To serve, give each person a fish package and serve sweet potatoes separately.

New Zealand

The native inhabitants of New Zealand are Maori people. They are Polynesian descendents who migrated to New Zealand in the fourteenth century and intermarried with native Tangata Whenua. Captain Cook, one of the first Europeans to set foot in New Zealand, brought with him pigs and potatoes, thus began the importing of animals and foods to the island. Every type of sheep, cat, possum, chicken, pig, dog, kangaroo, mouse, horse, and freshwater fish that lives in New Zealand was brought by humans. Today, with millions of sheep, exotic fruit, and a wonderful fishing industry, New Zealand is an island rich with amazing culinary treasures.

New Zealand was settled by the British who introduced farming and ranching. Under British rule, Polynesian foods and customs were of little interest to English settlers. An exception is the *hangi* (a feast, like a *luau*) that takes place in tribal villages. During the hangi, food is wrapped in burlap sacks and buried in the ground to cook over hot stones.

❧ White Fish Fritters

Fish is a key ingredient in this island cuisine.

Yield: serves 4

1 cup flour

1/2 teaspoon baking powder

1/2 teaspoons salt

1 egg

1/2 cup milk, more as needed

4 6-ounce fillets, firm white fish, such as trout, red snapper or sea bass, cut into 4 strips each

vegetable oil, as needed

lemon wedges for serving

Equipment: Medium mixing bowl, mixing spoon or whisk, tongs, medium skillet, spatula, paper towel

1. In mixing bowl, combine flour, baking powder, and salt. Mix well. Add egg and milk and whisk until batter is smooth (similar to pancake batter).

2. Heat 2 tablespoons oil in skillet over medium-high heat. Using fingers or tongs, dip each piece of fish into batter mixture, coat well, and shake off excess batter.

3. Place coated fish side-by-side into skillet over medium-high heat and fry until golden brown on both sides, 5–8 minutes, turning with spatula. Remove from skillet and drain on paper towel.

4. Serve at once on platter with lemon wedges.

Yaki Udon (Chicken and Vegetables with Noodles)

Yield: serves 4

2 tablespoons vegetable oil

1 pound boneless chicken breasts or thighs or tofu, **diced**

1 green cabbage, **trimmed, shredded**

1 carrot, trimmed, shredded

1 onion, trimmed, peeled, thinly sliced

1 green bell pepper, trimmed, thinly sliced

1 zucchini trimmed, thinly sliced

1 yellow squash, trimmed, thinly sliced

1 bunch broccoli spears, trimmed, separated, **blanched**

1 pound *Udon* noodles (available at Asian markets), cooked according to directions on package

2 tablespoon oyster sauce, more to taste (available at Asian markets)

Equipment: **Wok** or large saucepan, mixing spoon

1. Heat oil in wok or saucepan over medium-high heat. Add chicken or tofu and stir-fry until lightly golden, about 4–6 minutes. Add cabbage, carrot, onion, green bell pepper, zucchini, squash, and broccoli. **Sauté** until lightly cooked, about 8–12 minutes. Add more oil if necessary to prevent sticking.

2. Stir in noodles and toss well. Add 2 tablespoons oyster sauce, toss to coat, and add more oyster sauce to desired taste.

3. Serve warm.

Rock Cakes

Rock cakes are one of the oldest written recipes in New Zealand, dating back to 1861. The dough should be made to look like rocks, as rough as possible, similar to the English scone.

Yield: serves 6 or 8

1 cup all-purpose flour

1/2 teaspoon salt

1/2 cup butter or margarine

1/2 cup sugar

1/2 cup seedless raisins

2 tablespoons orange marmalade

1 egg, lightly beaten

Equipment: Flour **sifter**, large mixing bowl, mixing spoon, fork, greased or nonstick cookie sheet

1. Preheat oven to 425°F.

2. **Sift** flour and salt into mixing bowl. Blend in butter or margarine using clean hands, until mixture resembles fine bread crumbs.

3. Add sugar, raisins, and marmalade and mix well with spoon. Add egg and blend into flour mixture until stiff and rocky. Mixture must be stiff or it will lose shape when baking. Pull off golf-ball-sized chunks of dough and drop on cookie sheet about 1 inch apart. Do not smooth out dough pieces.

4. Bake in oven about 15 minutes or until lightly browned. Remove from oven and turn rock cakes bottom side up to cook.

5. Serve rock cakes as a snack with milk or tea.

Kiwi Sorbet (Dessert Sherbert)

Kiwis are a fruit of China originally known as Chinese gooseberries. During the 1950s, New Zealand began cultivating the fruit and for marketing reasons renamed the fruit kiwi. The new name is in honor of the New Zealand endangered and famous kiwi bird. Both are brown, short, plump, and fuzzy. Today, New Zealand is known as the kiwi capital of the world.

Yield: serves 4 to 6

1/2 cup sugar

1/2 cup water

7 kiwis, peeled, mashed (set aside one to slice for garnish)

3 tablespoons lemon juice or juice of 1 lemon

1 egg white, beaten to stiff peaks.

Equipment: Small saucepan, mixing spoon, medium metal bowl, aluminum foil

1. Place sugar and water in small saucepan and cook over medium heat about 2 minutes, stirring continually to dissolve sugar. Bring to boil and remove at once from heat. Cool to room temperature.

2. Place mashed kiwi and lemon juice in metal bowl. Add sugar mixture, and mix well. Cover with foil, place in freezer, and chill until slightly thickened, about 1 to 1 1/2 hours.

3. Remove from freezer. Mixing continually, add whipped egg whites. Cover with foil and return to freezer until firm, about 2 to 3 hours. When ready to serve, place in refrigerator for 5–10 minutes if mixture is too firm.

4. To serve, spoon sherbert into individual dessert bowls and garnish each with a slice of kiwi.

❧ *Pavlova* (Meringue Fruit Dessert)

Pavlova, a dessert named in honor of a world famous Russian ballerina, is very popular in both New Zealand and Australia. Pavlova is a meringue dessert with a moist sticky center, similar to marshmallow cream.

Yield: serves 6 to 8

4 egg whites, at room temperature

1/2 teaspoon salt

1 cup sugar

1 teaspoon cornstarch

2 teaspoons apple cider vinegar

1 1/2 cups heavy cream, whipped or 3 cups prepared frozen whipped topping, thawed, for serving

4 kiwis, peeled, sliced across, for garnish

Equipment: medium pie pan or plate, greased and lightly floured cookie sheet, medium mixing bowl, **egg beater** or electric mixer, small bowl, spoon or spatula

1. Preheat oven to 350°F.

2. *Make pattern*: place pie pan or plate upside down on greased and floured cookie sheet. Using clean finger trace around pie pan to make circle in flour. Set aside.

3. Place egg whites and salt in medium bowl. Using egg beater or electric mixer, whip into soft peaks. Add sugar, a little at a time, beating after each addition until smooth and glossy.

4. In small bowl mix cornstarch and vinegar until smooth. Using spoon or spatula **fold** into whipped egg whites until well blended. Pour whites into center of circle marked on cookie sheet. Using spoon or spatula spread meringue evenly to edges of circle, building up edges more than center.

5. Place on middle shelf in oven, reduce oven heat to 250°F, and bake until outside of meringue is firm and golden, about 1 hour. Remove from oven and cool. Do not cover or chill.

6. To serve, spread top and sides with whipped cream or whipped topping. Garnish top with kiwi slices.

Papua New Guinea and Western Guinea

The island of New Guinea was once colonized by Germany, the Netherlands, and England, separating the island into three different territories. After years of war and occupation, the territories have changed hands several times. The southeastern region, today, once occupied by Germany and Britain, is a unified country known as Papua New Guinea. The western half of the island, referred to as Western Guinea (Western Irian Jaya and Papua), is currently occupied and greatly influenced by the culture and cuisine of Indonesia.

For centuries people of Papua New Guinea lived in small remote villages, often unaware of neighboring communities due to the mountainous terrain. However, during the 1990s people began to migrate to ports and major centers, resulting in urbanization.

Papua New Guinea has lush rainforests and rich biological diversity. Today, nongovernmental organizations are focused on educating the people of Papua New Guinea about ecological effects of deforestation.

Pork, a favorite meat, is served with an assortment of vegetables on special occasions and during village feasts. The pig is roasted for many hours over hot stones set in a large hole in the ground called an earth oven.

The chief foods are starchy *sago* from pith of sago palm, yams, mangoes, passion fruit, pawpaws, bananas, pineapples, and coconuts. Fish, shellfish, and ocean vegetation are prepared simply with no fancy sauces or garnishes.

❧ Boiled Shrimp

Boiled shrimp are often cooked in the shell to preserve flavor. To be eaten, shrimp must first be cooked, then peeled. To peel, hold shrimp by tail with one hand and place thumbnail of other hand under legs, separating the shell and then pull off shell; it peels easily over and off. Shrimp are often eaten without removing the dark vein that runs along the back, especially if they are small, except they are cleaner when **deveined**, because in large shrimp the vein contains grit. Allow at least 1/2 pound per person of raw shrimp when serving shell-on boiled shrimp.

Yield: 4 to 6

3 pounds raw, headless shrimp, fresh or frozen (thawed)

2 quarts water

1 tablespoons salt

3 lemons, cut into wedges, for serving

Equipment: **Colander** or strainer, large saucepan, mixing spoon

1. Rinse shrimp in colander or strainer under cold water and drain well.
2. Heat water in saucepan over high heat. Add salt, bring to boil, and add shrimp. Water will cool when shrimp are added, return to boil, reduce heat to simmer, and cook about 3–6 minutes. Large shrimp take a little longer to cook. Very tiny shrimp cook almost immediately when they hit boiling water. Shrimp are done when meat becomes **opaque** white.

3. Remove at once from boiling water and rinse in colander or strainer under cold water or ice to stop cooking action.

4. Serve shell-on shrimp either warm or chilled. Provide an extra plate or paper to hold shells and extra napkins or damp towels and a lemon wedge.

Grilled Fish

On New Guinea, grilling is the common way to cook. To keep food moist and juicy, it is first wrapped securely in leaves, then placed over hot coals. In the following recipe we suggest using aluminum foil instead of leaves. Islanders always prepare whole, head-on, bone-in fish; we are using fish fillets instead. It is also easier to bake fish in the oven, but those who are more adventuresome can grill. (We suggest using rubber gloves or bags when working with jalapeno peppers.)

Yield: serves 6

4 onions, **trimmed**, peeled, **finely chopped**

1 pickled jalapeño pepper, trimmed, **cored, seeded**, finely chopped

3 cloves garlic, trimmed, peeled, **minced** or 1 teaspoon garlic granules

1 teaspoon ground **turmeric**

2 tablespoons fresh ginger, trimmed, peeled, minced or 2 teaspoons ground ginger

2 teaspoons lemon grass, finely chopped (also called sorrel) or juice of 1 lemon

1 cup grated unsweetened coconut, homemade (recipe page 138), or frozen (thawed), or canned

salt to taste

6 red snapper fillets 6–8 ounce each, trout, or other firm fish **fillets**

Equipment: Small mixing bowl, mixing spoon, 6 (8˝ × 10˝) foil sheets, 1 or 2 baking sheets

1. Preheat oven to 350°F.

2. Place onions, jalapeño, garlic, turmeric, ginger, lemon grass or juice, and grated coconut in small bowl. Mix well and set aside.

3. Place 6 foil sheets side-by-side on work surface. Place one fillet in center of each. Spread same amount of mixture equally over each fillet.

4. Wrap fillets in foil: bring 2 long edges of foil up over fillets, and holding them together, fold over several times and press each fold to tightly seal package. Bend ends over to make airtight.

5. Place packages of fish side-by-side, seam side up, on baking sheet (use 2 if necessary). Bake in oven about 25–30 minutes. Fish is fully cooked when flesh is **opaque white** and **flakes** easily when poked with a fork.

6. To serve, each person is given a fish package seam side up.

3

The Caribbean

The Caribbean islands, popular tourist destinations, are located off southeastern North America and northern South America. The islands include Aruba, Bahamas, Cuba, Curacao, Greater Antilles, Dominican Republic, Haiti, Jamaica, Puerto Rico, Tobago, and Trinidad, plus many smaller islands.

The language and cooking throughout the Caribbean are a fusion of many cultures: first European explores colonized the islands, followed by Africans brought by slave trades, and people from India brought as cheap labor to work the plantations.

The soul of Caribbean cooking is enhancing flavors of fresh-grown fruits and vegetables with island spices and herbs. Allspice, thyme, tamarind, and coriander all grow on the islands. Allspice grows in such abundance in Jamaica it is called "Jamaican pepper."

Unusual fruits native to the Caribbean are ackee, apricot, balata, breadfruit, guava, naseberry, avocados, passion fruit, mango, star apple, and water lemon.

For centuries tubers, root vegetables, such as yams, Malanga, sweet potatoes, and **cassava** have been an important nutrient source. Shiploads of slaves, on their long journey from Africa, survived on tubers. Other common foods throughout the Caribbean are calabaza (pumpkin), greens, coconuts, squash, corn, tomatoes, and your basic garden vegetables.

BAHAMAS

In 1692 the British established the first colonies in the Bahamas. In 1973, the 700 small islands, off the Florida coast, were granted independence from Britain.

The settlers brought with them their English foods and cooking traditions. They quickly combined dishes from home with spices of islands. The English added locally grown red peppers to traditional English pickled onions, and rum was added to enhance the flavor of fruitcakes.

✷ *Guava-Duff* (Guava Log with Sauce)

This recipe is like a jelly roll.

Yield: serves 10 to 12

30-ounces canned guavas (we recommend using Goya brand, available at Latino or Asian Markets)

Dough:

4 cups flour

4 tablespoons baking powder

1 egg

4 teaspoons granulated sugar

Guava Sauce:

1 cup water

2 tablespoons granulated sugar

1 cup butter, room temperature

1/2 teaspoon salt

1/2 cup butter, room temperature

1 cup milk

1 teaspoon cinnamon

1 teaspoon nutmeg

1 tablespoon granulated sugar

2 cups powdered sugar

1 teaspoon vanilla extract

1 teaspoon rum extract

Equipment: Sharp knife, cutting board, small spoon, small bowl, medium mixing bowl, electric mixer, mixing spoon, floured work surface, two 16″ ×12″ sheets of aluminum foil, small saucepan, mixing spoon, large stock pot with cover

1. Fill large pot with water and over high heat bring to boil.

2. Remove guavas from can, set juice aside. Slice each guava in half. Using small spoon, remove seeds and place them in saucepan. Add 1 cup water, 2 tablespoons sugar, and 3 tablespoons guava juice from can. Stir and set aside.

3. Coarsely chop guava halves and place in bowl; set aside.

4. *Prepare dough*: in mixing bowl combine flour, salt, 4 teaspoons sugar, and baking powder. Crumble in butter and stir in egg. Using electric mixer, mix well. Slowly add milk and mix until well blended. Transfer to floured work surface. **Knead** until stiff dough is formed.

5. Using rolling pin, roll dough into 10″ × 15″ rectangle. Evenly spread chopped guava chunks on dough surface. Sprinkle with cinnamon, nutmeg, and sugar. Roll up like a jelly roll log. Cut log in half and pinch dough at each end to prevent guava from seeping out.

6. Securely wrap each log separately in foil, tightly securing both ends to prevent leakage. Submerge foil-wrapped logs into boiling water, cover, and boil about 1 1/2 hours, adding hot water, if necessary, to maintain water level.

7. *Prepare guava sauce*: place guava seed mixture over medium-high heat, bring to boil, reduce heat, and simmer for 20 minutes, stirring frequently. Remove from heat and set aside to cool to room temperature. When cooled, **strain** into small bowl. Discard seeds and set strained liquid aside.

8. In mixing bowl, using electric mixer, mix butter and powdered sugar until fluffy. Beat in vanilla and rum extracts; blend well. Add strained guava juice and beat until smooth. Transfer to small serving bowl, cover, and place in refrigerator.

9. When logs are fully cooked, using tongs with oven mitts remove logs from water and place on work surface. Allow to cool slightly and carefully remove foil wrapping from each log. Place logs on serving platter.

10. To serve: while warm, cut into 1/4-inch slices. Ladle 1–2 tablespoons guava sauce over top of each serving.

❧ Banana Pudding

Bahamian puddings resemble cakes more than they do puddings.

Yield: serves 4 to 6

6 ripe bananas, peeled, mashed	1 tablespoon melted butter
1/2 cup all-purpose flour	1 teaspoon ground nutmeg
1 cup sugar	confectioner's sugar for garnish

Equipment: Large mixing bowl, mixing spoon, greased square cake pan

1. Preheat oven to 325°F.

2. Place bananas in mixing bowl. Add flour, sugar, butter, and nutmeg and mix well.

3. Pour batter in baking pan and bake in oven about 40 minutes until top is golden brown. Cool to room temperature, cut in squares, and sprinkle with confectioner's sugar.

4. Serve warm or cold as dessert.

🌿 *Conkies* (Sweet Coconut Snack)

Conkies are made each year on November 5, "Guy Fawkes Day," to celebrate the failed plot to blow up the British Parliament. Guy Fawkes, the leader of this plot, was executed. On the Islands conkies would be wrapped in banana leaves; we suggest aluminum foil.

Yield: makes 12

1 1/2 cups grated coconut meat, fresh (recipe page 138) or canned

1 cup pumpkin fresh, peeled, grated, or canned

1 cup sweet potatoes, **trimmed**, peeled, grated

1 1/2 cups brown sugar

1 teaspoon ground allspice

1 teaspoon ground nutmeg

1 teaspoon almond extract

1/2 cup seedless raisins

1/4 cup all-purpose flour

1 cup white or yellow cornmeal

1 teaspoon salt more or less to taste

1 cup melted butter or margarine

1 cup milk

water, as needed

Equipment: Large mixing bowl, wooden mixing spoon or electric mixer, 12 6-inch squares of aluminum foil, **steamer pan or basket**

1. Combine coconut, pumpkin, sweet potatoes, brown sugar, allspice, nutmeg, almond extract, raisins, flour, cornmeal, and salt in mixing bowl. Using spoon or electric mixer, mix well. Slowly add butter or margarine and milk and mix to smooth paste.

2. Place 2 tablespoons mixture into middle of each foil square. Fold in edges making tightly sealed package.

3. Place about 2 or 3 inches of water in steamer basket (water should not touch basket). Stack packages in steamer, bring water to boil over high heat, and cover tightly. Reduce heat to simmer and steam for 1 hour or until mixture in packages is thoroughly cooked. Frequently check to make sure water has not boiled out. If necessary, add more hot water.

4. To serve, open foil package and enjoy the conkie inside.

CUBA

Unlike hot and spicy cooking on the other Caribbean islands, Cuba adds *Sofrito* (recipe page 147) to enhance flavors of stews, soups, many meat dishes, and black beans. Meats and poultry are usually marinated in citrus juices, such as lime or sour orange juices. They are then roasted over low heat until the meat is falling-off-the-bone tender. Other common staples are root vegetables such as *yuca*, *malanga*, and *boniato* (available in Latino markets). Their flavor improves when marinaded in *mojo*, a mix of olive oil, lemon juice, sliced raw onions, garlic, cumin, and a little water. *Cafe con leche*, a favorite Cuban beverage, is made by combining strong coffee with warm milk.

La Sopa Fryoles Negros (Black Bean Soup)

We suggest adding sofrito (recipe page 147) to this recipe to enhance the flavor.

Yield: serves 6 to 8

2 cups dried black beans (washed and any foreign matter removed)

10 cups water

2 green peppers, **trimmed, cored, seeded, finely chopped**

1 onion, trimmed, peeled, finely chopped

4 cloves garlic, trimmed, peeled, **minced** or 1 tablespoon garlic granules

2 bay leaves

1/2 pound bacon, fried crisp, finely chopped

salt and pepper to taste

3 cups cooked rice (cooked according to directions on package)

Equipment: Large saucepan with cover or **Dutch oven**, mixing spoon

1. Add beans to water in large saucepan or Dutch oven and bring to boil over high heat.

2. Reduce to medium. Add green peppers, onion, garlic, bay leaves, bacon, and salt and pepper to taste. Mix well. Cover and cook about 2 hours or until beans are tender.

3. Remove from heat and discard bay leaves.

4. To serve, spoon cooked rice into each soup bowl and ladle the soup over top.

❧ *Frituras de Malanga* (Yam Fritters)

Malanga is starchy tropical tuber with a nutlike flavor. It has a yam-like shape and rough, fuzzy brown skin with patches of yellowish or pinkish flesh beneath. It is popular throughout the Caribbean and Latin American countries.

CAUTION: HOT OIL IS USED

Yield: serves 4 to 6

1 pound malanga or yams, **trimmed**, peeled, finely grated

1 egg

1 clove garlic, trimmed, peeled, **minced**

1 teaspoon parsley flakes

1 teaspoon vinegar

vegetable oil as needed

Equipment: Medium mixing bowl, mixing spoon, deep fryer with deep fryer thermometer or large saucepan, wooden spoon, metal spatula or metal tongs, paper towels, baking sheet pan, aluminum foil

1. In mixing bowl combine grated malanga or yams, egg, garlic, parsley, and vinegar and mix well.

2. Prepare to deep fry: ADULT SPUERVISION REQUIRED. Have ready several layers of paper towels on baking sheet. Fill deep fryer with oil according to manufacturer's directions or fill large sauce pan with about 3 inches of vegetable oil. Heat oil to 375°F on deep-fryer thermometer or place handle of wooden spoon in oil; when small bubbles appear around surface, oil is ready for frying.

3. Fry fritters in batches: carefully slip one heaping tablespoon of mixture into oil and using metal spatula or metal tongs press down to keep fritters submerged. Fry until golden brown. Using slotted spoon or metal tongs, remove fritters from fryer and place on paper towels to drain. Wrap fritters in foil to keep warm while frying remaining fritters.

4. Serve warm with soups and stews.

❧ *Arroz con Pollo* (Rice with Chicken)

Arroz con pollo can vary in consistency; some cooks prefer it soupy and others prefer a drier mix; either way it is delicious.

Yield: 4 to 6

2–3 pounds chicken, cut in serving-sized pieces

1/2 cup lime juice

3 cloves garlic, **trimmed**, peeled, **minced**

4–6 tablespoons vegetable oil

1 green pepper, trimmed, **cored, seeded, finely chopped**

1 onion, trimmed, peeled, finely chopped

1/2 cup raisins

2 bay leaves

1 cup tomato sauce, canned

4 cups chicken broth, homemade or canned

2 cups rice

salt and pepper to taste

1/2 cup sliced **pimento**, canned (drained)

2 cups green peas, fresh or frozen

4 eggs, hard-cooked, quartered, for garnish

2 limes cut into wedges for garnish

Equipment: Large skillet or **Dutch oven**, mixing spoon

1. Rub chicken pieces with lime juice and garlic, cover, refrigerate for 30 minutes.

2. Heat 2 tablespoons oil in skillet or Dutch oven over medium-high heat. Add chicken and brown on both sides, about 8 minutes per side. Add more oil as needed to prevent sticking. Remove browned chicken and set aside.

3. Add green pepper, onion, raisins, bay leaves, tomato sauce, broth, and rice to skillet. Mix well and bring to boil over high heat. Reduce heat to simmer and, return chicken pieces to mixture. Cover and cook until chicken and rice are done, about 25–30 minutes. Add salt and pepper to taste. Remove from heat. Remove and discard bay leaves. Sprinkle with pimento and peas and garnish with egg and lime wedges.

4. Serve from skillet.

⋇ *Masa Real* (Marmalade Tart)

Yield: 24 pieces

1 1/2 cups sugar

1 1/4 cups vegetable oil

1 egg

2 tablespoons vanilla extract

5 cups cake flour

2 1/2 tablespoons baking powder

1/2 teaspoon salt

1/2 cup milk

3 tablespoons cornstarch

3 cups guava or pineapple marmalade

all-purpose flour for work surface

1 egg, beaten

1 tablespoon milk

Equipment: Large mixing bowl, mixing spoon or electric mixer, medium bowl, wooden mixing spoon, small saucepan, floured work surface, rolling pin, medium baking sheet, **whisk** or fork, small bowl, pastry brush

1. Preheat the oven to 375°F.

2. *Prepare dough*: in large mixing bowl or electric mixer, cream together sugar and oil until smooth and fluffy, about 3 minutes. Add egg and vanilla and mix well.

3. In medium bowl, mix flour, baking powder, and salt together. Add flour mixture and milk alternately to sugar mixture, being careful not to over mix; just blend together. Cover and refrigerate for 2 hours.

4. *Prepare filling*: using wooden spoon, mix cornstarch with 1/2 cup marmalade to smooth paste in saucepan. Add remaining marmalade and blend well. Cook over medium heat until thick, stirring frequently. Set aside to cool.

5. Place dough on work surface and divide in half. Using as little flour as possible, roll each piece to fit bottom of baking sheet; about 1/2-inch thick.

6. Spread out a sheet of dough into pan and gently pull edges up to overlap top crust. Spread filling evenly over dough in pan. Cover with second sheet of dough. Press top and bottom edges together to seal.

7. *Prepare glaze*: in small bowl beat egg with milk. Using pastry brush, brush top piece of dough with glaze. Using fork tines, poke vent holes in top dough.

8. Bake for 20 minutes or until top crust begins to brown. Reduce temperature to 350°F and bake for 30 minutes more or until the top is firm and dry.

9. To serve, cool to room temperature and cut into squares.

Ajiaco (Pork and Vegetable Stew)

Yield: serves 6

1 1/2 pounds lean pork, cut into 2-inch cubes

1 pound pork bones

3 quarts water

3 yams or sweet potatoes, peeled, cut into chunks

2 ears of corn, fresh or frozen (cut crosswise into 4 pieces)

2 summer squash, **trimmed**, skin on, **coarsely chopped**

4 **plantains**, peeled, cut in chunks (if available)

2 tablespoons vegetable oil

1 onion, trimmed, peeled, coarsely chopped

1 green bell pepper, trimmed, **cored, seeded**, coarsely chopped

2 tomatoes, trimmed, coarsely chopped

3 cloves garlic, trimmed, peeled, **minced** or 1 tablespoon garlic granules

juice of 2 limes

salt and pepper to taste

3 cups cooked rice (prepared according to directions on package)

Equipment: Large saucepan with cover or **Dutch oven**, tongs, spoon, medium skillet

1. Place pork, bones, and water in saucepan or Dutch oven and bring to boil over high heat. With spoon, skim off any film that comes to the surface. Reduce heat to simmer, cover, and cook about 1 hour or until meat is tender. Remove and discard bones. Add yams, corn, squash, and **plantains**. Simmer about 30–35 minutes.

2. Heat oil in skillet over medium heat. Add onion, green pepper, tomatoes, and garlic. Stirring continually, fry about 3–5 minutes until soft. Add to stew, with lime juice and salt and pepper to taste, and mix well.

3. Serve ajiaco over cooked rice.

DOMINICAN REPUBLIC

The Dominican Republic is located on the eastern half of Hispaniola, which it shares with Haiti. Rule of this part of the island passed among French, Spanish, Haitians, and the United States. Then in 1924 it became an independent country. People are predominantly Spanish-speaking Catholics and are of mixed European and African descent.

Sugar is an important cash crop. Many islanders work plantations and processing plants owned by three international companies. The output of sugar has declined since the 1980s due to the increase of sugar alternatives and less people using sugar in their diets. A large portion of the labor force once employed by the sugar industry is now expanding the production of other food crops such as coffee, cocoa, rice, beans, and coconuts.

La Bandera (Rice, Red Beans, Stewed Meat, and Fried Green Plantains)

La Bandera, the national dish of the Dominican Republic, literally translates to "the Dominican Flag." La Bandera consists of four separate dishes: rice, red beans, stewed meat, and fried plantains.

Arroz (Rice)

The rice crust formed in the later part of this recipe is called *conco* and is considered a delicacy.

Yield: serves 4 to 6

2 cups white rice (cooked according to directions on package)

Equipment: Medium bowl, mixing spoon, medium nonstick saucepan

1. Place cooked rice in bowl, leaving 1-inch layer of rice in bottom of pan. Cover bowl of rice and keep warm.
2. Continue cooking remaining rice over medium-low heat until firm crust forms on bottom of pan, about 20–30 minutes.
3. To serve: scrape crusty rice from bottom of pan and plate separately.

Red Beans

Yield: serves 4 to 6

2 tablespoons vegetable oil

6 cups cooked red kidney beans, homemade or canned

1 red onion, **trimmed**, peeled, **finely chopped**

3 cloves garlic, trimmed, peeled, **minced**

1/2 teaspoon coriander

2 tablespoons tomato paste

2 cups chicken broth, homemade or canned, more as needed

salt and pepper to taste

Equipment: Medium saucepan, mixing spoon, potato masher

1. In medium saucepan heat oil over medium heat. Add onions and sauté until **caramelized**, about 10–12 minutes, stirring frequently.

2. Stir in garlic and coriander and sauté about 2–3 minutes until fragrant. Add kidney beans and 2 cups broth. Cook over medium heat about 15–20 minutes, stirring frequently.

3. Remove beans from heat. Using potato masher, mash beans until smooth. Return to heat, adding more liquid if necessary to prevent sticking. Stirring frequently, cook an additional 5 minutes to heat through.

4. Serve with arroz, guisade, and tostones.

Guisade (Stewed Meat)

Goat meat and stewing beef can be used in this recipe. In the Dominican Republic goats graze on wild oregano, giving a unique flavor to its meat. To duplicate the wild oregano flavor, we suggest the following marinade.

Marinade:

2 tablespoons oil

3 tablespoons lime juice

1 onion **trimmed**, peeled, **finely chopped**

3 teaspoons fresh oregano finely chopped or 1 teaspoon dried

salt and pepper to taste

Stewed meat:

2 tablespoons vegetable oil

3 pounds goat (available at Latino food markets) or stewing beef, cut into 1/2-inch cubes

3 onions, trimmed, peeled, **coarsely chopped**

6 cloves garlic, trimmed, peeled, **minced**

4 tomatoes, trimmed, coarsely chopped

2 green peppers, trimmed, **cored, seeded, julienned**

2 cups beef broth, homemade or canned

coriander, salt, and pepper to taste

Equipment: Small mixing bowl, mixing spoon, large plastic bag, medium skillet with cover

1. *Prepare marinade*: In small bowl combine oil, lime juice, onion, oregano, and salt and pepper to taste. Mix well.

2. Rub meat with marinade, place in baggie, and refrigerate overnight. Turn several times to evenly coat.

3. *Prepare stewed meat*: In skillet heat 2 tablespoons oil over medium-high heat. Add marinated meat. Stirring frequently, pan **sear** on all sides for about 3–5 minutes.

4. Reduce heat to medium. Add onions, garlic, tomatoes, and peppers. Stirring frequently, **sauté** about 3–5 minutes.

5. Stir in beef stock, bring to boil, cover, and reduce to simmer. Add coriander, salt, and pepper to taste. Cook for about 30–45 minutes for flavors to blend.

6. Serve with arroz, red beans, and tostones.

Tostones (Fried Green Plantains)

Yield: serves 4 to 6

6 green plantains

salt to taste

vegetable oil, as needed

Equipment: vegetable knife, medium skillet, slotted spoon or metal spatula, paper towels, small glass or spatula

1. Peel plantains by cutting through the skin lengthwise and opening with your fingers. Slice on an angle into 1/2-inch ovals.

2. Heat about 1/2 inch oil in skillet over medium heat. Fry plantain slices, a few at a time, turning frequently using slotted spoon or spatula, until golden brown, about 5 minutes. Remove from oil and drain on paper towels.

3. Use bottom of small glass or spatula flatten each plantain to about 1/2 its thickness. Add more oil to skillet if necessary and fry flattened plantains a second time until crispy. Remove from oil and drain on paper towels.

4. To serve, sprinkle tostones with salt to taste. Keep warm.

5. To serve La Bandera, plate rice, beans, and meat separately with tostones (plantains) served separately.

COCONUTS: HOW TO BUY AND OPEN

The following advice is for buying coconuts and making shredded coconut and coconut milk. To select a fresh coconut, shake it to feel sloshing of liquid inside. A cracked or an old coconut will be empty and dry.

1. Preheat oven to 400°F.

2. *Opening coconut*: Pierce brown eye-like spots at one end with sharp point, such as the head of a Phillips screwdriver or an ice-pick. Drain and discard coconut water. In some parts of the Caribbean coconut water is a popular drink; however, it is not to be confused with coconut milk which is made from adding water to the grated coconut meat (recipe follows).

3. Place coconut in oven for 15 minutes. Remove and wrap in clean kitchen towel. Carefully crack open with hammer and break away coconut meat from shell. If any coconut meat remains on shell return to oven for a few minutes.

Making Shredded Coconut

1. Grate white meat from brown shell using fine side of hand grater or peel meat from brown shell with vegetable peeler, then shred it in food processor or with a sharp knife. One coconut yields about 4 cups grated coconut.

Coconut Milk

Homemade coconut milk is at its best when freshly made. Even under refrigeration it quickly loses its flavor.

Yield: 1 1/2 to 2 cups

2 cups grated coconut meat (see previous recipe, or canned or frozen unsweetened shredded coconut is available at most supermarkets)

2 cups boiling water

Equipment: Small bowl, blender or food processor, 8-inch square of cheesecloth (surgical gauze can be used) or 8-inch square of clean nylon stocking

1. Place grated coconut in small bowl. Add boiling water and let set for 30 minutes. *If using a blender or food processor*, add boiling water and blend for 1 minute. Let cool for 5 minutes.

2. Strain liquid through cheesecloth or nylon. Squeeze and twist cloth to extract all milk from the coconut meat.

3. Repeat the process if additional coconut milk is needed.

Sweet Potato Balls

Yield: about 24 balls

2 pounds cooked sweet potatoes, peeled and **cubed**, fresh or canned, drained

1/2 cup coconut milk (previous recipe) or heavy cream

1/4 cup sugar, more as needed

2 egg yolks (refrigerate egg whites to use at another time)

2 tablespoons ground cinnamon for garnish

Equipment: Large mixing bowl, potato masher or electric blender, large saucepan, wooden mixing spoon, pie pan or flat plate

1. Place potatoes in mixing bowl and blend smooth with potato masher or in electric blender. Transfer potatoes to saucepan. Add coconut milk or cream, sugar, and egg yolk and mix well. Cook over medium heat, stirring continually until mixture pulls away from sides of pan. Remove from heat and let mixture sit until cool enough to handle. Shape into ping-pong-sized balls.

2. Place cinnamon into pie pan or flat plate and coat potato balls one at a time. Place side-by-side on platter and refrigerate.

3. Serve sweet potato balls cold as candy treat.

GRENADA

The British and French, the early explorers, left their mark on Grenada as they did throughout the Caribbean. Known as the "spice island" Grenada grows, harvests, and processes large amounts of spices. The aroma of spices fills the air surrounding the island.

Callaloo (Vegetable Stew with Greens)

Callaloo is the Caribbean name for one-pot stew. Some African one-pots are also called callaloo, and they are made with whatever is on hand.

Yield: serves 4 to 6

2 pounds spinach or kale, fresh, **trimmed**, washed, drained, **coarsely chopped**

6 cups water

1 cup celery, trimmed, coarsely chopped

1 cup okra, trimmed, sliced, fresh or frozen (thawed)

1 cup corn kernels, frozen (thawed)

1 onion, trimmed, peeled, coarsely chopped

1 cup green bell pepper, trimmed, **cored, seeded,** coarsely chopped

1 tablespoon sugar

2 cloves garlic, trimmed, peeled, **minced,** or 1 teaspoon garlic granules

1 jalapeno pepper or Scotch Bonnet pepper, seeded, **finely chopped**

salt and pepper to taste

Equipment: Large saucepan with cover or **Dutch oven**, mixing spoon

1. Place spinach or kale, water, celery, okra, corn, onion, bell pepper, sugar, garlic, and jalapeño in saucepan or Dutch oven and bring to boil over high heat. Reduce heat to simmer. Mix well, cover, and cook until tender, about 45–50 minutes. Add salt and pepper to taste and mix well.

2. Serve callaloo in individual bowls over rice, beans, or both.

✼ Spicy Nutmeg Chicken

Yield: serves 6 to 8

1/4 cup soy sauce

2 garlic cloves, **trimmed,** peeled, **minced**

1 onion, trimmed, peeled, **finely chopped**

1/2 teaspoon hot pepper sauce

1/4 teaspoon ground ginger

1/2 cup nutmeg syrup (Morne Delice island brand is recommended, available at international markets)

salt to taste

8 chicken wings, legs or thighs

Equipment: Medium bowl, mixing spoon, large sealable plastic baggie, medium baking casserole

1. Preheat oven to 375°F

2. In bowl combine soy sauce, garlic, onion, hot pepper sauce, ginger, nutmeg syrup, and salt to taste. Mix well.

3. Place chicken wings, legs, and thighs in plastic bag. Pour nutmeg syrup mixture over top. Seal and shake bag to evenly coat chicken pieces. Marinate in refrigerator for 1 hour, turning occasionally.

4. Transfer chicken with syrup mixture to baking pan and bake in oven about 30–40 minutes or until cooked through.

5. Serve warm as main dish with rice.

✼ Nutmeg Ice Cream

Yield: serves 6 to 8

2 cups milk

1 cup half-and-half

4 eggs

3/4 cup sugar

3/4 cup sweetened condensed milk canned

1 1/2 cups heavy cream

2 whole nutmegs, freshly grated or 2 tea-spoons ground nutmeg

Equipment: Large saucepan, mixing spoon, medium mixing bowl, **whisk** or electric mixer, ice cream freezer

1. Heat milk and half-and-half in saucepan over medium-high heat. Bring until bubbles form around edges but DO NOT BOIL. Reduce heat to low.

2. In medium bowl blend eggs and sugar using whisk or mixer. Add small amount of hot milk to egg mixture and mix well. Then add egg mixture to remaining hot milk in saucepan. Stirring continually, cook over low heat until thickened. Again, DO NOT BOIL. When thickened, remove from heat.

3. Add condensed milk and grated nutmeg. Mix well and cool to room temperature. Stir in heavy cream and refrigerate for 2 hours.

4. Transfer to ice cream freezer (continue according to manufacturer's directions).

5. Serve nutmeg ice cream as snack or dessert on sweet potato or pumpkin pie.

HAITI

Once a prosperous country, Haiti over the years has had its share of misfortunes both politically and economically. Today, Haiti is one of the poorest islands in the Caribbean. Most Haitians live off the land with their own small plot, once part of the large prosperous plantations.

﷽ Sweet Red Pepper Soup

Yield: serves 4 to 6

6 cups chicken broth, canned or homemade

4 red bell peppers, trimmed, **cored, seeded, finely chopped**

1 1/2 cups heavy cream or canned evaporated milk

2 tablespoons tomato paste

salt and pepper to taste

sprinkle of paprika for garnish

1/2 cup coconut milk, fresh (recipe page 138) or canned

Equipment: Medium saucepan, mixing spoon or **whisk**

1. Pour chicken broth into saucepan and bring to boil over high heat. Add peppers and mix well. Reduce heat to simmer, cover, and cook for 20 minutes. Add cream or evaporated milk, tomato paste, and salt and pepper to taste. Mix well. Bring to boil for 1 minute. Remove from heat, cool to room temperature, and refrigerate.

2. Before serving, stir in coconut milk and sprinkle with paprika.

3. Serve sweet red pepper soup cold, in individual bowls.

Tarte A L'oignon (Onion Tart)

Yield: serves 4 to 6

4 tablespoons butter

6 onions, **trimmed**, peeled, **finely chopped**

1/4 pound ham finely chopped

4 tablespoons flour

1/2 teaspoon sugar

1/3 cup canned condensed milk

1/2 cup Parmesan cheese, grated

salt and pepper to taste

8-inch pie crust, homemade or frozen, thawed

Equipment: Medium-large skillet, mixing spoon, 8-inch pie pan

1. Preheat oven to 350°.

2. In skillet, melt 4 tablespoons butter over medium-high heat and add onions. Stirring constantly, **sauté** until soft, about 2–4 minutes. Stir in ham and heat through.

3. Remove from heat and stir in flour and sugar. Stirring constantly, add milk and cheese. Add salt and pepper to taste.

4. Pour onion mixture into pie crust and bake for 30–40 minutes until firm and crust is lightly browned. Remove from oven and let cool for 20–30 minutes before serving.

5. To serve, cut into wedges.

Pois et Ris (Kidney Beans and Rice)

This is the national dish of Haiti.

Yield: serves 6

1 cup bacon, ham, or sausage, or combination **finely chopped**

3 cloves garlic, **trimmed**, peeled, **minced**

1/2 teaspoon ground thyme

2 cups kidney beans, homemade or canned (with juice)

1 cup hot water

2 cups cooked rice (cooked according to directions on package)

salt and pepper to taste

Equipment: Large skillet with cover or **Dutch oven**, mixing spoon

1. Heat bacon, ham, or sausage, or combination in skillet or Dutch oven, over medium-high heat. Add garlic and thyme and mix constantly until meat browns, about 4 minutes.

2. Add beans with juice, water, cooked rice, and salt and pepper to taste and mix well. Reduce heat to low and cook about 10 minutes, stirring frequently. Cover, remove from heat, and allow flavors to blend about 10 minutes.

3. Serve pois et ris in individual bowls

✌ Sweet Potato Pudding Cake

Yield: serves 4 to 6

1 cup cooked, mashed sweet potatoes, fresh or canned

2 ripe bananas, mashed

1 cup milk

2 tablespoons sugar

1/2 teaspoon salt

3 egg yolks, beaten (refrigerate whites to use another time)

3 tablespoons raisins, **finely chopped**

Equipment: Medium mixing bowl, mixing spoon or electric mixer, greased or nonstick 9-inch cake pan, cake rack

1. Preheat oven to 300° F.

2. Place sweet potatoes and bananas in mixing bowl and blend using spoon or electric mixer. Add milk, sugar, yolks, and raisins. Mix well.

3. Pour batter into cake pan and bake in oven for 45 minutes or until cake is set, firm to the touch, and top is golden brown. Remove from oven and place on cake rack to cool at room temperature.

4. Serve as dessert, cut into wedges.

JAMAICA

Today, Jamaicans are known for their music, happy-go-lucky life style, and their cuisine. They add their own unique flavors to the food they cook, such as callou and breadfruit porridge (recipe page 144).

A popular fruit is *ackee* or *akee*, which grows in such abundance it is called "free food." Akee grows throughout the Caribbean; however, it is not as popular as it is in Jamaica. This is probably because when not fully ripe when picked it is poisonous.

The akee fruit has an unusual history: it was brought to Jamaica from West Africa in 1778 by a slave ship. Then, Captain William Bligh of "Mutiny on the Bounty" fame brought the unknown plant to England, where the botanical name, *Blighia sapida*, was given in his honor. When properly harvested, akee is used as a vegetable, often mixed with savory ingredients such as pork, salt fish, onions, green peppers, eggs, and tomatoes.

Breadfruit Porridge

Yield: serves 4 to 6

1 breadfruit, skin removed, seeded, finely chopped (available at some supermarkets and international food markets)

8 cups water, more as needed

1/2 teaspoon salt

1/2 cup sweetened condensed milk

3/4 cup evaporated milk

1/2 teaspoon ground nutmeg, more as needed

1/2 teaspoon vanilla extract

sugar to taste

Equipment: Blender, medium-large saucepan, wooden mixing spoon

1. Place chopped breadfruit in blender (in batches if necessary) with just enough water to blend until smooth and **purée**.

2. Pour 8 cups water in saucepan and bring to boil over high heat. Remove from heat. Stirring constantly, add puréed breadfruit and salt. Return to medium-high heat and bring to rolling boil. Stirring frequently, cook about 10–15 minutes to thicken.

3. Stir in sweetened condensed milk, evaporated milk, 1/2 teaspoon nutmeg, vanilla extract, and sugar to taste. Reduce heat to medium-low. Continue cooking until smooth and cooked through, about 10–15 minutes. Stir frequently.

4. To serve, ladle into individual soup bowls and sprinkle a pinch of nutmeg on each serving.

Jerked Pork and Chicken

Jerked meat is made with pork or chicken in Jamaica. Beef is seldom used because it is too scarce and expensive.

Yield: serves 6 to 8

4 tablespoons ground allspice

2 onions, trimmed, peeled, **finely chopped**

2 green chili peppers or jalapeño peppers, **seeded**, finely chopped

3 cloves fresh garlic, trimmed, peeled, **minced** or 1 teaspoon garlic granules

1 teaspoon ground cinnamon

1 teaspoon ground or freshly grated nutmeg

6 bay leaves, crumbled

salt and pepper to taste

3 tablespoons vinegar

1 cup vegetable oil

2 pounds lean pork loin or pork shoulder, cut into strips, about 4-inches long and about 1-inch thick

1 chicken cut into serving-sized pieces

Equipment: Small mixing bowl, mixing spoon, rubber gloves or plastic wrap for hands, large bowl with cover or plastic bag, outdoor grill and tongs or roasting pan with cover

1. *Prepare marinade*: Place allspice, onions, chilies, garlic, cinnamon, nutmeg, bay leaves, salt, pepper, vinegar, and oil in bowl and blend to a paste-like mixture.

2. Wearing rubber gloves or plastic wrap, rub pork and chicken with mixture. Place pieces in bowl with cover or in plastic bag, seal, and refrigerate at least 2 hours. Turn frequently to coat evenly.

3. *Grilling*: Ready coals to medium heat. Place meat on grill as far from direct heat as possible. Cover grill and cook until done, about 2 hours. Using tongs, turn at least once during cooking.

4. OR *Oven roasting*: Preheat oven to 350°F. Place pork and chicken in roasting pan, cover, and roast for about 1 hour. Meat should be very well done. To serve, transfer meat to platter and serve with raw onion slices.

Stamp and Go

In Jamaica street vendors sell stamp and go at almost every bus stop. Bus riders are known to jump off the bus, buy a stamp and go, and get back on to continue their trip. In Jamaica stamp and go is made with salted codfish. In this recipe, we suggest fresh codfish or any firm white fish fillets (such as red snapper, bass, trout, halibut, or tilapia).

Yield: serves 4 to 6

4 codfish **fillets**, skin removed, fresh or frozen (thawed)

6 cups water

1 onion, **trimmed**, peeled, **finely chopped**

1 clove garlic, trimmed, peeled, **minced** or 1/4 teaspoon garlic granules

1/2 teaspoon ground thyme

2 eggs

salt and pepper to taste

1/2 cup all-purpose flour

1 teaspoon vinegar

2 tablespoons vegetable oil, more as needed

Equipment: Medium saucepan, **colander** or strainer, large mixing bowl, mixing spoon, small bowl, large skillet, pancake turner or metal spatula, paper towels

1. Place fillets in saucepan and cover with water. Bring to boil over high heat. Reduce heat to simmer and cook 10–12 minutes or until fish **flakes** easily with fork. Drain in colander or strainer; discard water. Transfer to large bowl and break into small pieces. Add onion, garlic, thyme, eggs, salt, and pepper to taste and mix until well blended.

2. Mix flour and vinegar in small bowl. Add to mixture and mix well.

3. Heat 2 tablespoons oil in skillet over medium-high heat. When hot but not smoking, drop teaspoons of mixture into skillet. Flatten to about 2 inches across, with back of spoon. Fry on both sides until golden brown, about 5 minutes per side. Remove patties from skillet and drain on paper towels. Continue frying remaining mixture, adding more oil if necessary.

4. Serve stamp and go hot or cold as a finger food with lime or lemon wedges.

PUERTO RICO

Puerto Rico is located in the northeastern Caribbean and is a self-governing territory of the United States. Spanish settlers greatly influenced the development of Puerto Rico: politically, culturally, and in the cuisine. African slaves brought with them their own survival and cooking traditions. Today, the cuisine of Puerto Rico is a blend of Spanish, African, and American cultures called *cocina criolla* (creole cooking).

Mofongo (Mashed Plantain Balls in Broth)

Mofongo is a traditional dish of Puerto Rico, made from fried green plantains or fried yucca.

Yield: serves 4 to 6

4 fried green plantains (prepare according to tostones [recipe page 137])

1/2 cup pork cracklings, crumbled (available at most supermarkets)

1 tablespoon garlic, **trimmed**, peeled, **minced**

salt and pepper, to taste

1 tablespoon olive oil

fresh cilantro leaves, **finely chopped**, for garnish

Equipment: Large mixing bowl, potato masher

1. Place warm tostones, pork cracklings, garlic, and olive oil in mixing bowl. Using clean hands or potato masher, mash until smooth. Add salt and pepper to taste. Take a handful of mixture and shape into tennis ball-sized balls. Set aside.

2. Serve as side dish or as a dumpling in chicken or beef broth. Sprinkle top with cilantro leaves for garnish.

Sofrito (Savory Sauce)

Sofrito is added to many dishes from soups to entrees to enhance flavor. Although prepared sofrito is readily available at supermarkets, most Puerto Ricans create this recipe from scratch and keep stored in an airtight glass or plastic container in the refrigerator or freezer.

Yield: 1 to 2 pints

2 medium green peppers, **trimmed**, seeded, **coarsely chopped**

1 red pepper, trimmed, seeded, coarsely chopped

2 tomatoes, trimmed, seeded, coarsely chopped

2 yellow onions, peeled, trimmed, coarsely chopped

1 head garlic, trimmed, peeled, **minced**

1 bunch cilantro leaves, washed, drained, trimmed, finely chopped

1/2 bunch parsley leaves, washed, drained, trimmed, finely chopped

olive oil, as needed

Equipment: food processor

1. Place green peppers, red peppers, tomatoes, yellow onions, garlic, cilantro, and parsley in food processor. Blend well. If necessary, add just enough olive oil to blend into a smooth paste.

2. To serve, add 1–2 tablespoons or to taste to recipes that serve 6–8 people.

TRINIDAD AND TOBAGO

The British were the last to rule the islands of Trinidad and Tobago before granting independence in 1962. Over the years immigrants from Spain, France, England, China, and India have brought with them customs and cuisine from their homelands, creating a **fusion** of tastes in Trinidad and Tobago.

Tobago does not have the same natural resources as Trinidad, the larger island, thus it relies more on tourism.

Fungi (Cornmeal Cake)

Fungi, also called *cou-cou* and *funchi*, is the Caribbean "comfort food." This recipe can be used for all Caribbean countries. When cold, fungi is sliced and eaten like bread.

Yield: serves 6

3 tablespoons butter or margarine, more as needed

1/2 cup onions, **trimmed**, peeled, **finely chopped**

1/2 cup okra, trimmed, **coarsely chopped**, fresh or frozen (thawed)

2 1/2 cups water

1 1/2 cups yellow stone-ground cornmeal

salt and pepper to taste

Equipment: Small skillet, wooden mixing spoon, medium saucepan with cover, greased or nonstick baking sheet, spatula

1. Melt 3 tablespoons butter or margarine in skillet over medium heat. Add onions and okra and cook for 5 minutes or until vegetables are soft, stirring frequently. Remove from heat and set aside.

2. Place water in saucepan and bring to boil over high heat. While stirring with wooden spoon, slowly pour in cornmeal. Reduce heat to low. Cover and cook for 10–12 minutes. Add onions, okra, and skillet scrapings and mix well. Add salt and pepper to taste. Increase heat to simmer and cook about 4 minutes more or until mixture pulls away from sides of pan.

3. Pour mixture into center of baking sheet. Using spatula, spread mixture out into smooth circle about 1-inch thick. Dot top with butter or margarine.

4. Serve fungi either warm or cold. The Islanders set fungi in the center of the table and everyone helps themselves.

Divkadgye Phodiyo (Breadfruit Fritters)

CAUTION: HOT OIL USED

Yield: serves 4 to 6

1 small breadfruit, **trimmed**, cut in half

3 teaspoons *asafetida* (available at Asian or Mexican markets)

4 teaspoons chili powder

2 teaspoons turmeric

4 tablespoons rice flour (available at Asian or Mexican markets)

salt to taste

vegetable oil for frying

Equipment: Cutting board or clear work surface, sharp knife, small mixing bowl, fork, deep fryer (use according to manufacturer's directions) or large saucepan, deep-fryer thermometer or wooden spoon, skimmer or metal tongs

1. Place breadfruit halves cut side down on work surface or cutting board. Using sharp knife, cut each half into 1/4-inch thick slices. Remove skin and cut each 1/4-inch slice into 4 equal wedge-shaped pieces.

2. In small bowl, using fork, mix together *asafetida*, turmeric, chili powder, and rice flour. Mix well. Coat breadfruit pieces one-by-one with mixture. Set aside.

3. Prepare to deep fry: ADULT SUPERVISION REQUIRED. Have ready several layers of paper towels on baking sheet. Fill deep fryer with oil according to manufacturer's directions or fill large saucepan with about 3 inches of vegetable oil. Heat oil to reach 375°F on deep-fryer thermometer or place handle of wooden spoon in oil; when small bubbles appear around surface, oil is ready for frying.

4. Fry breadfruit 3 or 4 at a time and carefully place in hot oil. Using metal tongs or **skimmer**, press to keep submerged for about 30 seconds or until golden brown. Remove and place on paper towels to drain.

5. Serve warm as snack or side dish.

✤ *Bammy* (Pan-Fried Bread)

Bammy, a flat, pancake-like bread, is a popular Caribbean snack. African slaves deserve the credit for creating bammies, not as a snack but as survival food. The slaves were given little to eat, so they turned simple greens or roots into nourishing and tasty meals.

Yield: serves 4 to 6

4 cups fresh **cassava** (yucca root) or yams, **trimmed**, peeled, finely grated

1 1/2 teaspoons salt

2 tablespoons vegetables oil, more as needed

Equipment: Medium mixing bowl, mixing spoon, 6-inch skillet, pancake turner or spatula, medium plate

1. Using mixing spoon, add cassava or yams and salt in medium bowl.

2. Heat 1 tablespoon oil in skillet over medium heat, swirling oil to cover bottom and about 1 inch up side.

3. Add 1 cup of cassava or yam mixture to skillet and press down with back of spoon to fill pan. When steam rises and edges pull away slightly from sides of skillet, press mixture flat again with back of spoon. Cook about 5–8 minutes. Remove from heat and turn over on plate. Using pancake turner or spatula, return bammy to skillet with uncooked side down. Cook about 5 minutes or until lightly browned. Repeat process until all mixture is used.

4. Serve bammies hot or cold.

4

Europe

The continent of Europe is divided into four regions (Northern Europe, Western Europe, Eastern Europe, and Southern Europe) plus the British Isles. The countries within each region tend to have similar terrain, climate, planting, growing and harvesting seasons. Europe is a cornucopia of cooking pleasures, from the northern Scandinavian countries to the Mediterranean Sea and from the Asian border on the east to the Atlantic Ocean on the west. For centuries, food and customs have evolved due to invasion, colonization, immigration, and travel.

Since World War II, efforts have been made by the European Union (EU) to unify the countries within the continent of Europe. Members of the EU were hopeful that through the Euro (monetary system) and a more universal rail system, progress would be made. So far only moderate success has been achieved. Many European countries recognize the need to join together to safeguard earth and respect the planet's natural resources. Their goal is to help protect and improve the quality of water and food sources throughout the continent.

To take a quick culinary trip through Europe, just visit the cheese case in the deli selection of your local supermarket. The following lists the most popular imported cheeses from Europe. The British Isles: from England: Stilton; from Ireland: Dubliner. Northern Europe: from Denmark: Fontina, Danish blue and Havarti; from Norway: *Jarslburg*. Western Europe: from France: Brie, Munster, Roquefort, and Port Salute; from the Netherlands: Edam and Gouda; from Switzerland: Swiss, Emmentaland Gruyere; from Germany: Bavaria Blu and Limburger. Southern Europe: from Italy: Mozzarella, Asiago, Parmesan, Ricotta, Gorgonzola, and Provolone; from Spain: Manchego; from Greece: Feta. Eastern Europe: from Russia: Tvork; from Poland: Bryndza.

THE BRITISH ISLES

Four countries make up The British Isles: England, Ireland, Scotland, and Wales. Before the term "British" was created in the late-eighteenth century, each country within the British Isles had its own history, language, and identity. Due to war and migration these countries became unified as part of the United Kingdom.

The mountains, the Atlantic Ocean, and the warm waters of the Gulf Stream influence the climate of the British Isles. Winter weather can range from being chilly and damp to hot and sticky, and sometimes there are a few days each year when the weather is sunny and warm with a blue sky. Food tends to be wholesome, nourishing, and robust, which goes well with the damp and foggy weather hovering over this region most of the time.

Many foods and beverages from the British Isles have traveled across the Atlantic and been adapted into other cultures: dark fruit cakes, plum puddings at Christmas time, tea, and Scotch whiskey are just a few.

Tea drinking became a part of English culture about 1600. It came from China by way of The Netherlands. Tea was expensive and heavily taxed, keeping it as a luxury available only for the privileged few. Today, tea drinking is a national pleasure and "taking afternoon tea" usually happens about 4 P.M. From the palace drawing room to the back rooms of factories and shops, everyone stops to drink tea. There are regional tea drinking practices, such as "cream tea" served in Devonshire, England, named after the clotted cream spread on the biscuits served with tea. In the industrial regions of northern England a heartier repast called "high tea" came about. When factory workers returned home they wanted a light supper to tide them over until a full meal was eaten. "High tea" is also called "meat or ham tea," where, as the name suggests, little meat pies are served with tea.

England

England, the largest nation within the British Isles, has a rich and unique history. However, today the cultures and customs of the English are very similar to the United States. As in America, most parents work five days a week, while weekends are a time to spend with family. Gardens both private and common are enjoyed throughout England. The gardens include rare and exotic flowers, topiaries, and on occasion vegetables. Many British people are known to be extremely polite with a unique and witty sense of humor.

Today, London, the metropolis of England, has one of the most diverse populations in the world where over 100 languages are known to be spoken. The cuisine of England is a cornucopia of different cultures. A well-known culinary contribution is the sandwich created in England by John Montagu, Earl of Sandwich. As legend goes he created this small meal that could be eaten with one hand, while he continued his nonstop gambling.

Scones (English Baking Powder Biscuits)

Scones and crumpets are traditionally served with afternoon tea. Scones are basically baking powder biscuits, usually served warm with a drizzle of jam.

Yield: serves 12

2 cups all-purpose flour

2 teaspoons double-action baking powder

1 tablespoon sugar

1/2 teaspoon salt

1/4 cup butter or margarine

2 eggs

1/3 cup half-and-half

Equipment: Flour sifter, large mixing bowl, wooden mixing spoon, small bowl, whisk, floured work surface, cookie cutter or firm water glass, nonstick or lightly greased baking sheet, pastry brush

1. Preheat oven to 450°F.

2. **Sift** flour, baking powder, sugar, and salt into mixing bowl. Using clean hands, blend in butter or margarine until mixture is crumb-like.

3. With **whisk**, beat eggs in small bowl and set aside 2 tablespoons. Add half-and-half to remaining eggs and mix well.

4. Make well in center of flour mixture. Pour in egg mixture and blend together, making an elastic dough just firm enough to handle, working it as little as possible. Transfer to work surface and pat flat to about 3/4 inch thick. Cut into rounds with cookie cutter or top rim or water glass. Lightly flour greased baking sheet and place scones side-by-side, at least 1 inch apart. Brush tops with remaining egg. Bake in oven 15 minutes or until golden brown.

5. Serve scones while still warm with plenty of jam and butter. They are delicious to eat at any time.

❧ Bubble and Squeak

Bubble and squeak got its name from the noise it makes while cooking. There is no standard or basic recipe to follow and quantities can vary according to whatever is on hand. You may do this or just follow the recipe as given.

Yield: serves 4 to 6

4 tablespoons vegetable oil, more as needed

3 cups cooked mashed potatoes, freshly made or instant potato flakes (prepared according to directions on package)

3 cups cabbage, **finely chopped**, boiled for 5 minutes, drained (discard water)

salt and pepper to taste

Equipment: Large skillet, mixing spoon, pancake turner or metal spatula, large plate

1. Heat 4 tablespoons oil in skillet over high heat. Add potatoes, cabbage, and salt and pepper to taste and mix well. Reduce heat to medium and cook until bottom is browned. Press down on mixture with pancake turner or metal spatula so it forms shape of flat cake.

2. Remove from heat, invert on plate, and slide back into skillet to brown other side. Add more oil along sides of skillet, if necessary, to prevent sticking. When browned on both sides, transfer to flat serving plate and cut into wedges.

3. Serve bubble and squeak hot, as either a main dish or as a side dish.

❧ Shepherd's Pie (Meat and Vegetable Casserole)

Traditionally, shepherd's pie was made with mutton or lamb. If the pie was made with beef, it was called cottage pie. Today any meat or poultry can be used, and the recipe is still called shepherd's pie.

Yield: serves 6 to 8

2 tablespoons vegetable oil, more as needed

2 onions, **trimmed**, peeled, **finely chopped**, sliced in thin rounds

2 carrots, trimmed, peeled, finely chopped, sliced in thin rounds

1/2 cup celery finely chopped

2 pounds ground beef

2 tablespoons all-purpose flour

1 cup beef broth

salt and pepper to taste

4 cups cooked mashed potatoes, freshly made or instant potato flakes (prepared according to directions on package)

1/2 cup melted butter or margarine

1/2 cup shredded Cheddar cheese

Equipment: Large skillet, mixing spoon, small bowl, greased, medium shallow baking casserole

1. Preheat oven to 350°F.

2. Heat oil in skillet over medium-high heat. Add onions, carrots, and celery. **Sauté** until onions are tender, about 3–5 minutes. Add meat and reduce heat to medium. Stirring constantly, cook until meat browns, about 8 minutes.

3. Add flour to beef broth in small bowl and mix to blend. Add to meat mixture and mix well. Season with salt and pepper to taste and remove from heat. Transfer mixture to baking pan and smooth top.

4. Combine mashed potatoes with 1/4 cup melted butter. Add salt and pepper to taste and mix well. Spoon potatoes on top of meat mixture. Drizzle with remaining butter and cheese. Bake in oven about 10 minutes, until potatoes begin to brown and cheese melts.

5. Serve sheperd's pie as a one-dish meal with plenty of bread for sopping.

Spotted Dick (Currant Pudding)

Spotted Dick also known as spotted dog is a sponge pudding with currants. Puddings are very popular throughout England and are also referred to as "puds" or "afters." Although most puddings are served after the meal as a dessert, some are eaten during the starter or main course such as Yorkshire pudding and black pudding.

Yield: serves 4

1/3 cup butter or margarine	pinch of salt
1/3 cup sugar	1/4 cup milk, more as needed
1 cup self-rising flour	2 eggs
1 teaspoon baking powder	1/2 cup currants

Equipment: Medium mixing bowl, electric mixer or mixing spoon, small bowl, sifter, medium heat-proof bowl, foil, **steamer pan**

1. In mixing bowl, using electric mixer or mixing spoon, blend together butter, sugar, and eggs until light and fluffy.

2. In small bowl sift together flour, baking powder, and salt. Slowly add flour mixture to butter-egg mixture and add 1/4 cup milk, more if necessary to keep mixture soft. Add currants and mix well.

3. Transfer mixture to heat-proof bowl, cover with foil, and place in **steamer pan**. Cook for about 2 1/2 hours or until firm to the touch.

4. Serve plain or add spoonful of warm vanilla pudding over each serving (instant or regular pudding mix).

Ireland

Ireland, an island, lies to the west of Great Britain and is part of the British Isles. Ireland is often referred to as the Emerald Island due to its lush green terrain.

Traditional Irish cuisine is considered farm-style cooking, made up of hardy soups and stews, homemade breads and, of course, potatoes. The Irish enjoy eating their potatoes roasted, fried, boiled, mashed, and added to soups and stews. They are also known for raising sheep, which provide some of the world's finest wool and succulent meat. Seafood is abundant.

The potato was introduced to Ireland from the "New World" and quickly became a staple crop. In 1845 The Great Potato Famine hit Ireland and is known as the worst famine of the nineteenth century. The source of the famine is believed to have been from *late blight*, a disease that destroys both the leaves and roots of the potato plant. Heavy dependence on the potato by the majority of the population, especially the poor, caused the death of thousands of Irish. Those who could immigrated to the United States and Canada in hopes of a better life. Despite this tragedy, the heart of the Irish prevailed, making those who remained in Ireland more determined than ever to rebuild their lives.

Trio of Peas (Three-Pea Sauté)

Peas, a healthy source of fiber, are very popular in Ireland. Adding tart lemon and tarragon gives a unique flair to this pea **sauté**.

Yield: serves 4

2 teaspoons vegetable oil, more as needed

1 cup snow peas, **trimmed**

1 cup sugar snaps peas, fresh, trimmed or frozen, thawed

2 cups frozen peas, thawed

1/2 teaspoon lemon **zest**, freshly grated

4 teaspoons lemon juice

1 1/2 teaspoons dried tarragon

2 teaspoons butter

salt and pepper to taste

Equipment: Medium nonstick skillet, wooden mixing spoon

1. Heat oil in skillet over medium-high heat. Add snow peas and sugar snap peas. Stirring constantly, cook for about 2–3 minutes.

2. Reduce heat to medium and stir in thawed peas. Add more oil if necessary to prevent sticking. Stirring occasionally, cook about 3–5 minutes or until peas are heated through and tender.

3. Remove from heat and stir in lemon zest, lemon juice, tarragon, and butter. Season with salt and pepper to taste.

4. Serve warm as a side dish.

Colcannon (Mashed Potatoes with Cabbage)

In the sixteenth century Spanish conquistadors found potatoes cultivated in Peru and brought them back to Europe. A meal is not complete unless *praties* (as the Irish call them) are on the table.

Yield: serves 4 to 6

3 cups green cabbage, **trimmed**, finely **shredded**

1 onion, trimmed, peeled, **finely chopped**

1/4 cup water

6 cooked potatoes, mashed or 4 cups prepared instant mashed potatoes (prepare according to directions on package)

1/4 cup milk

1/4 cup butter or margarine

salt and pepper to taste

Equipment: Medium saucepan with cover, mixing spoon

1. Place cabbage, onion, and water in saucepan, and bring to boil over high heat. Reduce to simmer, cover, and cook for about 8 minutes or until tender.

2. Add mashed potatoes, milk, butter or margarine, and salt and pepper to taste. Mix well to blend and heat through.

3. Serve colcannon warm, as side dish with meat, chicken or fish.

Irish Stew

Irish stew is the national dish of Ireland. To be authentic, it must be made with mutton or lamb, but other than that, there are as many ways to make Irish stew as there are Irish kitchens to cook it in. It is not necessary to use expensive cuts of meat for this recipe.

Yield: serves 4 to 6

2 pounds lamb, lean boneless neck or shoulder, cut into bite-sized chunks

6 potatoes, peeled, thinly sliced

3 onions, **trimmed**, peeled, thinly sliced

salt and pepper to taste

1/2 cup parsley, **finely chopped**

2 cups water, more as needed

Equipment: Medium pan with cover or **Dutch oven**, mixing spoon

1. Layer potatoes, lamb, and onions in saucepan or Dutch oven, beginning with potatoes and ending with onions on the top. Repeat several times. Sprinkle each layer with salt and pepper to taste and parsley.

2. Add water and bring to boil over high heat. Reduce heat to simmer, cover, and cook until lamb is tender, about 1 1/2 hours. Remove from heat and skim off any fat on top.

3. Serve Irish stew as a one-pot meal, with plenty of oatmeal bread for sopping (following recipe).

Oatmeal Bread

There is nothing more wonderful than the smell of homemade bread baking in the oven. Try our hardy oatmeal bread, which is easy and fun to make.

Yield: 1 loaf

2 cups old-fashioned oatmeal

1 1/2 cups buttermilk

1 cup flour, more as needed

1 teaspoon baking soda

1/2 teaspoon salt

1 tablespoon cream

Equipment: Large mixing bowl, aluminum foil, flour **sifter**, medium mixing bowl, floured work surface, greased baking sheet, oven mitts, pastry brush

1. Place oatmeal and buttermilk in large bowl. Mix well and cover tightly with foil. Set aside for about 2 hours.

2. Preheat oven to 350°F.

3. **Sift** flour, baking soda, and salt into medium bowl. Add to oatmeal mixture. Place on floured work surface and **knead** into smooth, stiff dough. Shape dough into round loaf, about 6 inches in diameter and about 2 inches thick.

4. Place on baking sheet and using floured knife, make 2 deep slashes, crisscrossing top. Bake in oven, about 45–50 minutes or until bread is golden brown. Using oven mitts, remove from oven. Cool 20 minutes and brush top with cream.

5. Serve *oatmeal bread* while still warm for the best flavor and with plenty of butter.

❦ **Bread and Butter Pudding**

Bread puddings are favorite desserts in most Irish homes. They are usually easy to make and require simple ingredients. The following recipe is a favorite of Irish children.

Yield: serves 4 to 6

1 teaspoon ground cinnamon

1/4 cup sugar

4 tablespoons butter or margarine, more or less as needed, at room temperature

5 slices crust-on white bread

1/2 cup golden raisins

2 cups milk

2 eggs

Equipment: Cup, nonstick or greased 8-inch baking pan, small mixing bowl, whisk or fork

1. Preheat oven to 350°F.

2. Add cinnamon to sugar in cup and mix well. Set aside.

3. Generously spread one side of each piece of bread with butter or margarine. Cut each in half, slicing diagonally. Arrange triangle slices in pan, slightly overlapping, with buttered side up and cut edges facing same direction, making a spiral. As you add bread, sprinkle with sugar-cinnamon mixture and raisins.

4. Place milk in small bowl. Add eggs and using whisk or fork mix to blend well. Pour milk mixture over bread and raisins in baking pan. Set aside for about 15 minutes for bread to absorb liquid. Bake in oven about 30 minutes, or until top is golden brown.

5. Serve the pudding while still warm in individual dessert bowls. It is eaten plain or with cream poured over it.

Scotland

Scotland is located on the northern third of the island of Great Britain. Traditional Scottish cooking was simple and used minimal spices, making it extremely bland. Then, during the Middle Ages, Mary, Queen of Scots, revolutionized Scottish cooking when she brought to Scotland a group of French chefs. They used their expertise to enhance the flavors of the cuisine.

During the last century Scotland has had an influx of immigrants from Italy, the Middle East, Pakistan, India, and most recently Poland. In recent years there has been a resurgence of fresh fruits and vegetables, while spices have been introduced by immigrant settlers from the Far East.

Feather Fowlie (Scottish Chicken Soup)

This recipe is an old Scottish chicken soup. The original recipe calls for *pot-posy*, which refers to the herbs and spices.

Yield: serves 6 to 8

2 1/2 to 3 pounds chicken, cut in serving pieces

6 cups water

1/4 cup parsley, **finely chopped**, fresh or dried

1 onion, **trimmed**, peeled, finely chopped

3 egg yolks (refrigerate whites to use at another time)

1/4 cup half-and-half

1 teaspoon ground **mace**

salt and pepper to taste

Equipment: Large saucepan with cover, mixing spoon, small bowl, fork or whisk

1. Place chicken pieces, water, parsley, thyme, onion, and celery in saucepan. Bring to boil over high heat. Reduce heat to simmer and cook about 1 1/2 hours, until chicken is tender.

2. Place eggs yolks, half-and-half, and mace in small bowl. Whisk until blended. Remove soup from heat. Transfer cooked chicken pieces to serving platter. Add egg mixture, and salt and pepper to taste to soup, stirring continually until well blended.

3. Serve soup in individual bowls first and then the chicken as the next course.

Teed Kettle (Salmon Hash)

Yield: serves 4 to 6

2 tablespoons butter or margarine

2 cups mushrooms, rinsed, **trimmed, coarsely chopped**

2 pounds boneless, skinless salmon fillets, cut into 2-inch squares

2 shallots, trimmed, peeled, **finely chopped**

pinch ground mace

salt and pepper to taste

2 cups chicken or vegetable broth, more as needed, homemade or canned

1 tablespoon fresh parsley, finely chopped, for garnish

Equipment: Medium skillet mixing spoon, medium saucepan, fork

1. Melt butter or margarine in skillet and add mushrooms. Stirring frequently, **sauté** until soft about 6–8 minutes. Set aside.

2. Place pieces of fish in saucepan and add shallots, mace, salt, and pepper to taste and enough broth to cover fish.

3. Bring to boil over medium-high heat. Reduce heat to simmer. Stirring occasionally, cook for 10–15 minutes or until fish is opaque and **flakes** easily when poked with fork. Add mushrooms and cook an additional 5 minutes.

4. Serve warm garnished with a sprinkle of parsley over top.

❧ Scots Shortbread

Shortbreads are quick and easy to make and are as sweet as it gets in Scotland, except for the smiles on young faces when they see someone has made shortbread. The following recipe is so easy it is goof-proof.

Yield: serves 6 or 8

1/2 cup butter or margarine, at room temperature

1/4 cup sugar

pinch of salt

1 cup flour

1/2 cup strawberry, raspberry, plum, or pineapple jam

Equipment: Mixing spoon or electric mixer, medium mixing bowl, buttered medium baking pan

1. Preheat oven to 350°F.

2. Using mixing spoon or electric mixer on medium, mix butter and sugar until light and fluffy. Add pinch of salt and flour a little at a time. Mix with spoon or mixer until mixture is crumble-like. Do not overmix.

3. Pat dough into baking pan with back of spoon or clean hands. Prick surface about 10 times with fork tines. Cut into 1 1/2-inch squares. Bake in oven until light brown, about 25 minutes.

4. While still warm, spread the top with jam of your choice.

5. Serve shortbread warm or cold as a cookie treat.

Wales

Wales is located on the Island of Great Britain with England to the east and the Atlantic Ocean and Irish Sea to the west. Throughout history, Wales has been known as a heavily industrialized nation with many jobs in manufacturing and mining. Over the last century, Wales has seen a decline in industrialization and an increase in service-oriented jobs.

The Welsh raise beef and dairy cattle; however, they are best known for the sheep they raise, for wool and meat. Similar to the rest of the British Isles, Wales is known for delicious seafood and an abundance of fisheries. A traditional breakfast, one of the most important meals of the day, would typically consist of eggs, cockles (small, edible salt water clams), bacon, sausage, and bread. The eggs would be dipped in ketchup, a commonly used and widely sought after breakfast condiment.

✿ Sticky Welsh Gingerbread

Nothing smells better than gingerbread baking in the oven, and most of the time the end result is as delicious as it smells. The following recipe has a shiny, sticky top and a spicy molasses taste, just like old-fashioned traditional gingerbread.

Yield: serves 8 to 12

1/2 cup butter or margarine

1 1/2 cups dark brown sugar

1 1/4 cups dark molasses

2 1/2 cups all-purpose flour

2 eggs, beaten

2 teaspoons ground ginger

1 tablespoon ground cinnamon

3 tablespoons warm milk

1 teaspoon baking soda

1/2 cup raisins

Equipment: Small saucepan, **whisk** or mixing spoon, large mixing bowl, electric mixer, greased 9-inch baking pan, rubber spatula

1. Preheat oven to 325°F.

2. Melt butter or margarine, sugar, and molasses in saucepan over low heat. Heat until sugar is dissolved and mix well. Remove from heat.

3. Place flour, eggs, ginger, cinnamon, milk, baking soda, and raisins in mixing bowl. Add butter mixture and mix with spoon or electric mixer until well blended.

4. Pour mixture into baking pan. Bake in oven for 45–50 minutes or until toothpick inserted in center of cake comes out clean.

5. To serve, allow to cool to room temperature before cutting into squares.

Caws Pobi (Welsh Rabbit or Rarebit)

There are legends about almost everything one eats in the British Isles, and the stories about Welsh rabbit or *rarebit* are no exception. One story says that an imaginative monk in a Welsh abbey created the dish by placing some stale bread and hard crumbly cheese near a blazing fire. The cheese melted over the bread and that was the beginning of Welsh rarebit. Another tale says that when a Welshman returned home from a hunting trip with nothing, his wife invented a dish with melted cheese and called it "Welsh rabbit."

Yield: serves 4 to 6

4 tablespoons butter or margarine

2 1/2 cups grated cheddar cheese, mild or sharp (do not use American processed cheese)

1/2 cup apple cider

2 egg yolks, beaten (refrigerate whites to use at another time)

2 teaspoons **prepared mustard**

salt and pepper to taste

6–8 slices white bread, toasted

sprinkle of paprika, for garnish

Equipment: Medium saucepan, mixing spoon

1. Melt butter or margarine in saucepan over medium-low heat. Add cheese, apple cider, egg yolks, mustard, and salt and pepper to taste. Stir constantly until mixture is well blended and smooth. Do not let mixture boil or bubble or it will become stringy and lumpy.

2. Arrange toast slices on individual plates and spoon cheese mixture over them. Sprinkle with paprika and serve at once.

3. Serve Welsh rarebit hot, as the main dish for lunch or supper. It is eaten with a fork.

NORTHERN EUROPE

Northern Europe includes the Scandinavian countries of Denmark, Norway, Sweden, Finland, and Iceland as well as the Baltic States of Estonia, Latvia, and Lithuania.

To survive through the cold, harsh winters, it was necessary to preserve meat and fish by smoking, drying, or salting. Preserving processes have been passed down throughout the years and are still used today. Most of the northern farming communities raise cattle, pigs, sheep, and reindeer as well as barnyard poultry: ducks, geese, and chickens. The most common fruits and vegetables grown are beets, potatoes, cucumbers, and apples while dill, parsley, and horseradish are the most popular seasonings. The cuisine of this region is pure and simple.

The Baltic States

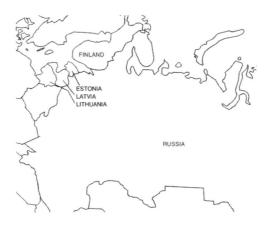

The Baltic States gained their independence from the Soviets in 1991. Estonia, Lithuania, and Latvia, on the Baltic Sea, share similarities in their cooking styles and traditions.

Estonian Cabbage Cream Soup

Yield: serves 4 to 6

4 cups cabbage, rinsed, **trimmed, coarsely chopped**

2 medium carrots, rinsed, peeled, **shredded**

8 cups vegetable broth, more as needed

1 medium zucchini, rinsed, trimmed, coarsely chopped

1 cup parsley root, trimmed, **finely chopped** (available at specialty food stores) (optional)

1 tablespoon soy flour (available in health food stores) or corn starch

2 tablespoons fresh dill, garnish

3 cups heavy cream

Equipment: Medium-large saucepan with cover, wooden mixing spoon, medium mixing bowl, whisk

1. In saucepan place cabbage, carrots, and add 8 cups vegetable broth. Over medium-high heat, bring to boil. Stirring, reduce heat to medium. Cover and cook 15–20 minutes or until vegetables are soft. Stirring frequently, add more broth if necessary to cover vegetables and retain soup consistency. Stir in zucchini and parsley root, cover and continue to cook 10–15 minutes longer.

2. Place flour in mixing bowl and slowly whisk in cream until smooth and well blended.

3. Stirring constantly, slowly add flour-cream mixture into soup. Cover and continue cooking 10–15 minutes more, stirring occasionally.

4. Serve warm in individual soup bowls. Garnish each serving with a sprinkle of dill.

Grybai Trookinti Grietineje ar Piene (Mushrooms Simmered in Sour Cream or Milk)

Mushrooms are very popular in Lithuania. During mushroom season, from early spring to late autumn, families can be seen combing the forests for mushrooms in a tradition called "mushrooming." With over 400 hundred varieties of edible mushrooms, cooks of Lithuania use them to add flavor to meat, fish, and potatoes dishes.

Yield: serves 4 to 6

1 pound fresh mushrooms, cleaned, sliced

1/2 cup sour cream, more as needed

6 tablespoons butter, more as needed

salt and pepper to taste

2 onions, **trimmed**, peeled, **finely chopped**

Equipment: Large skillet, wooden mixing spoon, bowl

1. Melt butter in skillet over medium-high heat. Add mushrooms. Stirring constantly, **sauté** until soft, about 5–8 minutes. Transfer mushrooms to bowl and set aside.

2. Add more butter to skillet. Stirring constantly, add onions and sauté until golden, about 3–5 minutes.

3. Return mushrooms to skillet with onions. Stirring constantly, cook an additional 3–5 minutes. Reduce heat to medium-low heat, stir in sour cream, and simmer 5 minutes. Stir frequently. Add salt and pepper to taste. Add more sour cream if mixture seems too dry.

4. Serve as side dish for lunch with hot potatoes or bread.

Denmark

Denmark, a Scandinavian country with over 443 islands, has a reputation for fine cheeses, pork products, and butter. Other leading foods are cereals and root crops.

Potatoes are a staple in the Danish diet and can be served boiled, peeled, and then sprinkled with dill or covered with a white sauce. For special occasions, such as Christmas Eve, Danes like potatoes with caramel sugar. Rice pudding, another favorite, once was served at the beginning of a traditional Christmas Eve dinner. However, today it is often served at the end of the meal with cherries or strawberries. Pork is the preferred meat and herring the preferred fish.

Ribbenstykke med Aebler (Apple and Prune Filled Spareribs)

Yield: serves 6 to 8

Rub:

1 teaspoon salt

1 teaspoon celery salt

2 tablespoons sugar

1 teaspoon cinnamon

6–8 pounds spareribs, cut into 8 equal racks

Gravy:

2 tablespoons flour

2 cups light cream, more as needed

1 pound apples, **cored**, peeled, **coarsely chopped**

1/2 pound prunes, pitted, found in most supermarkets

1/2 pound butter, melted, more as needed

salt and white pepper

warm water, as needed

Equipment: Small mixing bowl, medium mixing bowl, kitchen string, roasting or baking pan with cover or foil, oven mitts, medium saucepan, gravy boat

1. Preheat oven to 300°F.

2. *Make rub*: In small mixing bowl, combine salt, celery salt, sugar, and cinnamon. Mix well. Using clean hands coat both sides of spareribs with rub.

3. In medium mixing bowl, mix together apples and prunes. Cover surface of rack of lamb with mixture and place other rack over filling, making a sandwich. Tie two racks together to secure and retain filling. Repeat with remaining racks and filling.

4. Place ribs in roasting pan and cover with melted butter. Add enough water to generously cover bottom of pan. Cover and bake about 2 1/2 to 3 hours. If necessary, add more water as needed and occasionally baste with pan juices to prevent ribs from sticking. When ribs are tender, remove cover and cook additional 15–20 minutes or until brown.

5. Using oven mitts, remove ribs from oven. Transfer to serving platter, cover, and keep warm.

6. *Make gravy*: Transfer drippings from roasting pan to saucepan. Place saucepan over medium heat. Using whisk, slowly stir in light cream and flour, alternating until mixture is thick and smooth. If gravy becomes too thick add more cream. Bring mixture to simmer and remove from heat. Add salt and pepper to taste.

7. To serve, remove string from ribs and pour small amount of gravy over each serving of ribs. Transfer remaining gravy to gravy boat and serve over side dish of boiled potatoes.

Ris a L'amande (Rice Pudding)

This traditional rice pudding is often served on Christmas Eve. Mothers hide one whole almond in the pudding, and whoever finds it gets a special treat. An everyday version of rice pudding is to serve it with brown sugar and with cinnamon sprinkled on top.

Yield: serves 2 to 4

2 cups milk

1/3 cup rice

1 teaspoon vanilla

2 tablespoons sugar, more or less as needed

1 cup heavy cream

1 cup strawberry or cherry preserve or marmalade

1/4 cup water

2 tablespoons **finely chopped, blanched** almonds, for garnish

Equipment: Medium saucepan with cover, mixing spoon, small saucepan, individual soup bowls

1. Place milk in medium saucepan and bring to boil over medium heat. Mixing continually, add rice. Reduce to simmer, cover, and cook about 20 minutes or until rice is tender.

2. Remove from heat and add sugar and vanilla. Mix well and cool to room temperature.

3. When cooled, add heavy cream and mix well. Transfer to individual serving bowls and set aside.

4. Place strawberry or cherry preserve in small saucepan. Add water and mix well. Heat over medium heat until heated through. Spoon warm sauce equally over individual servings of rice pudding. Sprinkle each serving with almonds for garnish.

5. Serve pudding at once while sauce is still warm.

Finland

Finland has over 60,000 fish-filled lakes and is set among Europe's last great expanse of forest. The Finns love fishing and it is their favorite pastime, even during bitter cold winters. In summer or winter, Finland is a fisherman's paradise. Despite urbanization, most Finns maintain links with the land. Conservation and other green values are widely supported.

The neighboring countries of Russia to the east and Sweden and Denmark to the west have greatly influenced Finnish cooking. For example, the Swedish *smorgasbord* is set up with the Finnish version of appetizers; and from Russia they have adopted *borscht* (beet soup) (recipe page 231) and *blini* (cheese-filled pancake).

Porkkanasosekeitto (Cream of Carrot Soup)

Yield: serves 6 to 8

1 pound carrots, washed, **trimmed**, peeled, **coarsely chopped**

4 cups beef, chicken or vegetable broth, homemade or canned

2 tablespoons butter

2 tablespoons flour

4 cups milk

1 tablespoon sugar

salt and pepper to taste

2 tablespoons fresh parsley, coarsely chopped, for garnish

2 teaspoons nutmeg, or to taste, for garnish

Equipment: Large saucepan, wooden mixing spoon, food processor or potato masher, medium mixing bowl, individual soup bowls

1. Place carrots in saucepan and cover with broth. Bring to boil over medium-high heat. Reduce heat to simmer and cook until carrots are tender, about 20–30 minutes. Drain carrots and reserve 1 cup broth. Transfer carrots to food processor and purée until smooth or in mixing bowl, using potato masher, pound until smooth.

2. In same saucepan, melt butter over medium-high heat. Stirring constantly, add flour and mix well until smooth. Gradually stir in milk, bring to simmer, and cook for 10 minutes. Stir in reserved broth, carrot purée, sugar, and pepper. Cook until heated through, about 3–5 minutes. Add salt and pepper to taste.

3. To serve, transfer to individual soup bowls and garnish each serving with parsley and dash of nutmeg.

🌿 *Ristinnaulittu Sikka* (Racked Trout)

The original recipe for *ristinnaulittu sikka* (racked trout) calls for the fish to be nailed to a hardwood plank and grilled by reflected heat from an open fire. The flavor will be wonderfully authentic if you have a wire grill basked for holding the fish over an open fire made with hardwood chips. We suggest preparing the fish under the oven broiler. It will still be delicious, lacking only the wood-burning flavor.

Yield: serves 2 to 4

1 trout fish, 2–4 pounds, fresh or frozen, thawed, head removed, skin on, split open and boned (Frozen, whole, skin-on rainbow trout, available at most supermarkets, are often packaged bone-free. Many experienced fishmongers can bone fish from the inside.)

1/2 cup melted butter or margarine

1 teaspoon ground dry mustard

1/2 cup light brown sugar

1 teaspoon paprika

1 lemon cut in wedges for garnish

Equipment: Broiler pan, mixing spoon, metal spatula or pancake turner, oven mitts

1. Preheat oven broiler about 10 minutes before broiling fish.

2. Rub skin side of fish with melted butter. Open fish and lay on broiler pan with buttered skin side down.

3. Add ground mustard, brown sugar, and paprika to remaining butter. Mix well and coat flesh side of fish generously with mixture. Place fish about 6 inches under broiler heat and cook about 25 minutes or until golden brown.

4. Serve fish immediately, garnished with lemon wedges.

✿ *Rikkaat Ritarit* **(Fried Bread Dessert)**

Yield: serves 4 to 6

8 tablespoons almonds, **finely chopped**

8 tablespoons sugar

2 tablespoons all-purpose flour

1/2 teaspoon cinnamon

1 1/2 cups milk

2 eggs

12 slices white bread, crust trimmed off

4 tablespoons butter

Equipment: Small bowl, large mixing bowl, mixing spoon, large skillet, pancake turner

1. Place almonds and sugar in small bowl. Mix well and set aside.

2. Place flour, cinnamon, milk, and eggs in large bowl and mix until smooth. Dip each bread slice into mixture and coat on both sides. Sprinkle with almond-sugar mixture.

3. Heat 4 tablespoons butter or margarine, more as needed, in large skillet over medium heat. Add bread slices and fry on both sides until crisp and golden, about 5–8 minutes per side. Use pancake turner to turn bread slices over. Add more butter as needed for frying all the slices.

4. Serve warm with plenty of jam or applesauce; allow 2 or 3 slices per person.

Iceland

Iceland is an island in the North Atlantic Ocean between Europe and Greenland. Because of its unique location, just south of the Arctic Circle and on top of the Mid-Atlantic Ridge, it is known as the island of "fire and ice." Amazingly enough, Iceland is still known for growing fine fruits and vegetables.

🌿 *Ofnsteiktur fishkur meo lauk og osti* (Fish Casserole with Onions and Cheese)

Yield: serves 6 to 8

4 pounds firm white fish fillets, boneless, skinless, such as cod, halibut, trout, or red snapper, **coarsely chopped**

1/2 to 3/4 pound peas fresh, shelled or frozen, thawed

salt and pepper to taste

1/4 cup butter, more as needed

2 onions, **trimmed**, peeled, **finely chopped**

1 cup breadcrumbs, more as needed

4–6 new potatoes, boiled, thinly sliced

1/2 cup cheddar cheese, grated, more as needed

Equipment: Medium mixing bowl, medium baking casserole with cover or foil, medium skillet, wooden mixing spoon

1. Preheat oven to 350°F.

2. In mixing bowl, combine fish and peas. Using clean hands or mixing spoon, toss to mix well. Sprinkle salt and pepper to taste. Set aside.

3. In skillet, melt 1/4 cup butter over medium-high heat. Add onions. Stirring continuously, **sauté** until golden, about 2–3 minutes. Remove from heat and set aside.

4. Generously butter bottom and sides of casserole dish and sprinkle with 1/2 cup breadcrumbs. Layer sliced potatoes over bottom of casserole dish. Evenly spread layer of fish with peas on top. Cover with layer of sautéed onions. Sprinkle fish with layer of remaining breadcrumbs then sprinkle with cheese. Dot with small pieces of butter, cover with foil, and bake in oven about 20–30 minutes. Remove cover and bake uncovered for 10 minutes more.

5. Serve warm with garden salad.

🌿 *Mandarinu-ostakaka* (Mandarin-Orange Cheesecake)

Yield: serves 6 to 8

Cheesecake filling:

1 cup boiling water

2 1/2 teaspoons (1-pouch) lemon gelatin
Mandarin gelatin, topping:

2 teaspoons unflavored gelatin powder

5 tablespoons sugar

1 pound cream cheese, softened to room temperature

1 cup heavy cream, whipped

1 teaspoon vanilla extract

1/2 cup sugar
1 12-ounce can mandarin oranges, reserve 1/2 cup juice

2 tablespoons lemon juice

1 9-inch graham cracker pie crust

Equipment: Small mixing bowl, mixing spoon, medium mixing bowl, electric mixer, spatula, small saucepan, teaspoon

1. *Make cheesecake filling*: In small mixing bowl, stir lemon gelatin into boiling water and mix well. Set aside to cool. Refrigerate until gelatin has thick soupy texture, about 35–45 minutes.

2. In medium mixing bowl using mixing spoon or electric mixer beat cream cheese until smooth. Add vanilla extract and sugar and mix until well blended. Carefully fold lemon gelatin into cheese mixture. Fold whipped cream into cream cheese mixture. Pour mixture into graham cracker crust, smooth top, and refrigerate. Allow to cool for about 2–4 hours to set firmly.

3. *Make mandarin gelatin*: In small saucepan, warm reserved mandarin orange juice and lemon juice over medium-low heat. Once warm, remove from heat. Add unflavored gelatin powder and stir until completely dissolved. Cool, stirring occasionally.

4. *Assemble*: Once cheesecake is firm to the touch, remove from refrigerator and arrange mandarin orange sections in pattern over the top. Gently spoon mandarin orange gelatin mixture over top. Refrigerate to set and cool.

5. Serve cold, cut into wedges.

Norway

Norway is very mountainous and rugged, with only 3 percent of the land available for farming. A short growing season and long, cold winters make it necessary to store food for months, even years; smoked meats and cheeses, dried fruits, hard cookies and breads, cured fish, and root vegetables are just some of the foods Norwegians enjoy. Fish is served at most meals and plays an important role in the Norwegian diet. They enjoy their fish smoked and salted as well as fresh. Reindeer meat is popular and is often served along with cheese, boiled eggs, sour cream, berries, and waffles at breakfast. Lunch is simple and traditionally consists of a sandwiches, while dinner, served in the early evening, might consist of soup and meat or fish.

⁂ *Sot Suppe* (Sweet Soup)

Yield: serves 6 to 8

25 cloves	1 cup prunes, pitted
1 stick cinnamon	7 tablespoons tapioca
10 cups water	4 cups grape juice
1 cup raisins	2 cups sugar, more as needed
1 cup currants	1/2 cup lemon juice
1 cup dried apricots	3/4 tablespoons salt
1 cup dried cranberries	

Equipment: 1 6-inch square of cheese cloth with kitchen string, large sauce pan with lid, mixing spoon

1. Place cinnamon sticks and cloves in center of cheese cloth, fold over to form pouch, seal with string.

2. Place clove-cinnamon pouch in saucepan. Add water, raisins, currants, apricots, cranberries, and prunes. Over medium-high heat, bring to boil. Reduce heat to simmer and cook 20–30 minutes, stirring frequently. Stir in tapioca, grape juice, and sugar to taste. Cook until tapioca is completely dissolved, about 15–20 minutes.

3. Remove from heat. Add salt to taste and remove and discard spice bag. Set aside to cool. As mixture cools, add lemon juice.

4. Serve cold as dessert with dollop of vanilla ice cream or whipped cream.

⁂ *Toskakake* (Almond Caramel Topped Cake)

This easy-to-make almond and caramel topped cake is a favorite in most Scandinavian countries. Many, many years ago it was imported from Italy and made over in the Scandinavian cooking tradition. This cake can be served as a representative dessert from Norway, Denmark, or Sweden.

Yield: serves 10 or 12

3 eggs, room temperature	3 tablespoons milk
1 1/2 cups sugar (set aside 1/2 cup for topping)	1 teaspoon vanilla
1 1/2 cups all-purpose flour	1/2 cup heavy cream
1 1/2 teaspoons baking powder	1/2 cup chopped almonds, walnuts, or pecans
1 cup melted butter (set aside 1/3 cup for topping)	

Equipment: Large mixing bowl, **egg beater** or electric mixer, medium mixing bowl, **whisk** or mixing spoon, buttered 10-inch **springform pan**, small skillet, toothpick, oven, mitts, wire rack

1. Preheat oven to 350°F.

2. Mix eggs and 1 cup sugar with egg beater or electric mixer in large bowl until mixture is pale yellow and a ribbon forms when beaters are lifted, about 5 minutes.

3. Combine flour and baking powder in medium bowl. Mix well and **fold** into egg mixture using whisk or mixing spoon. Add 2/3 cup melted butter, milk, and vanilla and mix until smooth.

4. Pour into springform pan. Bake in oven, about 35–40 minutes.

5. *Prepare topping*: Place remaining 1/3 cup butter in skillet over low heat. Add remaining 1/2 cup sugar and cream and mix well. Increase heat to medium high. Bring to boil and cook about 2–3 minutes. Remove from heat and set aside.

6. To test cake doneness, insert toothpick in center and if it comes out clean, remove from oven using oven mitts. If toothpick is not clean, continue baking for a few more minutes until toothpick inserted comes out clean. Immediately pour hot topping over top. Sprinkle with nuts, return to oven, and continue baking until top is bubbly and golden brown, about 10 minutes. Using oven mitts, remove from oven and set on wire rack.

7. To serve, remove sides of pan and set cake on serving platter. Serve tosakake warm or at room temperature.

Sweden

Sweden has one of the highest standards of living in the world, despite its lack of usable land and harsh northern climate. Swedish cooks take pride in their foods and lovingly show off their national dishes. What better way to do this than with the *smorgasbord*, Sweden's most notable culinary contribution to the world? The smorgasbord is an appetizer table, loaded with several assortments of food, and is often able to satisfy a hearty appetite. The recipes in this section can all be used in the smorgasbord. Swedish baked goods reign supreme in taste and variety. Spices are added sparingly and hot peppers are almost unheard of in Swedish kitchens. Dill grows in many herb gardens and is used extensively in sauces and soups. Agriculture in Sweden concentrates on dairy products such as milk and cheese.

Among many festivals celebrated in Sweden, one takes place the first week of August; it is the beginning of crayfish season. Eating these little crustaceans is a national pleasure; there is no fancy way to cook or eat them. They are boiled in salty water for about 10 minutes until they turn bright red. Crayfish are eaten like miniature lobsters; the meat in the tail section is eaten and the heads are discarded.

Schmorr Gurken (Cucumbers with Bacon)

Cucumbers make great pickles and add a pleasant crunchiness to salads. The following Swedish recipe requires cucumbers to be cooked. This is an old Swedish recipe, yet new to many who have never eaten cooked cucumbers.

Yield: serves 4 to 6

2 medium cucumbers, **trimmed**, peeled, thinly sliced crosswise

1/2 teaspoon salt

4 slices lean bacon, **finely chopped**

1 tablespoon sugar

1 tablespoon vinegar

1 tablespoon flour

Equipment: Large plate, medium skillet with cover, mixing spoon, plate covered with paper towels, strainer, small bowl

1. Spread cucumber slices on plate and sprinkle with salt. Let stand for about 30 minutes.
2. Fry bacon in skillet over medium heat stirring frequently, until crisp, about 4–6 minutes. Set aside.
3. Transfer cucumbers to strainer. Rinse under cold water and drain well. Add to bacon in skillet.
4. Place sugar, vinegar, and flour in small bowl and mix well. Stir into cucumbers and bacon mixture. Cover and simmer, about 10–15 minutes or until heated through.
5. Serve *schmorr gurken* hot as a side dish with meat or chicken.

Gravlax (Marinated Salmon)

The term *gravlax* ("buried salmon") comes from the Middle Ages when fisherman would salt then bury salmon in the sand for fermentation. Today, salmon is only buried under salt and dill.

Yield: serves 6 to 8

2 1-pound salmon fillets, boneless, skin on, rinsed, patted dry

1/2 cup salt, more as needed

1/2 cup sugar, more as needed

2 tablespoons coarsely ground black pepper

4 sprigs fresh dill, more as needed

Equipment: Small mixing bowl, plastic wrap, large plastic sealable bag, cookie sheet, heavy-bottom saucepan, 3 16-ounce jars or cans with lids

1. In mixing bowl combine sugar, salt, and black pepper and mix well. Using clean hands, generously rub mixture into flesh side of each fillet. Using remaining salt and sugar mixture, rub into skin side of each fillet.

2. Place one fillet skin side down on large sheet of plastic wrap. Cover generously with fresh dill. Place second fillet over dill, skin side up. Wrap securely with plastic wrap. Place wrapped fish inside plastic bag and seal. Transfer to sheet pan and weigh down with bottom side of large skillet. To weight, place 2–3 16-ounce jars or cans on top.

3. Refrigerate for 48 hours, turning once or twice daily.

4. When ready to serve, discard dill and pour off accumulated moisture.

5. To serve, thinly slice and serve chilled or **sauté** in skillet along with gravlax sauce (next recipe).

Gravlax (Sauce)

3 tablespoons vegetable or olive oil

1 tablespoon red wine vinegar

1 tablespoon sugar

1/2 teaspoon salt

pinch white pepper

2 tablespoons prepared mustard, more to taste

2 tablespoons fresh dill, minced, more to taste

Equipment: Small mixing bowl, mixing spoon

1. In mixing bowl, stir together oil, red wine vinegar, sugar, salt, pepper, and mustard and mix well. Stir in dill. If necessary, adjust flavor by adding more mustard or dill.

2. To serve, transfer to a small serving bowl with spoon and use as condiment.

Kjottboller (Swedish Meatballs)

Swedish meatballs have gained popularity as an appetizer. It is probably because they are not only delicious but also small and easy to make and eat. Adding a touch of nutmeg makes them distinctly Swedish.

Yield: about 36 balls

1 pound ground lean beef

1/2 pound ground lean pork

1 cup breadcrumbs

2 teaspoons sugar

1/4 cup milk

1 egg

1 onion, **trimmed**, peeled, **finely chopped**

salt and pepper to taste

2 tablespoons vegetable oil, more as needed

3 tablespoons butter or margarine

3 tablespoons all-purpose flour

2 1/2 cups half-and-half, slightly warm

1 teaspoon ground nutmeg

Equipment: Large mixing bowl, clean hands or mixing spoon, large skillet, metal spatula or slotted spoon, medium or large baking pan, medium saucepan, **whisk** or mixing spoon

1. Place beef, pork, crumbs, sugar, milk, egg, onion, and salt and pepper to taste in large mixing bowl. Using clean hands or mixing spoon, blend well. Shape mixture into ping-pong-sized balls by rolling between the palms of your wet hands. (Rinse hands in cold water to prevent sticking.) Place balls side-by-side on clean work surface.

2. Heat 2 tablespoons oil in skillet over medium heat. Add meatballs, a few at a time, so they can be rolled around to brown evenly. Cook about 5 minutes; add more oil as needed. Using spatula or slotted spoon, remove and drain well. Transfer to baking pan and set aside.

3. Prepare sauce in saucepan. Melt butter or margarine over medium heat. Add flour and blend well using whisk or mixing spoon. Stirring continually, cook about 2 minutes until smooth and thick. Do not allow mixture to brown. Continue stirring and slowly add half-and-half. Bring mixture to simmer, turn heat to low, and cook about 5 minutes or until sauce thickens. Remove from heat and add salt to taste and nutmeg. Pour hot sauce over meatballs using spoon, and rotate meatballs to completely coat with sauce.

4. Serve kjottboller warm as an appetizer.

WESTERN EUROPE

The countries of Western Europe include Austria, Belgium, France, Germany, Luxembourg, Monaco, The Netherlands, and Switzerland. The cuisine of this region is the cornerstone of fine dining throughout the world. Elaborate and unique recipes from *escargo* (snails **sautéed** in garlic butter), introduced by the French, to the elaborate Austrian *sachertorte* (recipe page 178) have withstood the test of time. Even with migration, tourism, and fast-food chains opening in cities throughout Europe, cooking traditions unique to each country have remained consistent.

The climate of Western Europe is mild with a long growing season. The most popular food crops are sugar beets, grains, potatoes, tomatoes, onions, grapes, pears, and apples along with livestock, including cattle, pigs, sheep, and goats, geese, ducks, and chickens.

Austria

Austria was once the seat of the Holy Roman Empire followed by the long Hapsburg reign. Today, Austria is only a sliver of the land that it once occupied. The country has a unique history of storybook kings and queens, beautiful music, the romantic Blue Danube River, and the Viennese waltz. The cuisine of Austria has been influenced by other countries within the region and today is known as one of the most multicultural cuisines in Europe.

Austrians have always enjoyed coffee, midday snacks, and delicious desserts such as the famous *sachertorte*.

Sachertorte (Chocolate Cake)

Over 150 years ago, a very unusual war broke out in Austria that lasted nearly 7 years. It was the war of the *sachertorte*, a chocolate cake that became world famous. Two pastry chefs claimed to have created the original recipe, and the battle was taken to court. The case ended in a draw, and both parties were permitted to bake and serve the cake. To this day, the cake is one of Austria's national treasures. The following recipe is one version of this delicious cake.

A good-quality chocolate sauce to pour over the cake for frosting can be purchased at most supermarkets; however, if you'd like to make your own, the recipe follows.

Yield: serves 12 to 14

1/2 cup butter or margarine

1/2 cup sugar

6 eggs, **separated**

1 cup melted semisweet chocolate squares or chips, warm

1 cup all-purpose flour, **sifted**

1/2 cup strained apricot jam, warm, for frosting

1/2 cup semisweet chocolate sauce, for frosting, canned or homemade (recipe follows)

Equipment: Large mixing bowl, mixing spoon or electric mixer, medium mixing bowl, rubber spatula, buttered 9-inch **springform** pan, wax paper, scissors, oven mitts, wire rack

1. Place butter or margarine and sugar in large mixing bowl and using mixer or mixing spoon, blend until light and fluffy. Add egg yolks, one at a time, beating well after each addition. Slowly add chocolate and blend well.

2. Using clean and dry mixer, beat egg whites until stiff and peaks form. With spatula, gently fold half of egg whites into chocolate mixture and fold in half of flour. Slowly add remaining whites and flour and blend well.

3. Place springform pan on wax paper and, with a pencil, trace a circle around bottom of pan. Using scissors, cut out circle and butter one side of wax paper. Line bottom of springform pan with wax paper circle, butter side up. Sprinkle paper lightly with flour and tip pan to pour out extra flour. Pour mixture into springform and bake in oven, about 35 minutes or until toothpick inserted in center of cake comes out clean. Using oven mitts, remove from oven, cool on wire rack. Remove sides of pan and transfer to serving platter.

4. Spread apricot jam over top of cake. Pour chocolate sauce (next recipe) over top of cake and let sauce drip down and cover sides. Refrigerate to set.

5. Serve *sachertorte* cut in wedges with a dollop of whipped cream.

Chocolate Sauce

Yield: about 2 cups

1/4 cup butter

1/2 cup semisweet chocolate chips

1/2 cup sugar, more as needed

1/2 cup cream

pinch of salt

1 teaspoon vanilla

Equipment: Small saucepan, mixing spoon

1. Melt butter and chips in saucepan over low heat, mixing frequently. Add sugar to taste, cream, and salt. Mixing continually, increase heat to boil. Mix and remove from heat. Mix in vanilla.

2. Cool to room temperature and pour over *sachertorte*.

Belgium

The tiny fertile country of Belgium, north of France and west of Germany, is known for its wonderful vegetable gardens. Other claims to fame are waffles, french fries, mussels, brussels sprouts, and Belgian endive. The Belgian endive is a unique, lovely looking and tasting light-green vegetable. It is often eaten raw in salads or cooked in soups and stews. Brussels sprouts look like miniature cabbages and are easy to cook. It is said Belgium cuisine has the finesse of French cooking, yet served with German generosity.

✵ *Potage au Beligium* (Cream of Belgian Endive Soup)

Yield: serves 4 to 6

2 Belgian endives, **trimmed, cored, finely chopped**

1 white onion, trimmed, peeled, finely chopped

1 garlic clove, trimmed, peeled, **minced**

2 tablespoons butter

2 potatoes, washed, trimmed, peeled, finely chopped

2 cups chicken or vegetable broth

1 cup milk or heavy cream

salt and pepper to taste

chives, finely chopped, for garnish

dill sprigs, finely chopped, for garnish

Equipment: Medium-large saucepan, wooden mixing spoon, food processor or blender, soup tureen or large serving bowl with ladle

1. In saucepan melt butter over medium-high heat. Stir in endives, onion, and garlic. **Sauté** about 3–5 minutes or until soft, stirring frequently.

2. Stir in potatoes and broth, reduce heat, and simmer about 15 minutes or until potatoes are soft. Transfer to food processor or blender and blend until smooth. Transfer to soup tureen or a large serving bowl with ladle. Stir in milk or cream and salt and pepper to taste. Using whisk or mixing spoon, mix until well blended.

3. Serve hot or cold garnished with chives and dill in individual bowls.

Choux de Bruxelles (Brussels Sprouts)

Yield: serves 4 to 6

1/2 cup butter or margarine

1/2 teaspoon ground nutmeg

1 pound Brussels sprouts, fresh, **trimmed**, or frozen, thawed

salt and pepper to taste

Equipment: Medium skillet with cover, mixing spoon

1. Melt butter or margarine in skillet over medium-high heat. Add Brussels sprouts and mix to coat. Reduce heat to medium, cover, and cook for about 8 minutes, until tender but firm. Remove from heat and season with nutmeg and salt and pepper to taste.

2. Serve choux de bruxelles warm as a side dish with meat, chicken, or fish.

Pom Koek (Belgian Coffee Cake)

Yield: serves 6 to 8

3 cups flour

1 teaspoon salt

1/2 cup sugar

1 cup honey

1 teaspoon baking soda

1 cup hot coffee

1 teaspoon cinnamon

1 egg

1/4 teaspoon ground cloves

1/3 cup corn oil

Equipment: Medium mixing bowl, mixing spoon or whisk, large mixing bowl, rubber spatula, greased loaf pan (line bottom with parchment or wax paper), toothpick, oven mitts

1. Preheat oven to 350°F.

2. In medium mixing bowl, combine flour, sugar, baking soda, cinnamon, cloves, and salt. Using mixing spoon, lightly mix together.

3. In large mixing bowl, whisk together honey, coffee, and oil and mix well. Add egg and beat until smooth.

4. Using rubber spatula, gently fold flour mixture into egg mixture and blend well.

5. Pour batter into loaf pan and bake about 30 minutes or until toothpick inserted in center of loaf comes out clean. Using oven mitts, remove from oven and set aside to cool.

6. To serve, cut into thin slices, plate, and serve warm with butter.

France and Monaco

France is a country with a long history of talented and creative chefs. When Catherine de Medici left Italy for France to marry Henry II in 1533, she brought her personal chefs. They introduced *haute cuisine* (food made with rich sauces and elegant presentation) to the French court. From this the French perfected techniques and cooking skills still revered and practiced today.

Prior to the French revolution there was a separation of guilds between those who grew and sold raw foods and the chefs who prepared foods for the French elite. Following the French Revolution in 1789 the guild system was abolished, allowing chefs to both produce and cook culinary items without restraint.

French chefs are held in the highest esteem by professional chefs and *gourmands* (people who love good food). French cuisine has made several transitions, the most recent combining *haute cuisine* and *nouvelle cuisine* (simplified French cooking).

Grapes are the most important crop throughout France. The government encourages planting the best grapes to produce the highest-quality wines possible.

Monaco, the smallest French-speaking country, bordering the Mediterranean Sea, combines French and Italian cuisines, giving it a distinguished flavor. The following recipe of *soupe a l'oignon* is a favorite among both the French and the people of Monaco.

Soupe a L'oignon (Onion Soup)

Yield: serves 4

3 tablespoons butter or margarine

2 cups onions, **trimmed**, peeled, thinly sliced

4 cups beef broth

4 slices French bread cut 1/4 inch thick, crust on, toasted and cut to fit into individual soup bowls

1 cup Gruyere or Swiss cheese, **shredded**

1/2 cup Parmesan cheese, grated

Equipment: Large saucepan with cover or **Dutch oven**, mixing spoon, toaster, ladle, individual ovenproof soup bowls, baking sheet, oven mitts

1. Preheat broiler

2. Melt butter or margarine in saucepan or Dutch oven over medium heat. Add onions, cover, and cook, stirring frequently until limp about 3–5 minutes. Add beef broth, cover, and simmer about 10 minutes more.

3. To broil: set oven shelf 8 inches under broiler.

4. Ladle soup into four individual ovenproof bowls and sprinkle half shredded cheese equally among the bowls. Place one slice of toasted bread into each bowl, cover with equal amounts of remaining shredded cheese and equal amounts of Parmesan cheese. Place bowls on baking sheet and, using oven mitts, set under broiler about 5 minutes or until cheese is bubbly and light brown. Using oven mitts, remove bowls from oven and set on heat-proof surface. *Be careful; bowls are very hot.*

5. To serve, place bowls on individual serving plates and serve immediately. *Bon appetit.*

❧ *Ratatouille a la Nicoise* (**Vegetarian Stew**)

Every province and peasant has a different way of making *ratatouille*, a popular French vegetable casserole. Using the freshest vegetables from your garden or market is all that really matters. The dish is a blending of cooked vegetables, which should not be overcooked and mushy. This recipe originated in the port city of Nice and uses fresh locally grown vegetables. Cooking the vegetables with olive oil and garlic is typical style of Mediterranean French cooking.

Yield: serves 6

1/2 cup olive oil

4 cups eggplant, **trimmed**, peeled, cut into 1/2-inch chunks

salt and pepper, as needed

2 onions, trimmed, peeled, **coarsely chopped**

3 cloves garlic, trimmed, peeled, **minced** or 1 teaspoon garlic granules

2 green bell peppers, trimmed, **cored**, **seeded**, cut into thin strips

2 zucchinis, trimmed, cut into 1/4-inch rounds

1/2 teaspoon ground oregano

1/2 teaspoon ground thyme

3 bay leaves

4 tomatoes, **peeled**, cut into chunks or 2 cups canned whole tomatoes

Equipment: Large saucepan with cover, mixing spoon, **colander** or strainer, medium baking casserole, oven mitts

1. Preheat oven to 350°F.

2. Sprinkle eggplant with 1 teaspoon salt and set aside in colander or strainer in sink or over plate for 30 minutes.

3. Heat 2 tablespoons olive oil in saucepan over medium heat. Add onion and garlic and mix well. Cook until onions are soft, about 3–5 minutes. Transfer to casserole.

4. Rinse eggplant in colander or strainer under cold water and drain well. Return skillet to medium heat and add 2 tablespoons oil, eggplant, bell peppers, zucchinis, oregano, thyme, and bay leaves. Stirring frequently, reduce heat to simmer, cover, and cook for about 5 minutes. (Add more oil if necessary to prevent sticking.)

5. Remove bay leaves and discard. Transfer mixture to casserole and mix with onions. Cover top with tomatoes and add salt and pepper to taste. Drizzle lightly with oil and bake in oven for about 45 minutes or until top is browned. Remove from oven using oven mitts.

6. Serve hot as the main dish with plenty of crusty French bread and butter.

Truffles au Chocolat (Chocolate Candy)

Giving a gift of homemade truffles to friends and family is a wonderful treat; they are inexpensive and easy to make. Homemade truffles are far superior to the very expensive storebought truffles. Chopped nuts, dates, grated coconut, chocolate, butterscotch, white chocolate mini-chips, or candied cherries can be added to this recipe for a variety of textures and flavors.

Yield: about 12 pieces

4 ounces semisweet chocolate chips or bar	4 tablespoons butter or margarine
2 tablespoons water	3/4 cups confectioner's sugar
3 egg yolks (refrigerate whites to use at another time)	5 tablespoons cocoa

Equipment: Small saucepan, rubber spatula, mixing spoon, medium mixing bowl, wax paper, cookie sheet, small bowl, aluminum foil

1. **Melt chocolate** in saucepan over low heat. Add water and mix to blend. Remove from heat and pour chocolate into mixing bowl. Scrape out pan with rubber spatula. Add egg yolks, butter, and sugar. Mix until well blended. Refrigerate until firm, about 2 hours.

2. Remove mixture from refrigerator, using clean hands shape into ping-pong-sized balls. Place balls side-by-side on wax paper covered cookie sheet.

3. Place cocoa in small bowl and roll balls, one at a time, in cocoa until coated. Return balls to cookie sheet, cover with foil, and refrigerate until ready to serve.

4. Serve truffles as a candy treat. Wrap each in plastic wrap and store in a covered container; refrigerate.

✎ *Soufflé au Fromage* (Cheese Soufflé)

Yield: serves 2 to 4

2 tablespoons butter	1 3/4 cups shredded Swiss cheese
1/4 cup flour	salt and pepper to taste
1 cup milk	3 eggs separated

Equipment: Medium saucepan, mixing spoon, medium mixing bowl, electric mixer or whisk, rubber spatula, small greased ovenproof soufflé dish or baking casserole, oven mitts

1. Preheat oven to 350°F.

2. In saucepan over medium heat melt butter. Whisk or stir in flour and cook until smooth and bubbly. Stir constantly, cook about 1 minute. Stir in milk, a little at a time. Bring to boil, stirring constantly, 1 minute.

3. Reduce to medium-low heat. Stir in cheese, salt and pepper to taste and remove from heat. Whisk or beat in egg yolks one at a time.

4. Using whisk or electric mixer, beat egg whites in bowl until stiff. Using spatula or spoon, carefully fold egg whites into cheese mixture.

5. Pour into soufflé dish and bake about 25–30 minutes or until golden. Remove from oven using oven mitts.

6. Serve immediately as savory main dish with a side of fresh fruit.

Germany

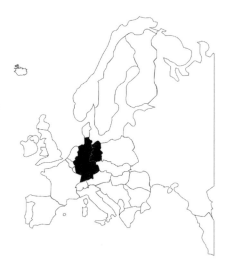

Germany is located in the middle of Western Europe. After years of war and political turmoil the country has transformed to a well-respected democracy.

German cuisine, often considered robust, varies from region to region. In recent years, however, German chefs have introduced *Neue Küche* (modern German cuisine), which focuses on healthier, lighter meals while maintaining the traditional German flavors.

Many Germans are known to love all meats including wild game, both four-legged and winged. Germans are famous sausage makers, producing over 1,500 different varieties with many available worldwide. Other creations of the German people include foods preserved through curing, salting, pickling, and smoking. The most popular are *sauerkraut* (fermented cabbage), *matjes* (pickled herring), and *sauerbraten* (roast beef cured in vinegar and red wine). Mustard, horseradish, and garlic, along with strong spices, are prevalent in German cooking.

❧ *Königsberger Klopse* (German Meatballs with Caper Sauce)

Yield: serves 4 to 6

Meatballs:

2 slices white bread, soaked in cold water

1 onion, **trimmed**, peeled, **finely chopped**

1 pound lean hamburger meat

Caper Sauce:

2 tablespoons butter or margarine

2 1/2 tablespoons flour

1 egg separated

2 tablespoons prepared mustard

salt and pepper to taste

4 cups water
2 cups beef broth

2 tablespoons milk

1 tablespoon capers, drained

Lemon juice to taste

Equipment: Large mixing bowl, plate or clean work surface, medium saucepan, slotted spoon, medium baking pan, medium-large saucepan, wooden mixing spoon, small mixing bowl

1. *Make meatballs*: Using clean hands, squeeze water from bread and place in mixing bowl. Add onion, hamburger meat, egg white and salt and pepper to taste. Mix well. With wet hands form into ping-pong-sized balls, place side-by-side on plate or clean work surface.

2. Pour water into medium saucepan. Add 1 teaspoon salt and bring to boil over medium-high heat. Add meatballs a few at a time; when they float to top they are done. Using slotted spoon, remove to baking pan, set aside, and keep warm.

3. *Make caper sauce:* In medium-large saucepan over medium-high heat, melt butter. Stirring constantly, add flour to make **roux**. Constantly stir to avoid lumps. Add beef broth. Bring

to a boil and cook about 5 minutes, stirring frequently. Remove sauce from heat and set aside.

4. In small mixing bowl, beat egg yolk with milk. Stir in 2 tablespoons of sauce mixture. Return to sauce in saucepan and heat over medium-low heat. Add capers and stir in lemon juice and salt and pepper to taste. Reduce heat to low, add meatballs to sauce, and cook about 5 minutes, stirring occasionally. Remove from heat and let stand about 5 minutes before serving.

5. Serve warm over rice or mashed potatoes.

Himmel und Erde (Cooked Potatoes and Apples)

This recipe, blending fruit and vegetables, is typical German country cooking, giving a sweet and sour flavor to the dish. Perhaps it is named *himmel und erde* (heaven and earth) because apples grow on trees toward the heavens and potatoes grow in the earth.

Yield: serves 6 to 8

2 pounds new red potatoes, washed, **trimmed**, quartered

6 cups water

1 tablespoon vinegar

2 pounds cooking apples, trimmed, peeled, cut into chunks

6 slices bacon, finely **diced**

1/2 cup breadcrumbs

salt and pepper to taste

Equipment: Medium saucepan with cover, medium skillet, mixing spoon

1. Place potatoes in saucepan and cover with water. Add vinegar and bring to boil over high heat. Reduce heat to simmer, cover, and cook about 10 minutes. Add apple chunks and mix well. Continue cooking until potatoes are tender but not mushy, about 10 minutes more. Drain well.

2. While the potatoes and apples are cooking, fry bacon in skillet over medium-high heat until crisp. Reduce heat to medium, add breadcrumbs, and mix well to coat crumbs. Fry about 2 minutes more to heat through.

3. Add bacon mixture to potatoes and apple mixture. Add salt and pepper to taste and toss gently. Transfer to serving bowl.

4. Serve himmel und erde hot as a side dish with meat, poultry, or fish.

The Netherlands

The Netherlands, also known as Holland, is the land of tulips, windmills, and canals. Hollanders, also referred to as the Dutch, live in a fish-lover's paradise. The Netherlands ("lowlands") is built on land reclaimed from the sea. Due to its location along the coast, fishing is a very important industry.

The Dutch are very proud of the tulips they grow and ship all over the world. They love their flowers, and pushcarts on every city street corner overflow with a mosaic of fresh-cut blossoms. These floral bouquets are sold alongside street vendors peddling their daily catch of herring, still glistening from the cold waters of the North Sea.

Fruits and vegetables are primarily grown under hothouse conditions (large glass buildings, used as a shelter from the cold).

The cheeses, Dutch chocolates, and pastries of the Netherlands are some of the world's best. Dutch cheeses are often nibbled on at the conclusion of the meal.

Dutch cuisine has international flavor, combining foods native to Western Europe with exotic spices of their former colony, Indonesia.

Hollandse Jachtschotel (Hunter's Pie)

Yield: serves 4 to 6

2 tablespoons butter, more as needed

2 onions, **trimmed**, peeled, **finely chopped**

1 pound cooked meat, such as lamb, roast beef, or ham, cut into bite-sized cubes

1 cup beef broth

1 bay leaf

1 teaspoon ground thyme

2 teaspoons ground cloves

salt and pepper to taste

3 tart apples, peeled, **cored**, thinly sliced

2 pounds potatoes, trimmed, peeled, boiled, mashed

1 cup cheese, grated, such as Edam or Swiss

Equipment: **Dutch oven** or large skillet, greased deep baking dish, oven mitts

1. Preheat oven to 350°F.

2. In Dutch oven or large skillet melt 2 tablespoons butter over medium-high heat. Add onions and **sauté** until soft, about 3–5 minutes. Reduce heat to medium, add meat, and heat through, about 3–5 minutes. Stir frequently. Stir in beef broth, bay leaf, thyme, and clove. Cover and simmer about 30 minutes. Add salt and pepper to taste. Remove and discard bay leaf.

3. Transfer mixture into baking dish and cover with layer of sliced apples. Top with mashed potatoes and place dabs of butter over top. Sprinkle with grated cheese. Bake uncovered about 20 minutes or until top is browned.

4. Serve warm as main dish with fresh garden salad.

⁂ *Curried Kool Sla Au Gratin* (Curried Cabbage with Cheese Casserole)

Yield: serves 6 to 8

3 pounds cabbage, **trimmed**, finely **shredded**

2 cups water

1 bay leaf

3 cloves garlic, trimmed, peeled, **minced** or
1 tablespoon garlic granules

1 onion, trimmed, peeled, **finely chopped**

8 tablespoons butter or margarine

1/4 cup all-purpose flour

1 cup milk

1 teaspoon curry powder

1 cup cheddar cheese, shredded

salt and pepper to taste

1/2 cup breadcrumbs

Equipment: Large saucepan with cover, mixing spoon, **colander** or strainer, medium saucepan, fork or **whisk**, large mixing bowl, nonstick or buttered medium baking casserole, oven mitts

1. Preheat oven to 375°F.

2. Place cabbage, water, bay leaf, garlic, and onion in large saucepan. Bring to boil over high heat. Reduce heat to simmer, cover, and cook about 10–15 minutes or until cabbage is tender. Remove from heat, drain well in colander or strainer, and discard liquid and bay leaf.

3. *Prepare sauce*: melt 4 tablespoons butter in medium saucepan over low heat, add flour, and mix until well blended. Increase to medium heat. Stirring constantly, slowly add milk. Cook

until mixture thickens. Do not boil. Remove from heat. Add curry powder, cheese, and salt and pepper to taste. Mix well.

4. Transfer cabbage to large mixing bowl and **fold** in sauce. Pour mixture into casserole. Sprinkle with breadcrumbs and dot with remaining butter or margarine. Bake about 10–15 minutes or until top is golden brown. Remove from oven using oven mitts.

5. Serve casserole as a side dish with meat, poultry, or fish.

🎄 *Speculaas* (Dutch Christmas Cookies)

Cookies of every shape and flavor are popular with Dutch children, all year long. *Speculaas* are easy to make and keep well in the cookie jar.

Yield: about 24 cookies

1/2 cup butter or margarine, at room temperature

1/2 cup light brown sugar, firmly packed

1 egg

2 cups all-purpose flour

2 teaspoons baking powder

1/2 teaspoon ground nutmeg

1/2 teaspoon ground cinnamon

1/2 teaspoon ground cloves

1/2 teaspoon salt

Equipment: Large mixing bowl, clean work surface, mixing spoon or electric mixer, medium mixing bowl, aluminum foil, sharp knife, nonstick or lightly greased cookie sheet, oven mitts

1. Combine butter or margarine and sugar in large mixing bowl. With mixing spoon or electric mixer, blend until smooth. Add egg, and mix well.

2. Place flour, baking powder, nutmeg, cinnamon, cloves, and salt in medium mixing bowl and mix well. Slowly add to butter mixture, mixing continually until soft dough is formed. Remove from mixer and transfer dough to work surface. Using clean hands, shape into a cylinder, or log shape, about 2 inches thick. Wrap in foil and chill in refrigerator about 1 hour, until firm.

3. Preheat oven to 350°F.

4. Unwrap foil and place dough on work surface. Cut into 1/4-inch-thick slices with sharp knife and place side-by-side on cookie sheet. Bake in oven about 15 minutes, until cookies are golden.

5. Serve speculaas with a glass of milk or cup of warm cocoa. Dutch children sometimes press or cut the cookie dough into different designs and shapes.

Switzerland

Switzerland, a tiny landlocked country, is situated between Italy, France, Germany, and Austria. Because of its location, the Swiss people speak German, French, Italian, and Romansh (a language descended directly from Latin). This diversity is reflected in their cuisine.

Most Swiss live in small cities and villages between the Alps and the Jura ranges. Cattle, sheep, and goats graze in the mountainous Alpine region, where wide-scale planting is impossible.

This small country has distinguished itself in banking and tourism along with precision products such as clocks. The cheeses, chocolates, wines, brandies, and liqueurs of Switzerland are enjoyed throughout the world.

Fotzelschnitte (Swiss-Style French Toast)

The story behind the name *fotzel slices* is still unknown but popular belief is that it stems from the homemaker's rule "Never throw away any bread." It is thought that to savor every "scrap of bread" grandmothers inspired this recipe to spruce up day-old bread.

Yield: serves 4 to 6

4 eggs

1 cup milk

1/2 teaspoon salt, to taste

12 slices stale rye bread

2 tablespoons butter or margarine, more as needed

sugar and cinnamon to taste

Equipment: medium mixing bowl, whisk, large skillet, spatula, serving platter

1. In mixing bowl whisk together eggs, milk, and salt.

2. Melt butter in skillet over medium-high heat.

3. Lay bread, one slice at a time, in egg mixture, to coat both sides. Fry each slice in skillet until golden brown on both sides. Add more butter as needed and fry in batches.

4. While toast is still warm, sprinkle each slice with sugar and cinnamon to taste. Serve immediately.

5. Serve warm with a slice of Swiss cheese, a dollop of applesauce, and a cold glass of milk.

Birchermuesli (Raw Granola)

This recipe originates from Dr. Bircher-Benner, a Swiss physician whose impact on healthy eating dates back to 1900. He introduced the idea of eating "foods of sunlight"; this meant eating uncooked foods based on their biological and natural ingredients.

Yield: serves 4

juice of 2 lemons

2 apples, rinsed, **cored, finely chopped**

4 tablespoons oatmeal flakes

1 cup berries such as blueberries, blackberries, or raspberries

1/2 cup mandarin oranges, fresh, peeled, sliced or canned, drained

1/4 cup nuts, such as hazelnuts or almonds, ground or finely chopped

honey or sugar to taste

Equipment: Medium mixing bowl, mixing spoon, serving bowls

1. Place chopped apples in mixing bowl, cover with lemon juice, toss well. Using clean hands or mixing spoon, stir in oatmeal flakes, berries, mandarins, and nuts. Add honey or sugar to taste.

2. Serve at room temperature in individual bowls with a dollop of yogurt.

Fondue (Melted Cheese)

The cheeses of Switzerland are legendary and many villages have their own cheese maker. For centuries, long before the Romans invaded the tiny country, the process of making cheese was already well established. Fondue, the national dish of Switzerland, shows off the excellent Swiss cheeses. Fondue, which means "to melt," is easy and fun to make and heavenly to eat. Do not use American processed cheeses because they do not melt properly.

Yield: serves 6 to 8

2 cups Gruyers cheese, **finely chopped**

2 cups Swiss cheese, finely chopped

1/2 cup all-purpose flour

3 cloves garlic, **trimmed**, peeled, **minced** or
  1 teaspoon garlic granules

2 cups pure apple juice

1 tablespoon lemon juice

1/2 teaspoon ground nutmeg

salt to taste

1 loaf Italian or French bread, with crust, cut
  into bite-sized chunks

Equipment: Medium bowl, medium saucepan with electric hot plate or electric fondue pot (use according to manufacture's directions), wooden mixing spoon, long-handled fondue forks or 12-inch skewers

1. Place Gruyere and Swiss cheeses in bowl, add flour, and toss to coat well.

2. Place garlic, apple juice, and lemon juice in saucepan or fondue pot. Heat to simmer. Add cheese, a handful at a time, stirring continually until melted. Add nutmeg and salt to taste.

3. To serve, cheese must be kept hot either over an electric hot plate or in an electric fondue pot. Each person has a plate of bread chunks. Place chunks, one-by-one, securely on fork tines or skewer and dip into pot to coat with melted cheese. Serve with an assortment of fresh fruit.

Bunder Gerstensuppe (Grison Barley Soup)

In this recipe *grison* is a special **marinated** dried beef made in Switzerland. Any dried chipped beef can be substituted.

Yield: serves 4 to 6

4 tablespoons butter or margarine

1 onion, **trimmed**, peeled, **finely chopped**

1 carrot, washed, trimmed, **diced**

1 leek washed, trimmed, **diced**

1 celery stalk trimmed, sliced

1/2 cup dried beef, **coarsely chopped**

1/2 cup smoked ham, chopped

1/2 cup barley

8 cups chicken broth, homemade or canned

1/4 teaspoon ground nutmeg

1/2 cup heavy cream

1/2 cup cooked white beans, also known as
  Great Northern beans, homemade or
  canned

salt and pepper to taste

Equipment: Large saucepan with cover or **Dutch oven**, mixing spoon

1. Melt butter or margarine in saucepan over medium heat. Add onions, carrots, leeks, and celery. Stirring occasionally, cook about 10–15 minutes or until soft. Add beef, ham, barley, and chicken broth and mix well. Bring to boil. Reduce heat to simmer, cover, and cook about 1 hour, stirring occasionally.

2. Add nutmeg, cream, cooked beans, and salt and pepper to taste. Heat through, about 3 minutes. Remove from heat.

3. Serve this hardy soup as a one-dish supper with crusty bread and cheese as the Swiss would after skiing in the Alps.

SOUTHERN EUROPE

The countries of southern Europe include Albania, Bosnia and Herzegovina, Croatia, Macedonia, Montenegro, Greece, Serbia, Slovenia, Italy, Portugal, and Spain.

The climate in the southern region tends to be warm and sunny year round. With warm temperatures, an abundant supply of olives, grapes, citrus fruits, and figs grow in this region. Most produce and barnyard animals, raised on small independent farms, are brought to open-air markets. Most people shop for fresh produce and meats on a daily or weekly basis. An abundance of livestock is raised, including pigs for meat, donkeys as beasts-of-burden, and sheep, goats, cattle, and water buffalo not only for meat, but also for milk. Similar to other countries around the world, tourism, along with migration, war, and invasion, have heavily influenced the cuisine of each country.

Fishing is another significant industry within this region with squid, eel, prawns, oysters, sardines, and fish creating unique flavors and dishes.

Albania

Albania is a small country located on the Balkan Peninsula across the Adriatic Sea from southern Italy. Although the land available for agriculture is minimal, a favorable climate and fertile soil along the coast makes farming important to the Albanians.

Wheat is a significant crop along with corn, oats, sorghum, and potatoes. Recently there has been a greater emphasis on the production of cash crops: cotton, tobacco, rice, sugar beets, sunflowers, fruits, and nuts.

Dairy products are a daily part of the Albanians' diet, especially their favorite drinks: yogurt and sour milk. Mint is a popular flavoring used in meat dishes, salads, and cold drinks.

✤ *Arapash* or *Harapash* **(Albanian Cornbread with Feta Cheese)**

There are two distinct classes within the country of Albania: the farmers and mountain-dwelling herders are in one class and then there is the urban upper class. Farmers and herders have a deep appreciation of bread. They have a tradition, in some households, where the father or male of the house starts the meal with breaking of bread before any other foods are placed on the table. It is believed the Turks, Greeks, and Italians influenced Albanian cooking.

Yield: serves 4 to 6

1 1/2 cups yellow cornmeal

12 ounces or 1 1/2 cups small-curd cottage cheese or 1 1/2 cups yogurt cheese (recipe page 308)

4 eggs, lightly beaten

1 cup green onions, **trimmed, finely chopped**

1/4 cup unsalted butter, melted

3/4 teaspoon dried thyme

1/4 teaspoon salt

4 ounces Feta cheese

Equipment: Medium mixing bowl, wooden mixing spoon or spatula, baking sheet, buttered medium tart pan with removable bottom, serving platter

1. Preheat oven to 375°F.

2. In mixing bowl, using mixing spoon or spatula, stir together cornmeal, cottage cheese or yogurt cheese, eggs, green onions, melted butter, thyme, and salt. Mix well.

3. Place prepared tart pan on baking sheet. Spoon mixture into prepared tart pan and spread evenly. Sprinkle top with feta cheese. Bake in oven until golden brown and slightly puffy, about 45 minutes. After cornbread is cooled, remove sides of tart pan and transfer to platter.

4. Serve warm, sliced into individual portions with soups or stews.

✤ *Emator* **(Puff Pastry with Nuts)**

Yield: makes 8 to 10 puffs

1/2 cup butter or margarine

1 cup water

1/2 cup sugar

1/2 teaspoon salt

1 cup all-purpose flour

4 eggs

1 teaspoon almond extract

1/2 cup **crushed** or **finely chopped** nuts: **blanched** almonds, pecans, or walnuts

Equipment: Medium saucepan, wooden mixing spoon, nonstick or greased cookie sheet, metal spatula or pancake turner

1. Preheat oven to 450°F,

2. Place butter or margarine, water, sugar, and salt in saucepan and bring to boil over medium-high heat. Add flour all at once, stirring vigorously with wooden spoon until mixture pulls away from sides of pan, about 2 minutes. Remove from heat and cool about 3–5 minutes. Add eggs, one at a time, beating after each. Mix in almond extract and nuts.

3. Drop by heaping tablespoons onto cookie sheet, about 2 inches apart, and bake about 10 minutes. Reduce heat to 325°F and continue baking an additional 10 minutes or until golden brown. Remove from baking sheet and set on platter to cool.

4. Serve emator as a snack with a glass of milk or tea.

Bosnia and Herzegovina, Croatia, Macedonia, Montenegro, Serbia, and Slovenia

A number of ethnic groups in the Balkan region were once part of Yugoslavia. Due to the breakup of Yugoslavia during the early 1990s, six countries declared their independence. The breakup of Yugoslavia was characterized by violence and war.

Even though the countries have declared independence, their cuisines, basically consisting of soups and stews, are similar and referred to as peasant food. Accompanying soups and stews are thick dark breads such as rye and pumpernickel.

This area of southern Europe is mountainous with little usable land. However, in recent years, many farmers have found it more profitable to raise and breed pigs, sheep, and poultry rather than growing cash crops.

The recipes in this section are traditional Balkan dishes eaten throughout the region.

❧ *Goulash* (Croatian Stew)

Although this stew is unique to Croatia, Goulash is very popular throughout this Slavic region.

Yield: serves 6 to 8

2 onions, **trimmed**, peeled, **coarsely chopped**

2 tablespoons vegetable oil, more as needed

1 cup water or beef broth, more as needed, homemade or canned

1 1/2 pounds beef: chuck or round, trimmed, cut into cubes

1/2 pound pork: shoulder or tenderloin, trimmed, cut into cubes

6 cups sauerkraut

2 tablespoons paprika

1 cup sour cream

Equipment: **Dutch oven** or large stock pot, wooden mixing spoon

1. In Dutch oven or stock pot, heat 2 tablespoons oil over medium-high heat. Add onions. Stirring constantly, **sauté** until soft, 2–3 minutes. Remove from heat. Using wooden spoon stir in paprika.

2. Add 1 cup water or beef broth and cubed meat. Cover and **braise** over medium heat about 1 to 1 1/2 hours or until meat is tender. Add more water or broth as needed to prevent sticking. Using wooden spoon, stir occasionally to prevent sticking.

3. Stir in sauerkraut and cook an additional 30 minutes. Remove from heat and stir in sour cream.

4. Serve warm with boiled potatoes.

❧ *Kisel Zelje* (Pickled or Fresh Cabbage Salad)

In this region, cabbage is an important staple, and often several dishes made with cabbage will be served at the same meal. During the summer months fresh cabbage salad is on every dinner table, and pickled cabbage salad is often eaten all winter long. When the following recipe is made with sauerkraut, it becomes the winter cabbage salad. When made with fresh cabbage, it is the summer salad.

Yield: serves 6 to 8

2 cups canned sauerkraut, rinsed to remove brine, drained well

or 2 cups fresh green cabbage, **trimmed**, finely **shredded**

2 cups carrots, trimmed, peeled, shredded

1 green pepper, trimmed, **cored, seeded, finely chopped**

1 onion, trimmed, peeled, finely chopped

6 tablespoons sunflower or olive oil

salt and pepper to taste

Equipment: Salad bowl, salad spoon, and fork or tongs

1. Place washed sauerkraut or fresh cabbage, carrots, green pepper, and onion in salad bowl. Add oil, toss using salad spoon and fork or tongs. Add salt and pepper to taste. (Salt is probably not needed with sauerkraut.)
2. Serve cabbage salad as a perfect starter to a Balkan meal. Serve with crusty bread.

Pogaca (Peasant Bread)

Yield: serves 6 to 8

4 cups self-rising flour

1/2 teaspoon salt

1/2 cup olive oil, more as needed

1 cup plain carbonated water (club soda)

Equipment: Large mixing bowl, mixing spoon, floured work surface, floured rolling pin, sharp knife, nonstick greased baking sheet

1. Preheat oven to 375°F.
2. Place flour, 1/2 cup oil and salt in mixing bowl. Mix well. Add carbonated water and mix to form soft dough. Transfer to floured work surface and **knead** about 5 minutes, adding more flour if necessary.
3. Using floured rolling pin, flatten dough into a 9-inch circle, about 1/2 inch thick. Sprinkle 1 tablespoon oil on each side of dough circle and place on baking sheet. Using sharp knife, make 3 1/4-inch-deep cuts, about 4 inches long, across top of bread. Bake about 45 minutes or until golden brown.
4. Serve bread warm with plenty of yogurt, cheese, or butter.

Greece

Greece, a mountainous peninsula with surrounding islands, is located between the Aegean and Ionian Seas.

Greek cooking is renowned for its simplicity and distinctive rich tastes. The waters around Greece are filled with fish, squid, prawns, octopus, and mussels, all important to the Greek diet. The most popular way to cook fish is simply with olive oil, tomatoes, and garlic. Great flocks of sheep are raised on the hilly countryside, making lamb the most important meat. Feta cheese is a farmer's cheese in Greece, white and crumbly with a distinctive salty taste. In Greece, feta cheese is spread on bread, served with the main meal, or as an appetizer with tomatoes, olives, and pickled peppers.

The hills of Greece are covered with sweet-smelling lemon trees and ancient, gnarled olive trees, making lemons, olives, and olive oil the most important ingredients in traditional Greek cooking.

Similar to other European countries, today fast-food chains are becoming popular, yet many people still prefer the traditional Greek cuisine.

Soupa Avgolemono (Lemon Soup)

Lemons are used in many dishes, and the national soup of Greece is *soups avgolemono*, lemon soup. In this recipe, the lemony broth is basic, and it is used for many different soups. Adding noodles, vegetables, lentils, or beans instead of rice creates an entirely new flavor and type of soup.

Yield: serves 4 to 6

8 cups chicken broth, homemade or canned

1/2 cup uncooked rice

1 tablespoon cornstarch

1 cup milk

2 egg yolks (refrigerate whites to use at another time)

1/2 cup lemon juice

1 tablespoon butter or margarine

2 teaspoons flat leaf parsley, **trimmed, finely chopped**

salt and pepper to taste

Equipment: Medium saucepan, mixing spoon, small bowl

1. Bring chicken broth to a boil in saucepan over high heat. Add rice, reduce heat to simmer, cover, and cook for 20 minutes, until rice is fully cooked.

2. Combine cornstarch, milk, and egg yolks in small bowl and mix well. Pour mixture into soup, mix well, and remove from heat. Stirring constantly, add lemon juice slowly to prevent soup from curdling. Add butter or margarine, parsley, and salt and pepper to taste. Mix well. Return to low heat and heat through.

3. Serve soup warm in individual bowls.

Kolokithia "Papoutsakia" (Stuffed Zucchini "Little Shoes")

This dish is popular throughout Greece. The name "little shoes" comes from how the zucchini look like little wooden shoes when stuffed.

Yield: serves 8

8 small zucchini, each about 6–8 inches long, washed, **trimmed**

1 tablespoon butter

2 green onions, trimmed, **finely chopped**

Sauce:

2 tablespoons butter

2 tablespoons flour

1 teaspoon paprika

4 tomatoes, trimmed, peeled, **seeded**, finely chopped

salt and pepper to taste
1 1/2 cups hot milk

1/2 teaspoon dry mustard

8 tablespoons feta cheese, crumbled and divided

Equipment: Medium saucepan, medium bowl of ice water, colander, melon scoop, sharp knife, small bowl, medium skillet, small saucepan, whisk, greased medium baking pan, oven mitts

1. Preheat oven to 375°F.

2. In saucepan place zucchini, cover with water, and cook for 15 minutes or until tender. Using slotted spoon remove zucchini and **shock** by placing in bowl with ice water.

3. Using a sharp knife, cut a 1-inch-wide slice, lengthwise, on each zucchini. Using melon scoop remove just enough pulp from each zucchini to retain shape. Finely chop pulp and set aside in small bowl.

4. Prepare stuffing: Melt butter in skillet over medium-high heat. Add green onions and **sauté** until soft, about 2–3 minutes. Stir in chopped zucchini pulp, paprika, tomatoes, and salt and pepper to taste. Cook until well blended and all ingredients are soft, about 3–4 minutes. Remove from heat and set aside.

5. Prepare sauce: Melt butter in saucepan over low heat. Stir in flour and blend well using whisk. Stir constantly. Remove from heat and gradually add hot milk. Stirring constantly return mixture to heat and cook until sauce is thick and smooth, about 3–5 minutes. Remove from heat and add mustard and 2 tablespoons feta cheese. Add salt and pepper to taste.

6. Using paper towels, pat dry zucchini. Arrange cut side up side-by-side in baking pan. Stuff each zucchini with tomato mixture, spoon sauce over each zucchini, and sprinkle tops with remaining feta cheese. Bake in oven, about 15–20 minutes or until golden brown on top. Remove from oven using oven mitts.

7. Serve warm as a main dish with rice or boiled potatoes.

🎋 *Salata* (Greek Salad with Dressing)

The true flavors of Greece, lemon juice, olives, olive oil, and feta cheese, are all combined in the following salad.

Yield: serves 6

6 tablespoons olive oil

juice of 1 lemon

3 cloves garlic, **trimmed**, peeled, **minced** or 1 teaspoon garlic granules

1 romaine lettuce, torn into bite-sized pieces

3 tomatoes, trimmed, cut in wedges

12 Greek black olives, in oil

1 onion, trimmed, peeled, thinly sliced

1/4 cup chopped flat leaf parsley, **finely chopped**

1/2 cup crumbled feta cheese

salt and pepper to taste

Equipment: Pint jar with tight-fitting lid, salad bowl, tongs or salad fork and spoon

1. Place oil, lemon juice, and garlic in jar. Tighten lid and shake well.

2. Place lettuce, tomatoes, olives, onion, parsley, and feta cheese in salad bowl. Pour on dressing from jar, add salt and pepper to taste, and toss gently, using tongs or salad fork and spoon.

3. Serve Greek salad at room temperature for best flavor.

🎋 *Melomacrons* (Honey Cake)

Greece has been known for its fine honey and the art of beekeeping since the second century BC. Honey is an important sweetener for desserts, cakes, and pastries. Every New Year is ushered in with the eating of honey cakes, a symbol of good luck, wealth, and health for the coming year. In a household with children, it is customary to insert one or two new drachmas (Greek coins) into the cake just before it is baked. The cake is not cut until midnight, when the New Year starts. Children finding the coins will have extra good luck, unless by mistake they should swallow one; then they are not so lucky.

Yield: makes 8 to 10 pieces

3 eggs

1 cup sugar

1 cup warm honey

1/4 cup vegetable oil

2 teaspoons baking powder

1 teaspoon baking soda

3 cups flour

1/4 teaspoon ground ginger

1/4 teaspoon ground cinnamon

1/4 teaspoon ground cloves

1 cup strong brewed tea, cold

Equipment: Large mixing bowl, mixing spoon or electric mixer, medium mixing bowl, **whisk**, flour **sifter**, nonstick or greased 9″ × 5″ loaf pan or nonstick or greased 9-inch **Bundt pan**, oven mitts

1. Preheat oven to 350°F. Place oven shelf on lowest brackets.

2. Place eggs, sugar, honey, and oil in large mixing bowl. Using spoon or electric mixer, mix until well blended.

3. **Sift** baking powder, baking soda, flour, ginger, cinnamon, and cloves into medium mixing bowl.

4. Mixing egg mixture constantly, add flour mixture alternately with tea until batter is lump-free and smooth.

5. Pour batter into prepared loaf or bunt pan. Bake on bottom shelf in oven about 50–60 minutes or until toothpick inserted into center of cake comes out clean. Remove from oven using oven mitts.

6. Serve honey cake with jam or fruit; it is usually not frosted.

Italy

Italy's culinary history can be traced back more than 2,000 years to the ancient civilization of Rome. With the fall of the Roman Empire came the decline of fancy cooking and feasting. It was not long before the interest in cooking was revived in Italy during the Renaissance along with art, literature, and music. Italy consists of 20 regions and for centuries did not exist as the nation we now know. After hundreds of years of regional differences, even erupting into violent wars, in 1861 Italy became a united country. Strong regional pride still exists, however, and Italians have one word for it, "*campanilismo*," meaning, "my region is the best." Even today each region jealously clings to its own culinary heritage, believing it is the best. Common ingredients in the north are butter and *risotto* (rice-like grain), while to the south, olive oil and tomatoes are preferred.

Fresh fruits and vegetables from Italy make their way to the rest of Europe, especially during the winter when fresh produce is not available in colder countries.

Cheeses are a very important part of Italian life and are a national product. There are hundreds of wonderful cheeses made not only from cows' milk but also from the milk of goats, ewes, and water buffalo. The most highly prized cheese is made from the milk of water buffalo, called *"mozzarella di buffalo."* The full name is stamped on the rind, and its production and distribution are tightly controlled by the government. Usually an Italian meal ends with an assortment of fresh fruits and cheeses.

Even today, with the increased popularity of fast food and tourism, when it comes to food, Italians remain true to their heritage.

Pasta e Fagiolio (Pasta and Bean Soup)

If Italy has a national soup it would be a tie between *minestrone* and *pasta e fagioli* made with noodles and beans.

Yield: serves 6 to 8

5 cups water

1 1/2 cups dried white beans: navy, baby lima, or northern

1 onion, **trimmed**, peeled, **coarsely chopped**

2 cups canned Italian-style tomatoes, with juice

1 cup celery, trimmed, **finely chopped**

1 cup carrots, trimmed, peeled, finely chopped

3 cloves garlic, trimmed, peeled, coarsely chopped, or 1 teaspoon garlic granules

1/2 pound cooked smoked ham, chopped

3 bay leaves

1/2 cup uncooked macaroni (shells, bows, or elbow shapes)

salt and pepper to taste

1/2 cup grated Parmesan cheese for garnish

Equipment: Large saucepan with cover or **Dutch oven**, mixing spoon

1. Place water and beans in saucepan or Dutch oven. Bring to a boil over high heat and continue to boil about 3–5 minutes. Remove from heat. Cover and set aside about 1 hour.

2. Add onion, tomatoes, celery, carrots, garlic, smoked ham, and bay leaves. Mix well. Return to boil over high heat. Reduce heat to simmer, cover, and cook until beans are tender, about 1 1/2 hours. Stir frequently.

3. Add macaroni and mix well. Cover and continue simmering until macaroni is tender, about 12 minutes. Remove and discard bay leaves before serving.

4. Serve hot soup in individual bowls with a side dish of Parmesan cheese for the guests to sprinkle into their soup. Serve crusty bread for sopping.

❧ *Rappini* (Sautéed Broccoli Rabe)

This vegetable is popular in both Italian and Asian cuisines. The vegetable itself has several names including *broccoli rabe* or *broccoli rape*, *rapini* or *rappini*, Italian turnip, or flowering Chinese cabbage. In preparing rappini, since the stalks are edible, it is essential to trim the stems at the base; use stock whole or cut into bite-sized pieces. **Blanch** in salted water and **shock** in ice water before cooking to remove some of the bitterness.

Yield: serves 4 to 6

2 tablespoons olive oil

1 red onion, **trimmed**, peeled, thinly sliced

2 cloves garlic, trimmed, peeled, **minced**

1 pound *rappini* or broccoli rabe, trimmed, **blanched, shocked, coarsely chopped**

1/4 cup chicken or vegetable broth homemade or canned

juice of 1/2 lemon

1/4 cup Italian green or black olives, pitted, sliced

1/2 cup cherry or grape tomatoes, rinsed, sliced in half

salt and fresh cracked black pepper, to taste

red pepper flakes, to taste

1/4 cup aged cheese, grated, such as Parmigiano Reggiano or Pecorino (optional)

Equipment: Large skillet with cover, wooden mixing spoon

1. Heat olive oil in skillet over medium-high heat. Stir in onion and cook until soft, about 2–3 minutes. Stir in garlic and **sauté** until both are golden brown, about 2–3 minutes. Stir constantly.

2. Reduce heat to medium. Add rappini and chicken or vegetable broth, cover, and stirring frequently, simmer until rappini is tender, about 6–8 minutes.

3. Uncover and cook until most liquid is evaporated. Pour lemon juice over rappini and stir in olives. Season with salt, black pepper, and red pepper to taste. Sprinkle cheese on top and melt.

4. Serve hot as side dish with pasta and meat or fish of choice.

❧ *Tiramisu* (Ladyfinger Icebox Cake)

Yield: serves 8 to 10

1 pound Mascarpone cheese (available at most supermarkets)

2 teaspoons hazelnut extract

1/4 cup sugar

1 cup heavy whipping cream

1 cup espresso or very strong black coffee, room temperature

2/3 cup bittersweet chocolate, shaved into small pieces

24 Italian ladyfingers

Equipment: 2 large mixing bowls, mixing spoon, electric mixer or whisk, 8″ × 8″ serving dish at least 2 inches deep, pastry brush

1. In mixing bowl, using mixing spoon, combine Mascarpone cheese, hazelnut extract, and sugar and mix well.

2. In separate bowl using electric mixer or whisk, whip cream until soft peaks form.

3. Gently **fold** Mascarpone mixture into whipped cream.

4. In serving dish layer 1/2 ladyfingers tightly on bottom of 8″ × 8″ pan. Using pastry brush, evenly brush half of espresso or strong coffee over ladyfingers. Spread half Mascarpone mixture on top of ladyfingers. Sprinkle half of shaved chocolate on top.

5. Layer remaining ladyfingers on top. Using pastry brush evenly coat ladyfingers with remaining espresso or strong coffee. Layer with remaining Mascarpone mixture and smooth using back of wooden spoon or spatula. Sprinkle remaining chocolate over top.

6. Cover with plastic wrap and store in refrigerator overnight.

7. Serve cut individual slices as a dessert with espresso or glass of milk.

Pastas and Sauces

When people think of Italian cooking, they think of pastas and sauces. All pastas regardless of shape or name are basically the same; they are simply made from a dough flour and water; sometimes eggs are added. There are many kinds of pastas all named after what they look like, such as ribbons, thimbles, butterflies, bows, angel hair. There are over 200 different noodle shapes and each with a different name. **Semolina,** a flour made from **durum wheat,** is the very best flour for pasta making. It is a high-protein, hard-wheat grain. Noodles made from semolina flour hold their shape, staying **al dente** longer when properly cooked. Cooked pasta should be firm when you bite into it, not soft and mushy. When cooking pasta it is best to taste from time to time while cooking to make sure it is just right. Remove from heat and drain at once; do not run cold water over pasta (starch in pasta allows sauce to thicken and cling to pasta); instead, add pasta to prepared sauce and serve immediately. Professional Italian chefs often add pasta to the sauce instead of adding sauce to the pasta. Note: cooking time will vary according to pasta thickness and whether it is dry, frozen, or freshly made. Freshly made pastas require less cooking time than dried pastas.

Sauces, the distinguishing factor in a dish, get their names from a variety of sources: a town, a region, a chef who first created it, a primary ingredient in the recipe, a fantasy, or a historical legend. Sauces distinguish dishes one region from another. For instance, in the Emilia-Romagna region, the local sauce is *ragu*, a sauce made with meat. In the Rome-Latium region, it is tomatoes and basil; in Lombardy, it is butter and the herb sage. The following are recipes for sauces to pour over pastas.

✣ **Primavera Sauce (Fresh Vegetable Pasta Sauce)**

Primava means "spring style" and the sauce is red made with any combination of vegetables.

Yield: serves 2 to 4

3 tablespoons olive oil

3 clove fresh garlic, **trimmed**, peeled, **minced** or 1 teaspoon garlic granules

3 tablespoons butter or margarine

1 cup zucchini, fresh or frozen, thawed, trimmed, thinly sliced

1 cup broccoli, fresh or frozen, thawed, **coarsely chopped**

1 cup onion, trimmed, peeled, coarsely chopped

2 green peppers, trimmed, **cored, seeded**, cut into strips

2 cups tomato sauce, homemade or canned

1/2 cup tomato paste

salt, pepper, and red pepper flakes to taste

1 pound pasta (cooked according to directions on package, keep warm); a few drops of oil tossed with pasta to keep it from sticking together

Parmesan cheese, grated, for garnish

Equipment: Large skillet, wooden mixing spoon, 2 forks

1. Heat oil in skillet over medium heat. Add garlic and **sauté** about 2 minutes. Increase heat to medium-high. Add butter or margarine, zucchini, broccoli, onions, and green peppers. Stir frequently and cook about 6 minutes or until vegetables are cooked through but still crisp.

2. Add tomato sauce and paste and mix well. Heat through, about 3 minutes. Add salt, pepper, and red pepper to taste.

3. Before serving add pasta to warm sauce in skillet. Mix thoroughly. With a fork in each hand, toss pasta to coat with sauce. Sprinkle with Parmesan cheese. Transfer to serving bowl and serve with extra cheese, extra red pepper flakes, green salad, and warm garlic bread.

✣ *Salsa al Limone* **(Lemon Crème Sauce for Pasta)**

Italian sauces are very easy to make and uncomplicated. This cream sauce is from the Amalfi coastal region of Italy.

Yield: serves 2 to 4

1 cup heavy cream

1/2 cup half-and-half

2 teaspoons dried red pepper flakes, more or less to taste

2 tablespoons lemon **zest**

1 pound pasta (cooked according to directions on package, keep warm); a few drops of oil

tossed with pasta to keep it from sticking together

1 cup Parmesan cheese, grated

1/2 cup fresh basil, **finely chopped**

salt and pepper to taste

Equipment: Medium saucepan, mixing spoon, large bowl, 2 forks

1. Place cream, half-and-half, 1 teaspoon red pepper flakes, and lemon rind in saucepan and cook over medium-low heat about 20 minutes. Stir frequently until liquid is slightly thick and reduced to about 1 cup.

2. Place sauce in pasta bowl and add pasta. With fork in each hand, toss pasta with and up-and-down rotating motion over the bowl, until pasta is completely covered with sauce. Sprinkle in 1/2 cup Parmesan cheese, basil, and salt and pepper to taste and continue to toss and coat pasta. Sprinkle top with remaining cheese, remaining red pepper flakes, more or less to taste, basil, and salt and pepper to taste.

3. Serve with extra cheese, red pepper flakes, green salad, and warm garlic bread.

Fettuccine Alfredo (Fettuccine Pasta with Creamy White Sauce)

Alfredo is a creamy white sauce which distinguishes it from the well-known Italian red sauce.

Yield: serves 2 to 4

1 cup butter or margarine at room temperature

1/2 cup heavy cream

1/2 cup grated Parmesan cheese

1 pound pasta (such as fettuccine; cooked according to directions on package); time the cooking so it can be drained and mixed with the sauce while still very hot

salt and pepper and ground nutmeg to taste

Equipment: Large heat-proof serving bowl, medium mixing bowl, wooden mixing spoon, oven mitts, heat-proof work surface, 2 forks

1. Warm serving bowl in the oven until ready to use.

2. Place butter or margarine in mixing bowl, and, using wooden spoon, beat until light and fluffy. Add cream, a little at a time, and mix until well blended. Add cheese by tablespoon, beating well after each addition.

3. Using oven mitts, remove heated serving bowl from oven and place on heat-proof work surface. Place drained cooked pasta in warm bowl and add cheese mixture. With fork in each hand, toss pasta in an up-and-down rotating motion over the bowl until pasta is well coated with sauce. Add salt, pepper, and nutmeg to taste and continue to toss and coat pasta.

4. Serve at once while very hot on individual plates with a side dish of extra grated cheese. Adding green salad with Italian dressing and warm garlic bread makes a wonderful meal.

Pana Untata (Garlic Bread)

Yield: serves 6 to 8

1 loaf French or Italian bread, split in half lengthwise

1/2 to 1 cup olive oil, melted butter, or melted margarine

3 cloves garlic, **trimmed**, peeled, **minced** or 1 teaspoon garlic granules

salt and pepper to taste

1/2 cup grated Parmesan cheese

Equipment: Bread knife, nonstick or greased baking sheet, small bowl, pastry brush or spoon

1. Preheat oven to 375°F.
2. Place both halves of bread on a baking sheet with cut sides up.
3. Place oil, butter, or margarine in a bowl, add garlic, and mix well. Using either pastry brush or spoon, spread mixture over cut side of bread. Sprinkle with salt, pepper, and cheese.
4. Just before serving, place in oven for 15 minutes or until top is golden and bread is heated through.
5. To serve bread hot, wrap in napkin or aluminum foil to keep warm, place in basket or on platter.

Portugal

Portugal is bordered by Spain to the east and the Atlantic Ocean to the west. The Portuguese have a long history of adopting culinary traditions from other countries. Centuries ago, when the route to India was discovered, many exotic spices from the Far East were brought to Europe by Portuguese sailing ships. The variety of spices include coriander, pepper, ginger, curry, saffron, and paprika. *Piri piri* (recipe page 16)

is a blend of spices unique to Portugal cooking. Portugal has a rich fishing industry with an abundance of oysters, eel, squids, prawns, crabs, cod, and sardines. The Portuguese like sardines, often dried or fresh, not out of the can as most people are accustomed to eating them.

Portugal is a country of hardy soups, stews, and casseroles that vary from region to region, day to day, and cook to cook. What the fishermen catch, what is at the market, in the garden, or on the pantry shelf, or how the cook is feeling can determine what will be tossed in the pot. Combining fish and seafood with meat in the same casserole or stew is traditional to Portuguese and Spanish cooking. Garlic is added with a "heavy hand," and no dish is complete without it.

❧ *Portuguese Arroz de Marisco* (Portuguese Seafood Stew with Rice)

This recipe calls for squid, which is also known as *calamari*. Calamari must be rinsed thoroughly inside and out then sliced into 1/4- to 1/2-inch rings.

Yield: serves 6 to 8

2 tablespoons olive oil, more as needed

1 onion, **trimmed**, peeled, **finely chopped**

4 cloves garlic, trimmed, peeled, finely chopped

1 pound shrimp, peeled, **deveined**

1/2 pound cod, bass, or white fish, boned, cut into 1-inch cubes

1/2 pound squid, rinsed, cut into 1/2- to 1/4-inch rings

2 16-ounce cans stewed tomatoes

2 cups water or vegetable broth homemade or canned

1 teaspoon paprika

1 teaspoon coriander

3 bay leaves

1 tablespoon parsley

salt and pepper

cayenne pepper, to taste

2 cups white rice, cooked (cooked according to directions on package), for serving

Equipment: Large stock pot with cover, wooden mixing spoon, fork

1. Heat 2 tablespoons oil in stock pot over medium-high heat. Add onions and garlic. Stirring constantly fry until soft, about 2–3 minutes.

2. Add tomatoes, water or vegetable broth, paprika, coriander, and bay leaves and bring to boil. Stir in seafood and return to boil. Reduce heat to simmer, cover, and cook, about 10–15 minutes or until fish flakes easily with a fork. Remove and discard bay leaves. Add salt, black pepper, and cayenne pepper to taste.

3. Serve warm in soup bowls. Mix rice with seafood or ladle seafood over rice and garnish with parsley.

🎋 *Pao* (Country Bread)

No Portuguese meal is complete without bread. In some Portuguese villages housewives still bring their freshly shaped loaves of bread to communal brick ovens to bake. The bread usually consists of only four ingredients. It is chewy and thick crusted because of vigorous hand **kneading** and brick-oven baking with intense steam heat. Not having a brick oven, the following cooking tip for crusty bread works very well in any household oven. Before preheating the oven, place an oven-safe pan of water (about 2 quarts) on the bottom shelf.

Yield: 2 round (8-inch) loaves

3 packages active dry yeast (each envelope 1/4 ounce)

1/2 cup lukewarm water (105°F–115°F), more as needed

1 cup **sifted** all-purpose flour, more as needed

2 teaspoons salt

Equipment: Large mixing bowl, wooden spoon, kitchen towel, floured work surface, 2 oiled medium round cake pans, roasting pan with 2 quarts water for steaming, oven mitts

1. Combine yeast with 1/2 cup warm water and 1 cup flour in large bowl. Beat with wooden spoon until smooth. Cover bowl with towel and set in warm place. Let dough rise until spongy and doubled in bulk, about 25–35 minutes.

2. Stir yeast mixture down. Add 1 cup water, salt, and 6 cups flour, 1 cup at a time, making a stiff but workable dough. Transfer to floured work surface and **knead** vigorously for 5 minutes or until smooth and elastic. Shape dough into ball and place in warm, lightly greased bowl. Cover with towel, set in warm place, and let rise until double in bulk, about 1 hour.

3. Place dough on floured work surface and **punch down**. Knead for 5 minutes. Divide dough into two pieces, knead each about 3 minutes and shape into balls. Place each ball in cake pan and dust top lightly with flour. Cover with towel and set in warm place to rise until double in size, about 45–50 minutes.

4. Place 2 quarts water in roasting pan and place in oven on bottom shelf for steaming.

5. Preheat oven to 450°F.

6. When oven is hot and steamy, place pans of bread on middle shelf, using oven mitts to protect hands. Bake for 15 minutes, then lower heat to 400°F. Bake bread, about 20–30 minutes or until browned and hollow sounding when tapped.

7. Serve pao warm with butter as an accompaniment to any meal.

Spain

In a country where being thin was once a sign of poverty, every meal except breakfast is robust and filling. Spanish food is colorful but not too spicy using garlic, paprika, olives, and olive oil as seasonings. Favorite main course foods are seafood, in particular salted cod, smoked sausages, and **stewed** meat. Rice, beans, and fresh produce are also served in abundance. Spanish wine is well received around the world, and wine grapes are an important crop.

History has played a significant role in the development of food in Spain. The occupation of the country from 711 AD to 1492 by the Moors, who were Muslims from northwestern Africa, brought great agricultural treasures and methods to the Iberian Peninsula. For example, the Moors introduced advanced irrigation techniques, which made increased agricultural production possible. They also brought rice, figs, almonds, citrus fruits, peaches, and bananas and planted them in Spain. The Muslim Moors introduced the spices of the East to Spain, including cumin and aniseed, which are still used extensively today. In turn, the Spanish Conquistadors are responsible for introducing spices of the Far East to the Americas while bringing back peppers, potatoes, tomatoes, and chocolate to all of Europe.

Gazpacho (Grilled Tomato Soup with Vegetables)

For centuries, the very poorest Spanish peasants ate "bread and water" soup called *gazpacho*. Today it is world famous and considered very classy, eaten by rich and poor alike. The old, traditional gazpacho is made with stale bread soaked in olive oil and tomato juice. Over the years the recipe has changed somewhat, with the same delicious results. A quick and easy way to make gazpacho is to combine 1 cup fresh salsa (available at all supermarkets) with 2 cups tomato juice, V8, or Bloody Mary mix, mix well, chill, and serve as directed here.

Yield: serves 4 to 6

1/2 cup tomato **trimmed**, peeled, **finely chopped**

1/2 cup cucumber, trimmed, peeled, finely chopped

1/2 cup green pepper, trimmed, **cored, seeded,** finely chopped

1/2 cup celery, trimmed, finely chopped

2 cloves garlic, trimmed, peeled, **minced** or 1/2 teaspoon garlic granules

1 tablespoon apple cider vinegar

1 tablespoon olive oil

4 cups tomato juice

salt and pepper to taste

4 green onions, trimmed, finely chopped, for garnish

Equipment: 1/2-gallon jar or container with tight-fitting cover

1. Place tomato, cucumber, green pepper, celery, garlic, vinegar, oil, tomato juice, and salt and pepper to taste in jar. Cover tightly and shake well. Refrigerate until ready to serve.

2. When ready to serve, shake well and pour into individual bowls, making sure chopped vegetables are in each bowl. Sprinkle each serving with green onions.

3. Serve gazpacho very cold. Small dishes of chopped **hard-cooked eggs** and croutons can be served and sprinkled in the soup for added flavor.

Croquetas (Ham Croquets)

Croquetas are an appetizer, or as the Spanish call them, *tapas*. Dinner is not eaten until very late, usually between 9 and 11 P.M. Tapas are savory dishes, served between work and dinner.
CAUTION: HOT OIL IS USED

Yield: serves 4

2 tablespoons olive oil, more as needed

4 tablespoons flour

1 cup milk

1 teaspoon ground nutmeg

1/2 pound precooked ham, ground or **minced**

1 egg

2 cups breadcrumbs, more as needed

salt to taste

Equipment: Medium skillet, wooden mixing spoon, plate, 2 small soup bowls, fork or whisk, baking sheet covered with paper towels, deep fryer or medium heavy-bottomed saucepan, metal slotted spoon or metal tongs

1. In skillet heat 2 tablespoons oil over medium-high heat. When oil bubbles around edge of pan remove from heat. Using wooden spoon stir in flour until mixture becomes smooth and well mixed.

2. Return pan to medium heat and slowly stir in milk. Stir constantly until mixture is smooth. Stir in nutmeg and ham. Stirring constantly, cook until mixture is thickened, about 2–3 minutes. Set aside to cool.

3. When mixture is cool, using clean hands, form egg-shaped croquets. Place side-by-side on plate.

4. Beat egg in small bowl, using fork or whisk. Place breadcrumbs in second small bowl. Place side-by-side on work surface.

5. Dip croquets, one at a time, into beaten egg. Coat well and then roll in breadcrumbs to cover. Press breadcrumbs into croquet. Return to plate and place side-by-side.

6. Prepare to deep fry: ADULT SUPERVISION REQUIRED. Have ready several layers of paper towels on a baking sheet. Fill deep fryer with oil according to manufacturer's directions or fill a medium heavy-bottomed saucepan with about 3 inches of vegetable oil. Heat oil to reach 375°F on deep-fryer thermometer or place the handle of a wooden spoon in the oil; if small bubbles appear around surface, oil is ready for frying.

7. Fry croquets one at a time: Carefully slip one into oil and using metal spatula or metal tongs, press down to keep submerged for about 30 seconds. When golden brown or when croquet floats to surface, using metal spatula or metal tongs remove and place on paper towel to drain. Keep warm until ready to serve.

8. Serve warm as tapas.

EASTERN EUROPE

Eastern Europe includes Armenia, Belarus, Bulgaria, Czech Republic, Georgia, Hungary, Moldova, Poland, Romania, Russia, Slovakia, and Ukraine.

After decades of Soviet dictatorship and influence, Eastern Europe has been recovering from political turmoil, an unproductive economy, and environmental damage, most notably from an explosion at the Chernobyl Nuclear Power plant in 1986. To this day, the Eastern European countries are working to decontaminate the land, to improve their economy, increase tourism, and encourage nations to join the established European Union.

The countries within Eastern Europe have varied climates due to terrain and geographical location, affecting what grows within each country. The basis of the peasant food in Eastern European countries stems from the rural population living in a harsh climate. Hardy soups and stews are made with dried and stored produce and/or seasonal vegetables. To the north, cold-weather crops such as potatoes, sugar beets, rye, oats, cabbage, and hardy wheat are grown. To the south a greater variety of crops requiring more sunlight is possible: fruit trees, corn, sunflower seeds, soybeans, and grapes. Throughout the region, goats, cattle, chickens, sheep, and pigs are the most popular livestock raised. Hunting wild game is still an important source of food.

In the cities most people purchase produce and meat at their local markets, while in small provincial villages most people grow their own vegetables in small hothouse gardens and perhaps raise a cow, pig, and a few chickens for their own milk, meat, and eggs. The cuisine of Eastern Europe is robust and filling.

Armenia and Georgia

Armenia and Georgia are neighboring countries situated between the Black Sea and the Caspian Sea. The terrain is mostly mountainous, where the weather is hot in the summer and extremely cold in the winters. The cuisine of this region is strongly influenced by flavors of the Middle East, Russia, and Turkey. The favorite foods are lamb, eggplant, yogurt, and a favorite bread called *lavash*. The most commonly used spices are saffron, cinnamon, fresh mint, and coriander.

Vosp (Red Lentil Soup)

It is believed lentils were brought to Armenia by merchants of the "Silk Road," a vast network of trade routes established by the Han Dynasty in 114 BC. Lentils along with spices and extravagant luxury goods such as silk, rubies, pearls, satins, and diamonds were traded along this 5,000-mile route.

Yield: serves 4 to 6

1 cup red lentils, rinsed

1/2 cup coarse milled bulgur (bulghour) (available at Middle Eastern food markets and supermarkets)

8 cups beef or vegetarian broth, homemade or canned

1/2 cup parsley, **trimmed, finely chopped**

1 teaspoon fresh mint leaves, trimmed, finely chopped

1/2 teaspoon dried sweet basil

2 tablespoons butter

1 onion, trimmed, peeled, finely chopped

Equipment: Large stock pot or saucepan with cover, wooden mixing spoon, medium skillet

1. In large stock pot or saucepan, boil broth over medium-high heat. Add lentils, bulgur, parsley, mint leaves, and sweet basil. Cover and simmer 30–45 minutes or until lentils and bulgur are tender. Stir occasionally.

2. Melt butter in skillet over medium-high heat. Add onions and **sauté** about 2–3 minutes or until golden. Stir frequently. Add onions to soup mixture about 5–10 minutes before serving. Add salt and pepper to taste and mix well.

3. Serve warm with lavash (recipe page 293).

Chanakhi (Braised Lamb Casserole)

Yield: serves 4 to 6

1 pound boneless lamb, cut into 2-inch cubes

1 1/2 pounds potatoes, washed, **trimmed, coarsely chopped**

1/2 pound tomatoes, trimmed, coarsely chopped

3/4 to 1 pound eggplant, trimmed, peeled, coarsely chopped

1/2 pound string beans, trimmed or frozen, thawed

1 onion, trimmed, peeled, **finely chopped**

salt and pepper to taste

1 tablespoon, fresh parsley or fresh coriander, finely chopped or 1 teaspoon dried

2 cups water

Equipment: Medium greased or nonstick baking casserole with cover, oven mitts, hot pad or trivet

1. Preheat oven to 350°F.

2. Place lamb, tomatoes, eggplant, string beans, onions, and parsley or coriander into casserole and gently toss to mix. Season with salt and pepper to taste. Add water, cover, and bake about 1 1/2 to 2 hours or until meat is tender and cooked through.

3. To serve, carefully place casserole on hot pad or trivet in center of table. Serve with lavash or dark bread such as rye or pumpernickel

Apricot Candy

Yield: serves 8 to 10

2 pounds dried apricots, **minced**

1 cup water

blanched whole, almonds as needed

1 cup sugar, more as needed

butter or margarine, as needed

Equipment: Medium-large saucepan, wooden mixing spoon, baking sheet covered with wax paper, small bowl, plastic wrap

1. Place apricots and water into saucepan and bring to boil. Reduce to simmer and cook until apricot mixture thickens. Stir frequently. Using wooden mixing spoon, stir sugar into apricots and simmer an additional 10–15 minutes. Remove from heat and set aside to cool.

2. Have ready 1 cup sugar in small bowl. Using buttered hands (to prevent sticking) form apricot mixture into ping-pong-sized balls. Between palms of hands flatten each ball into 1/2-inch-thick rounds. Set side-by-side on baking sheet. Place an almond in center of each ball. Dip in sugar to coat all sides. Return to baking sheet, cover with plastic wrap, and refrigerate until ready serve.

3. Serve as dessert treat or midday snack.

Bulgaria

The terrain of Bulgaria is very diverse with plains, plateaus, hills, mountains, gorges, and deep river valleys. Due to fertile soil and excellent weather, Bulgarians are able to grow a variety of fruits, vegetables, and herbs.

The Turks to the southeast of Bulgaria invaded, conquered, and occupied the country for 500 years. The dietary habits of the Muslim-Turkish people were enforced; thus, Bulgarian foods reflect this influence.

Bulgarians are credited with being the first to produce yogurt, which they made from the milk of their sheep.

Kisselo Mleka (Homemade Yogurt)

Throughout many east European and Middle Eastern countries yogurt is an important part of the daily diet. It is used in and on everything from soups to desserts to cooling drinks. Yogurt is very easy to make, needing no complicated equipment. A **candy thermometer** (available at most supermarkets) is helpful for checking the temperature of the milk. If the milk is too hot, the culture will die, and if it is too cold, nothing will happen. It takes a spoon of "starter" yogurt for each pint of milk. The spoon of starter must come from fresh live yogurt culture called **acidophilus**. Acidophilus is available at most supermarkets and all health food stores. Once the fresh warm milk begins to ferment, with the help of the starter, it becomes the "culture." Each time a fresh batch of yogurt is made, set aside a spoonful to become the starter for the following batch. This recipe would be fun to do at home or as a class project.

Yield: about 2 cups

2 cups whole milk

2 tablespoons fresh commercial live yogurt starter

Equipment: Medium heavy-bottomed saucepan, mixing spoon, **candy thermometer**, large heat-proof glass or enamel bowl with cover, bath towel with heating pad

1. Place milk in saucepan and bring to boil over high heat (for smooth yogurt, the milk must come to a boil.) When milk froths and starts to boil over, quickly remove pan from heat. Reduce to medium heat and return pan to heat for 2 minutes more. Remove from heat and set pan on heat-proof work surface.

2. Milk must cool down to between 95°F and 110°F. This cooling takes about 1 hour at room temperature. Use candy thermometer to check. With spoon, carefully skim off any skin that forms on milk.

3. Transfer 1 cup warm milk to bowl, add 1 tablespoon yogurt starter, and mix to blend. Add remaining 1 cup milk and mix well. Cover and wrap bowl in bath towel, place on heating pad and set heat on low. Leave undisturbed about 10 hours. When set, refrigerate 4 hours before using.

4. Serve yogurt on salads, in recipes, or on desserts or add fresh fruit and eat as a healthy snack.

✣ *Lassi* (Iced Yogurt Beverage)

Yield: 2 drinks

1 cup plain yogurt

1 cup water

2 cups crushed ice

1 1/2 tablespoons sugar or honey

1/4 teaspoon **rose water** (available at most supermarkets and Middle Eastern markets)

sprig of mint for garnish

Equipment: small bowl, mixing spoon, tall glass for serving

1. Place yogurt and water in bowl and mix well.

2. Fill each glass with about 1 cup of ice.

3. Add yogurt, sugar or honey, and rosewater and mix well. Garnish each glass with sprig of mint.

4. Serve lassi as a refreshing and nourishing drink on a hot day. This same drink, made with mangoes, is popular in India.

Tarator Soup (Walnut Yogurt Soup)

Yield: serves 6

1/2 cup walnuts, **finely chopped**

6 cloves garlic, **trimmed**, peeled, finely chopped or 2 teaspoons garlic granules

5 teaspoons olive oil

5 cups yogurt

1 medium cucumber, trimmed, peeled, finely chopped

salt and pepper to taste

1/2 cup fresh mint or fresh parsley, trimmed, finely chopped, for garnish

Equipment: Electric blender, large bowl with cover, rubber spatula, mixing spoon, ladle or large spoon

1. Using blender, mix walnuts with garlic. Add olive oil, a little at a time, making a smooth paste.
2. Transfer to large bowl, using spatula to scrape out mixture. Add yogurt, cucumber, and salt and pepper to taste; mix well. Cover and refrigerate.
3. Serve cold. Mix well and ladle into individual bowls and sprinkle each with mint or parsley.

Czech Republic and Slovakia

In 2003 Czechoslovakia split, forming two countries: the Czech Republic and Slovakia. Prior to Communist rule, Czechs and Slovaks were known as some of the finest cooks in Europe. Before World War II, they were frequently hired to manage kitchens in many wealthy homes in surrounding countries.

One pastry that has been exported by immigrating Czechs and Slovaks is *kolaches* or *kolachkes* (recipe page 224). Many Czech and Slovak communities in the United States have kolache festivals and contests to find the best kolache makers. Popular fillings are meat, cheeses, vegetables and sweetmeats. Kolaches can be made either with open tops or folded over and sealed.

Zemakove Placky (Potato Pancakes)

Yield: serves 4 to 6

4 cups peeled, raw, grated potatoes, well drained

2 eggs, well beaten

1 tablespoon flour

1/4 teaspoon baking powder

salt and pepper to taste

2 tablespoons butter or margarine, more as needed

applesauce, as needed, for garnish

sour cream, as needed, for garnish

Equipment: Medium mixing bowl, mixing spoon, large skillet or griddle, pancake turner or metal spatula, baking sheet

1. Preheat oven to 150°F.

2. Place drained potatoes and eggs in mixing bowl and blend well. Add flour, baking powder, and salt and pepper to taste.

3. Melt 2 tablespoons butter or margarine in skillet or on griddle over medium-high heat. Drop mixture by tablespoonfuls onto skillet and spread with back of spoon, making each pancake about 4 inches across. Brown on both sides. Transfer fried pancakes to baking sheet and keep in warm oven until ready to serve. Repeat using all the mixture and adding more butter or margarine if necessary to the pan.

4. Serve pancakes with applesauce and sour cream for added flavor.

Vareniky (Stuffed Dumplings)

Yield: serves 4 to 6

Filling:

2 tablespoons vegetable oil

1 onion, **trimmed**, peeled, **finely chopped**

1 pound lean ground beef

Dough:

1 cup flour, more as needed

1 cup semolina

2 tablespoons fresh parsley, finely chopped

1/2 teaspoon marjoram

salt and freshly ground pepper to taste

1/8 teaspoon baking powder

1 egg

1/2 cup milk, more as needed

water as needed

1/2 cup butter, melted, more as needed   2 lemons, sliced into wedges

Equipment: large skillet, wooden mixing spoon, large bowl, spatula, floured work surface, floured rolling pin, sharp knife or pizza cutter, large saucepan, slotted spoon, covered serving dish

1. *Filling*: In skillet heat oil over medium-high heat. Add onions. Stirring constantly, **sauté** about 2–3 minutes or until golden. Stir in ground beef and brown about 4–6 minutes. Stir frequently. Remove from heat, add parsley, marjoram, and salt and pepper to taste. Mix well and set aside.

2. *Dough*: In large mixing bowl mix together flour, semolina, and baking powder. Make small well in center of flour mixture. Add egg and 1/2 cup milk. Using mixing spoon or clean hands, gradually combine flour with milk-egg mixture. Continue working in flour, adding more milk if needed. Mix until dough is firm.

3. Transfer dough to floured work surface and knead about 2–3 minutes. Using rolling pin, roll out until dough is about 1/8 inch thick. Using sharp knife or pizza cutter, cut dough into 2″ × 2″ squares.

4. Spoon tablespoon of filling mixture into center of each square of dough. Fold dumpling in half to form triangle. Pinch sides to seal in filling mixture.

5. In large saucepan, fill about 2/3 full with water and add 2 teaspoons salt. Over high heat, bring water to boil, reduce heat to simmer, and add dumplings a few at a time. Boil about 5–7 minutes or until tender. (Dumplings will rise to the surface when done.) Remove with slotted spoon and place in serving dish with cover. Pour melted butter over top of each dumpling.

6. Serve warm. Garnish with lemon wedges and a side of boiled potatoes.

Hungary

Hungary is located on a flat, fertile plain. Hungarians are originally nomadic Magyars who arrived and settled in this region around 896 AD. They brought with them *bogrács*, a large cauldron used for cooking food over an open fire. Bogrács, still found in many households today, are used to make traditional Hungarian dishes including *goulash*, also known as *Pörkölt*.

During the sixteenth and seventeenth centuries when Turks invaded Hungary, they introduced the red pepper plant from which they made paprika. The use of paprika quickly became popular among shepherds, peasants, and aristocrats alike. This red powder is made from grinding dried sweet red pepper, ranging in color from vibrant orange-red to a deep red. Hungarian paprika, available throughout the world, has a sweet yet hot flavor.

❧ *Bogracs Gulyas* (Hungarian Goulash)

Goulash is Hungary's most famous national dish; it can be either a stew or a soup. Originally cooked in large iron caldrons, called bogracs, over the open fire by shepherds, known as *gulya*, it came to be known as *bogracs gulyas*. There are as many different ways to make goulash as there are sheep roaming the vast Hungarian plains.

Yield: serves 6

2 tablespoons vegetable oil

1 1/2 pounds beef, round steak, or boneless chuck, cut into 1-inch **cubes**

2 onions, **trimmed**, peeled, **coarsely chopped**

3 cloves garlic, trimmed, peeled, **minced** or 1 teaspoon garlic granules

4 cups beef broth, homemade or canned

1 cup canned **stewed** tomatoes

2 teaspoons Hungarian paprika (available at all supermarkets)

1 teaspoon caraway seeds

2 bays leaves

2 potatoes, washed, trimmed, peeled, cut into 1-inch cubes

2 carrots, washed, trimmed, cut into 1/2-inch slices

2 green peppers, trimmed, **cored, seeded**, cut into 1-inch pieces

salt and pepper to taste

Equipment: Large saucepan with cover or **Dutch oven**, mixing spoon

1. Heat oil in saucepan or Dutch oven over medium-high heat. Add beef and cook, stirring constantly, about 5 minutes or until brown. Reduce heat to medium. Add onions and garlic and cook about 5 minutes or until onions are soft. Mix well. Add beef broth, tomatoes, paprika, caraway seeds, and bay leaves. Mix well. Bring to boil and reduce heat to simmer. Cover and cook about 1 hour.

2. Add potatoes, carrots, green peppers, and salt and pepper to taste. Mix well, cover, and simmer an additional 20 minutes or until vegetables are tender. Before serving, remove and discard bay leaves.

3. Serve in individual bowls with chunks of crusty bread for dunking. Both a fork and spoon are needed to eat goulash.

❧ *Huszarcsok* (Sugar Cookies)

Yield: serves 8 to 10

2/3 cup unsalted butter	1 1/3 cups flour
1/3 cup sugar	1/3 cup walnuts, **finely chopped**
3 eggs	1/3 cup raspberry jam

Equipment: Medium mixing bowl with cover or plastic wrap, electric mixer or wooden mixing spoon, nonstick cookie sheet, small bowl, fork or whisk, pastry brush, spoon

1. Preheat oven to 350°F.

2. In medium mixing bowl, using electric mixer or mixing spoon, mix together butter and sugar. Beat well. Add 1 egg yolk (reserve white), 1 egg, and flour. Blend well. Cover mixture, chill in refrigerator for 45 minutes.

3. Remove mixture. Using clean floured hands, pinch off dough and shape into ping-pong-sized balls. Place balls 1 inch apart on cookie sheet. Using clean finger, make 1/2-inch-deep depression into top of each ball.

4. In small mixing bowl, using fork or whisk, beat 1 egg with reserved egg white. Using pastry brush, coat each cookie with beaten eggs. Sprinkle top of each cookie with nuts. Bake about 12–15 minutes or until golden. Set aside to cool. Using small spoon, fill depression on top of each cookie with about 1/2 teaspoon raspberry jam.

5. Serve cookies with coffee or glass of milk.

Poland

Poland, a low-lying country, borders the Baltic Sea. The Polish terrain has always been good for growing crops and raising livestock.

With the fall of Communism in 1989, Poland began to see a revival of traditional cooking. Traditional Polish food is considered to be robust and filling and is often thought of as comfort food. At one time the Polish people believed a meatless meal was simply a snack or "going hungry." Similar to people throughout most of the world, Poles have become more health-conscious, serving smaller, lighter portions. Popular Polish meals include freshwater fish, ham, pork, sour cream, dark breads, mushrooms, cucumbers, noodles and dumplings, buckwheat groats, wild game, and rich cakes. A favorite simple salad is cucumbers combined with sour cream.

Kluski Z Kapusta Po Polski (Polish Noodles and Cabbage)

Yield: serves 4 to 6

1/4 cup butter or margarine

1 cup onion, **trimmed**, peeled, **coarsely chopped**

4 cups green cabbage, trimmed, coarsely chopped

1 teaspoon caraway seeds

8 ounces wide egg noodles (cooked according to directions on package, drained well)

salt and pepper to taste

1/2 cup sour cream

Equipment: Large skillet with cover, mixing spoon

1. Melt butter or margarine in skillet over medium-high heat. Add onions and **sauté** until soft, about 2–3 minutes. Stirring frequently, add cabbage, reduce to medium, cover, and cook about 10 minutes or until tender.

2. Add caraway seeds, noodles, and salt and pepper to taste and mix well. Remove from heat.

3. Add sour cream and mix thoroughly. Return to low and heat through, about 3 minutes.

4. To serve, transfer to platter and eat while hot. This dish is very filling and can be the main meal almost anywhere, but in Poland, it is only a side dish.

Pan-Fried Mushrooms

Wild mushrooms grow especially well in northern Europe. Throughout the Polish country-side mushroom hunts had been a favorite family pastime until Russia's Chernobyl nuclear power plant accident in the spring of 1986. Since then, wild mushroom picking has been banned in many parts of Poland and neighboring countries. However, mushrooms are still a popular food in Poland.

Yield: serves 4 to 6

1 pound medium-sized whole mushrooms, wipe lightly with paper towels, trim and discard stems

2 eggs, beaten

1/2 cup water

1 cup dried breadcrumbs, more as needed   1/4 cup butter or margarine, more as needed

salt and pepper to taste

Equipment: 2 small bowls, **whisk** or fork, work surface covered with wax paper, large skillet, slotted spoon, serving platter

1. Place breadcrumbs in small bowl.

2. Place egg and water in a separate small bowl. Using whisk or fork, mix well. Dip mushrooms, 2 or 3 at a time, into egg mixture and then into bowl with crumbs. Coat evenly on all sides. Carefully remove mushrooms and set side-by-side on wax paper. Repeat until all mushrooms are dipped and coated.

3. Melt 1/4 cup butter or margarine in skillet over medium heat. Add mushrooms, a few at a time, leaving room to turn. Fry until golden brown on all sides. Add butter or margarine as needed to prevent sticking. Using slotted spoon, remove mushrooms and transfer to platter, keep warm. Repeat until all mushrooms are fried.

4. Serve pan-fried mushrooms as an appetizer or side dish.

Apricot *Kolachkes* (Pastry Filled with Apricot Preserves)

Yield: makes 4 to 5 dozen

Filling:

1 12-ounce jar apricot preserves

1/2 cup walnuts or pecans, **finely chopped**

Pastry Dough:

1 cup butter, room temperature

1/4 teaspoon ground cinnamon

1/4 teaspoon ground nutmeg

1/4 teaspoon ground cloves
8-ounce package cream cheese, room
    temperature

2 tablespoons sugar

2 cups all-purpose flour
1 tablespoon water

To assemble: powdered sugar, sifted, as needed for garnish

1 large egg, lightly beaten

Equipment: Medium bowl, mixing spoon, electric mixer or large mixing bowl, clean and lightly floured work surface, rolling pin, 3-inch round cookie cutter, small bowl, small spoon, pastry brush, large greased or nonstick cookie sheet, oven mitts, spatula, wire rack

1. Preheat oven to 350°F.

2. *Make filling*: In medium bowl combine apricot preserve, walnuts or pecans, cinnamon, nutmeg, and cloves. Mix well and set aside.

3. *Make pastry dough*: blend butter and cream cheese together in electric mixer set on medium-high or in large mixing bowl using mixing spoon. Slowly add sugar and blend until creamy and smooth. Reduce electric mixer to low or stir in flour, a little at a time, until well blended.

4. On work surface, roll dough out until about 1/8 inch thick. Using cookie cutter, cut dough into rounds.

5. In small bowl, combine egg and water and mix well. Set aside.

6. *To assemble:* Spoon 1/2 teaspoon apricot filling into center of each pastry round. Using pastry brush, brush edges of dough with egg and water mixture. Fold opposite sides to center, slightly overlapping edges and pinch to seal. Place side-by-side on cookie sheet. Bake in batches for 10–12 minutes or until golden brown. Remove from oven using oven mitts. Transfer to wire racks and sprinkle with powdered sugar. Allow to cool.

7. Serve as snack or dessert with milk or coffee.

Romania

Romania is located between Bulgaria and Moldova on the Black Sea. Romanian food has been influenced by the Italians and the Turks who at various times controlled this Eastern European country. A traditional staple of the Romanian diet has been *mamaliga*, a cornmeal mush.

Main meals often include tangy soups, sausage, and vegetables. Their sausage is often made with black pepper, an important Romanian seasoning.

Mamaliga (Cornmeal Porridge)

Romanian porridge, mamaliga, is eaten at almost every meal. When mamaliga cools it becomes firm and is sliced like bread. The slices are sometimes fried in a skillet or dipped in egg, similar to French toast. Mamaliga can be eaten with cheese, spread yogurt, or dipped in a spice mixture and eaten as a snack. As a sweet dish, mamaliga can be topped with cinnamon, sugar, and cream. Another popular Romanian way of eating mamaliga is topped with stewed apples, poppy seeds, and honey.

Yield: serves 4 to 6

3 1/2 cups water

1 teaspoon salt

1 cup yellow cornmeal

2 tablespoons butter or margarine

1 cup sour cream

Equipment: Medium saucepan with cover, **whisk** or mixing spoon, greased medium baking dish

1. Preheat oven to 450°F.

2. Place water in saucepan. Add salt and bring to a boil over high heat. Stirring continually, slowly add cornmeal and reduce to simmer. Add butter or margarine and mix well. Cover and cook for about 15 minutes or until all water is absorbed and mixture is thick. Stir frequently to prevent sticking. Remove from heat.

3. Pour mixture into baking dish and spread top with sour cream. Place in oven about 6–8 minutes, until top is golden. Remove from oven.

4. Serve mamaliga hot from baking dish. It is eaten at any meal, day or night. It is also eaten cold, cut into squares, or sliced and fried.

❧ *Sarmale* (Stuffed Cabbage)

Stuffed cabbage is popular throughout Eastern Europe. The basic recipe is the same using cabbage, minced meat, rice, and onions with variations in seasonings.

Yield: serves 6 to 8

2 tablespoons vegetable oil, more as needed

1 pound carrots, **trimmed, finely chopped**

1 pound onions, trimmed, peeled, finely chopped

1/4 cup fresh parsley, trimmed, finely chopped

3 tablespoons tomato paste

3 1/4 cups long-grain rice, cooked according to directions on package

2 pounds ground pork or beef

1/2 teaspoon dried dill, trimmed, finely chopped

salt and pepper to taste

1 medium head cabbage, trimmed

2 cups canned stewed tomatoes

2 tablespoons vinegar

2 tablespoons sugar

boiling water, as needed

Equipment: Large skillet, mixing spoon, medium bowl, heavy-bottomed stock pot with cover or **Dutch oven**, metal tongs, **colander**, small bowl

1. In skillet heat 2 tablespoons oil over medium heat. Add carrots, onions, parsley, and tomato paste. Stirring frequently, cook about 3–5 minutes or until vegetables are soft. Transfer to medium bowl and add cooked rice. Mix well.

2. In same skillet, heat 2 tablespoons oil over medium-high heat. Add meat. Stirring constantly, **sauté** about 3–5 minutes or until lightly browned. Remove from heat and transfer to bowl with vegetable-rice mixture. Add dill and salt and pepper to taste. Mix well. Set aside to cool.

3. Carefully separate cabbage leaves and place in stock pot or Dutch oven with about 2 inches of water. Bring to boil, cover, and cook 5–10 minutes or until leaves are soft and flexible.

4. Using tongs, transfer cabbage leaves to colander set in sink. Leave enough cabbage leaves in stock pot or Dutch oven to cover bottom. When leaves in colander are cool enough to handle, take leaves, one at a time, and cup in hand. Fill each with 2 tablespoons meat mixture. Encase meat mixture on all sides with cabbage leaf and roll up. Place cabbage rolls folded side down into stock pot or Dutch oven. Repeat until all of meat mixture is used.

5. Place stewed tomatoes, vinegar, and sugar in small bowl. Mix well and pour over stuffed cabbages. Place any remaining cabbage leaves over top.

6. Add just enough boiling water to cover cabbage rolls. Bring to boil over medium-high heat. Cover, reduce to simmer, and cook about 25–30 minutes.

7. Serve warm as main dish. Ladle pan juices over each serving.

Russia, Belarus, Moldova, and Ukraine

Russia, Belarus, Moldova, and Ukraine are neighboring countries, all formerly part of the USSR. The cuisines and cooking techniques are very similar and stem from Slavic traditions. The term Slavic refers to people who migrated to this region of the world during the sixth century.

The dissolution of the Soviet Union has greatly changed this region. Although most people thought of Russia and the Soviet Union as being one and the same, Russia was just one of 15 Soviet republics that are now independent. Russia is still a very large country covering almost one-sixth of the earth's surface.

Many Russians love *smetana* (sour cream), and they seem to use it in and on everything. Dill is the national herb of Russia, and it grows in almost every garden. Pickled beets, pickled cucumbers, and dried mushrooms are in almost every kitchen pantry. Garlic is used with a "heavy hand" and is spread on bread like butter, peanut butter, or jam. During the summer months, the most popular salad is tomato slices tossed with sliced cucumbers, a dollop of sour cream, and a sprinkle of dill. Dark, dense breads, commonly known as black bread or pumpernickel, are often served with *borscht* (recipe page 231), the most popular Russian soup. Borscht, originally a Ukrainian dish, is popular throughout all of Eastern Europe; however, it varies from country to country.

Machanka (Pork Stew)

Yield: serves 4 to 6

2 tablespoons vegetable oil, more as needed	salt to taste
2–3 pounds pork chunks with rib bones	1 onion, **trimmed**, peeled, **coarsely chopped**
2 cups beef broth or water, more as needed	2 cups sour cream
2 bay leaves	

Equipment: Large skillet, tongs, **Dutch oven** or large saucepan with lid, wooden spoon, whisk

1. Heat oil in skillet over medium-high heat. Add pork chunks and fry in batches until golden brown. Using tongs turn meat and brown on all sides.

2. Transfer pork to Dutch oven. Add 2 cups broth or water, bay leaves, and salt to taste. Bring to boil over medium-high heat. Reduce heat to simmer and cover and cook 30–45 minutes or until meat is tender.

3. In skillet, heat 2 tablespoons oil over medium-high heat. Add onions. Using wooden spoon stir constantly and **sauté** until soft, about 2–3 minutes. Whisk in sour cream and 1/2 cup broth or water into onions and mix well.

4. Pour sour cream mixture over meat in Dutch oven. Using tongs to turn meat, coat all sides. Cook an additional 10–15 minutes or until heated through. Remove and discard bay leaves.

5. Serve warm with boiled potatoes or potato pancakes (recipe page 219).

Grechnevaia Kasha (Buckwheat Groats)

There are several different kinds of groats (grains) that can be used to make *kasha*, Russian porridge: **millet**, oats, or pearl barley. In Russia buckwheat groat is the most popular grain for making kasha. Kasha is used in place of potatoes and is usually served with meat.

Yield: serves 4 to 6

2 tablespoons butter or margarine	1 egg
1 onion, **trimmed**, peeled, **finely chopped**	1 teaspoon salt
2 cups buckwheat groats (available from most supermarkets and health food stores)	2 cups boiling water

Equipment: Small skillet, mixing spoon, medium mixing bowl, greased medium baking dish, oven mitts

1. Preheat oven to 375°F.

2. Melt 2 tablespoons butter or margarine in skillet over medium heat. Add onion and fry until soft, about 3–5 minutes. Set aside.

3. Place groats, egg, and salt in mixing bowl and mix well. Transfer to baking dish. Slowly add as much boiling water to groats as they will absorb, stirring constantly. (They should not be soupy or too dry.) Add onion and pan scrapings and mix well. Bake in oven 30 minutes or until groats are tender. Using oven mitts remove from oven.

4. Serve kasha like mashed potatoes, with chicken or meat gravy.

❧ *Omelet Smetanoi* (Omelet with Sour Cream)

Yield: serves 2 to 4

4 eggs, more as needed	2 tablespoons flour
2 tablespoons fresh parsley, **trimmed, finely chopped** or 1 tablespoon dry flakes	3/4 cup hot milk
	1 cup sour cream
1 tablespoon butter or margarine, more as needed	salt and pepper to taste

Equipment: Small mixing bowl, fork or **whisk**, cup, 6-inch skillet with cover, heat-proof plate

1. Place 4 eggs in small bowl and mix in parsley. Melt 1 tablespoon butter or margarine in skillet over medium heat and add half egg mixture. Swirl pan to coat. Cover and cook until set, about 3 minutes. Transfer omelet to warm plate. Add 1 tablespoon butter or margarine and make a second omelet exactly like the first. When done, stack it on top of the first omelet. Pour any pan drippings over and keep warm.

2. Separate 2 eggs and place yolks in cup (refrigerate whites to use at another time).

3. Melt 2 tablespoons butter or margarine in skillet over medium-low heat. Add flour and mix until smooth. Add hot milk, stirring continually until blended. Mix in sour cream and egg yolks and blend well. Stirring continually until smooth and thick, season with salt and pepper to taste. When ready to serve, pour hot sauce over egg omelets.

4. Serve with pumpernickel or black bread for sopping up the sauce. In Russia omelets are eaten at any time, day or night.

✤ **Russian Black Bread**

Yield: 2 loaves

4 cups rye flour

3 cups all-purpose flour, more as needed

1 teaspoon sugar

1 teaspoon salt

2 cups all bran cereal

2 tablespoons caraway seeds, crushed

2 teaspoons instant coffee powder

2 teaspoons onion powder

1/2 teaspoon fennel seed, crushed

2 0.25 ounce packages active dry yeast

2 1/2 cups water

1/4 cup vinegar

1/4 cup dark molasses

1 ounce unsweetened chocolate

1/4 cup butter or margarine

Equipment: Medium mixing bowl, wooden mixing spoon, large mixing bowl, medium saucepan, electric mixer or wooden mixing spoon, rubber spatula, floured work surface, dish towel, large greased bowl, 2 greased 8-inch round cake pans, wire racks

1. Preheat oven to 350°F.

2. In medium mixing bowl, combine rye and all-purpose flour. Using wooden spoon, mix well.

3. In large mixing bowl combine 2 1/2 cups flour mixture, sugar, salt, cereal, caraway seed, coffee powder, onion powder, fennel seed, and yeast.

4. In medium saucepan, combine 2 1/2 cups water, vinegar, molasses, chocolate, and butter. Warm mixture over low heat (120°F–130°F). Stir until chocolate and butter mixture is melted and smooth.

5. Gradually stir chocolate mixture into dry ingredients in large mixing bowl. Using electric mixer or mixing spoon, blend well until smooth. Using rubber spatula, occasionally scrape sides of bowl.

6. Add remaining 4 1/2 cups flour mixture, a little at a time, forming soft dough that holds together. Transfer to floured work surface and cover dough with dish towel; let rest 15 minutes. **Knead** dough until smooth and elastic, about 10–15 minutes.

7. Place in greased bowl and turn until all sides are coated. Cover with dish towel and let rest in warm place. Allow to rise until double in size, about 1 hour.

8. Transfer dough to floured work surface. Divide in half and shape each half into ball about 5 inches in diameter. Place each ball into center of cake pan. Cover with dish towel and let rise until doubled in size, about 1 hour. Bake for 40–45 minutes or until crust is firm. Remove from pans and set on wire racks to cool.

9. Serve slices of bread, well buttered, with soups or stews.

🎗 *Borscht* (Vegetarian Beet Soup [Cold])

Many Russian cooks have their own way of making *borscht*. The following recipe is a simple version of beet borscht. Usually vegetarian borscht is eaten cold and is very refreshing on a hot summer's day. Adding a cold boiled potato or hard-cooked egg to each serving of soup is not unusual and makes the borscht more filling. Freshly chopped chives sprinkled over the soup gives it a little more flavor and adds a hint of color.

Yield: serves 2

2 cups beets, cooked and **cubed** or sliced beets, canned, including 3/4 cup juice (if necessary, add water to make 3/4 cup juice)

juice of 1 lemon

1 tablespoon sugar, more or less to taste

salt and pepper to taste

2 tablespoons sour cream

Equipment: Medium bowl, mixing spoon

1. Place beets with juice in bowl and add strained lemon juice and sugar. Mix well to blend and dissolve sugar. Chill until ready to serve.

2. Serve borscht cold in individual soup bowls with a **dollop** of sour cream in each serving. Have plenty of bread and butter to eat with it.

🎗 *Russki Salat* (Russian Salad)

Russian salads contain cooked vegetables and often include cooked meat, poultry, or fish. The salad dressing is simply oil and vinegar. This recipe is a wonderful way of using leftovers.

Yield: serves 4 to 6

1 cup **diced** cooked ham, beef, sausage, chicken, turkey or combination

2 cups beets, peeled, and diced, homemade or canned (drained)

2 cups potatoes, diced, homemade or canned, skin on or peeled

1 cup beans of your choice, homemade or canned (drained)

1 onion, **trimmed**, peeled, diced

1 fresh cucumber, trimmed, thinly sliced

3 hard-cooked eggs, sliced

6 gherkins (small sweet pickles), **coarsely chopped**

salt and pepper to taste

cruets of oil and vinegar, for garnish

Equipment: Salad bowl, tongs or salad fork and spoon

1. Mix all ingredients in salad bowl. Add salt and pepper to taste and gently toss with tongs or salad fork and spoon.

2. Serve salad in individual bowls with cruets of vinegar and oil. Let each person blend and add oil and vinegar to taste.

❧ *Sibierskie Pelmeni* (Siberian Meat Dumplings)

Yield: serves 4 to 6

Pastry:

1 cup flour

4 tablespoons vegetable oil

Filling:

butter or margarine as needed

1 onion, **trimmed**, peeled, **finely chopped**

Sauce:

1/2 cup lemon juice or vinegar

6 tablespoons water

1/2 teaspoon salt

1 cup cooked beef, ham, sausage, or chicken finely chopped

salt and pepper to taste

6 cups boiling water
1 tablespoon chopped fresh parsley or 1 teaspoon dry flakes

Equipment: Medium mixing bowl, mixing spoon, floured work surface, clean kitchen towel, floured rolling pin, medium skillet, medium saucepan, slotted spoon, cookie cutter or firm water glass, fork

1. *Prepare pastry*: place 1/2 cup flour in mixing bowl. Add oil, water, and salt and mix until dough holds together. Transfer to work surface. Using clean hands, **knead** remaining flour into dough until smooth and elastic. Transfer to bowl, cover, and chill for 1 hour.

2. Using rolling pin, roll dough out on work surface until pie crust thin, adding more flour to prevent sticking if necessary. Cut dough into 3-inch circles with cookie cutter or top rim of water glass. Stack circles and cover with slightly damp towel until ready to fill.

3. *Prepare filling*: melt 3 tablespoons butter or margarine in skillet over medium heat. Add onion and **sauté** for 3 minutes until soft. Add meat and mix well. Cook an additional 3 minutes. Season with salt and pepper to taste. Remove from heat and set aside.

4. Place tablespoon of filling on each circle of dough. Wet finger with water and rub it along the edge. Fold dough over filling making a half circle. Press edges firmly together using fork tines. Continue filling all circles of dough. Set aside on lightly floured work surface.

5. Keep water boiling in saucepan over high heat. Reduce to medium heat and add dumplings a few at a time. Cook about 15 minutes. Remove with slotted spoon, drain well, and place in bowl.

6. *Prepare sauce*: melt 1/2 cup butter in small saucepan over medium heat. Add lemon juice or vinegar and parsley flakes and mix well. Pour butter mixture over dumplings when ready to serve.

7. Serve warm as the main dish or as an appetizer or snack.

❧ *Sharlotka* (Apple Charlotte Dessert)

Sharlotka is a classic Russian dessert. The original recipe calls for slices of buttered bread instead of breadcrumbs. The Russians are masters with "leftovers," thus the following recipe is a great way to use stale bread.

Yield: serves 4 to 6

1/2 cup butter or margarine

4 cups breadcrumbs

1/4 cup sugar, more or less to taste

4 cups cooked apple slices, homemade or canned

Equipment: Large skillet, mixing spoon, medium bowl, nonstick or buttered 8-inch baking pan, wax paper

1. Preheat oven to 350°F.

2. Melt butter or margarine in skillet over medium heat. Add breadcrumbs and mix well to brown evenly. Add 1/4 cup sugar. Reduce to low heat and mix well to blend. Cook for 2 minutes and remove from heat. Set aside.

3. Place cooked apples in mixing bowl and add just enough sugar to sweeten (canned apples are usually sweetened, so no additional sugar is needed). Mix well.

4. Cover bottom of baking pan with about 1/4-inch layer of crumbs. Alternate layers of apples and crumbs, ending with crumbs on top. Butter a piece of wax paper that will fit over top of pan. Place buttered side of paper on top of crumbs. Bake in oven about 20 minutes or until golden brown. Remove wax paper.

5. Serve sharlotka hot or cold as dessert. It is delicious with ice cream.

✌ 5 ✌

Latin America

Latin America includes Central America and South America. The countries within Central America are Belize, Costa Rica, El Salvador, Guatemala, Honduras, Nicaragua, and Panama. The countries within South America include Argentina, Bolivia, Brazil, Chile, Columbia, Ecuador, French Guiana, Guyana, Paraguay, Peru, Suriname, Uruguay, and Venezuela. Mexico, part of North America, is included in this section because of its cultural affinity with the other countries.

When European explorers and settlers arrived in this part of the world they were greeted by settlements of Aztecs and Mayans. Later slave traders brought shiploads of Africans to work the land. All made their mark on the cultures and culinary mosaic of Latin America.

The settlers brought with them foods and cooking methods new to the natives. Garlic, onions, cinnamon, and rice were brought by the Spanish who also showed them frying as a new way of cooking.

The introduction of new foods worked both ways. Foods brought back to Europeans were tomatoes, cocoa, pineapples, pumpkins, peanuts, sweet potatoes, and squash. The Spanish returned to Spain with cocoa beans, where sugar was added, making chocolate as we know it today.

Hot spices, beans, and rice are important to Latin American cooking as well as major cash crops of corn, wheat, rye, mangos, pineapples, papaya, cotton, yucca, **plantains**, tobacco, bananas, bell peppers, tomatoes, peanuts, coffee, sugarcane, and citrus fruits.

Avocado trees are native to Latin America and their fruit is especially rich in vitamin C. Avocados are used in and on everything from soups to desserts.

> **Buying avocados**: press the skin slightly, if it gives, the avocado is ripe. It should be soft, not mushy. The nut inside should not rattle when the fruit is shaken. If the avocado is still very firm when you buy it, it will ripen at room temperature in a day or two.
>
> **Preparing avocados**: slice lengthwise, rolling knife around large nut in center, and twist halves apart. The flesh can be eaten right out of the shell-like skin with a spoon or it can be peeled, sliced, **diced**, and mashed. If avocados are very ripe, they are easy to mash, using the back of a fork or potato masher. After peeling an avocado, sprinkle the flesh with lemon juice to prevent browning.

In Latin America, *maize* (corn) is the most important grain. How it is cooked varies from country to country and from cook to cook. Tortillas, cornmeal flat bread, are "the stuff of life."

Peppers grow extremely well in the warm climate. Chili peppers come in all sizes and all degrees of hotness. The smaller the pepper, the hotter it is. The most common peppers are *jalapeños*, *chile rellenos*, and *habaneros*.

Popular herbs and spices are tamarind, **cilantro**, oregano, *achiote*, garlic, nutmeg, ginger, cloves, cinnamon, and chili peppers.

Flan (recipe page 272), a dessert made with a variety of flavors, is extremely popular throughout all of Latin America.

The geography, as much as the history, influenced the cuisine of this region. Latin America is one of the most ecologically diverse areas in the world with waterfalls, rivers, desserts, mountains, and the amazing Amazon Rainforest.

Animals are just as diverse as the land, including but not limited to llamas, anacondas, piranhas, jaguars, vicuñas, and tapirs. Traditional farm animals raised throughout Latin America are goats, pigs, cattle, horses, and donkeys as well as all barnyard animals.

Throughout Latin America people of mixed European and indigenous ancestry are known as *Mestizo*.

In most large cities the lifestyle of the affluent is continental with strong European influences. Today, much of Latin American cooking is a blending of the ancient with the new. Many families prepare and eat the same indigenous food of their ancestors, however, using modern cooking equipment and techniques.

Open-air markets are common through small towns and villages where vendors sell everything from fresh produce to souvenirs, colorful fine-wool hats, scarves, and clothing to beautiful handcrafted housewares.

CENTRAL AMERICA

Belize

Belize is located on the Caribbean coast in northern Central America. The country gained its independence from the British Empire in 1981 and is the only country in Latin America where English is the official language. Sugar and citrus are the leading crops grown for export, while the top industry for development is agriculture followed by eco-tourism and tourism.

Belizean Habanero Sauce

CAUTION: use rubber gloves when working with hot peppers.

Yield: serves 6 to 8

1 tablespoon vegetable oil

1 onion, **trimmed**, peeled, **coarsely chopped**

1 cup carrots, trimmed, **finely chopped**

2 cups water

4 habanero chilies, trimmed, seeded, finely chopped

3 tablespoons lime juice

3 tablespoons white vinegar

salt to taste

Equipment: Large skillet, mixing spoon, food processor, medium glass jar with lid

1. In skillet, heat oil over medium-high heat. Add onion. tsirring constantly, **sauté** until soft, about 2–3 minutes.

2. Stir in carrots and water and bring to boil. Reduce to simmer and cook until carrots are soft. Remove from heat.

3. Stir in chilies, lime juice, vinegar, and salt.

4. Transfer to food processor and **purée** until smooth. Transfer to glass jar and seal.

5. To serve, place jar of condiment with spoon on table and allow each person to add desired amount to soups, stews, and meat or fish dishes.

Costa Rica

Costa Rica ranks fifth in the world and first among the Americas in reducing environmental stresses to human health, protecting ecosystems and natural resources. Due to its commitment to environmental issues Costa Rica is a popular destination for world travelers. It is also known as one of the most stable democracies in Latin America. "Ticos" (people from Costa Rica) successfully grow and export fine-quality coffee, bananas, sugar cane, rice, corn, and cocoa. Geographically, the country is a fishing paradise, with 125 miles of coastline along the Caribbean Sea and over 600 miles along the Pacific Ocean.

Tortilla Soup

Yield: serves 6

2 tablespoons vegetable oil, more as needed   3 corn tortillas, cut into 1/2-inch-wide strips

1 onion, **trimmed**, peeled, **finely chopped**

6 cloves garlic, trimmed, peeled, finely chopped or 2 teaspoons garlic granules

2 stalks celery, trimmed, finely chopped

1 cup boneless, skinless, finely **diced** raw chicken

4 cups chicken broth, homemade or canned

1 cup canned **stewed** tomatoes

1 teaspoon chili powder

1 teaspoon cumin

1 tablespoon chopped fresh **cilantro**

1 bay leaf

salt and pepper to taste

1/2 cup sour cream, more or less, for serving

2 avocados, peeled, **seeded, cubed,** more or less, for serving

1/2 cup shredded Monterey Jack cheese, more or less for serving

Equipment: Large saucepan or **Dutch oven**, slotted mixing spoon, paper towels

1. Heat 2 tablespoons oil in saucepan or Dutch oven over medium-high heat. Add tortillas. Mix well and fry until crisp. Remove tortillas with slotted spoon, drain on paper towels, and set aside.

2. Heat 2 tablespoons oil in saucepan or Dutch oven over medium-high heat. Add onion, garlic, celery, and chicken. Mix well and **sauté** for about 3 minutes until onions are soft. Add chicken broth, tomatoes, cumin, chili powder, cilantro, and bay leaf and bring to boil. Reduce heat to simmer, stir frequently, and cook for 30 minutes. Remove and discard bay leaf. Add salt and pepper to taste.

3. To serve, place a few tortilla strips in bottom of individual soup bowls and pour over hot soup. Serve with remaining chips, sour cream, avocado, and cheese in separate bowls to add to soup if desired.

Gallo Pinto (Black Beans and White Rice)

The name *gallo pinto* means "spotted rooster" due to the beans and bean juice giving it a spotted or speckled appearance.

Yield: serves 6 to 8

2 tablespoons canola or other vegetable oil

1 onion, **trimmed**, peeled, **finely chopped**

2 garlic cloves, trimmed, peeled, **minced**

1 teaspoon ground cumin

1 teaspoon ground coriander

1/2 teaspoon ground ginger

3 tablespoons Worcestershire sauce

3 cups cooked white rice, cooked according to directions on package

2 cups cooked black beans, homemade (cooked according to directions on package) or canned, drained, rinsed

salt and fresh ground pepper to taste

fresh cilantro, for garnish

sliced green onion, for garnish

Equipment: Large skillet, mixing spoon

1. In skillet, heat oil over medium-high heat. Add onions. Stirring constantly, **sauté** until soft about 2–3 minutes. Add garlic and sauté an additional 3–5 minutes or until onions are golden brown.

2. Stir in cumin, coriander, ginger, and Worcestershire sauce and mix well.

3. Stir in drained black beans and cooked rice. Stir frequently, until heated through. Add salt and pepper to taste.

4. Serve hot in individual bowls. Sprinkle each serving with cilantro and green onion for garnish.

❧ *Tamal Asado* (Cheese Bread)

Tamal asado is a traditional recipe from Costa Rica.

Yield: serves 10 to 12

1 1/2 cups cornmeal

3 cups milk

3/4 cup sugar

1/2 cup margarine or butter, melted

1 cup white cheese, grated, such as Monterrey Jack or Chihuahua (available at Latino food markets)

2 eggs

1 teaspoon vanilla extract

Equipment: Large mixing bowl, mixing spoon or electric mixer, medium nonstick baking pan, oven mitts, sharp knife

1. Preheat oven to 350°F.

2. In mixing bowl, using spoon or electric mixer, slowly add milk, sugar, margarine or butter, cheese, eggs, and vanilla to cornmeal. Mix until well blended and firm.

3. Transfer to baking pan and with palm of hand press down on dough until mixture is smooth. Bake about 1 hour or until mixture is firm and golden. Using oven mitts remove from oven and cool to room temperature.

4. Using sharp knife, cut into little squares.

5. Serve as a snack or breakfast treat with *café con leche* (coffee with milk).

El Salvador

El Salvador is situated along the "Pacific Ring of Fire," a horseshoe-shaped area in the Pacific Ocean where earthquakes and volcanic activity are frequent. Therefore, the country experiences its share of natural disasters including drought and mudslides and numerous ecological challenges.

Within the last few decades, El Salvador has made tremendous strides to increase trade relations throughout the world. Today, coffee, sugar, and corn are the main agricultural exports. El Salvador is also known for the production of textiles and apparel.

El Salvador was once part of the Mayan territory. It was invaded by the Aztecs and then the Spanish. Today, El Salvadorians are predominantly a *mestizo* people and the cuisine blends the Mayan culture with a Spanish influence.

✸ *Pupusas* (Cheese-Filled Cornmeal Patty)

Pupusas are fundamental to El Salvadorian cooking, so much so that November 13th has been declared "National Pupusa Day."

Yield: serves 4 to 6

2 cups corn flour (*Masa harina*, available at all supermarkets)	1 cup water, more if needed

Filling:

	2 tablespoons vegetable oil, more as needed
1/2 cup mozzarella cheese, **shredded**	1 zucchini, **trimmed**, finely grated
1/4 cup sour cream	

Equipment: Medium mixing bowl, mixing spoon, **colander**, small mixing bowl, 1 tablespoon, skillet, spatula, large sheet of foil

1. In medium bowl, mix together cornmeal flour and water to form dough. Using clean hands, knead until firm dough has formed, adding more water if necessary. Set aside to rest 5–10 minutes.

2. Prepare filling: place zucchini in colander and allow to drain for about 30 minutes. Using hands, squeeze out excess liquid and transfer zucchini to bowl.

3. Stir in sour cream and mozzarella cheese to zucchini and mix until well blended. Set aside.

4. Using hands, flatten golf-ball-sized pieces of dough into disc. Place 1 tablespoon of mixture into center of each piece. Fold over and pinch ends together to secure filling. Using palm of hands flatten until about 1/2-inch thick. Be careful filling does not spill out.

5. Heat 1–2 tablespoons oil in skillet over medium-high heat. Reduce heat to medium and fry pupusas in batches, until lightly browned on each side, about 2–3 minutes. Remove from pan and drain on paper towels. Wrap in foil to keep warm until ready to serve.

6. Serve warm as snack or with soups and stews.

✸ *Curtido Salvadoreno* (El Salvadoran Vegetable Slaw)

Yield: serves 4 to 6

1 medium cabbage, **trimmed, finely chopped**	1/2 teaspoon red pepper flakes (optional)
2 carrots, trimmed, **shredded**	1 teaspoon oregano
1 onion, trimmed, peeled, finely sliced	2 teaspoons olive oil
1/4 cup white vinegar	1/2 cup water
2 teaspoons light brown sugar	salt to taste

Equipment: Large saucepan, colander or strainer, large bowl, mixing spoon, small bowl, metal tongs or salad fork and spoon

1. In saucepan **blanch** cabbage in boiling water for about 1 minute, transfer to colander or strainer to drain.

2. In large bowl, using hands or mixing spoon, toss together cabbage, carrots, and onion and set aside.

3. In small bowl stir vinegar into brown sugar and mix well. Add red pepper flakes, oregano, olive oil, water, and salt to taste Mix well. Pour vinegar mixture over cabbage mixture, using tongs or salad fork and spoon. Toss to mix well. Place in refrigerator and chill for 2 hours.

4. Serve *curtido* chilled with warm pupusas (previous recipe).

Guatemala

After years of civil war, Guatemala has finally regained some political stability, specifically with a democratic election in 2007. Within recent years, signing the free trade agreements with United States, Mexico, and China has helped increase Guatemala's production of textiles and apparel.

Similar to other Central American countries, Guatemala is a blend of Mayan traditions with strong Spanish influences. Traditional Mayans who live in rural highlands still create handwoven textiles.

Arroz Guatemalteo (Guatemalan-Style Rice)

Yield: serves 4 to 6

2 tablespoons vegetable oil

1 onion, **trimmed**, peeled, **finely chopped**

3 cloves garlic, trimmed, peeled, **minced** or 1 teaspoon garlic granules

1 cup uncooked rice

2 carrots, trimmed, finely chopped

1 green pepper, **cored, seeded,** finely chopped

2 1/2 cups water

1/2 cup green peas, fresh or frozen (thawed)

salt and pepper to taste

Equipment: Medium skillet with cover, mixing spoon

1. Heat oil in skillet over medium-high heat. Add onions and garlic and **sauté** until soft, about 3–5 minutes. Add rice, carrots, and green pepper. Stirring constantly, cook an additional 3 minutes. Add water and bring to boil. Reduce to simmer, cover, and cook about 20–25 minutes until water is absorbed and rice is tender.

2. Add peas and salt and pepper to taste. Mix well and **fluff** with fork.

3. Serve rice as a side dish with meat.

❧ *Pollo en Pepian Dulce* (Mayan Chicken Fricassee)

Yield: serves 6 to 8

3 1/2- to 4 pound chicken, cut into serving-sized pieces

3 cups chicken broth, more as needed, home-made or canned

1 tablespoon sesame seeds

1/2 cup *pepitas* (Mexican pumpkin seeds, available at Latino food markets)

3 red bell peppers, **trimmed, cored, seeded, coarsely chopped**

1 14.5-ounce can diced tomatoes

1 onion, trimmed, peeled, coarsely chopped

2 cloves garlic, trimmed, peeled, **minced**

2 tablespoons vegetable oil

3/4 cup orange juice

1/2 cup lime juice

1/2 teaspoon ground allspice

salt and freshly ground pepper, to taste

1/4 cup seedless raisins, soaked in water for 15 minutes, drained, for garnish

1/4 cup slivered almonds, for garnish

Equipment: **Dutch oven** or heavy-bottomed large saucepan with cover, tongs, large plate, medium bowl, blender or food processor, strainer, small bowl, large skillet, wooden mixing spoon

1. Place chicken pieces in Dutch oven or heavy-bottomed saucepan. Add chicken broth, more as needed to cover. Over medium-high heat, bring to boil. Reduce to medium heat, cover, and simmer until chicken is tender, about 30 minutes. Using tongs, remove chicken pieces and set on plate. Pour broth into bowl and set aside.

2. In blender or food processor finely grind sesame and pumpkin seeds. Strain ground seeds into small bowl and discard residue in strainer.

3. Return ground seeds to blender or food processor. Add red peppers, tomatoes, onion, and garlic. Blend to coarse **purèe**.

4. In skillet heat oil over medium-high heat and add purée. Reduce to medium heat. Using mixing spoon, stir constantly and add 1 cup reserved chicken broth, orange juice, lime juice, allspice, and salt and pepper to taste. Mix well. Cook for 3–5 minutes to heat through.

5. Return chicken to Dutch oven or heavy-bottomed saucepan. Pour over puree, cover, and simmer until chicken is tender and cooked through, about 15 minutes. Add more broth if necessary.

6. To serve, transfer chicken with sauce to warm serving platter and sprinkle with almonds and raisins. Serve with plain white rice or *arroz Guatemalteo* (recipe page 243).

Honduras

Honduras is bordered by the Caribbean Sea on the north and the Pacific Ocean to the south. Although the land is rich and fertile with lush rainforests and a variety of plants and animals, the mountainous terrain prevents large-scale farming. Over the past decade Honduras has lost vast amounts of rainforest due to slash and burn farming techniques, illegal logging, forest fires, and natural disasters. In recent years Hondurans have increased environmental awareness and improved farming techniques.

Bananas, coffee, sugarcane, seafood, beef, and timber are all essential to the economy.

❧ *Chiles Rellenos* (Stuffed Chili Peppers)

Yield: serves 4 to 6

6 poblano chilies, fresh or canned (available at most supermarkets and Latino food stores)

1/2 pound Monterey Jack cheese, **shredded**

1 teaspoon cumin

3 eggs, beaten

1/2 cup milk

salt and pepper to taste

Equipment: **Egg beater**, nonstick or greased medium baking pan, medium bowl, mixing spoon

1. Preheat oven to 350°F.
2. Cut chilies down one side, remove seeds, and rinse. Fill each chili with cheese and place side-by-side in baking pan.
3. Add cumin to eggs and milk in medium bowl and mix well. Pour mixture over stuffed chilies. Sprinkle with salt and pepper to taste.
4. Bake in oven about 25 minutes or until eggs are set.
5. Serve warm with rice and beans.

✤ *Chayotes Maria* (Spicy Pepper with Cream Sauce)

Yield: serves 4 to 6

4 quarts water

2 teaspoons salt

6 *chayotes*, washed, trimmed, seeded, cut in 1/4-inch slices (available at Latino food markets)

Sauce:

1/3 cup flour

3 cups milk

1 cup evaporated milk

1/2 cup sour cream

1 1/2 tablespoons chopped fresh parsley

1/2 cup green onions, trimmed and minced

salt and pepper to taste

Equipment: Large saucepan with cover, small bowl, **whisk**, medium nonstick saucepan, tongs, cutting board, sharp knife

1. In saucepan bring 4 quarts water and salt to boil over medium-high heat. Add chayotes. Cover, reduce to simmer, and cook until tender, about 5–8 minutes. Transfer to serving bowl, cover, and keep warm.
2. *Prepare sauce*: In small bowl, whisk together flour and 1/2 cup milk; mix until smooth.
3. In saucepan, stir together remaining milk and evaporated milk. Stirring constantly, bring to simmer over medium heat. Gradually whisk in flour mixture. Stirring constantly, simmer until sauce thickens, about 3–5 minutes. Reduce to low. Stirring constantly, cook an additional 2 minutes.
4. Remove from heat. Stir in sour cream, parsley, green onions, and salt and pepper to taste. Pour over chayotes.
5. Serve immediately as side dish with meat or fish.

Mexico

Mexico is located directly south of the United States with the Pacific Ocean to the west and the Gulf of Mexico to the east.

Regional differences in Mexico vary in climate, terrain, and cooking. Northern Mexico is similar to the southwestern United States. Cattle and goats are raised, cheese is produced, and wheat is grown. In central Mexico, corn, beans, capsicums, root vegetables, and fruits are grown while the predominant livestock are goats, pigs, turkeys, and chickens. Small patches of corn can be seen growing on steep mountain sides throughout this region. In the southern region and along the Yucatan Peninsula, cooks integrate tropical fruits, vegetables, and seafood in a cooking style derived from Aztec and Mayan cultures. Along the Pacific Coast tropical fruits, vegetables, fish, and seafood prevail.

Mexico is divided not only by regions but also by class. Foods of the wealthy are very continental, with French flavors, sauces, and cooking techniques. Mexican food, if properly prepared, is neither greasy nor fatty. It is actually low in calories, high in nutrition, flavorful, and not necessarily hot (spicy).

Over the past few decades, the rapid increase of industrialization in Mexico has had a substantial impact on the country's environment. Very few of Mexico's original tropical rainforests are still standing. In recent years, however, environmental awareness has improved and the government has taken steps to reduce pollution and illegal use of forests.

✤ **Atole (Mexican Cornmeal Beverage)**

Atole is an ancient Mexican beverage with roots from pre-Columbian times. Warm drinks with cornmeal are found throughout Central America and are especially popular in the evening. The consistency can vary from a porridge consistency to a liquid drink.

Yield: serves 4

5 cups milk or water

1/2 cup *Masa harnia* (available at Latino food markets)

1/4 cup brown sugar or *piloncillo* (available at Latino food markets)

1/2 teaspoon ground cinnamon

1 teaspoon vanilla

Equipment: saucepan, wooden mixing spoon

1. In saucepan, mix together milk or water, *masa harina*, sugar or *piloncillo*, and cinnamon. Mix well.
2. Place saucepan with mixture over medium heat. Bring to boil, reduce to medium-low heat, and continue cooking until thickened, about 5 minutes.
3. Remove from heat, stir in vanilla, and mix well.
4. To serve, pour into individual mugs and serve immediately.

✤ *Champurrado* (Chocolate Atole)

Champurrado is traditionally whisked with a wooden utensil called a *molinillo* and the drink is mixed until frothy.

Make atole according to previous recipe and **whisk** in 4 ounces of Mexican chocolate (available at Latino markets) until completely dissolved. Adjust sugar to taste.

✤ **Tortillas (Mexican Flat Bread)**

Since prehistoric times women of Mexico have soaked corn kernels in water with lime, ground this mixture to a paste, and hand-patted dough into an edible plate, the tortilla. Tortillas can be stuffed or topped with a cornucopia of meats and vegetables. In almost every Mexican village, no matter how small, there is a bakery, *una tortillaria*, that makes tortillas. Tortillas can be made from either *masa harina* (corn flour) or wheat flour.

Yield: makes about 12

2 cups *masa harina* (corn flour)

1 teaspoon salt

1 cup warm water, more or less

Equipment: Medium mixing bowl, floured work surface, rolling pin or tortilla press, kitchen towel or wax paper, large cast-iron skillet, pancake turner or metal spatula

1. Place flour and salt in mixing bowl. Add water, a little at a time, until mixture holds together to make stiff dough. Divide into 12 equal balls and flatten each into thin 6-inch circles with rolling pin or in tortilla press. Stack under towel until ready to fry.

2. Heat dry skillet over medium-high heat and fry tortillas one by one. When they bubble and are light brown, about 2 minutes, turn over and cook other side about 1 minute. When done, wrap in wax paper or kitchen towel.

3. Serve tortillas warm for the best flavor and stack them in towel or napkin to keep them soft and warm. In Mexico, tortillas are eaten as bread.

Guacamole (Avocado Dip)

Avocados, often called "poor man's butter" for their creamy rich meat, make a great substitute for high-cholesterol foods such as sour cream, mayonnaise, and butter. The most popular way to eat avocados is in the avocado side dish, guacamole.

Yield: makes 2 cups

2 avocados, peeled, pit removed, **finely chopped** or mashed

1 tablespoon lemon juice

1 tomato, **trimmed**, finely chopped

1 onion, trimmed, peeled, finely chopped

salt to taste

1/4 teaspoon hot red pepper sauce, more or less to taste

Equipment: Medium bowl, mixing spoon

1. Place avocados in mixing bowl, add lemon juice, and mix well to keep avocado from browning. Add tomato, onion, salt to taste, and red pepper sauce. Refrigerate until ready to serve.

2. Serve guacamole as an appetizer with tortillas, on shredded lettuce as a salad, or as a side dish with meat.

Salsa (Red Tomato Sauce)

Mexican cooking includes many sauces, which are either added to or served with most dishes. They are usually made with tomatoes, herbs, spices, chiles, and peppers. Both chiles and peppers have been used for centuries.

Yield: about 2 cups

2 tablespoons vegetable oil

1 onion, **trimmed**, peeled, **finely chopped**

1 clove garlic, trimmed, peeled, finely chopped

2 ripe tomatoes, trimmed, **peeled, seeded,** finely chopped

1 pickled jalapeño, **cored**, seeded, finely chopped (available at most supermarkets and Latino food markets)

1/2 teaspoon sugar

1 tablespoon chopped fresh **cilantro** or 1/2 teaspoon ground cilantro

salt and pepper taste

Equipment: Medium skillet, mixing spoon

1. Heat oil in skillet over medium-high heat. Add onion and garlic. Stirring constantly, **sauté** until onion is golden, about 3 minutes. Add tomatoes, jalapeño, and sugar. Bring to boil. Reduce heat to simmer, mix well, and cook for about 5 minutes or until mixture is well blended.

2. Add coriander and salt and pepper to taste and remove from heat. Cool to room temperature and refrigerate.

3. Serve salsa in small bowl as condiment to add flavor to Mexican dishes. It is also a great dip for tortilla chips.

✷ *Arroz a la Mexicana* (Mexican Rice)

Mexican rice is a blending of native Mexican and Spanish cooking. The Spanish brought rice to what is now Mexico and the indigenous peoples enlivened it with tomatoes and chiles.

Yield: serves 4 to 6

2 tablespoons vegetable oil

1 cup uncooked long grain rice

1 clove garlic, **trimmed**, peeled, **finely chopped**

salt to taste

1/2 cup onion, trimmed, peeled, finely chopped

1/2 cup tomato, trimmed, finely chopped

1/2 teaspoon ground cumin

3 cups chicken broth, homemade or canned

1 cup peas, frozen (thawed)

Equipment: Medium saucepan with cover or **Dutch oven**, mixing spoon

1. Heat 2 tablespoons oil in saucepan or Dutch oven over medium-high heat. Add rice and cook about 3–5 minutes. Stir continually.

2. Add garlic, salt, onion, tomato, cumin, and chicken broth and mix well. Bring to boil. Reduce to simmer, cover, and cook about 30 minutes, until rice is tender.

3. Remove cover, add peas, mix well, and heat through.

4. Serve as the main meal or as a side dish with *picadillo* (next recipe).

✷ *Picadillo* (Spiced Ground Meat)

There are many ways to make picadillo; it can be mildly seasoned or fiery hot. Picadillo is eaten with rice and beans, as a crispy taco filling, or rolled in tortillas.

Yield: serves 6 to 8

2 tablespoons vegetable oil

1 cup onions, **trimmed**, peeled, **finely chopped**

2 pickled jalapeño peppers, **cored, seeded,** finely chopped (available at most supermarkets or Latino markets)

1/4 cup vinegar

2 pounds lean ground beef or pork or combination

1/2 cup raisins (optional)

4 cups chopped whole tomatoes

salt and pepper to taste

Equipment: Large saucepan or **Dutch oven**, mixing spoon

1. Heat oil in saucepan or Dutch oven over high heat. Add onions, jalapeños, 2 tablespoons vinegar, ground meat, and raisins. Mix well. Reduce heat to simmer and continue cooking until meat is lightly browned, stirring to keep crumbly.

2. Add tomatoes, remaining vinegar, and salt and pepper to taste. Mix well. Bring to boil, mix well, and reduce heat to simmer. Cook until thickened, about 20 minutes.

3. Serve picadillo hot over rice or beans.

❧ *Bacalao a la Visciana* (Mexican Fish Stew)

Yield: serves 4 to 6

1 pound salt cod, soaked in water for 24 hours, gently rinsed, broken into large chunks

1 pound new potatoes, **trimmed**, rinsed, quartered

1/4 cup olive oil, more as needed

2 cups white onions, trimmed, peeled, **finely chopped**

3 garlic cloves, trimmed, peeled, **minced**

2 14.5-ounce canned diced tomatoes

1/4 pound ham, chopped

1/4 cup flat leaf parsley, trimmed, chopped

1 teaspoon black pepper

1/8 teaspoon cinnamon

Pinch ground cloves

1 4–6-ounce can pickled jalapeños, sliced, juice reserved

salt to taste

12 pimento stuffed green olives, sliced in half, for garnish

Equipment: Large saucepan, fork, colander or strainer, **Dutch oven** or heavy-bottomed saucepan, mixing spoon, large baking casserole dish, oven mitts

1. Preheat oven to 300°F.

2. Place potatoes in saucepan, cover with water, and bring to boil. Reduce to medium heat and cook until potatoes are tender when pierced with fork, about 15–20 minutes. In colander, drain potatoes and set aside.

3. In Dutch oven or heavy-bottomed saucepan heat olive oil over medium-high heat. Add onions and reduce heat to medium-low. Stirring frequently cook until **caramelized**, about 15–20 minutes. If necessary add more oil to prevent sticking.

4. After onions are caramelized, stir in garlic and tomatoes. Stirring constantly, cook over medium-high heat until mixture thickens, about 10–15 minutes.

5. Add ham, parsley, pepper, cinnamon, clove, potatoes, and jalapeños with juice into tomato mixture and mix well. Using mixing spoon, gently fold in cod. Add salt to taste. Transfer to casserole dish, sprinkle with olives, and bake about 15–20 minutes. Remove from onion using oven mitts.

6. Serve warm over rice. Serve with a basket of tortillas for sopping (recipe page 248).

Nicaragua

Nicaragua, a relatively small country, is tucked between Honduras on the north and Costa Rica to the south. It is bordered by the Caribbean Sea to the east and the north Pacific Ocean to the west. Largo de Nicaragua, the largest lake in Central America, is located here and is home to the world's only freshwater sharks. Nicaragua is heavily dependent on agriculture to sustain its economy.

Red beans and rice are fried together with onions to make, perhaps, the most common dish in Nicaragua, *gallo pinto* (recipe page 239). If additional flavoring is needed, hot sauce, a readily available condiment, is placed on the table for each person to add as desired to kick it up a notch. Fruits are commonly used for making candies, puddings, and fruit drinks.

✤ *Nacatamales* (Nicaraguan Meat- and Vegetable-Filled Tamales)

Yield: serves 6 to 8

Dough:

6 cups *masa harina* (available at Latino food markets)

1 cup solid shortening (we suggest Crisco)

1 tablespoons salt

Filling:

3 pounds pork butt, **cubed**

3/4 cup rice, soaked in warm water for 30 minutes, drained, set aside

salt and pepper to taste

1/2 pound potatoes, **trimmed**, peeled, sliced into 1/4-inch rounds

1/2 cup sour orange juice (available at Latino food markets)

4 cups chicken stock, more as needed, home-made or canned

1 onion, trimmed, peeled, sliced into 1/4-inch rounds

2 bell peppers, trimmed, peeled, sliced into 1/4-inch rounds

2 tomatoes, trimmed, sliced into 1/4-inch rounds

1 bunch mint, finely chopped

Equipment: Large mixing bowl, electric mixer, wet towel, large bowl, clean work surface, 12 banana leaves (hard spine removed, cut into 10-inch squares, available at international markets) and kitchen string or 12 pieces aluminum foil cut into 10-inch squares, **steamer pan**

1. Place masa harina and shortening in mixing bowl. Using electric mixer, mix on low to incorporate shortening into masa harina. Mixture should have mealy texture. Continue mixing on low and add sour orange juice and enough chicken broth to make soft, moist dough (similar to texture of mashed potatoes).

2. Increase speed to medium-high and mix 2–3 minutes until mixture is light and fluffy. If necessary add more chicken stock. Cover with wet towel and set aside to rest for 30 minutes.

3. In a separate bowl combine pork and drained rice. Season with salt and pepper to taste.

4. *To assemble*: lay 1 banana leaf smooth side up on work surface. Place 1 cup of dough in center of leaf. Using clean, moist hands, slightly flatten. Top with 1/2 cup pork and sprinkle 1 tablespoon rice over top. Layer 1–2 slices of each: potatoes, onions, bell peppers, and tomatoes. Sprinkle top with mint. Using palm of hand, gently press down to make 4-inch square.

5. Fold top edge of banana leaf down over filling. Fold bottom leaf up. Fold sides inward to make package. Be careful not to wrap too tightly or filling will squeeze out. Securely tie with string from both directions. If using foil, wrap *nacatamales* by folding over edges to seal.

6. *To steam*: Place nacatamale packages in steamer basket, seam side down. Set steamer over boiling water, cover tightly, reduce heat to medium, and cook 3–4 hours, adding more hot water as needed to keep from boiling dry. Remove from heat.

7. To serve, each person unwraps nacatamales revealing filling to eat with fork or hands.

🍌 *Maduro en Gloria* (Heavenly Bananas)

Recipes for baked bananas are found throughout Latin America. Sometimes they are called *banana celeste*. Sometimes fruit juice is added instead of coconut milk or cream; the end result is heavenly.

Yield: serves 4 to 6

6 bananas, peeled, cut in half lengthwise

1/2 cup melted butter

1 cup cream cheese (at room temperature)

1/2 cup light brown sugar

1 teaspoon cinnamon

1 cup coconut milk or heavy cream

Equipment: Buttered medium shallow baking pan, medium mixing bowl, mixing spoon or food processor

1. Preheat oven to 350°F.
2. Place banana slices cut side up, side-by-side in baking pan. Pour melted butter over top.
3. Place cream cheese, sugar, and cinnamon in bowl and blend together, using either mixing bowl and spoon or in food processor.
4. Spread half mixture over bananas in pan, then place remaining banana slices cut side down on top, sandwich fashion. Spread remaining mixture over bananas and cover with coconut milk or cream.
5. Bake in oven about 20 minutes or until top is lightly brown and bubbly. Do not overcook.
6. Serve warm for dessert directly from baking pan.

Panama

The tiny country of Panama, separating Central America and South America, has emerged as a focal point in the world of trade and commerce since the digging of the "Big Ditch." The Panama Canal was built in 1914 to decrease the travel time for ships crossing between the Atlantic and Pacific Oceans.

Many farmers have their own small farms, which they still work as their ancestors did before them. Most agriculture takes place on the eastern side of the country, where mountains give way to plains, making cattle raising and farming possible. Along the Pacific Coast, fishing is an important industry for Panamanians.

In spite of thousands of ships passing through the canal loaded with people from every country on earth, there is hardly any foreign influence on Panamanian cooking.

Escabeche (Pickled Fish and Vegetables)

Escabache is often made with *corvina*, a fish known throughout the waters of Panama. If corvina is not readily available white sea bass, speckled sea trout, black drum, mackerel, or tuna will work just as well.

Yield: serves 4 to 6

2 pounds white fish fillet, cut into 2-inch pieces, washed, drained, patted dry

2 tablespoons vegetable or canola oil, more as needed

3 onions,**trimmed**, peeled, thinly sliced

2 cloves garlic, trimmed, peeled, **minced**

3 bay leaves

3 dried red peppers

1/2 tablespoon whole black peppercorns

1/4 tablespoon ground cumin

1/4 tablespoon ground marjoram

1 cup vinegar

Equipment: Large skillet, spatula, mixing spoon, paper towels, glass or Pyrex bowl with tight-fitting lid or plastic wrap

1. In skillet heat 2 tablespoons oil over medium-high heat. Add fish and fry until flesh becomes firm and **opaque** white, about 2–3 minutes. Remove from skillet and drain on paper towels. Set in glass or Pyrex bowl and set aside.

2. Add more oil to skillet if necessary. Over medium-high heat **sauté** until onions become soft, about 2–3 minutes. Add garlic and sauté for an additional 2–3 minutes. Stir in bay leaves, red peppers, black peppercorns, cumin, marjoram, and vinegar and mix well. Reduce heat to medium-low and cook for 2–3 minutes. Remove from heat and cool to room temperature.

3. Pour vinegar mixture over fish in bowl. Cover tightly with lid or plastic wrap. Remove bay leaves before serving.

4. To serve, serve as appetizers over shredded lettuce.

SOUTH AMERICA

The countries in South America include Argentina, Bolivia, Brazil, Chile, Colombia, Ecuador, French Guiana, Guyana, Paraguay, Peru, Suriname, Uruguay, and Venezuela.

The Amazon region in South America belongs mostly to Brazil, followed by Peru. Lesser amounts are owned by Colombia, Venezuela, Ecuador, Bolívar, Guyana, French Guyana, and Suriname.

This huge region is home to an extremely large number of exotic birds and animals found nowhere else on this planet. The world's largest river basin with one-fifth of the world's fresh water is in the Amazon. Yet, what happens in the Amazon Rainforest affects everyone on this planet. Today, it is in danger of destruction; therefore, saving the rainforest is a worldwide ecological challenge.

Important crops in South America are wheat, corn, sugar cane, grapes, citrus, fruits, and soy beans. The grapes are used to make wine. Cattle raising is one of the leading agricultural productions on the continent. Argentina's meat is world famous and an important part of the country's economy.

Argentina

Argentina, located at the southern tip of South America, is bordered by the Chilean Andes to the west; Bolivia and Paraguay to the north; and Uruguay, Brazil, and the South Atlantic Ocean to the east. Argentina is home to some of the world's tallest mountains, expansive deserts, and impressive waterfalls. The land supports heavy agricultural production, making it very prosperous by South American standards.

Argentine cooking is very European, especially influenced by early Spanish and Italian settlers. Traditional Old World cooking methods are combined with locally grown produce. The cooking lacks the strong indigenous influence found in most other South and Central American countries.

Tea, also called *mate* or *yerba*, is an Argentine specialty. It was originally brewed by the Guarani Indians. Tea is made of the leaves and stems of a South American holly tree. The leaves are used for at least 10 brewings, with the fourth or fifth brewing considered the best. Some people add sugar and cream.

Argentina is well known for fine wine and tender beef.

Pastel de Papa (Vegetarian Potato and Lentil Casserole)

Yield: serves 4

2 tablespoons vegetable oil, more as needed

3/4 cup white onion, **trimmed**, peeled, **finely chopped**

2 green onions, trimmed, finely chopped

1 cup dried lentils homemade (cooked according to directions of package), drained

1/2 cup red bell peppers, trimmed, **cored, seeded**, finely chopped

1 tablespoon cumin

1 pinch cayenne pepper

salt and pepper to taste

6 potatoes, peeled, washed, boiled (keep warm)

2 tablespoons butter, at room temperature, more as needed

1/2 cup milk, more as needed

1/4 cup Parmesan cheese, grated, more as needed

1/2 teaspoon nutmeg

1 egg

Equipment: Large skillet, mixing spoon, large mixing bowl, potato masher or electric mixer, large nonstick baking casserole

1. Preheat oven to 375°F.

2. In skillet, heat 2 tablespoons oil over medium-high heat. Stirring constantly, **sauté** onions until soft, about 2–3 minutes. Add green onions and red bell peppers. Stirring constantly, cook an additional 1–2 minutes until soft. Add more oil if necessary to prevent sticking.

3. Stir in lentils and reduce heat to medium-low. Add cumin, cayenne, and salt and pepper to taste and mix well. Cook until heated through. Remove from heat and set aside.

4. Prepare mashed potatoes: place boiled potatoes in mixing bowl and, using potato masher or electric mixer, mash well. Mixing continually, slowly add butter, milk, and Parmesan cheese. Mix until smooth. Add nutmeg and salt and pepper to taste. Add egg and mix well.

5. Spread half mashed potatoes into bottom of casserole, using spatula or wooden spoon to smooth down. Evenly spread layer of lentil mixture over mashed potatoes, then spread remaining mashed potatoes over top. Add several dollops of butter.

6. Bake 20–30 minutes or until top is golden brown.

7. Serve warm as vegetarian entrée or as side dish with meat or fish.

❧ *Huevos al Nido* (Eggs in a Nest)

Yield: serves 6

6 medium firm tomatoes, trimmed

2 tablespoons butter or margarine

1 onion, **trimmed**, peeled, **finely chopped**

1/2 cup mushrooms, fresh or canned, drained, finely chopped

1/2 cup cooked ham, finely chopped

1/2 cup bread crumbs

salt and pepper to taste

1/2 cup green peas, fresh, shelled or frozen, thawed

6 eggs

4 teaspoons Parmesan cheese

4 cups cooked rice (cooked according to directions on package)

Equipment: Tablespoon, small bowl, paper towels, medium skillet, strainer, nonstick or greased medium baking pan

1. Preheat oven to 350° F.

2. Cut tops off all tomatoes, about 1/2 inch down. Using spoon, carefully scoop out **pulp** and place in bowl. Place scooped-out tomatoes upsidedown to drain on paper towels.

3. Melt 2 tablespoons butter or margarine in skillet over medium-high heat. Add onion and mushrooms. **Sauté** about 3–5 minutes. Stir continually until soft and cooked through.

4. Using strainer, drain tomato juice from pulp. (Refrigerate juice to use at another time.) Add tomato pulp, ham, breadcrumbs, and salt and pepper to taste to onion mixture and mix well. Cook to heat through, about 3 minutes. Remove from heat, add peas, and mix well

5. Spoon mixture into scooped-out tomatoes, leaving about 1/2 inch of space at top of each. Set filled tomatoes in baking pan. Break eggs, one at a time, and place one on top of each filled tomato. Sprinkle with salt and pepper to taste and Parmesan cheese. Bake in oven about 20 minutes or until eggs are cooked to desired doneness. Tomatoes should be tender but still firm.

6. Serve stuffed tomatoes while warm on bed of rice.

Bolivia

Bolivia, a landlocked country bordered by Peru and Chile to the west, Brazil to the north, Paraguay to the east, and Argentina to the south, was part of the rich Inca Empire. Bolivia is a struggling country and underdeveloped in many ways. Most Bolivians are indigenous, living much as their ancestors have for centuries. Two important crops, quinoa seeds and oca roots, are native to Bolivia and for many years could only be found in this country. Today, however, quinoa is grown in other Latin American countries as well as Canada and even the United States. These two foods provide the mainstay in many Bolivians' diets. Quinoa seeds are roasted and boiled into porridge that has a nutty flavor.

The national food of the Bolivians is *chuno* (dehydrated potatoes). The potatoes are spread out on the ground at the first frost, frozen at night, and then thawed under the hot sun. During the day they become soggy and are then trampled on by family members, who squeeze out any moisture. Freezing, thawing, and stomping is repeated until nothing is left except hard little potato nuggets that can be stored for years without spoiling. This process was probably the first freeze-dry method of preserving food, dating back to the Incan Empire.

Caliente Pollo con Vinagre (Bolivian Hot Pickled Chicken)

Yield: serves 6 to 8
CAUTION: use rubber gloves when handling hot peppers

3 pounds chicken breast, cut into 2- to 3-inch chunks

2 onions, **trimmed**, peeled, finely sliced

2 medium habenero peppers, trimmed, **seeded, finely chopped**

3 medium carrots, trimmed, quartered

1 red bell pepper, trimmed, **cored**, seeded, **coarsely chopped**

1/2 cup olive oil

1 cup red wine vinegar

2 bay leaves

1/4 teaspoon nutmeg

salt and pepper to taste

Equipment: **Dutch oven** or heavy-bottomed saucepan, mixing spoon

1. Combine all ingredients in Dutch oven or heavy-bottomed saucepan. Bring to boil over medium-high heat. Reduce heat to simmer for 30–40 minutes or until chicken is tender. As mixture is cooking, use mixing spoon to skim off foam that forms on surface.

2. To serve, remove and discard bay leaves. Serve warm over rice with tortillas for sopping.

Papas y Elotes (Potatoes and Corn)

Yield: serves 4 to 6

2 tablespoons vegetable oil

3 cloves garlic, **trimmed**, peeled, **minced** or 1 teaspoon garlic granules

2 onions, trimmed, peeled, **finely chopped**

1 fresh green chili pepper, **cored**, **seeded**, and finely chopped (available at most supermarkets and Latino food stores)

1 tablespoon ground cumin

1 teaspoon dried hot red pepper flakes, to taste

salt and pepper to taste

4 cups chopped tomatoes, trimmed, fresh or canned

1 tablespoon sugar

2 cups corn kernels, fresh (cooked, cut off cobs), frozen (thawed), or canned (drained)

6 boiled potatoes (egg size), quartered, fresh or canned

1 cup sour cream for garnish

Equipment: Large skillet with cover, mixing spoon

1. Heat oil in skillet over medium-high heat. Add onions, garlic, green chili, cumin, red pepper flakes, and salt and pepper to taste. Mix well. **Sauté** about 3 minutes until onions are soft.

2. Add tomatoes and sugar, mix well, and bring to boil. Add corn and potatoes and mix well. Reduce heat to simmer, cover, and cook about 15 minutes, stirring frequently to prevent sticking.

3. Serve *papas y elotes* hot in a bowl with a dish of sour cream to spoon over it and warm tortillas for sopping.

❧ *Salteñas* (Meat Turnovers)

The original *salteña* is believed to have been created by Juana Manuela Gorriti. The story goes that Juana, born in Salta, Argentina, was exiled to Bolivia. Living in poverty, in order to survive, she created the first salteña. The recipe was a hit and the legacy of Juana lives on with the nickname salteña (also means female citizen from Salta, Argentina).

On many city street corners in Bolivia vendors sell salteñas as a mid-morning snack. The pastry is made with basic pie crust dough and any ready-made crust can be used.

Yield: serves 4

2 tablespoons vegetable oil

2 onions, **trimmed**, peeled, **finely chopped**

3 cloves garlic, trimmed, peeled, finely chopped or 1 teaspoon garlic granules

1/2 pound ground lean beef

1/4 cup tomato paste

1/2 teaspoon ground hot red pepper, more or less to taste

1/4 cup **pitted**, sliced green olives

2 **hard-cooked eggs**, peeled, finely chopped

salt and pepper to taste

4 9-inch unbaked pie crusts, homemade or frozen, thawed

1 egg, beaten

Equipment: Large skillet, mixing spoon, cup, fork, nonstick or lightly greased baking sheet, spoon or pastry brush

1. Heat oil in skillet over medium-high heat. Add onions and garlic and **sauté** until soft, about *1* 3 minutes. Add meat, mix well, and cook about 5 minutes until meat is no longer pink. Add tomato paste, red pepper, olives, rice, eggs, and salt and pepper to taste. Mix well. Cook for 3 minutes and remove from heat.

2. Have cup of water handy. Place 4 pie crust rounds side-by-side on work surface and pile meat mixture equally on each, keeping to one half of crust. Leave 1-inch margin along curved edge. Fold unfilled side over filling, joining curved edges to make a half circle. To seal edges together, dip finger into cup of water and run it along inside curved edges. Using back of fork tines, press edges firmly together, poking each top about 4 or 5 times with fork tines. Place pastries side-by-side on baking sheet and refrigerate about 30 minutes.

3. Preheat oven to 400°F.

4. Bake in oven for 10 minutes, reduce temperature to 350°F, and continue baking an additional 12–15 minutes or until tops are golden brown.

5. Serve salteñas hot or cold as a snack or full meal. They are excellent to take on picnics or in a lunch box.

Brazil

Brazil, the largest country in South America, is bordered by the Atlantic Ocean to the east. All countries of this region except Chile and Ecuador border Brazil. The largest portion of the rainforest runs through Brazil, providing this country with a variety of biodiversity, including unique foods and an abundance of fish.

Indigenous peoples showed the Portuguese settlers how to make **manioc** flour from **cassava** (yucca). Fresh yucca roots, once peeled, can be boiled, baked, or fried and are usually lightly seasoned with salt. Another popular way to eat manioc is to create flour or meal, which is then seasoned and called *farofa*. The seasoned manioc meal is used as a condiment and sprinkled over everything from soups to vegetables, similar to how Italians use Parmesan cheese.

Freijoada (Feijoada) (Meat Stew with Black Beans)

In Brazil the national dish is *freijoada*, a stew made by cooking a variety of meats together with black beans. For special feast days as many as 15 different meats are combined with black beans. Sausage, pork, bacon, tongue, beef, and pig's feet or ear are basic ingredients, although for everyday eating no more than 4 or 5 meats are customary. Traditionally freijoada is served with a rice dish called *arroz Brasileira*, orange salad called *laranja*, and shredded greens called *couve a mineira*.

Yield: serves 6

2 cups dried black beans (**reconstitute** according to directions on package)

3 cups water, more as needed

1/2 pound sausage, cut into 1-inch pieces

1/2 pound beef, cut into 1-inch cubes (any cut of meat)

1/2 pound pork, cut into 1-inch cubes (any cut of meat)

3 slices bacon, cut into 1-inch pieces

1 jalapeño, or green chili pepper, **trimmed, seeded,** and **finely chopped** (to handle peppers, wear rubber gloves or put hands in plastic bags)

1 tomato, trimmed, finely chopped

3 cloves garlic, trimmed, peeled, **minced** or 1 teaspoon garlic granules

salt, pepper, and ground red pepper to taste

1 orange, halved, cut into 1/4-inch rounds, for garnish

Equipment: Large saucepan with cover or **Dutch oven**, mixing spoon, small skillet

1. Place drained, soaked beans with water in large saucepan or Dutch oven and bring to boil over high heat. Reduce heat to simmer, cover, and cook about 40–50 minutes or until beans are tender; stir frequently.

2. Add sausage, beef, and pork and mix well. Cover and cook over medium heat about 45 minutes. Stir frequently and add more water if necessary to prevent sticking.

3. In small skillet, fry bacon over medium for 5–7 minutes or until crisp. Add jalapeño, tomato, and garlic and mix well. Reduce heat to simmer and cook 2 minutes. Add bacon and vegetables to meat mixture and add salt, pepper, and red pepper to taste.

4. Serve over rice and garnish with orange slices.

Couve a Mineira (Shredded Greens)

Yield: serves 6

4 cups water

3 pounds kale, collard greens, or spinach, washed, drained, **trimmed, shredded**

1/2 pound bacon, **finely chopped**   salt and pepper to taste

Equipment: Large saucepan with cover, wooden mixing spoon, **colander** or strainer, large skillet, tongs

1. Place water in saucepan and bring to boil over high heat. Add greens. Using wooden spoon, push down to cover with water. Return to boil, reduce heat to simmer, cover, and cook about 3 minutes. Drain greens in colander or strainer, then rinse under cold water to stop cooking action.

2. Place bacon in skillet over medium-high heat and fry until crisp, about 3 minutes. Reduce heat to medium, add greens, and season with salt and pepper to taste. Using tongs, turn greens to mix with bacon and cook about 3 minutes, until greens are cooked through.

3. Serve *couve a mineira* as a side dish with *feijoada*.

❧ *Pao de Queijo* (Brazilian Cheese Bread)

Tapioca and manioc flour are made from cassavas. Brazilians are very fond of manioc flour and sprinkle it on almost everything. Note: *Pao de queijo* instant bread mix is available at most Latino food markets.

Yield: serves 4

1 cup water

1 cup milk

1/2 cup vegetable oil

1 teaspoon salt

1 pound package tapioca starch (available at Asian or Latino food markets, sold in 450-gram package (1 pound)

2 eggs

2 cups Parmesan cheese, grated

Equipment: Large saucepan, wooden mixing spoon or electric mixer, large mixing bowl, greased or nonstick baking sheet pan,

1. Preheat oven to 350°F.

2. In saucepan over medium-high heat add water, milk, oil, and salt. Stirring constantly, bring to boil. Remove from heat and transfer to mixing bowl, add tapioca starch and mix well with wooden spoon or electric mixer. Set aside to cool.

3. Mixing continually with mixing spoon or electric mixer add eggs and Parmesan cheese and mix well.

4. Transfer dough to lightly floured work surface. Using clean hands, knead until dough is smooth and firm.

5. Using slightly greased hands, roll dough into golf-ball-sized balls and place about 1 inch apart on baking sheet.

6. Bake in oven for about 15–20 minutes or until lightly browned.

7. Serve warm as an appetizer or snack.

❧ *Brigadeiros* (Chocolate Balls)

Yield: makes about 10 to 12

1 14.5-ounce can sweetened condensed milk

1/4 cup unsweetened cocoa powder

1 tablespoon butter or margarine

6 tablespoons chocolate sprinkles, more as needed, for coating

Equipment: Medium saucepan, mixing spoon, flat dinner plate, 10–12 paper or aluminum mini-cupcake cups, serving platter, plastic wrap

1. Place sweetened condensed milk, cocoa powder, and butter in saucepan and mix well. Stirring constantly, cook over medium-low heat for 6–8 minutes or until mixture pulls away from sides of saucepan. Remove from heat and cool to room temperature.

2. Using greased hands, shape candy into 1-inch ping-pong-sized balls. Spread chocolate sprinkles on plate, rolling each ball to coat evenly. Add more sprinkles if needed. Place each ball in individual paper or foil candy cup.

3. Place cups side-by-side on platter, cover with plastic wrap, and refrigerate to chill, about 2–4 hours.

4. Serve chilled as dessert.

Chile

Chile, a Europeanized nation, is a long narrow strip of land with a 2,600-mile coastline along the South Pacific Ocean. It is bordered by the Andes Mountains to the east and Peru and Bolivia to the north. Grapes were introduced to Chile and now are an important crop grown to produce excellent wine. Due to its location along the coast, fish and shellfish are vital industries within Chile.

Pebre, a popular sauce-like condiment, is often added to barbequed meat and is spread on bread in lieu of butter. It is made of onions, vinegar, olive oil, garlic, chili, and **cilantro**.

Uminitas (Corn Casserole)

Yield: serves 4 to 6

4 cups corn kernels, frozen, thawed

2 eggs, beaten

1 teaspoon all-purpose flour

salt and pepper to taste

4 tablespoons melted butter or margarine

1/2 cup shredded cheddar cheese

Equipment: Medium mixing bowl, mixing spoon, medium baking pan

1. Preheat oven to 350°F.
2. Place corn kernels, eggs, flour, and salt and pepper to taste in mixing bowl. Mix well.
3. Swirl melted butter or margarine around baking pan to coat bottom and sides. Add half of corn mixture, 1/4 cup cheese, and then remaining corn mixture. Sprinkle remaining cheese over top. Bake about 30 minutes or until top is bubbly and brown.
4. Serve hot as a side dish with meat, poultry, or fish.

Cazuela (Little Pot with Meat and Vegetables)

Yield: serves 10 to 12

3 tablespoons vegetable oil, more as needed

1 red bell pepper, **trimmed, seeded, cored, coarsely chopped**

1/2 teaspoon cayenne pepper

3 onions, trimmed, peeled, coarsely chopped

2 pounds boneless chicken, cut into 2-inch-cubes

10 cups chicken broth, homemade or canned

2 zucchini, trimmed, sliced into 1/4-inch rounds

1 10-ounce package frozen corn, thawed

1 10-ounce package frozen green beans, thawed, cut in half

1 cup frozen peas, thawed

1 fennel bulb, trimmed, coarsely chopped (available at international markets)

1/2 cup rice

1 teaspoon cumin

2 sprigs mint, **finely chopped**

2 tablespoons parsley, finely chopped

2 potatoes, peeled, **cubed**, boiled, drained (set aside and keep warm)

1 egg beaten

2 tablespoons cider vinegar

10–12 lime wedges, for serving

Equipment: Stock pot, mixing spoon, large mixing bowl, potato masher, ladle

1. Heat oil in stock pot over medium-high heat. Add red bell pepper, cayenne pepper, and onions. Stirring constantly, **sauté** for 5–7 minutes or until soft.

2. Stir in chicken and broth and bring to boil. Reduce heat to simmer and cook about 30–35 minutes.

3. Stir in zucchini, green beans, corn, peas, fennel, rice, cumin, mint, and parsley. Stirring occasionally, simmer an additional 30–40 minutes.

4. In mixing bowl, using potato masher, mash together potatoes, egg, and vinegar. Add to soup mixture and mix well. Season with salt and pepper to taste. Cook an additional 10 minutes to heat through.

5. Serve warm in individual soup bowls with limes wedges for squeezing juice into soup.

Colombia

Colombia, in the northwestern part of South America, is the South American link to Panama and the rest of Central America. The extensive coastal region is rich in fish and shellfish. Tropical fruits and vegetables flourish in the hot, humid, sea-level climate. On the mountain plateaus, where it is cooler, grow the agricultural treasures of Colombia. Coffee beans grown here are considered some of the finest and are exported throughout the world. Potatoes also grow well in this mountainous region. Outstanding corn with huge white kernels and unusual purple corn with a delicate flavor and aroma grow on many plots of cultivated land.

For many years, pockets of people lived in almost complete isolation due to inadequate ways to cross the mountains. Each region developed its own style of cooking using foods that were readily available.

❧ *Humas Enolla* (Corn Dish)

Yield: serves 4 to 6

4 cups corn kernels, freshly grated or frozen, thawed

1/2 cup all-purpose flour

4–6 tablespoons butter or margarine

1 onion, **trimmed**, peeled, **finely chopped**

1 green bell pepper, trimmed, **cored, seeded**, finely chopped

2 pickled jalapeños, trimmed, **seeded**, finely chopped

1/4 teaspoon ground red pepper, more or less to taste

1/2 cup half-and-half

salt and pepper to taste

Equipment: Medium mixing bowl, mixing spoon, large skillet

1. Preheat oven to 325°F.

2. Place corn and flour in mixing bowl, mix well, and set aside.

3. Melt butter or margarine in skillet over medium-high heat. Add onion, green pepper, and jalapeños and mix well. **Sauté** until onions are soft, about 3 minutes. Add corn. Stirring frequently, cook about 5 minutes or until corn is tender. Add red pepper, half-and-half, and salt and pepper to taste. Reduce heat to low, adding more butter if necessary to prevent sticking. Cover and cook an additional 10 minutes.

4. Serve as a side dish with meat or fish.

❧ *Tortas de Cacao* (Colombian Cacao Cakes)

Yield: serves 10 to 12

3/4 cup powdered cocoa

11/2 cups flour

1 tablespoon baking powder

1 pinch salt

1/2 cup butter, at room temperature

1 cup sugar

3 eggs

2/3 cup milk

1 teaspoons vanilla

Equipment: Medium mixing bowl, sifter, large mixing bowl, mixing spoon or electric mixer, greased and lightly floured or nonstick muffin tins, oven mitts, toothpick, wire rack

Preheat oven 375°F.

1. In medium mixing bowl, sift together cocoa, flour, baking powder, and salt. Set aside.

2. In large mixing bowl cream butter using mixing spoon or electric mixer set on medium. Slowly add sugar and blend until light and fluffy. Add eggs, one at a time, and mix well. Set mixer on low and slowly add flour mixture. Add milk and vanilla and mix until smooth.

3. Transfer to muffin tins, filling each cup 2/3 full. Bake about 20–25 minutes or when toothpick inserted in muffin comes out clean. Using oven mitts, remove pan from oven and transfer muffins to wire rack to cool.

4. Serve warm as a dessert or breakfast treat.

Ecuador

Ecuador, a small country situated in the northwest of South America, sits right on the equator. There are three main regions of Ecuador, each producing its own food, affecting what the people eat. Along the warm coast and rivers, the main source of food and income is from fish and shellfish. In the cooler jungles they grow coffee and certain flowers, and in the mountainous elevations they grow grains and cold climate vegetables.

🌿 *Locro de Ecuador* (Ecuadorian Vegetable Stew)

Yield: serves 4 to 6

2 tablespoons butter or margarine

2 onions, **trimmed**, peeled,**coarsely chopped**

2 cloves garlic, trimmed, peeled, **minced**

2 2 jalapeños trimmed, seeded, **finely chopped**

1 cup tomato juice, more as needed

1 cup corn, frozen, thawed

1 cup peas, frozen, thawed

16 oz. pumpkins, canned or frozen, thawed

4 medium potatoes, trimmed, washed, peeled, coarsely chopped

1 cup milk

3/4 cup grated *gruyère* cheese or Mozzarella   rice for serving
  cheese, grated

  Equipment: **Dutch oven** or large heavy-bottom saucepan, mixing spoon

1. Melt butter or margarine in Dutch oven or large saucepan over medium-high heat. Add onions and garlic. Stirring constantly, **sauté** for 2–3 minutes. Add Aja peppers, mix well, and sauté about 1 minute.

2. Stir in tomato juice, corn, peas, pumpkins, and potatoes and mix well. Cover and cook over medium heat about 25–30 minutes. If necessary, add more tomato juice to prevent drying out.

3. Remove from heat and stir in milk and cheese.

4. Serve over rice as main vegetarian dish or as side dish with meat or fish.

✣ *Quindin* (Coconut Pudding)

We suggest adjusting the quantity of sugar to suite your taste.

Yield: serves 6

1/4 cup butter (at room temperature)

1 cup sugar

1/2 teaspoon cinnamon

8 egg yolks (at room temperature; refrigerate whites to use at another time)

1 cup half-and-half

1/4 cup grated coconut, homemade (see recipe page 138), frozen or canned

  Equipment: Large mixing bowl, electric mixer, mixing spoon, 6 buttered heat-proof custard cups, baking pan large enough to hold 6 cups

1. Preheat oven to 325°F.

2. Combine butter, sugar, and cinnamon in large mixing bowl, with electric mixer or mixing spoon, and beat until light and fluffy. Add egg yolks one at a time, mixing constantly. Add half-and-half, mixing until mixture thickens and forms a ribbon when dripping off spoon, about 5–7 minutes.

3. **Fold** coconut thoroughly into egg mixture and spoon evenly into custard cups, filling each about 3/4 full.

4. Fill baking pan with 1 inch of water, place filled custard cups into water, and place in oven. Bake about 50 minutes or until firm and golden. Remove from oven and cool to room temperature.

5. Run small knife around inside of each cup to loosen custard. Turn over cups, one at a time, on individual plates to release pudding. Refrigerate until ready to serve.

6. Serve puddings cold for dessert and add **dollop** of whipped topping.

Guyana and French Guiana

Guyana and French Guiana are situated on the northeast coast of South America separated by Suriname.

Guyana was originally settled by the Spanish then taken over by the Dutch. The British gained possession in 1814 bringing a large influx of African and East Indians with them to work the plantations. The most important culinary influences have been a **fusion** of East Indian, Caribbean, African, and Chinese cuisines.

French Guiana, today, is an overseas region of France and the Euro is used for currency. African and French influences have given a strong Creole flavoring to the cuisine.

Roti (Guyana and French Guiana Flat Bread)

This is another version of the popular Indian flat bread.

Yield: serves 4 to 6

2 cups water	water, as needed
1/4 teaspoon baking powder	corn oil or vegetable oil, as needed
1/4 teaspoon salt	

Equipment: Sifter, large mixing bowl, rolling pin, work surface, kitchen towel, griddle or large heavy-bottomed skilled

1. Sift flour, baking powder, and salt into large mixing bowl. Working flour mixture with clean hands, add just enough water to make stiff dough.

2. Separate dough into 4–6 equal balls. Using rolling pin, flatten each, one at a time, into pancake shape on lightly floured work surface. Stack and cover with kitchen towel, about 30 minutes.

3. To fry: Lightly oil griddle or skillet over high heat about 1–3 minutes or until hot. Reduce to medium and fry one dough patty at a time. When edges bubble, about 2–3 minutes, turn over and cook other side until golden brown. Add more oil as needed to prevent sticking. Keep warm until ready to eat.

4. Serve *roti* warm with soup or stew to eat as sopping bread.

Paraguay

Paraguay, a landlocked country, is located between Brazil, Bolivia, and Argentina. The terrain is mostly grassy plains and wooded hills to the east and low marshes to the west.

The cuisine of Paraguay has many similarities to that of other South American countries. As in Argentina, *mate*, a tea, is the preferred beverage.

Humitas (Corn and Squash Medley)

Yield: serves 6

3 cups corn, frozen, thawed

2 eggs

1/2 cup milk

1/2 teaspoon sugar

2 tablespoons butter or margarine

2 Serrano peppers, **trimmed, finely chopped**

1 onion, trimmed, peeled, finely chopped

3/4 cup winter squash, trimmed, peeled, finely chopped

1/2 cup Parmesan cheese, grated

salt and pepper to taste

Equipment: Food processor, spatula, medium bowl, medium skillet, mixing spoon

1. Place corn in food processor. Add eggs, milk, and sugar and puree until well blended. Using spatula, transfer mixture to medium bowl. Set aside.

2. In medium skillet, heat butter or margarine over medium-high heat. Add peppers and onions. Stirring constantly, **sauté** for 2–3 minutes until soft. Add squash and bell peppers and reduce heat to medium-low. Stirring frequently, cook until squash is soft, about 8–10 minutes.

3. Add corn mixture and mix well. Add salt and pepper to taste and cook for about 5 minutes to thicken. Sprinkle in cheese and stir well.

4. Serve as side dish with meat, poultry, or fish.

Flan de Naranjo (Orange Pudding)

Yield: serves 2–4

2 eggs, separated (refrigerate whites to use at another time)

3 tablespoons sugar

1 pint whole milk

1 tablespoon cornstarch

1 4-ounce canned Mandarin oranges, drained

cinnamon to taste, for garnish

Equipment: Small saucepan, mixing spoon, small serving bowl

1. In small saucepan, mix egg yolks, sugar, and milk. Stirring constantly, cook over medium heat, until mixture thickens to custard consistency, about 3–5 minutes. Set aside to cool.

2. Place orange pieces in small bowl and pour custard over them. Sprinkle with cinnamon and refrigerate for about 1 hour.

3. Serve in individual dessert bowls.

Lengua de Res (Roasted Cow's Tongue)

Tongue is an inexpensive yet very tasty meat. It is eaten not only throughout Latin American, but also the rest of the world. Along with cow tongue, calf, ox, and lamb tongue are equally tasty. Tongue may be purchased in many butcher shops, either smoked or pickled.

Yield: serves 6 to 8

1 cow or calf tongue (available at most meat markets or Latino food markets), approximately 3 pounds, washed well and drained

2 bay leaves

1 teaspoon salt, more as needed

1 teaspoon pepper, more as needed

2 tablespoons olive oil or vegetable oil, more as needed

2 onions, **trimmed**, peeled, **finely chopped**

3 cloves garlic, trimmed, peeled, finely chopped

2 green (Anaheim or similar) chilies, roasted, peeled, **seeded, coarsely chopped**

5 large tomatoes, peeled, **diced** or 16-ounce can diced tomatoes

1 cup tomato paste

1 tablespoon fresh thyme, finely chopped or 1 teaspoon dried, crushed

3 tablespoons capers finely chopped or pitted green olives, finely chopped

1 tablespoon fresh oregano, finely chopped or 1 teaspoon dried, crushed

Kosher salt and freshly ground pepper, to taste

Equipment: 2 large saucepans with covers, tongs, sharp knife, mixing spoon

1. Place tongue in large saucepan and cover with water (at least 2 inches above tongue). Add bay leaves, salt, and pepper. Bring to boil over high heat, cover, and reduce to medium. Cook for 20 minutes per pound (or 60 minutes for 3 pounds) of tongue. Remove from heat.

2. Using tongs, place tongue on work surface. While tongue is still very warm, using sharp knife, skin tongue and discard peeling.

3. Slice across tongue into 1/2-inch thick slices. Cover and keep warm.

4. In second large saucepan, heat 2 tablespoons oil over medium-high heat. Add onions and garlic. Stirring constantly, **sauté** until soft, about 2–3 minutes.

5. Stir in tomatoes, thyme, oregano, chili peppers, tomato paste, capers, and salt and pepper to taste. Mix well. Stirring occasionally, cook 10 minutes over medium heat. Remove and discard bay leaves before serving.

6. To serve, slightly overlap tongue slices on warm serving platter. Cover with sauce and serve as main course.

Peru

Peru is located on the western coast of South America, with Ecuador and Columbia to the north, Brazil to the east, and Bolivia and Chile to the south. With the Pacific Ocean bordering Peru to the west, seafood and fishing are major industries for exporting.

It is believed potatoes were native to Peru, where pre-Incan (before 1100 AD) and Incan (about 1100–1500 AD) civilizations cultivated and developed more than 200 varieties. "Irish" potatoes were imported to Europe by way of Spain from Peru, so they are actually Peruvian. Today, there are more than 1,000 varieties of potatoes. Peruvians cook potatoes in many interesting ways, blending Spanish flavors with cooking skills handed down from their pre-Colombian ancestors.

Peru is home to several unique animals including llamas, alpacas, guanacos, and vicuñas. Although all four are known for their fine wool, the llamas, in particular, play an important role in the lives of farmers because they are beasts of burden, sources of clothes, and providers of meat and milk.

Llapingachos (Potato Cakes)

Yield: serves 6

6 boiled potatoes, peeled, mashed or 6 cups prepared instant mashed potatoes

1/4 cup butter

2 onions, **trimmed**, peeled, **finely chopped**

2 cups shredded cheddar cheese

salt and pepper to taste

2–4 tablespoons vegetable oil

Equipment: Large mixing bowl, mixing spoon, large skillet, pancake turner or metal spatula

1. Place mashed potatoes in mixing bowl and set aside.

2. Melt butter in skillet over medium-high heat and add onions. **Sauté** until soft, about 3 minutes. Add onions, pan scrapings, and cheese to potatoes and mix well. Season with salt and pepper to taste. Divide mixture into 12 patties.

3. Heat 2 tablespoons oil in skillet over medium-high heat. Add patties and fry until golden brown on both sides, about 4 minutes each side. Add more oil as needed to prevent sticking. Keep in warm place until ready to serve.

4. Serve the patties warm or cold as a side or main dish. Peanut sauce (recipe follows) is often served with patties.

Salsa de Mali (South American Peanut Sauce)

Traditionally *salsa de mali* is served with potato patties. In Peru it is made with fresh peanuts, but we suggest adding peanut butter for smoother, quicker sauce.

Yield: about 2 1/2 cups

2 tablespoons vegetable oil, more as needed

1 onion, **trimmed**, peeled, **finely chopped**

1 clove garlic, trimmed, peeled, finely chopped or 1/2 teaspoon garlic granules

2 tomatoes, trimmed, **peeled**, finely chopped or 1 cup canned whole tomatoes (and juice)

1/2 cup chunky peanut butter

salt and pepper to taste

Equipment: Medium skillet, mixing spoon

1. Heat oil in skillet over medium-high heat. Add onion and **sauté** until soft, about 3–5 minutes. Add garlic, tomatoes, and peanut butter. Mix well to blend and cook until heated through. Add salt and pepper to taste.

2. Serve warm over *llapingachos* (previous recipe).

Frittata (Purple Potato and Zucchini Omelet)

Yield: serves 6 to 8

12 eggs

2 tablespoons butter or margarine, more as needed

3 cups purple potatoes, **trimmed**, cut crosswise into 1/4-inch thick rounds (available at Latino food markets)

salt and pepper to taste

1 cup zucchini, trimmed, cut crosswise into 1/4-inch thick rounds

2 cloves garlic, trimmed, peeled, **minced**

1 tablespoon fresh parsley or 1 teaspoon dried

1 tablespoon fresh chives or 1 teaspoon dried

1 teaspoon dried tarragon

1 teaspoon dried chervil

Equipment: Large mixing bowl, **whisk**, medium saucepan, strainer or colander, large nonstick skillet with cover, spatula, plate

1. Break eggs into large mixing bowl, whisk to blend. Set aside.

2. Place potatoes in saucepan, cover with water, add 1 teaspoon salt and bring to boil over medium-high heat. Reduce heat to simmer and **parboil** potatoes for 10–15 minutes. Drain in strainer or colander, set aside.

3. Melt 3 tablespoons butter or margarine in skillet over medium heat. Stirring frequently, add parboiled potatoes and **sauté** 5–10 minutes. Poke potatoes with fork to test doneness. Transfer to plate, cover, and keep warm.

4. Using same skillet, melt 3 tablespoons butter or margarine. Add zucchini and garlic and sprinkle in parsley, chives, tarragon, and chervil. Mix well. Using spatula, stir frequently and sauté until cooked through, about 5–8 minutes.

5. Return potatoes to skillet, adding more butter if necessary to prevent sticking. Toss with zucchini and garlic mixture. Pour eggs over top and add salt and pepper to taste. Cover and cook until omelet is firm and pulls away from sides of pan. Transfer to serving platter.

6. Serve for breakfast or lunch, cut into wedges with a dollop of sour cream.

Suriname

Suriname, located on the northeastern coast of South America, is the smallest country within this region and was originally settled by the Netherlands to develop and grow plantains of coffee beans, sugar cane, and cotton. It is one of the four countries in Latin America where Spanish is not the official language, rather the people speak Dutch. Most land is covered by the rainforest. Suriname has established wildlife reserves and increased eco-tourism over the past decade.

Pom (Chicken and Malanga Casserole)

As legend goes, the recipe for *pom* was brought to Suriname by Jewish settlers. The Jewish community of Suriname is said to be the oldest in the Americas, dating back to the 1500s. The original recipe called for mashed potatoes; however, the new residents of Suriname decided to use a popular tuber root, similar to cassava called *tayer*. Soon the alternative recipe caught on and tayer became the preferred ingredient to use throughout the Jewish community. Chicken fat is the preferred cooking oil used by Orthodox Jews.

Yield: serves 4 to 6

1 tablespoon, nutmeg, freshly grated, more as needed

1 teaspoon salt and pepper, as needed

1 pound chicken, cut into serving-sized pieces

1/4 pound pastrami (available at international markets), **finely chopped**

3 tablespoons butter or margarine, more as needed

3 yellow onions, **trimmed**, peeled,**coarsely chopped**

16-ounce can coarsely chopped tomatoes

1 cup chicken broth, homemade or canned

2 tablespoons palm sugar (also known as coconut sugar, available at Latino food markets)

2 pounds grated malanga root (*pomtayer*), frozen, thawed (available at international markets)

1/3 cup celery leaves, trimmed, finely chopped

juice of 2 oranges

juice of lemon

Equipment: Small mixing bowl, large skillet, mixing spoon, colander or strainer, plate, large mixing bowl, medium baking casserole dish, buttered

1. Preheat oven to 350°F.

2. Make rub: combine nutmeg, salt, and pepper in small mixing bowl. Rub chicken pieces with nutmeg mixture. Cover and set aside.

3. Melt 2 tablespoons butter or margarine in skillet over medium-high heat. Add chicken and **sauté** until lightly browned on all sides, about 5–10 minutes. Add pastrami, onions, tomatoes with juice, chicken broth, and palm sugar. Mix well and heat through. Remove from heat. Using tongs, remove chicken pieces and set aside on plate. Transfer cooking liquid to large mixing bowl.

4. Add malanga root to reserved chicken broth mixture. Add celery leaves, orange juice, and lemon juice and mix well.

5. Transfer half of malanga mixture to casserole. Using spatula spread evenly over bottom. Layer chicken pieces over top. Spread evenly to cover with remaining malanga mixture. Place several dollops of butter or margarine over top. Bake for 1 1/2 hours. Check occasionally to test doneness. If mixture is dry, add a little butter or margarine.

6. Serve as main dish with a side of rice.

Matjeri Masala (Curried Fish)

This recipe is a classic Indian curry dish with a unique Surinamese touch: *habanero* peppers are added.

Yield: serves 6 to 8

2 tablespoons vegetable or sunflower oil, more as needed

2 pounds fish fillets (trout, red snapper, sea bass, or any firm white-flesh fish)

1 onion, **trimmed**, peeled, **coarsely chopped**

3 garlic cloves, trimmed, peeled, **minced**

2 tablespoons curry powder (*masala*, available at supermarkets)

2 habanero peppers, trimmed, seeded, finely chopped

1/2 teaspoon sugar

1 cup water

salt and pepper to taste

Equipment: Large skillet, spatula, serving bowl

1. Heat oil in skillet over medium-high heat and add fish. Using spatula to turn, fry until cooked through and golden brown on both sides, about 10–12 minutes. Transfer to serving bowl, cover, and keep warm.
2. Add onions, garlic, and hot peppers to skillet, adding more oil as needed to prevent sticking. **Sauté** until soft about 2–3 minutes.
3. Stir in curry powder, water, sugar, and salt and pepper to taste and mix well. Reduce to simmer and cook 4–6 minutes, stirring occasionally. Pour mixture over fish in serving bowl.
4. Serve warm as main dish with white rice.

Uruguay

Uruguay, a small country bordering the South Atlantic Ocean, is located east of Argentina and south of Brazil. Most of the usable land is devoted to raising animals and growing crops. The most popular meat in Uruguay is beef and is cooked in many forms: roasted on a spit, grilled, pan-fried, and cooked into a hardy stew.

Mate, a tea, is popular here as well. Since Argentina and Uruguay are so similar in customs and food, they can be considered sister countries. Thus, recipes can be interchanged to fit your needs.

❧ *Dulce de Leche* (Sweet Milk)

A sweet dessert, popular in Uruguay and all over South America, is called *dulce de leche* and is made from sugar and milk.

Yield: 20 candies

1 14.5-ounce can sweetened condensed milk   1/2 cup **finely chopped** nuts: pecan, peanuts, walnuts, or almonds

Equipment: **Double boiler** with cover, pie pan, plate covered with wax paper

1. Fill bottom pan of double boiler with about 3 inches of water. Bring to boil over high heat.

2. Pour sweetened condensed milk into top pan, cover, and set over pan of boiling water. Allow water to boil for about 5 minutes. Reduce heat to medium and cook for about 2 1/2 to 3 hours. Carefully and frequently check water level in bottom pan to make sure it does not boil dry. Keep kettle of hot water on stove to add to bottom pan to prevent from drying out.

3. When milk is thick, remove from heat and cool to room temperature. Refrigerate for about 1 hour.

4. Place nuts in pie pan. Take tablespoon of cooled milk, roll into ball, then roll in chopped nuts. Place balls side-by-side on wax paper. Cover and refrigerate.

5. Serve as a candy treat. They keep well for several weeks if refrigerated.

Yucca with Tangerine and Grapefruit Sauce

Yield: serves 4 to 6

1 1/2 pounds yucca, fresh or frozen, **trimmed, coarsely chopped**

3 tablespoons lime juice

2 6-ounce cans mandarin oranges, drained

1 pink seedless grapefruit, peeled, cored, membrane removed, diced

1 red onion, trimmed, peeled, thinly sliced

1 bunch chives, trimmed, coarsely chopped

1 tablespoon parsley, trimmed, coarsely chopped

1 tablespoon cilantro leaves, trimmed, **julienned**

garlic granules, to taste

salt and pepper, to taste

Equipment: Large saucepan, colander, large salad bowl, medium mixing bowl, tongs or salad fork, spoon

1. Place yucca in saucepan, cover with water, and bring to boil over high heat. Reduce to simmer and cook until yucca is translucent, about 45–50 minutes. Remove from heat and keep in water. When cool, drain in colander and transfer to salad bowl.

2. In medium mixing bowl, add lime juice, mandarin oranges, grapefruit sections, red onion, chives, parsley, and cilantro. Mix well. Add garlic, salt and pepper to taste.

3. Pour lime and fruit mixture over yucca. Using tongs or salad fork and spoon, toss well.

4. Serve chilled as appetizer or side dish.

Venezuela

Venezuela, an oil-rich nation, is located on the northern coast of South America bordered by Columbia to the southwest, Brazil to the south, and Guyana to the east.

In many pockets of the Amazon region, indigenous peoples live pretty much as they have for hundreds of years, eating what they can forage from the forest or grow by slash and burn farming techniques. Their lives remain untouched by modern society except for the occasional anthropologist, missionary, or government census taker.

In direct contrast to the isolated groups of indigenous peoples are the modern cities, such as Caracas, which thrive on oil money. Although oil is important to the Venezuelan economy, most people in the country are involved in agriculture. Fish and shellfish are also important exports in Venezuela.

Pabellon Criollo (Sliced Steak with Rice and Black Beans)

Pabellon means flag, and this national dish is tricolored like the Venezuelan flag.

Yield: serves 6

2 pounds skirt or flank steak

2 cups water

4 bay leaves

1/4 cup olive oil

1 onion, **trimmed**, peeled, **finely chopped**

6 cloves garlic, trimmed, peeled, **minced** or 2 teaspoons garlic granules

2 cups **stewed** tomatoes, homemade or canned

salt and pepper to taste

4 cups rice (cooked according to directions on package, keep warm for serving)

4 cups cooked black beans, homemade (see page 239) or canned, heated through for serving

Equipment: Medium saucepan with cover or **Dutch oven**, sharp meat knife, large skillet

1. Place meat, water, and bay leaves in saucepan and bring to boil over high heat. Reduce heat to simmer, cover, and cook for about 1 1/2 hours until meat is tender. Remove cover and set pabellon aside to cool in pan juices for about 1/2 hour.

2. Remove meat from pan, place on work surface, and cut into 1/4-inch-thick slices. Set aside any remaining pan juices and discard bay leaves.

3. Heat oil in skillet over high heat. Add onion and garlic and **sauté** until onion is soft, about 3–5 minutes. Add tomatoes, remaining pan juices, and salt and pepper to taste. Mix well. Add meat and simmer until heated through, about 10 minutes.

4. To serve pabellon arrange sliced meat in middle of large platter with cooked rice along one side and black beans along opposite side; hence, a three-color effect.

6

The Middle East

During the nineteenth century, the term "Middle East" was coined to reflect the region's relative location to Europe. Some people extend the boundaries of the Middle East farther west and east, but for this book, it stretches from Egypt in the west, to Iran in the east, Turkey in the north, and the Indian Ocean in the south. Middle Eastern countries are Egypt, Israel, Lebanon, Syria, Jordan, Saudi Arabia, Yemen, Oman, United Arab Emirates, Qatar, Bahrain, Kuwait, Iraq, Iran, Cyprus, and Turkey.

Middle Eastern cookery is distinctive, rich, and subtle in flavor. Spices are not only used to season food but also for the natives' medicinal and therapeutic purposes. Spices used in abundance include fennel, **cilantro**, mint, parsley, **cardamom**, ginger, nutmeg, and **turmeric**. In addition, favorite fruits and vegetables include cucumbers, eggplant, garlic, lettuce, onions, tomatoes, zucchini, oranges, and lemons. Frequently used grains and legumes are **bulgur** wheat, chickpeas, **lentils**, rice, whole wheat flour, and fava or broad beans known as *ful medames*. The most common nuts are almonds and pine nuts.

Due to strict Islamic dietary laws, only animals that have been slaughtered by one first asking God's permission through prayer are permitted to be eaten. Other foods that are forbidden are pork and animals that have not been slaughtered according to Muslim tradition. Jewish dietary laws are explained in the Israel section (see page 295).

Popular drinks include fruit juices, tea, coffee, camel's milk, soda, yogurt mixed with water, and sweet waters flavored with edible flowers.

Except for the inhabitants of Cairo, Beirut, and other metropolitan areas, most Muslims retain traditional eating practices. Often eating utensils are not used; instead soup is sipped from the bowl and food is eaten with clean fingers of the right hand. After platters of food are placed on low tables, the family and guests gather around on floor cushions to enjoy the meal. Many recipes within this section require rolling the food into little balls, making it is easier to eat with the fingers of your right hand.

CYPRUS

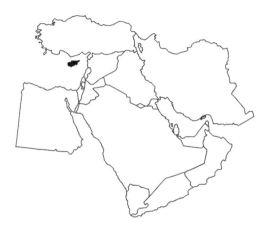

Cyprus is an island nation in the eastern Mediterranean Sea. A large number of Cypriots are involved in agriculture. In the fertile plains between their mountain ranges potatoes, wheat, barley, vines, vegetables, grapes, and citrus fruits are grown. Sheep, goats, donkeys, and cattle are raised. Dairy farming is important here because of the demand for yogurt and cheeses. The cooking habits of Cyprus are similar to its neighbors, Greece and Turkey, yet Cypriots have added some foods and a cooking style definitely their own.

Polpikilo (Mixed Vegetables)

In this recipe, potatoes, a main crop in Cyprus, are used along with other fresh vegetables.

Yield: serves 6

1 eggplant, **trimmed**, cut into 1/2-inch thick slices

salt and pepper to taste

1/4 cup corn or vegetable oil

2 cups soft white bread, **finely chopped**

3 cloves garlic, trimmed, peeled, **minced** or 1 teaspoon garlic granules

2 cups new potatoes, trimmed, thinly sliced

2 cups zucchini, trimmed, cut into 1/4-inch slices

2 tomatoes, trimmed, thinly sliced

1/2 to 1 cup water

Equipment: **Colander** or strainer, paper towels, 2 1/2-quart baking dish

1. Preheat oven to 350°F.
2. Place slices of eggplant in colander, sprinkle with salt, set aside in sink or over plate for about 30 minutes. Rinse well and pat dry with paper towels.

3. Pour 1/8 cup oil in baking dish and swirl to coat bottom and sides. Add 1 cup chopped bread and half of the garlic. Cover with eggplant slices, add layers of potatoes, zucchini and tomatoes, and season with salt to taste. Repeat layering, ending with tomatoes. Sprinkle remaining bread, garlic, 1/2 cup water, remaining oil, and salt and pepper to taste over tomatoes.

4. Bake in oven for about 1 1/2 hours, until vegetables are tender. Add more water if necessary. The dish should be fairly moist but not soupy.

5. Serve hot or at room temperature, as a vegetarian main dish or with meat, fish, or poultry.

EGYPT

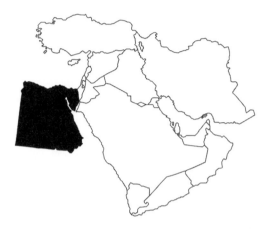

Egyptians have cultivated nature's bounty for thousands of years. Organized agriculture along the Nile in northern Africa began around 6000 BC. Egyptians discovered the leavening process that makes bread rise and how to preserve fish through salting and drying. Ancient wall paintings in the pyramids depict these wonders in minute detail, and supplies of food have been found intact in these ancient pharaohs' tombs, adding a great deal to our knowledge of what was eaten.

Today, Egyptians live among sand dunes, pyramids, camel caravans, and magnificent art and architecture. The foods rural Egyptians enjoy have changed little over the years. The growing season has become year-round because of the irrigation provided by the Aswan Dam, completed in 1971. Now Egyptians grow rice, sugar cane, and melons in the summer; corn in the fall; wheat in the winter; and a variation of these and other crops, such as onion and beans, during the spring. Throughout the rural areas, little kitchen gardens are found alongside many homes, supplying a few fresh vegetables for daily use. Sustaining the Egyptian economy, however, are cash crops of sugar cane, cotton, wheat, and other grains.

Most people buy foodstuffs at the colorful open air markets selling everything imaginable. People live quite well, and city dwellers enjoy foods from around the world. The use of silverware, china, and napkins is commonplace in urban homes.

❧ *Ful Mesdames* (Brown Fava Beans)

The national dish of Egypt is *ful mesdames*, or brown fava beans. It is as old as the pyramids and is said to have been eaten by the pharaohs. Fava beans can be eaten for breakfast, lunch, and supper by desert nomads as well as wealthy sheiks.

Yield: serves 2 to 4

2 tablespoons olive oil, more as needed

2 cups cooked brown fava beans, dried (cooked according to directions on package) or canned (drained), available at most supermarkets and health food stores

3 cloves garlic, trimmed, peeled, **finely chopped** or 1 teaspoon garlic granules

salt and pepper to taste

2–4 **hard-cooked eggs**, peeled, for garnish

1/2 cup chopped parsley, for garnish

1 lemon quartered, for garnish

Equipment: Medium saucepan, mixing spoon

1. Heat 2 tablespoons oil in saucepan over medium heat. Stir in beans, garlic, and salt and pepper to taste. Mix well. Cook until heated through, about 8–10 minutes. Add oil if necessary to prevent sticking.

2. Serve in individual bowls. Place a hard-cooked egg in each bowl, cover with hot beans, sprinkle with parsley, and serve lemon wedges on side.

❧ *Bamia* (Lamb and Okra Stew)

Yield: serves 6

2 tablespoons vegetables oil, more as needed

2 onions, **trimmed**, peeled, **finely chopped**

4 cloves garlic, trimmed, peeled, **minced** or 2 teaspoons garlic granules

2 pounds lean lamb or beef, cut into 1-inch **cubes**

4 cups chopped okra, fresh (trim ends) or frozen

3 tomatoes, trimmed, **peeled**, cut in cubes or 2 cups canned **stewed** tomatoes, drained, chopped

1/2 cup tomato sauce

1 teaspoon ground **cilantro**

1/2 teaspoon ground **cardamom**

salt and pepper to taste

4 cups water, more as needed

juice of 1 lemon

Equipment: Large saucepan with cover, mixing spoon

1. Heat 2 tablespoons oil in saucepan over medium heat. Add onions and garlic and **sauté** until soft, about 3–5 minutes. Mix well. Increase heat to medium-high. Add meat and brown on all sides, stirring frequently; add more oil if necessary, to prevent sticking.

2. Stir in okra, tomatoes, tomato sauce, cilantro, cardamom, and salt and pepper to taste. Add just enough water to cover meat and vegetables. Bring to boil, reduce to simmer, cover, and cook about 1 1/2 hours or until meat is tender and sauce is thick but not dry. If too dry, add more water; stir frequently. Remove from heat and stir in lemon juice.

3. Serve *bamia* in individual bowls. Plenty of flat bread is needed to sop up stew.

Kosheri (Lentils, Rice, and Macaroni Stew)

Throughout Egyptian cities, *kosheri* street vendors ladle out portions of rice, lentils, and macaroni from huge vats. Customers help themselves to toppings of fried onions and spicy tomato sauce. This recipe produces a popular, nourishing, and filling meal.

Yield: serves 4 to 6

1 cup cooked brown **lentils** (cooked according to directions on package)

1 cup elbow macaroni (cooked according to directions on package)

1 cup rice (cooked according to directions on package)

2 tablespoons vegetable oil

2 cups onion, **trimmed**, peeled, **coarsely chopped**

1 1/2 cups chunky-style spaghetti sauce, homemade, canned or bottled

2 tablespoons distilled white vinegar

1 teaspoon crushed red pepper, to taste

1/2 cup water

salt and pepper to taste

Equipment: **Colander** or strainer, large mixing bowl, medium skillet, mixing spoon, small and medium serving bowls

1. Drain cooked lentils and cooked macaroni in **Colander** or strainer and place in large mixing bowl. Add cooked rice, gently toss, and set aside in warm place.

2. *Prepare fried onions*: heat oil in skillet over medium heat. Add onions and mix well. **Sauté** until tender and slightly browned, about 2–3 minutes. Remove from heat, transfer to small serving bowl, and set aside.

3. *Prepare tomato sauce*: using same skillet, combine spaghetti sauce, vinegar, red pepper, water, and salt and pepper to taste. Mix well. Bring to boil over high heat. Reduce to simmer and cook for 3–5 minutes. Remove from heat, place in serving bowl, and keep warm.

4. To serve, ladle 1/2 cup, more or less, lentils, rice, and macaroni mixture into individual bowls. Add your own toppings of fried onions and tomato sauce.

Khoshaf 'ar' 'asali (Pumpkin Pudding)

The original recipe uses fresh pumpkin, but we suggest using canned pumpkin since it is available year-round.

Yield: serves 6 to 8

216-ounce cans pumpkin, mashed

sugar to taste

1/4 cup raisins

1/4 cup grated coconut

1/4 cup slivered almonds

ground cinnamon to taste

cardamom to taste

Equipment: Medium nonstick saucepan, mixing spoon

1. Place pumpkin in saucepan and simmer over medium-low heat. Add sugar to taste (about 1/2 cup) and continue cooking about 15–20 minutes until sugar is dissolved and pumpkin is cooked through.

2. Remove from heat and let cool. Add raisins, coconut, almonds, cinnamon, and cardamom to taste.

3. Serve in individual bowls with a dollop of whipped cream.

IRAN

Iran is an oil-rich nation, deriving much of its revenue from oil exports. The country, formerly known as Persia, is one of the oldest continuous civilizations in the world, dating back to 4000 BC. The people, foods, and language of Iran are known as Persian.

Spices were brought by camel caravans of Muslim traders and ships traveling to Europe across the Indian Ocean from the Far East. Many of the unique spices introduced to Persians are still used in today's cooking.

Iranians love their yogurt and it is eaten in many ways: cheeses (recipe page 308), drinks, desserts, or simply as a sauce over other foods.

✒ *Khorak-e Mai Sefid* (Pan-Fried Fish)

In many cultures holiday traditions require the eating of special foods. An important Iranian holiday is the New Year (*no ruz*), celebrated with the arrival of spring. The combination of *khorak-e mahi sefid* (pan-fried fish) **fillets** with *sabzi pollo* (green herb rice) is traditionally eaten then.

Yield: serves 4 to 6

1 cup all-purpose flour

salt and pepper to taste

4 or 6 fish **fillets**, about 8 ounces each, rinsed, patted dry

4–6 tablespoons butter, margarine, or **ghee**

lemon wedges for garnish

Equipment: Plate, large skillet, pancake turner or metal spatula

1. Combine flour and salt and pepper together on plate.

2. Coat each fillet with seasoned flour and shake off excess.

3. Heat 4 tablespoons butter, margarine, or ghee in skillet over medium-high heat, swirling pan to coat bottom. Pan-fry fillets on both sides until golden brown, about 6 minutes per side. Add more butter, margarine, or ghee and reduce heat to medium if necessary.

4. Serve with wedges of lemon and *sabzi pollo* (recipe page 290).

✒ *Chelo Kabab* (Ground Meat Patties)

The *chelo kebab* is the national dish of Iran. It is served over a bed of rice.

Yield: serves 4 to 6

1 pound ground lamb or beef

2 eggs

1 onion, **trimmed**, peeled, **finely chopped**

1/4 teaspoon ground cinnamon

3 cloves garlic, trimmed, peeled, **minced**

1/4 teaspoon marjoram

salt and pepper to taste

Equipment: Medium mixing bowl, shallow baking pan or broiler pan

1. Preheat boiler.

2. In medium mixing bowl combine meat, eggs, onion, cinnamon, garlic, marjoram, and salt and pepper to taste. Using clean hands or mixing spoon, mix well. Take a handful of mixture and shape into a very fat hot dog; continue until all mixture is used. Place side-by-side in shallow baking pan or broiler pan. Broil on each side 4 minutes or until desired doneness.

3. Serve warm over bed of *sabzi pollo* (recipe follows) with a dollop of yogurt for each serving.

🌿 *Sabzi Pollo* (**Green Herb Rice**)

Adding fresh herbs to rice gives it a wonderful fragrant flavor.

Yield: serves 4 to 6

1/2 cup green onions, **trimmed, finely chopped**

1/4 cup fresh dill weed, trimmed, finely chopped or 2 tablespoons dried dill

1/2 cup fresh parsley, trimmed, finely chopped or 1/4 cup dried flakes

1/2 cup fresh **cilantro**, trimmed, finely chopped or 1/4 cup dried cilantro

1/2 cup butter, margarine, or **ghee**

4–5 cups cooked rice (cooked according to directions on package)

Equipment: Medium bowl, mixing spoon, large skillet with cover

1. Combine onions, dill weed, parsley and cilantro in bowl and mix well.

2. Heat butter, margarine, or ghee in skillet over medium heat. Swirl pan to coat bottom. Pour in 1/2 cooked rice and sprinkle with 1/2 herb mixture. Add remaining rice and sprinkle with remaining herb mixture. Do not mix. Cover and steam over low heat for 30 minutes.

3. Serve hot from skillet as a side dish with pan-fried fish (recipe page 289).

🌿 *Koofteh Tabrizi* (**Tabriz Meatballs**)

According to Iranian legend, the finest meatball makers are in the city of Tabriz, in northwestern Iran, where all kinds of surprises are stuffed into apple-sized meatballs. It is not unusual to find a filling of prunes, walnuts, or **hard-cooked** eggs. Highly accomplished Tabriz cooks have been known to make giant meatballs stuffed with whole chickens.

Yield: serves 4 to 6

2 pounds ground lean beef or lamb

4 onions, **trimmed**, peeled, **finely chopped**

2 eggs, lightly beaten

2 cups cooked rice (cooked according to directions on package)

Fillings:

2 dried apricots or **pitted** prunes, soaked 1 hour in warm water

salt and pepper to taste

1/4 teaspoon nutmeg

1/4 teaspoon cinnamon

2 walnut halves

1 egg, hard-cooked and shelled

2 cups *each* water and tomato paste

Equipment: Large mixing bowl, mixing spoon, greased medium baking pan

1. Preheat oven to 350°F.

2. Place meat, half of chopped onions, eggs, rice, salt, pepper, nutmeg, and cinnamon in mixing bowl. Mix well with clean hands and shape into apple-sized balls. Press one of the fillings into each meatball, seal, and shape the meatball again. (You will have 2 meatballs with apricots or prunes, 2 with walnuts, one with egg, and one with raisins.) Place meatballs side-by-side in baking pan.

3. Combine remaining onions, water, and tomato paste and mix well. Pour over meatballs and bake for 1 hour, turning at least once and **basting** with sauce.

4. Serve meatballs with side dish of cooked rice or vegetables.

﷼ *Khoresht-e Fesenjan* (Chicken in Pomegranate Sauce)

Khoresht, **stewed** meat or fowl served with rice, is the mainstay of Middle Eastern cooking. Made with a variety of meats and vegetables, a hostess often serves platters of several different khoreshts at a single feast. The queen of all stews is called *fesenjan*. It is prepared with great care for special occasions made with syrupy sauces from juices of fruits such as pomegranates. Pomegranates are found throughout the Middle East; they are not only used for cooking but the juice is as popular with natives as orange juice is with Americans. Persians have used the wood of the pomegranate tree for fuel, bark for tannic acid, and roots for medicine; juice is used for dyes; the fruit is depicted in carpet and fabric designs; and the pomegranate is a symbol in poetry. The following recipe combines **stewed** chicken with syrupy pomegranate juice.

Yield: serves 6

5 tablespoons butter, margarine, or **ghee**

6 boneless and skinless chicken breasts

2 onions, **trimmed**, peeled, **finely chopped**

1 cup chicken broth

1 cup water

2 cups **finely ground** walnuts

1 cup pomegranate syrup or genuine grenadine syrup

1/2 cup sugar, more or less to taste

1/2 teaspoon salt

1/2 teaspoon **turmeric**

1/4 teaspoon cinnamon

1/4 teaspoon nutmeg

1/4 teaspoon black pepper

2 tablespoons lemon juice, more or less to taste

Equipment: Large saucepan with cover or **Dutch oven**, mixing spoon, small saucepan

1. Melt butter, margarine, or ghee in saucepan or Dutch oven over medium-high heat. Add chicken breasts and cook until light brown on both sides, about 4 minutes per side. Add onions, chicken broth, and water and bring to boil. Reduce heat to simmer, cover, and cook for about 30 minutes.

2. *Prepare sauce*: place nuts, syrup, sugar to taste, salt, turmeric, cinnamon, nutmeg, black pepper, and lemon juice in small saucepan and mix well. Cook for about 3 minutes, until heated through. Pour mixture over chicken breasts and continue cooking chicken uncovered for about 30 minutes more until sauce thickens.

3. To serve, arrange chicken breasts on platter over a mound of cooked white rice and top with sauce.

❧ *Sholeh Zard* (Iranian Rice Pudding with Nuts)

Yield: serves 4 to 6

1/2 teaspoon saffron

1/4 cup hot water

2 cups white rice, cooked according to directions of box, cover and keep warm

2 cups sugar or to taste

4 tablespoons vegetable or canola oil

1/2 cup rosewater (available at international food markets or Middle Eastern markets)

2 tablespoons crushed pistachio, more as needed for garnish

2 tablespoons crushed almonds, more as needed for garnish

1/2 teaspoon crushed cinnamon, garnish

Equipment: cup, spoon, mixing spoon, medium oven-proof nonstick baking dish with cover

1. Preheat oven to 350°F.

2. Place saffron in cup and stir in water until saffron is softened, about 3–5 minutes. Set aside.

3. Add sugar, saffron water, oil, 2 tablespoons pistachios, 2 tablespoons almonds, and rosewater to rice. Mix well. Transfer to baking dish and cover and bake for 30 minutes.

4. Serve warm as dessert in individual serving bowls. Garnish with sprinkles of pistachios, almonds, and cinnamon.

IRAQ

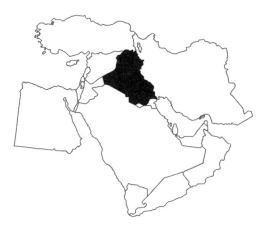

Iraq is an oil-rich nation with an ancient past. In the most recent millennium Iraq was divided into five cultural areas: Kurdish and various Christian people in the north,

Sunni Islamic Arabs in the central region, Shi'a Islamic Arabs in the south, and Marsh Arabs, a nomadic people, located in the marshlands.

In northeastern Iraq in the Kurdistan area, archeologists have uncovered 12 levels of a town called Jarmo. It is thought to be one of the oldest agricultural communities where farming was the way of life. Milling stones for wheat and fire-blackened stones where bread was baked have been found at even the lowest levels of the dig and date back 9,000 years. To this day, some Kurdish women still bake bread over fires in a 9,000-year-old, time-honored way.

From Jarmo similar agricultural practices radiated out to the better soils between the Tigris and Euphrates rivers, the site of ancient Mesopotamia. The soils between these two rivers are still the best agricultural areas in Iraq.

Nan-e Lavash (Flat Bread)

Yield: about 15 pieces

1/2 package dry activated yeast granules	1 teaspoon salt
1 1/2 cups lukewarm water	2 teaspoons vegetables oil
2 1/2 cups all-purpose flour	1 cup yellow cornmeal

Equipment: Cup, large mixing bowl, mixing spoon, floured work surface, kitchen towel, rolling pin, wax paper, 3 or 4 nonstick or greased baking sheets, small bowl

1. In cup, dissolve yeast in 1/2 cup of lukewarm water.

2. Combine 2 cups flour, salt, and oil in mixing bowl. Make well in center, add yeast mixture, remaining 1 cup water, and mix well. Transfer to work surface and **knead** dough until smooth and elastic for about 5 minutes.

3. Place dough in lightly greased mixing bowl, cover with towel, and set in warm place to double in bulk for about 1 1/2 hours.

4. Pinch off tennis-ball-sized pieces of dough and roll into balls. Repeat, using all the dough. Set 2 inches apart on baking sheets. Cover with towel and return to warm place to double in bulk, about 30 minutes.

5. Preheat oven broiler to high.

6. To bake, place flattened breads side-by-side on baking sheets and place under broiler heat for 15–20 seconds or until breads are crisp and brown.

7. Serve bread with Middle Eastern dishes. It keeps well wrapped in plastic.

Tepsi Baytinijan (Traditional Iraqi "Casserole")

Yield: serves 8 to 10

1 pound ground beef or lamb	salt and pepper to taste

1/2 cup vegetable oil, more as needed

2 eggplants, **trimmed**, peeled, cut across into 1-inch round slices

2 potatoes, trimmed, peeled, washed, sliced into 1-inch rounds

1 onion, trimmed, peeled, sliced into 1-inch rounds

6 garlic cloves, trimmed, peeled, **minced**

3 tablespoons tomato paste

2 1/2 cups water

2 tomatoes, washed, trimmed, sliced

Equipment: Medium mixing bowl, medium plate, nonstick large skillet, slotted spoon or tongs, baking sheet covered with several layers of paper towels, small bowl, wooden mixing spoon, measuring cup, greased large casserole dish or large baking pan, piece of foil to cover baking pan

1. Preheat oven to 350°F.

2. In medium bowl, combine ground meat with salt and pepper to taste. Using clean hands, make ping-pong-sized meatballs. Set on plate, cover, and refrigerate until ready to fry.

3. Heat 1/2 cup oil in skillet over medium-high heat. In batches, cook eggplant on both sides until lightly golden, about 3–5 minutes. Using tongs or slotted spoon remove from skillet and transfer to paper towels to drain.

4. Using same skillet, add more oil if necessary and cook potatoes on both sides until lightly golden, about 3–5 minutes. Using tongs or slotted spoon remove from skillet and transfer to paper towels to drain.

5. Using same skillet, add more oil if necessary and add sliced onions. Stirring frequently, **sauté** until soft, about 3–5 minutes. Using tongs or slotted spoon remove from skillet and transfer to paper towels to drain.

6. Using same skillet, add more oil if necessary and add meatballs one at a time and fry on all sides until lightly browned, about 5–8 minutes. Using tongs or slotted spoon, remove from skillet and transfer back to plate.

7. *Prepare for baking*: In small mixing bowl add tomato paste and crushed garlic to water and mix well. Set aside.

8. In baking dish or large baking pan, arrange eggplant pieces, slightly overlapping (if necessary to fit in pan). On top of eggplant, layer potato slices, then layer tomatoes on top of potatoes, and sprinkle with sautéed onions. Add meatballs and arrange evenly over top.

9. Cover with foil and bake in oven for about 45 minutes. Remove foil and bake uncovered for 10–15 minutes longer, until lightly browned and all vegetables are cooked through.

10. Serve warm over rice as main entrée.

ISRAEL

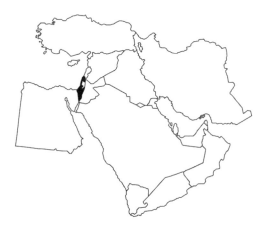

The foods of Israel are a blend of many cultures. Jewish people have immigrated from all around the world, even Asia, making Israel the land of a thousand and one flavors. The Israeli people follow many ancient practices, rituals, and laws handed down from generation to generation. The "strictly Kosher" dietary laws concerning selection, preparation, and eating of food dates back to Moses more than 3,000 years ago. These laws are deeply woven into Jewish religion and family life. The dietary laws were originally established for health reasons. Although today Israel has modern refrigeration, ice, healthful food and sanitation, ancient customs of not combining dairy with meat and not eating shellfish and certain animals continue to be practiced.

In many cultures food plays an important part in celebrations, festivals, and special days of remembrance. Traditionally flat unleavened bread called *matzo* is eaten during Jewish Passover as a reminder of the Jew's hurried flight from Egypt, when there was not time for the bread to rise. Today matzo is eaten at any time and matzo meal flour is available at most supermarkets.

✿ Chicken Soup with *Knaidlach* (Matzo Ball Dumplings in Chicken Soup)

Yield: serves 6 to 8

Matzo balls: (For quick matzo balls, a mix is available at most supermarkets)

2 tablespoons vegetable oil

2 eggs, slightly beaten

Soup:

1 chicken, cut into serving-sized pieces

1 cup matzo meal (available at most supermarkets)

2 tablespoons water

10 cups water, more as needed

2 ribs celery, **trimmed, coarsely chopped**

2 onions, trimmed, peeled, coarsely chopped

2 carrots, trimmed, coarsely chopped   salt and pepper to taste

Equipment: Medium mixing bowl, fork or **whisk**, plastic wrap to cover, large saucepan with cover, slotted spoon, medium roasting pan with cover, ladle

1. *Prepare dumplings*: Place oil and eggs in mixing bowl and mix well. Add matzo meal and water to egg mixture. Stirring constantly with fork or whisk, blend well. Add salt and pepper to taste. Cover and refrigerate until soup is ready.

2. *Prepare soup*: Place chicken, 10 cups water, celery, onion, and carrots in saucepan. Bring to boil, cover, reduce heat to simmer, and cook about 1 hour or until chicken is tender. Add salt and pepper to taste.

3. With slotted spoon transfer chicken and vegetables to roasting pan. Add 2 cups broth, cover, and keep warm. Keep remaining broth warm in saucepan over low heat.

4. Remove matzo ball mixture from refrigerator. Using clean hands or two spoons, form 6–8 balls, about 2 inches in diameter. Carefully drop balls one at a time into chicken soup, until all mixture is used.

5. Increase heat under soup to medium-high. Cover and reduce heat to simmer for about 20–30 minutes or until matzo balls float to surface of soup.

6. To serve matzo balls, place one in each soup bowl and ladle hot broth over it. Remove chicken and vegetables from oven, transfer to a large platter, and serve after soup with side dishes of potatoes and vegetables.

❧ *Mandelbrot* (Almond Cookies)

In this *mandlebrot* recipe it is necessary to bake the cookies twice in order to get a crisp, crunchy texture.

Yield: 18 slices

3 eggs, beaten   1/4 teaspoon salt

1/2 cup sugar   1/2 teaspoon ground ginger

1 1/2 cups all-purpose flour   1 teaspoon ground cinnamon

1 teaspoon baking powder   1/2 cup almonds, **finely chopped, blanched**

Equipment: Large mixing bowl, **egg beater** or electric mixer, nonstick or greased medium oven-proof loaf pan, **serrated knife**, nonstick or plain cookie sheet

1. Preheat oven to 350°F.

2. Place eggs and sugar in large mixing bowl. Using egg beater or electric mixer, blend well. Add flour, baking powder, salt, ginger, cinnamon, and almonds and mix well.

3. Pour into loaf pan and bake about 45 minutes or until golden. Remove from oven and cool before using serrated knife to slice into 1/2-inch-thick pieces.

4. Reduce oven heat to 200°F.

5. Place slices side-by-side on cookie sheet and return to oven to dry out. Bake about 20 minutes on each side or until very dry and lightly toasted.

6. Serve mandelbrot as a cookie snack. It keeps indefinitely when stored in an airtight container.

☙ Lukshen Kugel (Noodle Pudding)

Kugels are hot puddings made with noodles, potatoes, and some vegetables. They are staple side dishes in many Israeli homes, and every cook has a special way of making *kugel*.

Yield: serves 6 to 8

3 eggs

1/2 cup sugar

1/4 teaspoon salt

1/4 teaspoon cinnamon

8 ounces medium noodles, cooked, drained (cook according to directions on package)

1/2 cup raisins

2 cups small-curd cottage cheese

1/2 cup sour cream

1 apple, **trimmed**, peeled, grated

1 teaspoon vanilla

3 tablespoons butter or margarine

Equipment: Large mixing bowl, wooden mixing spoon, large greased baking pan or casserole

1. Preheat oven to 350°F.

2. Place eggs, sugar, salt, and cinnamon in mixing bowl and mix well. Stir in cooked noodles, raisins, cottage cheese, sour cream, grated apple, and vanilla.

3. Pour noodle mixture into greased baking pan and smooth down with back of wooden mixing spoon. Bake in oven about 1 hour or until top is browned. Remove from oven and cool about 20 minutes.

4. Serve kugel as a side dish with meat or chicken. Kugel is delicious when cooled to room temperature.

☙ Kichels (Biscuits)

Yield: about 18 pieces

1 cup butter or margarine, room temperature

1 cup sugar

2 eggs

2 cups self-rising flour

Equipment: Large mixing bowl, mixing spoon, rolling pin, floured work surface, 2 nonstick or lightly greased cookie sheets, small bowl, fork, pastry brush

1. Preheat oven to 375°F.

2. Blend butter or margarine, sugar, and 1 egg in mixing bowl. Add flour. Using clean hands knead into stiff dough.

3. Using rolling pin, roll dough about 1/4-inch thick on floured work surface. Cut into 2″ × 4″ pieces. Place pieces side-by-side on cookie sheet about 1 inch apart. Beat remaining egg in small bowl, using fork. Lightly brush egg over tops of dough pieces. Bake for about 15–20 minutes or until puffy and golden.

4. Serve *kichels* as snack. They are great to dunk in milk or cocoa, and they keep well in a covered jar.

✌ *Tzimmes Fleishig* (Stewed Carrots with Meat)

There are many ways to prepare carrots and there are popular recipes for both meat and vegetarian dishes in Israel. When meat is added, the dishes are called *fleishig*, and when they are made or served with milk or dairy, vegetarian dishes are *milchig*. This recipe can be made with or without meat.

Yield: serves 4 to 6

1 pound lean brisket of beef, cut in small **cubes**

4 cups carrots, sliced, fresh, **trimmed** or frozen, thawed or canned, drained

1/2 cup light brown sugar

2 cups water, more as needed

1/2 cup all-purpose flour

Equipment: Medium saucepan with cover or **Dutch oven**, mixing spoon

1. Place beef, carrots, sugar, and 1 1/2 cups water in saucepan or Dutch oven. Bring to boil over high heat, reduce heat to simmer, cover, and cook until tender, about 1 hour. If necessary add more water to prevent sticking.

2. Mix 1/2 cup of remaining water with flour making smooth paste. Add to beef and carrots, mix well, and simmer about 15 minutes. Season with salt and pepper to taste.

3. Serve *tzimmes* as main dish with side dishes of potatoes or rice and bread.

✌ *Halvah* (Traditional Jewish Candy)

Yield: serves 6 to 10

1 cup honey

2 cups *tahini* (recipe page 312 or available at Middle Eastern markets)

1 cup powdered milk

1 teaspoon vanilla extract

Equipment: Medium saucepan, wooden mixing spoon, 8-inch square cake pan lined with wax paper or aluminum foil, sharp knife

1. In medium saucepan over medium-high heat, bring honey to boil. Remove from heat.

2. Stir in tahini until well blended and smooth.

3. Stir in powdered milk and vanilla.

4. Transfer to cake pan, using back of wooden mixing spoon spread across bottom until smooth and even. Allow to cool.

5. To serve, turn candy onto a cutting board and peel off wax paper or foil. With a sharp knife cut into 2-inch squares. Store in airtight container.

JORDAN

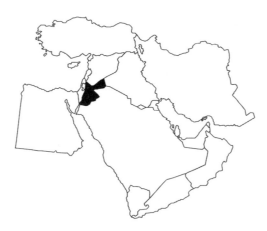

Jordan is a small, almost landlocked country. The only seaport is Aqaba on the Gulf of Aqaba. The economy is largely agricultural, despite the fact that only 10 percent of the land is usable for farming. Jordanians grow fruits and vegetables in their fertile mountainous areas to the west. Other principal crops include wheat, barley, and **lentils**. Nomadic Bedouins herd camels, goats, and sheep in the desert areas beyond the mountains to the east. More than half of the Jordanians live in the cities.

Jordanians' eating patterns differ somewhat from our own. Bread, white cheese, ripe olives, *hoomis* (recipe page 312), and *ful*, a bean dish (recipe page 286), are an interesting breakfast combination. Lunch is the main meal of the day. Meat, rice with nuts, and vegetable side dishes are commonly served.

Mansaf (Lamb in Yogurt Sauce)

Yield: serves 6 to 8

4 cups yogurt, homemade (recipe page 216) or store bought

clarified butter or *ghee* (recipe page 79), as needed

1 onion, **trimmed**, peeled, **coarsely chopped**

1 1/2 teaspoons **turmeric**

1/2 teaspoon ground allspice

2 teaspoons ground cinnamon

4 pounds lamb shoulder or lamb shank, cut into bite-sized pieces and reserve bones

water as needed

salt and pepper to taste

1/2 cup pine nuts, for garnish

1/2 cup almonds, for garnish

4 cups cooked rice, such as jasmine or basmati (cook according to directions on package)

Equipment: Large heavy-bottomed saucepan or **Dutch oven**, wooden mixing spoon, large stock pot with cover, slotted spoon, sieve, small skillet, small bowl, serving platter

1. Place yogurt in heavy-bottomed saucepan or Dutch oven and bring to boil over medium-high heat. Using wooden mixing spoon, stir constantly in one direction to prevent sticking. When yogurt comes to boil, remove from heat and set aside.

2. In stock pot over medium-high heat, melt 6 tablespoons butter. Add onions and stir constantly using wooden spoon. Fry until soft, about 2–3 minutes. Stir in turmeric, allspice, and cinnamon and **sauté** until well blended, about 2–3 minutes.

3. Place chunks of lamb with bones into stock pot with sautéed onions; add enough cold water to cover. Over medium-high heat bring water to boil. Skim, remove, and discard fat using ladle. Reduce heat to medium, cover, and boil until lamb is tender, about 45 minutes to 1 hour. Remove lid and over medium-high heat allow liquid to reduce by half. Add salt and pepper to taste.

4. Remove lamb using slotted spoon and set aside. Using sieve strain and reserve onions. Reserve 2–3 cups lamb stock and add to yogurt mixture. Mix well. Stir in meat and onions to yogurt mixture. Over medium-high heat bring mixture to boil and cook until sauce is thickened and heated through, about 5–8 minutes.

5. In skillet over medium-high heat, melt 2 tablespoons butter and add pine nuts and sliced almonds. Using wooden spoon, stir constantly and sauté until golden brown, about 2–3 minutes. Transfer from skillet to small bowl and set aside for garnish.

6. To serve, spoon warm yogurt with meat mixture over cooked rice. Garnish top with sautéed nuts and serve with bread.

Date and Nut Fingers

Yield: About 16 pieces

2 eggs, lightly beaten

1 cup sugar

2 cups walnuts or pecans, **finely chopped**

1 cup dates, finely chopped

1 cup candied cherries, finely chopped

1 teaspoon vanilla

1/2 cup all-purpose flour

1 teaspoon baking powder

Equipment: Large mixing bowl, mixing spoon, sifter, nonstick or greased medium baking pan

1. Preheat oven to 350°F.

2. Combine eggs and sugar in mixing bowl and mix until smooth. Add nuts, dates, cherries, and vanilla and mix well.

3. **Sift** flour and baking powder into mixture. Mix well. Pour into baking pan and spread evenly over bottom. Bake about 45 minutes or until lightly browned. Cut into finger-length strips while still warm.

4. Serve as a cookie or candy snack.

LEBANON AND SYRIA

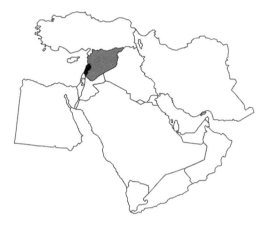

Lebanon is a tiny fertile country nestled on the Mediterranean Sea on Syria's eastern shore. Both countries are fertile and natives produce most of their own fresh fruits and vegetables that are essential to their diet. *Kibbeh* is the national dish of Lebanon and a very popular dish throughout the Middle East. Bulgur is one of the essential ingredients in kibbeh as well as in a *tabbouleh*, a special salad of this region. Bulgur is a cracked wheat grain with a nutty texture.

Baba Ghannooj (Eggplant Dip)

Sometimes called "poor man's butter," *baba ghannooj*, a popular Mediterranean spread, is a tasty dip to serve with raw vegetables, like carrots and celery sticks.

Yield: about 2 cups

1 eggplant (about 1 pound)

1 clove garlic, **trimmed**, peeled, **minced** or 1/4 teaspoon garlic granules

juice from 2 lemons

2 tablespoons sesame oil, more as needed

salt to taste

1 tablespoon **finely chopped** parsley, for garnish

Equipment: Fork, medium baking pan, oven mitts, medium bowl with cover, potato masher or electric blender

1. Preheat oven to 450°F.

2. Poke eggplant skin with fork tines in about 8 places. Place in baking pan and cook in oven until soft and tender, about 30–40 minutes. Remove from oven and, when cool enough to handle, cut in half. Scoop out meat and discard skin.

3. Place eggplant meat, garlic, lemon juice, 2 tablespoons oil, and salt to taste in medium bowl or blender. Blend mixture to smooth paste, either using potato masher or electric blender. If mixture is too dry add another tablespoon of oil. Cover and refrigerate until chilled, about 1–2 hours. When ready to serve, sprinkle with 1 tablespoon of remaining oil and parsley.

4. Serve in small bowl as dip for vegetables, chips, crackers, or chunks of flat bread.

Tabbouleh (Cracked Wheat and Parsley Salad)

Yield: serves 6

1 cup **bulgur** (available at some supermarkets and most health food stores)

1 cup hot water, more as needed

3 tomatoes, **trimmed**, peeled, **finely chopped**

1 bunch green onions, trimmed, finely chopped

1 1/2 cups parsley, trimmed, finely chopped

1/2 cup finely chopped fresh mint leaves or 3 tablespoons dried leaves

1/4 cup olive oil

1/2 cup lemon juice

salt and pepper to taste

leaf lettuce leaves, washed and patted dry, for garnish

Equipment: Small mixing bowl, mixing spoon, strainer, medium bowl

1. Place bulgur in small bowl and add enough hot water to just cover grains. Set aside for about 20 minutes, until water is absorbed and bulgur is tender. Drain through strainer and squeeze out excess water using back of spoon. Place bulgur in medium bowl and add tomatoes, green onions, parsley, and mint.

2. Mix oil and lemon juice in small bowl and add salt and pepper to taste. Pour over tomato salad and toss to mix well. Refrigerate until ready to serve.

3. Serve *tabbouleh* in bowl surrounded with lettuce leaves. Each person spoons mixture onto leaf and rolls it up, eating lettuce and all.

Fried Kibbeh (Hamburger Balls)

Kibbeh is the very popular hamburger of Syria and Lebanon made with ground meat, usually lamb, and cracked wheat (**bulgur**). The ingredients are blended until smooth and lump-free by either pounding in a **mortar** with a **pestle** or passing, several times, through the fine blade of a meat grinder. For the following recipe, ask the butcher to grind meat extra fine. Fine grain bulgur (resembling grains of sand) is available at most health food and all Middle Eastern food stores.

Yield: serves 4

1/2 cup fine grain bulgur (cracked wheat)	2 tablespoons water
1 pound finely ground meat (preferably lamb)	salt and pepper to taste
1 onion, **trimmed**, peeled, **finely chopped**	2 tablespoons olive oil, more or less as needed

Equipment: Strainer, medium mixing bowl, medium skillet, spatula

1. Place cracked wheat in strainer and rinse with cold running water. Drain well. Transfer to medium mixing bowl and add meat, onion, water, and salt and pepper to taste. Using clean hands, mix well until blended and lump-free. Divide into 4 equal parts and, using wet hands, shape each into an oblong patty.

2. Heat oil in skillet over medium-high heat. Add patties and fry until browned and well done (about 5 minutes on each side). Add more oil if necessary to prevent sticking.

3. Serve each person *kibbeh* with a side dish of beans and rice.

Inib im-khullal (Spiced Grape Relish)

Yield: 6 pint jars

3 cups sugar	1/2 teaspoon ground cinnamon
1 cup white vinegar	1/2 teaspoon sweet basil
1/2 teaspoon cardamom seeds	4 pounds seedless white grapes, washed, stemmed, and cut in half lengthwise
3/4 teaspoon ground nutmeg	
1/2 teaspoon ground ginger	

Equipment: Large nonstick saucepan, wooden mixing spoon, candied thermometer or small glass of water, 6 one-pint jars

1. Place sugar, vinegar, and spices in saucepan over medium-high heat. Stirring frequently, boil for 10–12 minutes or until mixture has thickened. To test doneness, candied thermometer will reach 234°F. Or, using wooden spoon take small amount of syrup and drop into glass of water; if sugar mixture holds together it is ready. Remove from heat and let cool until mixture thickens, about 30–45 minutes.

2. Reheat over medium-low heat until small bubbles appear around top edge of mixture. Stirring constantly, add in grapes and cook until grapes are tender but not soft, about 3–4 minutes. Transfer grape mixture to the pint jars, seal, and store in dry cool place for 2 days before serving.

3. Serve as relish with meat or fish.

✤ *Ma'mounia* (Dessert)

This nourishing pudding, *ma'mounia*, dates back to the ninth century when camel caravans were the only means of travel between ancient cities. Traveling back through time and to other Mediterranean cities, one finds many variations and different names for this sweet dish, but they're all basically the same. In Syria ma'mounia is often served for breakfast. **Semolina**, an ingredient in this recipe, is a by-product of wheat flour. There are two kinds of semolina: one made from regular wheat used in puddings (the kind needed for this recipe), and **durum wheat** semolina, used in pasta making.

Yield: serves 4 to 6

3/4 cup sugar

2 cups water

1/2 cup butter or margarine

1 cup semolina (made from regular wheat, not durum wheat)

1/2 cup each raisins and slivered almonds

1/4 teaspoon salt

1 cup heavy cream, whipped, or yogurt for garnish

Equipment: Small saucepan, wooden mixing spoon, medium saucepan

1. Heat sugar and water in small saucepan and bring to boil. Stirring frequently with wooden spoon, reduce to simmer for about 10 minutes or until mixture thickens.

2. In medium saucepan melt butter or margarine. Add Semolina and cook over low heat, stirring continually for about 3 minutes to heat through.

3. Pour sugar mixture, raisins, almonds, and salt into semolina. Increase heat and bring to boil. Reduce heat to simmer and stir continually until thick, about 5 minutes. Remove at once from heat.

4. Serve warm or cold in individual dessert bowls. Serve with side dishes of either whipped cream or yogurt to spoon over it.

SAUDI ARABIA

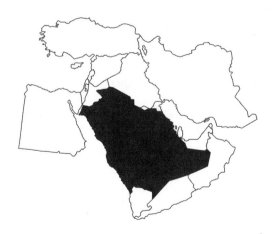

Saudi Arabia, an oil-rich country, occupies most of the Arabian Peninsula. Most Saudis are Sunni Muslim and they are known for their hospitality. There is a large group of Bedouin nomads that traditionally live in the desert and raise livestock and camels. Desert nomadic Bedouins generally eat little meat; however, when guests arrive, an animal is killed, stuffed, and roasted for the occasion. Camel's milk is an important part of the Bedouins' diet. (Milk is usually warmed and rarely served cold.) A popular rice, called *basmati*, is imported from Pakistan. Often a little clarified butter and onion are mixed with the rice to enhance flavor.

In the cities, the variety of foods available and the methods of cooking are very different. Wealthy city dwellers have the foods of the world at their fingertips. They use modern kitchen equipment and, of course, have ovens in which to bake foods.

Yalanchi (Stuffed Tomatoes)

This stuffed tomato dish has a typical Middle Eastern stuffing used to fill all kinds of vegetables as well as grape and cabbage leaves.

Yield: serves 6

6 medium-large, firm, ripe tomatoes

2–4 teaspoons olive or vegetable oil

1 onion, **trimmed**, peeled, **finely chopped**

1/2 cup raisins, soaked in warm water
   10 minutes, drained

1/2 cup pine nuts

1/2 teaspoon ground cinnamon

2 1/2 cups rice (cooked according to directions
   on package)

salt and pepper to taste

Equipment: Paper towels, large skillet, mixing spoon, teaspoon, nonstick or greased 9-inch baking pan

1. Preheat oven to 350°F.

2. Cut a slice from top of each tomato, about 1/4 to 1/2 inch down. **Core** and finely chop tops. Scoop out tomatoes and turn upsidedown on paper towels to drain. Refrigerate **pulp** to use at another time.

3. Heat 2 tablespoons oil in large skillet over medium-high heat. Add onion and cook until soft, about 3 minutes; stir frequently. Add chopped tomato tops, raisins, pine nuts, and cinnamon and mix well. Reduce heat to simmer for about 2 minutes. Remove from heat and add cooked rice and salt and pepper to taste. Mix gently until well blended.

4. Fill tomatoes with mixture and set side-by-side in baking pan. Dab remaining oil on tomatoes so they are well greased. Bake in oven until tender but still firm, about 25 minutes.

5. Serve warm or at room temperature for best flavor.

❧ *Lahooh Bel Loaz* (Almond Pancakes)

Yield: serves 8 to 10

Pancakes:

1 cup milk

4 eggs, well beaten

1 cup all-purpose flour

1 teaspoon salt

1 tablespoon vegetable oil, more as needed

Filling:

1 tablespoon cardamom

1 cup confectioner's sugar

2 cups almonds, roasted and finely ground

slivered almonds and confectioner's sugar for garnish

yogurt for serving

Equipment: Large mixing bowl, electric mixer or **whisk**, small mixing bowl, mixing spoon, nonstick medium skillet, ladle, baking pan, kitchen towel, serving platter

1. In medium mixing bowl, add milk to eggs and slowly stir in flour and salt. Blend until smooth. Heat 1 tablespoon oil in skillet over medium-high heat. Using ladle, pour only enough batter into skillet to make thin pancake. Tip skillet from side-to-side until batter covers bottom of pan. Brown pancake on each side and stack, slightly overlapping on baking pan and cover with towel. Set aside and keep warm. Continue until all batter is used, adding more oil as needed.

2. In small bowl stir together confectioner's sugar, almonds and cardamom. Mix well and set aside.

3. Sprinkle 2 tablespoons filling mixture over surface of pancake and roll-up one at a time. Place side-by-side on serving platter.

4. Serve warm and garnish with slivered almonds, confection's sugar mixture, and dollop of yogurt.

TURKEY

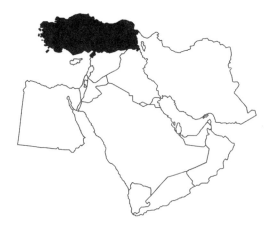

Turkey is in both Europe and Asia and it has been influenced by both regions, but the food is more similar to that from the Middle East. Turkish food, in particular sweets and coffee, are outstanding. Turkey gave us *shish kabobs* and *pilaf* (rice dish). Olive oil and butter are the preferred cooking oils. Commonly used seasonings include garlic, parsley, dill, mint, bay leaves, oregano, pepper, allspice, cinnamon, and paprika. Fresh vegetables are preferred. Some favorites are eggplant, tomatoes, cucumbers, green peppers, and okra. Drying and pickling of fruits and vegetables preserve summer's bounty. Agriculture is an important part of the Turkish economy. In some areas up to three growing seasons are possible, producing a wide variety of fruits, grains, and vegetables. Most of the world's supply of hazelnuts comes from Turkey. Interestingly, world-famous Turkey coffee is only served at special times. Coffee is too expensive to drink daily, and so tea is the national beverage of Turks.

Imam Bayildi (Vegetarian Stuffed Eggplant)

This dish, *Imam bayildi*, literally means, "the Imam fainted." As the legend goes, a certain Imam (Muslim religious leader), after observing a holy day and ending a long fast, was so taken with the delicious aroma of this dish, he fainted dead away.

Yield: serves 4

4 small eggplants, washed, patted, dry, **trimmed**

1/8 cup olive oil or vegetable oil

2 onions, trimmed, peeled, **coarsely chopped**

3 cloves garlic, trimmed, peeled, **minced** or 1 teaspoon garlic granules

2 green peppers, trimmed, **seeded, coarsely chopped**

2 tomatoes, trimmed, peeled, coarsely chopped

1/2 cup tomato paste

1/2 cup parsley, trimmed, **finely chopped**

salt to taste

2 cups water, more or less as needed

Equipment: Potato peeler, large skillet, mixing spoon, large baking pan (big enough to hold 4 eggplants and water)

1. Preheat oven to 375°F.

2. Cut 1-inch-deep slice from stem end down length of each eggplant. With small spoon, scoop out **pulp**, leaving about 1/4-inch wall around sides. Set scooped-out pulp aside. Sprinkle inside of shell with salt and turn upsidedown on work surface for about 1 hour to drain.

3. Heat oil in skillet over medium-high heat. Add eggplant pulp, onions, garlic, and peppers. Mix well and fry until onions are soft. Reduce heat to simmer and stir in tomatoes, tomato paste, and parsley. Add salt to taste, mix well, and simmer for 3 minutes longer. Remove from heat.

4. Rinse eggplants to remove salt. Pat dry and place side-by-side in baking pan. Fill each with eggplant mixture. Pour about 1 inch of water in baking pan with eggplants and bake in oven for 45 minutes or until eggplants are tender when poked with a fork.

5. Serve hot or cold as a main dish. Each person is served an entire eggplant.

❧ Yogurt Cheese

This recipe for yogurt cheese is very easy to make. Thick yogurt is a standard food in almost all Islamic countries throughout the Middle East. A bowl of yogurt is brought to the table with almost all meals.

Yield: Depends on amount used

Plain yogurt

Equipment: Mesh filter: **colander** or strainer, cheese cloth, or clean nylon stocking

Pour plain yogurt (as much as you need) into mesh filter and let it drain for about 8 hours at room temperature.

Following are two easy ways to make a mesh filter:

1. Line strainer or colander with cheese cloth about the size of a handkerchief. (Surgical gauze can also be used.) Set strainer or colander on top of a slightly smaller pan and allow yogurt to drain free of liquid. Discard liquid.

2. A clean nylon stocking (panty hose) with reinforced top cut off makes a great filter. (You might need help holding the stocking top open while you fill it with yogurt.) Only the foot part of the stocking will be filled with yogurt. Tie leg part over kitchen sink faucet, allowing yogurt-filled bottom part to hang freely and drain.

3. To serve, remove yogurt cheese from container used for draining and transfer to serving bowl. Use as you would cream cheese.

❧ *Yayla Corbasi* (Vegetarian Yogurt Soup)

Yield: serves 4 to 6

1/4 cup white rice

4 cups water

salt to taste

3 tablespoons all-purpose flour

2 cups plain yogurt

1 egg

1 tablespoon butter or margarine

1 tablespoon fresh mint, **finely chopped**, for garnish

Equipment: Medium saucepan, mixing spoon, small mixing bowl, small saucepan

1. Place rice, water, and salt in medium saucepan and bring to boil over medium-high heat. Reduce to medium heat and cook 20 minutes or until rice is tender.

2. Place flour, yogurt, and egg in bowl. Mix well.

3. Stir in 3 tablespoons of hot liquid from soup mixture to yogurt mixture and mix well.

4. Gradually add yogurt mixture to soup mixture in saucepan and mix well. Stirring constantly, bring to boil. Reduce heat to simmer and cook 10 minutes.

5. In small saucepan melt butter or margarine over medium to low heat. Add mint and stirring constantly cook about 1 minute to release aroma. Remove from heat.

6. Serve warm in individual soup bowls with a small amount of mint butter drizzled over the top of each serving.

Shish Kabob (Meat Grilled on a Skewer)

Turkish soldiers invented the *shish kabob*. As the legend goes, the soldiers speared chunks of lamb with their swords and cooked the meat to perfection over open fires. Today, shish kabobs are **marinated**, threaded on skewers, and then grilled or broiled. It is best to cook meat and vegetables on separate skewers, as the meat takes longer to cook.

Yield: serves 4

1 pound lamb, boneless shoulder, cut into 1-inch chunks

1/4 cup lemon juice

2 tablespoons olive or vegetable oil

Salt and pepper to taste

1/2 teaspoons dried oregano flakes

2 green bell peppers, **trimmed**, **seeded**, cut into 1-inch chunks

2 onions, trimmed, peeled, each cut into 4 wedges

1 cup eggplant, trimmed, coarsely chopped into 1-inch chunks

Equipment: Medium mixing bowl, mixing spoon, 8 metal 10–12-inch skewers, broiler pan, oven mitts

1. Place lemon juice, oil, salt, pepper, and oregano in medium bowl. Mix well and add meat chunks. With clean hands make sure meat is well coated. Cover and refrigerate for about 4 hours, stirring frequently. Remove meat from **marinade**; set both aside. Preheat broiler or grill to hot.

2. Alternate chunks of green pepper, onion, and eggplant on 4 skewers.

3. Thread meat on 4 remaining skewers.

4. Place meat kabobs on broiler pan and broil in oven about 3 inches under heat for about 5 minutes. Using oven mitts, turn kabobs and **baste** with marinade. Broil for about 5 minutes more. Carefully place vegetable kabobs on broiler with meat kabobs. Brush all sides with marinade. Broil vegetables for about 5 minutes until golden brown or desired doneness.

5. Serve one meat and one vegetable kabob to each person and eat right off the skewer.

✵ Simple *Halva*

This dessert is a favorite among Turkish women since it makes a special gift to give to a friend or is a symbolic offering of devotion.

Yield: serves 6 to 8

4 tablespoons butter

1 cup cream of wheat

2 cups warm water

1/2 cup seedless raisins

1 cup nuts: pecans, almonds, or walnuts, **finely chopped**

Equipment: Medium skillet, wooden mixing spoon, 9-inch square baking pan

1. Melt butter in skillet over medium heat and add cream of wheat. Stir continually until it is golden brown, about 3–5 minutes.

2. Add water and sugar. Mixing continually, bring to a simmer, and cook until mixture thickens, about 10 minutes. It will turn quite thick. Remove from heat and add raisins and 1/2 cup nuts. Mix well. Pour mixture into baking pan. Using back of spoon, spread evenly.

3. Halva is like a thick pudding. Sprinkle the remaining 1/2 cup nuts on top. It is served and eaten with a spoon.

YEMEN, OMAN, UNITED ARAB EMIRATES, QATAR, BAHRAIN, AND KUWAIT

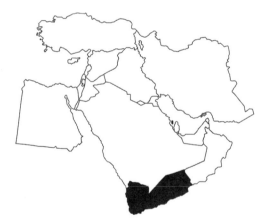

The following countries are all on the Arabian peninsula and share borders with Saudi Arabia. Each is a separate political entity, yet the countries share cultural heritage, including eating habits. All recipes from the Arabian peninsula are interchangeable. Crops that can be found in most of the following Middle Eastern countries include dates, limes, mangos, melons, wheat, bananas, and onions, which are grown in irrigated fields. Livestock raised include sheep, chickens, and goats.

Yemen

In 1990 North and South Yemen were united. Yemenites used to be some of the poorest people in the world. During 1996, an economic reform was launched with the help of the International Monetary Fund and the World Bank. Fishing is important to the Yemenites as well as raising livestock: mostly sheep, goats, and cattle. Some of the poorer Yemenites seldom eat meat; however, soup bones are customarily used for flavoring soups, such as lentil soup (recipe page 314).

Oman

The exploration of gas in Oman has improved the economy but during the slump in oil prices in 1998 Omanis began to diversify the economy by improving tourism and the development of natural gas. For centuries, fishing has assisted with improving the economy as well. Most fishing is done in the Gulf of Oman and the Arabian Sea.

United Arab Emirates

Oil exports have made this nation one of the wealthiest in the world. Most of the people live in the coastal cities. Grains have to be imported, however, by using pumping irrigation systems. The country is nearly self-sufficient in the growing of fruit and vegetables.

Qatar

Qatar is another oil-rich nation on the eastern coast of the Arabian peninsula. Most Qataris are city dwellers. Food has to be imported due to the lack of water and fertile soil. However, Qatar's economy is stable due to the abundance of oil reserves.

Bahrain

Bahrain is an island off the Arabian Peninsula in the Persian (Arabian) Gulf. The north and northwestern coasts have date groves and vegetable gardens, which are possible due to the springs and wells that provide artesian water. Although this is the fastest-growing nation in the Middle East, the depletion of both oil and underground water are major long-term concerns.

Kuwait

Located on the coast of the Persian Gulf, the name Kuwait means "fortress built near water." This small but powerful country is an oil-rich nation. In addition to oil production, Kuwait uses irrigation techniques to grow fruit, vegetables, and grains for livestock. The fishing industry is being revitalized, having been neglected after the discovery of oil. Prawns are the main catch in the Persian Gulf. Most of the land is desert, however, and oil money is what allows Kuwait to import its food.

❧ *Limonada* (Lemonade)

Lemon and lime are used in popular drinks in the Middle East. Here is a favorite recipe, nice and cold for a hot day.

Yield: 10 servings

1 1/2 cups lemon or lime juice with seeds removed (soak fruit in hot water before squeezing fruit for greatest yield)

1/2 cup corn syrup, or to taste

2 teaspoons orange blossom water (optional) (available at Middle East food stores)

8 12-ounce bottles of clear carbonated water

10 glasses with crushed ice

10 mint sprigs for garnish

Equipment: Pitcher, long stirring spoon

1. Place lemon or lime juice in pitcher, add syrup and orange blossom water, and mix well.
2. Pour about 1/4 cup mixture into each glass filled with crushed ice and fill to the top with carbonated water. Garnish each glass with a mint sprig.

❧ *Tahini* (Sesame Paste)

Yield: about 4 cups

5 cups sesame seeds (available at most super-markets and all international food markets)

1 1/2 cups olive or vegetable oil, more as needed.

Equipment: cookie sheet, metal spatula, oven mitts, blender or food processor, rubber spatula, plastic bowl with cover

1. Preheat oven to 350°.
2. Spread sesame seeds onto cookie sheet.
3. Toast seeds for 5–10 minutes, shaking seeds frequently with spatula. Do not allow to brown.
4. Using oven mitts, remove from oven and cool for 20–25 minutes.
5. Transfer seeds to blender or food processor and add oil. Blend for about 2 minutes. Turn off blender or food processor and using rubber spatula, mix to check consistency. Continue to blend until mixture is thick and smooth. Add more oil as needed to make a smooth, pourable texture. Store covered in plastic bowl in refrigerator.

❧ *Hoomis* (Chickpea Spread)

Hoomis, also spelled *hummus*, *homus*, and *humus* refers to **chickpeas** (also known as garbanzo beans) and to the following spread. Chickpeas are an important food throughout the Middle East.

Yield: 2 1/2 cups

2 cups cooked chickpeas, homemade (cook according to directions on package) or canned, with reserved liquid

2 tablespoons lemon juice

4 tablespoons *tahini*, homemade (recipe page 312) or bottled (available at most supermarkets)

1 teaspoon salt

3 cloves garlic, **trimmed**, peeled, **minced** or 1 teaspoon garlic granules

1/4 teaspoon ground red pepper (optional)

1 teaspoon olive oil or sesame oil for garnish

1 teaspoon finely chopped fresh parsley for garnish

Equipment: Electric blender, spoon or spatula, small bowl

1. Using blender, blend chickpeas, lemon juice, *tahini*, salt, and garlic until mixture is lump-free and resembles smooth paste.

2. Transfer to small bowl. Drizzle with oil and sprinkle with parsley and ground red pepper (optional).

3. Serve hoomis as a spread on pita bread or crackers or as a dip with raw vegetables such as carrot and celery strips, cut broccoli or cauliflower, cherry tomatoes, etc.

Cumin-Curry Tuna Salad with Dates and Chickpeas

In Oman this salad is made with purslane, a small salad green that is very popular in the Arab countries. As a substitute, mixed greens work very well. Tuna, abundant in the Gulf of Oman and the Arabian Sea, is the preferred fish in this region.

Yield: serves 2 to 4

2 8-ounce tuna steaks

2 teaspoons ground cumin

2 teaspoons curry powder, to taste

1 teaspoon paprika

salt to taste

2 tablespoons vegetable oil

2 cups mixed salad greens

2 tomatoes, **trimmed**, thinly sliced

1 onion, trimmed, peeled, thinly sliced

1 large mild red chili pepper, **seeded, finely chopped**

1/2 cup canned chickpeas, drained, rinsed

6 dates, pitted, quartered

1/3 cup olive oil

3 tablespoons fresh lemon juice, or to taste

Kosher salt to taste

Equipment: Clean work surface, nonstick skillet, spatula, cutting board, medium salad bowl, salad fork and spoon or tongs, 2–4 salad plates, sharp knife

1. On clean work space, season tuna steaks with ground cumin, curry powder, paprika, and salt to taste.

2. Heat 2 tablespoons vegetable oil in skillet over medium-high heat. Add tuna and cook for about 2 minutes on each side or until desired doneness. Transfer to cutting board.

3. In salad bowl, combine salad greens, tomato, onion, chili pepper, chickpeas, dates, olive oil, and lemon juice. Using salad spoon and fork or tongs, toss to mix well.

4. Using tongs or salad fork and spoon, divide salad among individual salad plates.

5. Using knife, cut tuna steaks into 1/4-inch slices and place on top of each salad.

6. To serve, sprinkle with kosher salt.

❧ *Shourba Bilsen* (Thick Lentil Soup)

This dish is particularly popular in Yemen.

Yield: serves 6

1 pound soup bones, beef or lamb

8 cups water

2 cups brown **lentils**

2 onions, **trimmed**, peeled, **finely chopped**

3 cloves garlic, trimmed, peeled, **minced** or
 1 teaspoon garlic granules

2 cups **stewed** tomatoes, homemade or canned

1/4 cup finely chopped **cilantro** leaves or
 3 tablespoons dried cilantro

salt and pepper to taste

Equipment: Large saucepan with cover or **Dutch oven**, mixing spoon

1. Rinse soup bones and place in saucepan with water. Bring to boil over high heat, then reduce to simmer.

2. Add lentils, onions, garlic, tomatoes, cilantro, and salt and pepper to taste. Cover and cook for 1 1/2 hours, stirring frequently to prevent sticking.

3. Serve hot in individual soup bowls. If there is meat on bones, eat it as well as the rich and nutritious bone marrow.

❧ Baked Guavas with Mushrooms and Olives

Yield: serves 6

6 large guavas, washed, patted dry, **trimmed**

1 tablespoon vegetable oil

1 cup mushrooms, trimmed, **coarsely chopped**

1/2 onion, trimmed, peeled, **finely chopped**

1/2 cup pitted green olives, coarsely chopped

4 teaspoons fresh dill weed finely chopped or
 1/2 teaspoon dried dill

salt and pepper to taste

1 tablespoon sesame seeds

Equipment: Sharp knife, melon ball scoop or small spoon, medium-large skillet, wooden mixing spoon, shallow medium baking pan (to hold 6 guavas), 1 sheet of foil to cover

1. Preheat oven to 325°F.

2. Prepare guava for stuffing: cut thin slice from top of each guava (about 1/4 inch.) With melon ball scoop or small spoon, remove and discard seeds. Set guavas aside.

3. Heat oil in skillet over medium-high heat. Stir in mushrooms, onion, olives, dill, and parsley. Stirring frequently, cook until vegetables are soft, about 3–5 minutes. Add salt and pepper to taste. Remove from heat and let cool.

4. Spoon stuffing mixture into each guava, filling to top. Place stuffed guavas side-by-side into baking dish. Sprinkle sesame seeds over top of each. Cover with foil and bake about 1 hour or until guavas are tender.

5. Serve warm as a side dish or main course.

Stuffed Dates, Figs, and Prunes

Stuffed dried fruit are popular sweet treats throughout the Middle East. They are tasty and wonderfully colorful when set in individual, mini paper cups or each wrapped in colored waxed tissue. Colored waxed tissue is available at most craft stores.

Yield: 30 pieces

10 **pitted** large whole dates

10 pitted large whole figs

10 pitted large whole prunes

2 cups confectioner's sugar

1 teaspoon almond extract

1 egg white (refrigerate yolk to use at another time)

30 whole pecans or walnuts or combination, more or less

1/2 cup sugar

Equipment: **Steamer pan**, large mixing bowl, mixing spoon, sharp knife, foil, cookie or baking sheet

1. Steam figs and prunes until soft, about 5 minutes over boiling water. Drain on paper towels to cool.

2. Place confectioner's sugar, extract, and egg white in bowl and mix well.

3. Cut fruit, making a slice halfway through each fruit. Fill each fruit cavity with about 1/4 teaspoon of mixture, then press whole pecan or walnut half onto filling so top side of nut shows.

4. Place sugar in flat dish and roll each filled fruit in it. Place side-by-side on foil and refrigerate until set, about 2 hours.

5. Serve as sweet snacks, box assortments, or stuffed fruits to give as gifts. They will keep refrigerated in covered containers for about 3 months; they can also be frozen.

Almond Biscuits

Yield: makes about 21

1/2 cup butter, margarine, or **ghee**	1 cup all-purpose flour
1/2 cup sugar	1/2 cup **crushed or finely ground** almonds
1 egg	1/2 cup sugar
1 teaspoon almond extract	21 whole almonds

Equipment: Large mixing bowl, mixing spoon, clean hands, flat dish, nonstick or greased cookie sheet

1. Preheat oven to 400°F.
2. Blend butter, margarine, or **ghee** with sugar in mixing bowl. Add egg and almond extract and mix well. Add flour and ground almonds and **knead** into stiff dough. Pinch off pieces and roll into ping-pong-sized balls between palms of hands.
3. Place sugar in flat dish and roll balls in sugar to coat. Press balls flat between hands. Place on cookie sheet and place an almond on top of each.
4. Bake in oven for about 10 minutes, until edges are browned.
5. Served almond biscuits as a cookie treat with tea or milk.

Fruit Balls

Yield: about 24

1/2 cup **pitted** dates, **finely chopped**	1/2 teaspoon ground cinnamon
1 cup seedless raisins, finely chopped	2 tablespoons lemon juice
1/2 cup prunes, finely chopped	1/2 cup grated coconut, homemade (recipe page 138), frozen, or canned
1/2 cup dried apricots, finely chopped	
1 cup almonds, finely chopped	

Equipment: Medium mixing bowl, flat dish

1. Mix dates, raisins, prunes, apricots, and almonds in medium bowl. Add cinnamon and lemon juice and mix well. Roll into ping-pong-sized balls using clean hands.
2. Pour coconut in a flat dish. Roll the fruit balls in coconut and press well between your hands. Set finished balls on flat plate or pan and refrigerate.
3. Serve as a midday snack.

7

North America

The United States and Canada, two neighboring countries, plus Mexico (covered in the Latin America section), make up the continent of North America. Mexico is included with the Latin American section because its cooking and culture are more closely related to the countries of Latin America than to Canada and the United States. Today, however, there is a considerable overlap in culture and cuisine between Mexico and its northern neighbors.

The United States and Canada have vast differences in climate, terrain, vegetation, and soil. Both countries are subdivided: Canada into 10 territories and 3 provinces and the United States into 50 states.

The rich history of both countries dates back to the early fifteenth century when European explorers boarded ships bound for the New World. Soon after discovering the vast land was rich and fertile, settlers from throughout Europe flooded into the new world. They brought with them a plethora of foods and cooking traditions from their homelands. As they arrived on the eastern shores of the New World many settlers began to build towns and cities while others explored the lands to the west, discovering unique plants, foods, and animals. As immigrants settled, they learned which areas were best to grow crops according to the climate and terrain. Today, the cooking of both nations reflects the mixed heritage of its many settlers and immigrants.

CANADA

Canada, located north of the United States (except for Alaska to the northwest), is bordered by three oceans with the Pacific Ocean to the west, North Atlantic to the east, and Arctic Ocean to the north. Canada is the second largest country in the world with the longest coastline in the world.

The majority of early Canadian settlers were French and British. Early settler cooking was simple; it depended upon what the people could catch, hunt, raise, and store. Fortunately, there was an abundant supply of wild game, birds, and fish. Canadians cooked wholesome stews and thick and nourishing soups of dried beans and peas and salted and smoked fish and meats. Old world cooking skills of France and Great Britain were used by the settlers to prepare the natural foods of their new homeland.

In recent years large numbers of Asians have immigrated and settled in Canada along the Pacific Coast, bringing with them the cuisine of their homelands.

Canada has regions that are known for different agricultural products. British Columbia grows exceptional fruits and nuts. Wild blueberries, wild mushrooms, along with a delicious asparagus-like fern called the fiddlehead (00) grow in the province of New Brunswick. Alberta raises prized grain-fed beef, Ontario is known for wild rice, and Quebec is known for cheese and maple syrup; some of the finest wheat grows on the western plains. Along with wheat, Canada is a leading exporter of fish and shellfish. The extensive coastline stretching over 151,000 miles along with thousands of fresh water lakes makes Canadian fishing industry one of the richest in the world.

✧ Cream of Fiddlehead Soup

Fiddleheads, also known as ostrich ferns in some parts of the world, resemble the curled ornamentation of a fiddle. Fiddleheads are a traditional dish of Quebec, and Tide Head, New Brunswick, claims to be the fiddlehead capital of the world.

Yield: serves 4 to 6

2 cups fiddleheads, **trimmed**, washed, drained,

1 tablespoon butter, more as needed

2 shallots, **trimmed**, peeled **finely chopped**

1/2 cup carrots, trimmed, finely chopped

1/2 cup leeks, trimmed, finely sliced (use white part only)

2 quarts, chicken or vegetable broth, home-made or canned

1 cup heavy cream

2 egg yolks

Equipment: Small saucepan, colander or strainer, large saucepan, mixing spoon, medium mixing bowl, whisk

1. Place fiddleheads in small saucepan and cover with water. Over medium-high heat bring to boil. Reduce heat to simmer and parboil for 5–10 minutes to remove any acidity. Drain in colander or strainer. Set aside.

2. Melt butter in saucepan over medium-high heat and add shallots. Stirring constantly, **sauté** until soft, about 2–3 minutes. Add carrots, leeks, and fiddleheads. Stirring frequently, cook additional 8–10 minutes. Add broth and salt and pepper to taste. Bring to boil, reduce heat to simmer, and cook for 30–35 minutes.

3. In mixing bowl, whisk together heavy cream and egg yolks.

4. Stirring constantly, to prevent curdling, slowly pour mixture into soup. Reduce heat to low and cook until heated through, about 6–8 minutes.

5. Serve immediately in soup bowls.

❧ *Coquilles Saint Jacque*

This recipe can be made in one large baking dish or individual **ramekins** (available in the kitchen supply section of some supermarkets and all department stores).

Yield: serves 4 to 6

6 tablespoons butter or margarine, more as needed

3 tablespoons all-purpose flour

1/2 teaspoon salt

1 1/2 cups heavy cream

24–30 medium-large fresh scallops

1 quart chicken or vegetable broth, homemade or canned

1 cup mushrooms, **trimmed**, sliced

1 cup breadcrumbs

6 slices Swiss cheese

Equipment: Heavy-bottomed saucepan, whisk, medium saucepan, slotted spoon, medium skillet, mixing spoon, 5 oven-proof ramekins about 4–5 inches in diameter and 1 inch deep, oven mitts

1. *Prepare sauce*: melt 6 tablespoons butter or margarine in heavy-bottomed saucepan over medium heat. Slowly whisk flour into melted butter or margarine until well blended. Whisking continually to prevent lumps, slowly add heavy cream. Mixture should be smooth. Remove from heat and set aside.

2. *Prepare scallops*: in medium saucepan, bring broth to boil over high heat. Add scallops, bring to boil, reduce heat to medium, and cook for about 3 minutes or until scallops are **opaque white**. Immediately remove from heat. Using slotted spoon, remove scallops and place in bowl. Set aside to cool. Discard liquid or refrigerate for another use.

3. *Prepare mushrooms*: melt 2 tablespoons butter or margarine in skillet over medium-high heat. Add sliced mushrooms and **sauté**, stirring frequently, until soft, about 5–7 minutes. Transfer to bowl and set aside.

4. Using same skillet, melt 8 tablespoons butter or margarine over medium heat. Remove from heat and stir in 1 cup bread crumbs. Add more butter or margarine if necessary to make mixture soupy. Set aside.

5. *To assemble*: cover bottom of baking dish or each ramekin with thin layer of buttered bread-crumbs. Place 4–5 scallops side-by-side on top of bread crumbs. Sprinkle sliced mushrooms over scallops. Cover generously with sauce. Place slice of Swiss cheese over top of each and sprinkle with remaining buttered breadcrumbs. Place under broiler for 10–15 minutes to heat through and make top golden. Remove using oven mitts.

6. Serve warm as main dish.

❧ Blueberry Corn Fritters

Yield: serves 4 to 6

1 1/2 cups all-purpose flour	2 tablespoons sugar, or to taste
2 teaspoons baking powder	3/4 cup cream-style canned corn
2 eggs, separated	1/2 cup blueberries, fresh or frozen, thawed and drained
3/4 cup milk	
1 teaspoon salt	2–8 tablespoons butter or margarine

Equipment: flour **sifter**; large mixing bowl; electric mixer, mixing spoon, or **whisk**; medium bowl; large skillet; metal spatula or pancake turner

1. Place flour and baking powder in sifter.

2. Combine egg yolks, milk, salt, and sugar in large mixing bowl and mix well. Slowly **sift** in flour mixture. Stir continually using mixer, spoon, or whisk until smooth and lump-free. Add corn and blueberries and blend well.

3. Place egg whites in medium bowl and beat with mixer or whisk until stiff. Gently **fold** whites into batter using whisk or mixing spoon.

4. Melt 2 tablespoons butter or margarine in skillet over medium-high heat. Drop batter by tablespoonful into pan and flatten slightly with back of spoon. Make each fritter about 3 inches across. Cook about 5 minutes on each side, until golden brown. Add more butter or margarine if necessary.

5. Serve fritters warm with maple syrup or blueberry jam. They are excellent to serve for breakfast or brunch with bacon, sausage, or ham and eggs.

❧ Maple Syrup Shortbreads

Canadian forests provide a wealth of wonderful products. None is more precious than one of nature's greatest gifts, maple syrup. Millions of gallons of this amber goodness are harvested each year. The sap of the stately sugar maple begins to run at the first breath of warm weather, and it is as cold and clear as spring water, flowing for only a few brief weeks in early spring. Harvested drop by drop, it takes 40 gallons of sap to yield only 1 gallon of pure maple syrup.

Yield: makes about 36

1/2 cup (1 stick) unsalted butter or margarine (at room temperature)

1/4 cup sugar

1 cup all-purpose flour

3/4 cup firmly packed brown sugar

1/2 cup pure maple syrup

1 tablespoon butter or margarine (at room temperature)

1 egg (at room temperature)

1/2 cup chopped walnuts

Equipment: Large mixing bowl, mixing spoon or electric mixer, greased medium baking pan, medium mixing bowl

1. Preheat oven to 350°F.

2. *Prepare cakes*: cream butter and sugar together in large mixing bowl, using spoon or mixer, until light and fluffy. Add flour, a little at a time, mixing continually, and blend well. Do not form into ball. Pat mixture into baking pan. Bake in oven until light brown about 25 minutes. Remove from oven and set aside.

3. *Prepare topping*: in medium bowl blend brown sugar, maple syrup, and butter. Add egg and vanilla and mix until smooth. Pour evenly over shortbread and sprinkle top with walnuts. Return to oven and bake until topping sets, about 20 minutes. Cool before cutting into squares.

4. Serve *shortbreads* as snack. They keep well in an airtight container and also make lovely special-occasion food gifts.

❧ Canadian Apple Cake

Two Canadian products that are both plentiful and popular are apples and maple syrup; this recipe contains both.

Yield: serves 8 to 10

1 1/2 cups **sifted** all-purpose flour	1 egg, beaten
1/2 cup sugar	3 apples, peeled, **cored**, finely sliced
2 teaspoons baking powder	1/2 teaspoon ground cinnamon
1/2 teaspoon salt	2 tablespoons butter or margarine
1/2 cup vegetable shortening	2 tablespoons maple syrup
1/2 cup milk	

Equipment: Flour **sifter**, large mixing bowl, knives or pastry blender, mixing spoon, greased medium cake pan

1. Preheat oven to 375°F.

2. **Sift** flour, 3 tablespoons sugar, baking powder, and salt in mixing bowl. Cut in shortening with 2 knives or pastry blender. Add milk and eggs, using mixing spoon, and mix to form soft dough.

3. Spread dough smoothly in cake pan and place overlapping slices of apples in rows on dough. Mix remaining sugar and cinnamon and sprinkle over apples. Dot with butter or margarine. Bake about 50 minutes or until toothpick comes out clean when inserted in cake. Remove from oven and pour maple syrup over top.

4. Serve Canadian apple cake while slightly warm, cut into squares or wedges.

❧ Hot Apple Cider

Yield: serves 12 to 20

2 quarts apple juice	1/2 tablespoon ground cloves
2 quarts cranberry juice	1 lemon, sliced into rings
1/2 cup light brown sugar	2 oranges, cut into quarters
3 sticks cinnamon	3 tablespoons whole cloves

Equipment: Large saucepan, mixing spoon

1. Heat apple juice, cranberry juice, brown sugar, cinnamon, ground cloves, and lemon slices in saucepan over high heat. Bring to boil and mix well. Reduce heat to simmer and cook for 15 minutes.

2. Poke whole cloves, polka-dotted fashion, into skin side of orange wedges. Add to cider and continue cooking an additional 5 minutes. The cloves and orange wedges enhance flavor as well as provide a decorative garnish.

3. Serve warm apple cider in cups. It is a great cold-weather party beverage.

UNITED STATES

Throughout the United States people from similar cultures, sharing common interests, often settled near one another in regions, communities, and neighborhoods. They found comfort and a sense of belonging by keeping the same cooking and eating customs they grew up with. Neighborhood "mom and pop" restaurants were first to share foods of their heritage. Today, regional and community cookouts, cook-offs, and festivals take place to showcase heritage and regional differences. For example, Scandinavians in the Midwest have community fish boils, cooking fish as their ancestors have done for centuries. In the south-central states, people travel to small Louisiana towns to sample crawfish prepared the Cajun way. There are festivals for everything, from garlic tastings and *grunion* in California to Italian and Greek food festivals on the streets of New York.

The United States soil is rich, with fruitful orchards, fertile plains, and enormous herds of cattle-roaming grasslands. An increased awareness of ecological issues has greatly influenced the farming and agricultural markets over the past decade. America continues to research and develop more efficient farming techniques as well as improve the quality of foods by using organic methods to grow vegetables.

❧ Chicken Fried Steak Texas Style with Cream Gravy

Chicken fried steak, popular in Texas and other Southern states, is battered and fried similar to fried chicken.

Yield: serves 4

1 egg	1/2 teaspoon salt
1/4 cup milk	1/2 teaspoon pepper
4 6–8-ounce beef cutlets or a 1 1/2- to 2-pound round steak, **tenderized**	vegetable oil

1 cup all-purpose flour

Equipment: Small bowl, whisk, shallow pie pan, wax paper, large cast-iron or heavy-bottomed skillet, wooden spoon, metal tongs or long handled fork, paper towels

1. In small bowl whisk together egg and milk. Mix well and set aside.
2. In shallow pan, combine flour, salt, and pepper. Lightly coat culets in flour on both sides and shake off excess. Dip each cutlet in egg and milk mixture then back in flour. Set aside on wax paper.
3. Prepare to fry: Have ready several layers of paper towels on baking sheet. Fill skillet with oil until about 1/2 inch deep. Heat over medium-high heat and test readiness by placing handle of wooden spoon in oil; if small bubbles appear around surface, oil is ready for frying.
4. Using metal tongs or long-handled fork, one by one carefully place cutlets in skillet. Fry until golden brown on both sides. Reduce to low heat, cover, and cook about 4–5 minutes until cutlets are cooked through. Using tongs, transfer cutlets to paper towels to drain; keep warm. Reserve pan drippings for cream gravy.
5. Serve immediately with cream gravy (next recipe) over top.

❧ **Cream Gravy**

3 tablespoons flour	3/4 cup water
3/4 cup milk	salt and pepper to taste

1. Using same skillet, drain all but 2 tablespoons cooking oil in skillet. Heat oil over medium-high heat. Stirring constantly, sprinkle in 3 tablespoons flour. Continue stirring and cook until flour is lightly browned. Stirring constantly, slowly add milk and water. Reduce to low heat and cook until gravy reaches desired thickness. Add salt and pepper to taste.
2. Serve immediately over chicken fried steak.

❧ *Jambalaya* (Cajun Sausage with Rice and Vegetables)

Jambalaya originated in New Orleans. It was a result of settlers attempting to recreate *paella* (a popular Spanish rice and seafood dish). There are two types of Jambalaya in New Orleans: Cajun and Creole. The Creole version originated in the New Orleans French Quarter and uses tomatoes whereas the Cajun version is from Louisiana's low-lying swamp country where the flavor is smokier and spicier and tomatoes are omitted.

Yield: serves 8 to 10

2 tablespoons vegetable oil, more as needed

1 pound *andouille*, Cajun or other spicy sausage, sliced into 1/4-inch rounds

1 cup celery, **trimmed, finely chopped**

2 cups green bell peppers, trimmed, finely chopped

2 cups onion, trimmed, peeled, finely chopped

2 jalapeño peppers, trimmed, **seeded**, finely chopped

4 garlic cloves, trimmed, peeled, **minced**

1 cup canned diced stewed tomatoes with juice

1/2 cup tomato paste

2 bay leaves

1 3/4 quarts chicken broth, homemade or canned

1/2 teaspoon red chili flakes

salt and pepper to taste

1 1/2 cups long-grain rice

1 tablespoon chopped fresh basil or 1 teaspoon dried

1 1/2 pounds medium shrimp, peeled, **deveined**

chopped green onion, for garnish

Equipment: Large stock pot with cover, wooden mixing spoon

1. In stock pot, heat oil over medium-high heat. Add sausage, stir frequently, and cook until lightly browned on both sides.

2. Add celery, bell peppers, and onions. Stirring occasionally, **sauté** until soft, about 6–8 minutes. Add more oil if necessary to prevent sticking. Stir in jalapeños and garlic and cook an additional 5 minutes. Stir in tomatoes, tomato paste, bay leaves, chicken broth, chili flakes, and salt and pepper to taste. Stir in rice and cover. Bring to boil over medium-high heat, reduce heat to medium, and cook about 15–18 minutes or until rice is tender.

3. Stir in basil and shrimp and cook an additional 5–7 minutes or until shrimp are **opaque white**. Remove and discard bay leaves.

4. Serve in individual soup bowls with green onion sprinkled over each serving.

Beef Jerky

Preserving meat was necessary for early pioneers traveling across the United States and Canada. *Jerky*, made from deer, elk, buffalo, or beef became popular and is still a favorite trail and snack food. Originally sun dried, the oven can effectively dry meat with similar results. Set oven to lowest heat; remember, you are not cooking the meat, just drying it out. The **marinade** for the following jerky recipe is to flavor the meat, not **tenderize** it. Worcestershire sauce and hot red sauce can be added, more or less to taste.

Yield: 10 to 20 pieces

1–2 pounds lean beef, such as round steak, fat **trimmed**; place in freezer for about

30 minutes till firm. Slice with grain (not across grain) in strips, 1/8 inch thick.

1 capful liquid smoke (available at some
    supermarkets and all international markets)

3 teaspoons garlic granules

2 teaspoons ground oregano

2 teaspoons thyme

2 teaspoons salt

1 tablespoon pepper

2 teaspoons soy sauce

    Equipment: Glass or plastic bowl, wire cake rack, aluminum foil

1. Preheat oven to lowest heat, about 150°F.

2. Mix liquid smoke, garlic, oregano, thyme, salt, pepper, and soy sauce in bowl. Using clean hands, rub mixture on meat strips making sure to coat each piece. Refrigerate for about 1 hour.

3. Place strips side-by-side on wire rack and place in oven (place a sheet of foil on shelf under meat rack to catch drippings). Make wedge of rolled foil to keep oven door open about 3 inches to release moisture. Keep meat in oven at least 12 hours or overnight.

4. In the morning check meat: if it is brittle, it is done. If it bends without breaking, leave it in for another couple of hours. When dry, store in airtight container.

5. Serve beef jerky as an easy-to-carry, quick-energy snack.

Roasted Garlic

Gilroy, California, is considered "The Garlic Capital of the World" and holds a yearly festival celebrating the joys of garlic. This festival brings people from all over the country. Garlic is known to have many health benefits and enhances the flavor of many dishes. An easy and fun way to serve garlic is in the following recipe.

    Yield: serves 8 to 10

1 cup garlic cloves, trimmed, peeled, separated
    (peeled garlic is available by the jar in most
    supermarkets)

olive oil cooking spray

    Equipment: Nonstick baking sheet

1. Preheat oven 375° F.

2. Place garlic on baking pan and generously coat all sides with cooking spray.

3. Bake in oven about 25–35 minutes or until cloves feel soft when pressed.

4. Serve as snack, spread over warm French bread or mash and serve along with sour cream as topping for baked potato.

℥ Whoopie Pie

Whoopie pies are popular throughout New England. They are like a sandwich but made with two soft cookies with a fluffy white filling, about the size of a hamburger.

Yield: makes 8–9 pies

1/2 cup solid shortening

1 cup firmly packed light brown sugar

1 egg

2 cups all-purpose flour

1 teaspoon baking powder

1/4 cup cocoa

1 teaspoon baking soda

1 teaspoon salt

1 teaspoon vanilla extract

1 cup milk

filling (recipe follows)

Equipment: Large bowl, electric mixer or mixing spoon, medium bowl, sifter, nonstick baking sheet, oven mitts, wire rack

1. Preheat oven to 350° F.

2. In large bowl, using electric mixer of mixing spoon, mix together shortening, sugar, and egg.

3. In medium bowl sift together flour, baking powder, cocoa, baking soda, and salt. Stirring constantly, add to shortening mixture, alternating with milk, a little at a time. Add vanilla extract and beat until smooth.

4. To form each cookie, drop 1/4 cup batter onto baking sheet. Using back of spoon, spread batter into 4-inch circles leaving 2 inches between each cookie. Bake 15 minutes or until cookies are firm to touch. Using oven mitts, remove from oven. When cool enough to handle, transfer to wire rack. Continue baking in batches until 16–18 cakes are made.

5. Prepare filling below.

6. When cookies are completely cool, spread generous amount filling on flat side of cake. Top with another cookie, pressing down gently to distribute filling evenly. Repeat with all cookies and filling to make 9 pies.

7. Serve as delicious dessert or wrap individual pies in plastic wrap and store in freezer or refrigerator for later use.

Filling:

1 cup solid vegetable shortening

1 1/2 cups powdered sugar

2 cups marshmallow fluff

1 1/2 teaspoons vanilla extract

Equipment: Medium bowl, electric mixer or mixing spoon

1. In medium bowl, using electric mixer of mixing spoon beat together shortening, sugar, and marshmallow fluff. Stir in vanilla extract until well blended. Set aside.

2. Use as directed in whoopie pie recipe.

✸ Boston Brown Bread

Boston brown bread is traditionally eaten with Boston baked beans. The bread is not baked; instead batter is poured into cans and steamed. For this recipe use two empty cans with one end smoothly removed, thoroughly washed (labels removed), and dried.

Yield: makes 2 loaves

2 cups buttermilk	1 cup white, fine ground cornmeal
1/2 cup dark molasses	3/4 teaspoon baking soda
1 cup seedless raisins	1 teaspoon salt
1 cup rye flour	1 tablespoon butter or margarine (at room temperature)
1 cup whole wheat flour	

Equipment: **Egg beater** or electric mixer, large mixing bowl, wooden mixing spoon, **sifter**, 2 clean cans (2 1/2-cup size, one end removed), wax paper, aluminum foil, string or tape, wire rack to fit inside large saucepan with cover, oven mitts, wax paper-covered work surface

1. Place about 2 quarts water in tea kettle and bring to boil over high heat.

2. Using egg beater or mixer, mix buttermilk and molasses about 5 minutes until well blended. Add raisins.

3. Place rye and whole wheat flours, cornmeal, baking soda, and salt into flour sifter. **Sift** into buttermilk mixture, a little at a time; stir continually until well blended.

4. Spread softened butter or margarine over inside bottom and sides of cans. Pour mixture equally into prepared cans. Cover each can loosely with greased wax paper (greased sides down), allowing room under wax paper for bread to rise. Cover wax paper loosely with large piece of foil, pulling tightly around outside of each can. Place filled cans on rack in saucepan. Set saucepan on stove and add enough boiling water to reach about 3/4 up sides of cans. Set on high heat and bring water to boil. Reduce to low heat, cover, and steam bread about 2 1/2 hours.

5. Using oven mitts, carefully remove cans, one by one, from water and place on work surface. Carefully remove foil and wax paper from hot cans. Turn cans upside down, turning bread out on wax paper-covered work surface.

6. To serve, allow bread to cool before slicing into about 1/2-inch-wide pieces. Refrigerated, the bread keeps well, if wrapped, about 10 days.

✌ Apple Pie

Nothing is more American than Fourth of July and apple pie. This has been said more times, in more places, in more songs, and in more movies and stage plays than one can imagine. Ever since Johnny Appleseed headed west, dropping his seeds on the way, apples have been the all-time, all-American favorite food.

Yield: serves 6 to 8

1 1/2 cups light brown sugar

2 1/2 tablespoons all-purpose flour

1/4 teaspoon salt

1/2 teaspoon ground cinnamon

1/2 teaspoon ground nutmeg

1/2 teaspoon ground cloves

5 tart apples (such as Granny Smiths) peeled, **cored**, finely sliced

2 tablespoons butter or margarine

1 teaspoon vanilla extract

2 unbaked 9-inch pie shells in oven-proof pie pans, homemade or frozen, thawed, one shell to be used for lattice top (see next recipe)

Equipment: Small-sized bowl, mixing spoon, fork

1. Preheat oven to 350°F.

2. Combine brown sugar, flour, salt, cinnamon, nutmeg, and cloves in small bowl and mix well.

3. Layer apple slices in pie shell and sprinkle with dry mixture, starting with apples and ending with mixture. Dot top with butter or margarine and sprinkle with vanilla extract.

4. For lattice top, cut dough into 1/2-inch strips and place half strips from left to right, about 1 inch apart, over apples. Repeat with remaining strips, placing from top to bottom at right angles to the first. Wet ends and press together with pie crust edge. Using fork tines make track marks around edge, sealing lattice top with bottom crust.

5. Bake in oven about 45 minutes, until top crust is golden brown. If pastry edge starts to brown too quickly, cover with strip of aluminum foil.

6. Serve warm or with ice cream for a grand dessert.

✌ Pie Crust

You have heard the expression "easy as pie"? Well, the following two pie crusts are foolproof, easy, and quick to make.

Yield: serves 6 to 8

1 1/2 cups flour

1/2 cup vegetable oil

1 teaspoon salt

1/4 cup cold water

Equipment: Spoon, 9-inch pie pan, aluminum foil, uncooked dried beans or rice for weight, oven mitts

1. Preheat oven to 450°F.

2. Place flour, oil, salt, and water in pie pan, and, using clean hands, blend mixture into ball. Pat dough out to cover bottom and sides of pie pan. Using fork, prick bottom 3 or 4 times.

3. To prebake pie crust before adding filling, cut a circle of foil to cover bottom and weigh down with uncooked dry beans or rice.

4. Bake about 10 minutes. Using oven mitts, remove from oven. Remove beans or rice and foil, return to oven, and bake until golden brown, about 10 minutes more.

5. Remove from oven, cool to room temperature, and fill with favorite filling.

※ Marionberry Cobbler

Marionberries are cultivated in Oregon and named after Marion County, where they are grown. They are exported and can be found at most international markets fresh or in jam.

Yield: serves 4 to 6

Filling:

1 teaspoon lemon **zest**

1 1/2 cups granulated sugar

1/4 cup packed brown sugar

Biscuit topping:

5 tablespoons cold unsalted butter, cut into small pieces

1 cup all-purpose flour

2 tablespoons yellow cornmeal

1 teaspoon cinnamon

1 1/2 tablespoons cornstarch

6 cups marionberries, washed, **trimmed**

2 tablespoons sugar

1 1/2 teaspoons baking powder

1/2 teaspoon salt

1/2 cup milk

1/2 teaspoon vanilla

Equipment: Large bowl, greased large oven-proof baking dish, food processor or medium bowl and mixing spoon, oven mitts, wire rack

1. Preheat oven to 375° F.

2. *Make filling:* Place lemon zest, granulated sugar, brown sugar, cinnamon, and cornstarch in large bowl. Add berries and toss to coat. Transfer to baking dish and spread evenly across bottom.

3. *Make biscuit topping:* In food processor or medium bowl with mixing spoon blend together flour, cornmeal, sugar, baking powder, salt, and butter until mixture resembles coarse meal. Stirring constantly, add milk and vanilla and mix until mixture forms dough.

4. Drop biscuit topping by rounded tablespoons onto berry filling. Bake in oven for 35–40 minutes or until topping is golden and cooked through. Using oven mitts, remove from oven and set on wire rack to cool.

5. Serve warm with scoop of vanilla ice cream on top.

✳ Peanut Brittle

During the Civil War, an infant was left an orphan after his slave mother was killed. The infant grew up with a love for the soil, reading, learning, and determined he would help make the world a better place to live. George Washington Carver grew up to receive world acclaim while head of the department of agriculture of Iowa. He made hundreds of useful products from peanuts and sweet potatoes, such as the following well-known peanut candy.

Yield: serves 6 to 8

1 tablespoon butter or margarine, more as needed

1 1/2 cups sugar

1/2 cup shelled, skinned peanuts

Equipment: Medium metal pie pan, 12-inch square aluminum foil, small heavy-bottomed saucepan or skillet, wooden mixing spoon

1. Line bottom and sides of pie pan with foil, wrapping foil over pan's top edge to secure foil. Grease foil generously with butter or margarine. Lay peanuts on foil and shake pan to spread evenly over bottom.

2. Melt sugar in saucepan or skillet over high heat, but do not mix until sugar begins to melt, about 3 minutes. Reduce heat to medium and stir constantly with wooden spoon until all sugar is dissolved. Carefully remove pan from heat and pour hot mixture over peanuts, using wooden spoon to make sure they are well covered. Cool to room temperature, peel peanut brittle from foil, and break into serving-sized pieces. To crush peanut brittle, first wrap in foil and completely cover with clean kitchen towel.

3. Serve peanut brittle as a candy treat. Store in covered jar.

✳ Pecan Pralines

Pecan trees thrive throughout the South, and there are many wonderful ways of using nuts. Pecan pralines are popular and easy to make.

Yield: makes about 4 dozen

2 cups sugar

2 teaspoons white corn syrup

1 cup firmly packed light brown sugar

1/2 cup butter (do not substitute margarine)

1 cup milk

4 cups pecans, broken in small pieces

Equipment: Medium heavy-bottomed saucepan, wooden mixing spoon, 2 tablespoons, wax paper-covered work surface

1. Place granulated and brown sugar in saucepan. Add milk, corn syrup, and butter, and, stirring continually, bring to rolling boil over medium-high heat. Reduce to low heat and cook about 20 minutes, stirring frequently. Add nuts and mix well. Increase heat to medium and cook

until mixture barely drops off spoon when lifted up, about 20 minutes. Stir frequently to prevent sticking. Remove from heat.

2. Quickly and carefully drop candy by tablespoon onto wax paper. Use-second spoon to scoop candy off first spoon. Each drop should form about 2-inch patty. When cool, remove from paper and store in airtight container or wrap each in plastic wrap.

3. Serve as a candy treat.

Bibliography

Casas, Penelope. *¡Delicioso! The Regional Cooking of Spain*. New York: Alfred A. Knopf, 1996.

Corey, Helen. *Helen Corey's Food from the Biblical Lands*. Terre Haute, IN: CharLyn Publishing House, 1989.

———. *The Art of Syrian Cooking*. Terre Haute, IN: CharLyn Publishing House, 1962.

Day, Harvey. *Indian Vegetarian Curries*. Rochester, VT: Thorsons Publishing Group, 1982.

Helou, Anissa. *Mediterranean Street Food*. New York: HarperCollins, 2002.

Jaffrey, Madhur. *From Curries to Kebabs: Recipes from the Indian Spice Trail*. New York: Clarkson Potter, 2003.

Jenkins, Nancy Harmon. *Cucina Del Sole*. New York: HarperCollins, 2007.

Kander, Simon, and Henry Schoenfeld. *The Settlement Cook Book*. 3rd ed. New York: Simon & Schuster, 1976.

Kochilas, Diane. *The Glorious Foods of Greece*. New York: HarperCollins, 2001.

Krohn, Norman. *Ody., Menu Mystique*. New York: Jonathan David Publishers, 1983.

Kurihara, Harumi. *Harumi's Japanese Cooking*. New York: Berkley Publishing Group, 2006.

Levy, Faye. *Feast from the Mideast*. New York: HarperCollins, 2003.

Marks, Copeland, and Aung Thien. *The Burmese Kitchen*. New York: M. Evans and Company, 1994.

McClane, A. J. *The Encyclopedia of Fish*. Canada: Holt, Rinehart & Winston, 1977.

Nguyen, Andrea. *Into the Vietnamese Kitchen*. Berkeley, CA: Ten Speed Press, 2006.

Polemis, Aphrodite. *From a Traditional Greek Kitchen*. Summertown, TN: The Book Publishing Company, 1992.

Ramqzani, Nesta. *Persian Cooking: A table of Exotic Delights*. New York: Quadrangle Books, 1974.

Rieley, Elizabeth. *The Chef's Companion*. New York: Van Nostrand Reinhold Company, 1986.

Roden, Claudia. *Arabesque: A Taste or Morocco, Turkey, and Lebanon*. New York: Penguin Books, 2005.

Rombauer, Irma, and Marion Rombauer Becker. *Joy of Cooking*. Indianapolis: Bobbs-Merrill Company, 1975.

Sahni, Julie. *Classic Indian Cooking*. New York: William Morrow and Company, 1980.

———. *Indian Regional Classics*. New York: William Morrow and Company, 1998.

Trang, Corinne. *Essentials of Asian Cuisine*. New York: Simon & Schuster, 2003.

Volokh, Anne, and Mavis Manus. *The Art of Russian Cooking*. New York: Macmillan, 1983.

Wilson, Ellen Gibson. *A West African Cook Book*. New York: M. Evans and Company, 1971.

Woodward, Sarah. *The Ottoman Kitchen*. Brooklyn, NY: Interlink Publishing Group, 2002.

WEB SITES

Africa: www.congocookbook.com
England: www.woodlands-junior.kent.sch.uk/customs/questions/festfood.htm
Indian Food Kitchen: http://www.top-indian-recipes.com
South African Cooking: www.3men.com/south.htm
International:
www.cdkitchen.com
www.fairtradecookbook.org
www.recipezaar.com
http://recipes.wuzzle.org
www.whats4eats.com

Index

Index

Atole (cornmeal beverage) (Mexico), 248
Australia, 115–17
Austria, 178–79
Avgolemono (lemon soup) (Greece), 199
avocados: about, 235–36; *guacamole* (avocado dip) (Mexico), 249

Baba Ghannooj (eggplant dip) (Lebanon and Syria), 301–2
Babute (curried beef meatloaf) (Democratic Republic of Congo), 41
Bacalao a la Viscaina (fish stew) (Mexico), 251–52
Bahamas, 128–30
Bahrain, 310, 311
Baked Guavas with Mushrooms and Olives (Middle East), 314–15
Baki, 82
Balkan States, 196–98
Baltic States, 164–65
bamboo shoots, bamboo shoots with ground meat (China), 76
Bamia (lamb and okra stew) (Egypt), 286–87
Bammy (pan-fried bread) (Trinidad and Tobago), 149–50
Banana Pudding (Bahamas), 129–30
bananas: baked bananas (Ivory Coast), 24; baked banana with coconut (Ghana), 19; banana porridge (Malaysia and Singapore), 96; banana pudding (Bahamas), 129–30; beans and plantain medley (Burundi and Rwanda), 51; heavenly bananas (Nicaragua), 254
Bangladesh, 72–73
beans: beans and plantain medley (Burundi and Rwanda), 51; black beans and white rice (Costa Rica), 239–40; black bean soup (Cuba), 131; black-eyed pea balls (Burkina Faso), 15–16; brown fava beans (Egypt), 286; *feijoada* (meat stew with black beans) (Brazil), 262; kidney beans and rice (Haiti), 142–43; for *La Bandera* (red beans, rice, stewed meat, and fried plantains) (Dominican Republic), 136; *pasta e fagiolio* (pasta and bean soup) (Italy), 203; Russian salad, 231; sliced steak with rice and black beans (Venezuela), 280–81
Beans and Plantain Medley (Burundi and Rwanda), 51
beef: beef jerky (United States), 325–26; beef stew (Zimbabwe), 68; chicken fried

steak Texas style with cream gravy (United States), 323–24; Croatian stew, 197; curried beef meatloaf (Democratic Republic of Congo), 41; curry in a hurry (Somalia), 61–62; *feijoada* (meat stew with black beans) (Brazil), 262; German meatballs with caper sauce, 186–87; grilled beef (Pakistan), 102–3; grison barley soup (Switzerland), 193; ground meat patties (Iran), 289–90; Hungarian goulash, 221; Hunter's pie (Netherlands), 188–89; meat baked in batter (Australia), 116–17; meat patties (Pakistan), 102; meat stew (Burkina Faso), 15; Nigerian melon seed soup (Nigeria), 28; peanut and meat stew (Mali and Mauritania), 26; *picadillo* (spiced ground meat) (Mexico), 250–51; Russian salad, 231; *salteñas* (meat turnovers) (Bolivia), 260–61; Siberian meat dumplings (USSR), 232; sliced steak with rice and black beans (Venezuela), 280–81; stewed carrots with meat (Israel), 298; stuffed cabbage (Romania), 226–27; Swedish meatballs, 176–77; Tabriz meatballs (Iran), 290–91; *teriyaki* marinated beef (Japan), 89–90; traditional Iraqi "casserole," 293–94
Beef Jerky (United States), 325–26
Belgium, 180–81
Belize, 237–38
Benin, 13–14
Berbere (mixed spices) (Djibouti and Eritrea), 52
berries: blueberry corn fritters (Canada), 320–21; marionberry cobbler (United States), 330
beverages: *atole* (cornmeal beverage) (Mexico), 248; chocolate *atole* (Mexico), 248; ginger drink (Guinea), 21; hot apple cider (Canada), 322; iced yogurt beverage (Bulgaria), 217–18; lemonade (Middle East), 312; peanut milk (Ghana), 20
Bhapa Ilish Patey (steamed fish fillets) (Bangladesh), 72–73
Birchermuesli (raw granola) (Switzerland), 192
Biryani (lamb in yogurt) (Malaysia and Singapore), 96–97
Biryani **Rice** (Malaysia and Singapore), 97–98
biscuits: almond biscuits (Middle East), 315–16; scones (English baking powder biscuits), 153
black beans: black beans and white rice (Costa Rica), 239–40, 252; black bean soup (Cuba), 131; *feijoada* (meat stew with black beans)

336

Index

About the Authors

LOIS SINAIKO WEBB has been in the food business ever since opening her restaurant in Seabrook, Texas, where she was cook-owner for more than 15 years. Lois closed the restaurant allowing herself time to write and travel. Her articles appeared in numerous food service publications. On a trip to the People's Republic of China, Lois was invited to teach American cooking to 54 chefs in the northern Jilin Provence. For many years Lois was Catering Coordinator for Villa Capri Restaurant in Seabrook, Texas. She was responsible for providing recipes and procedures necessary for cooks and staff to handle multicultural weddings and special events. Lois is a member of Professionals in Culinary Arts (a Houston culinary group). Lois is the co-author of *Multicultural Cookbook for Students* (1993) and is the author of *Holidays of the World* (1995) and *Multicultural Cookbook of Life-Cycle Celebrations* (2000), all by Oryx Press.

LINDSAY GRACE ROTEN was born and raised in Houston, Texas. She received her Bachelor of Science degree in Business Management from Birmingham-Southern College in Birmingham, Alabama. Throughout her life she has enjoyed writing short stories and poetry. While in college Lindsay honed her creative writing skills. Upon graduating in 2001 Lindsay traveled to Svir Stroy, Russia, as one of several Global Justice Volunteers. During this time she taught English, computer, and sports to orphans ages 8–16. While in Russia, Lindsay studied and researched justice issues affecting Russian orphans. Lindsay has developed a passion for exploring and experiencing a variety of cultures and the fusion of their ethnic foods. She has lived throughout the United States and is currently teaching English at Clear Creek High School in League City, Texas.